Economic Poisoning

CRITICAL ENVIRONMENTS: NATURE, SCIENCE, AND POLITICS

Edited by Julie Guthman, Jake Kosek, and Rebecca Lave

The Critical Environments series publishes books that explore the political forms of life and the ecologies that emerge from histories of capitalism, militarism, racism, colonialism, and more.

Economic Poisoning

*Industrial Waste and the Chemicalization
of American Agriculture*

Adam M. Romero

UNIVERSITY OF CALIFORNIA PRESS

University of California Press
Oakland, California

Library of Congress Cataloging-in-Publication Data

Names: Romero, Adam, author.
Title: Economic poisoning : industrial waste and the chemicalization
    of American agriculture / Adam M. Romero.
Other titles: Critical environments (Oakland, Calif.) ; 8.
Description: Oakland, California : University of California Press,
    [2022] | Series: Critical environments : nature, science, and
    politics; 8 | Includes bibliographical references and index.
Identifiers: LCCN 2021014008 (print) | LCCN 2021014009 (ebook) |
    ISBN 9780520381551 (cloth) | ISBN 9780520381568 (paperback) |
    ISBN 9780520381575 (epub)
Subjects: LCSH: Factory and trade waste—California. | Pesticides—
    Environmental aspects—California. | Agricultural chemicals
    industry—California.
Classification: LCC TD897.75.C2 R66 2022 (print) |
    LCC TD897.75.C2 (ebook) | DDC 363.738/49809794—dc23
LC record available at https://lccn.loc.gov/2021014008
LC ebook record available at https://lccn.loc.gov/2021014009

Manufactured in the United States of America

31 30 29 28 27 26 25 24 23 22
10 9 8 7 6 5 4 3 2 1

To all who have mixed their hands with the soil

Contents

Illustrations

Preface

Dear Ms. Carson,

I wish I was writing with better news. You once asked what future historians will think of contaminating the entire world just to ward off a few insect species, and I'm writing to let you know that many of us are still truly astonished, as you were, by our distorted sense of proportion.[1] You wondered how intelligent beings could purposefully spread poisons that brought death and disease even to our own kind. You wondered how intelligent beings could instigate an endless chemical war against nature and contaminate (hu)mans' total environment with compounds that alter the material fabric of humanity. You wondered how intelligent beings justified these practices despite their rationales collapsing the moment you examined them. Even in hindsight, answers to these questions are not simple or straightforward, and scholars are still trying to come to grips with them. Nevertheless, money, power, arrogance, fear, and the stories we keep telling ourselves are a good shorthand.

The environmental movement that you helped unleash with your eloquent book raised important questions and concerns about the impact of pesticides on environmental and human health.[2] A few years after you left us new environmental laws were passed, and a new agency was developed to help make our air more breathable and our water more drinkable. In 1972, that new agency banned DDT and many of the other organochlorine compounds that you wrote about, and this ban is still viewed by many as an unequivocal environmental victory.[3] Yet the metabolites of those compounds still haunt us today and likely will for so long that we might as well think of it as forever.[4] And now, more pesticides—some much more toxic than DDT—are used than ever before. The problem was that banning DDT did nothing to change the structure of US agriculture or the government institutions that championed chemicalized agriculture. Therefore, it did not change how chemical companies profited from the manufacture of industrial poisons. It did not knock the "gods of profit and productivity" from their perch, nor did it decrease the need for toxic chemicals in agriculture; it merely substituted one class of toxic chemicals for another class of chemicals even more toxic to farmworkers.[5] Our war against nature trudged on, just with a new set of chemical weapons.

Your book also helped catalyze a back-to-the-land food movement that sought alternatives to many of the problems of chemicalized agriculture that you described.[6] Now you can find organic and local food in most grocery stores. But despite people's best intentions, over the last few decades this has led to organic farming and food movements that continue to reify the production of systemic inequality. Now our food system is bifurcating into one for the rich and one for the poor, allowing critics of industrial agriculture to believe that they can seclude themselves from the harms that the widespread use of economic poisons entails. But this head-in-the-sand approach will not bring about the systemic agricultural change that is needed; instead it simply allows harmful practices to continue alongside less harmful ones and still subjects people who look like me to increased harm.

It seems like people only read part of your book or took from it the part of its message that resonated with them most. It seems that despite your impassioned pleas, people cared more about the silencing of birds than the suffering of people who grew and harvested our agricultural abundance. It still feels that way. We remain the most agriculturally productive nation in the world, yet millions of our children go to bed hungry every night, and many of the people who grow and harvest our food cannot afford to eat it themselves or to pay for basic health care.[7] Even the farmers who are left have a hard time making ends meet. And now climate change is throwing us for a loop. Something is still terribly wrong with our agriculture, and it only seems to be getting worse.

Many who read this letter will call me delusional and say that the agricultural systems we have now have to be this way, that the end will eventually justify the means, and that without widespread pesticide use we will all starve. But the prevention of famine and hunger has never been the most compelling reason pesticides are used, despite claims to the contrary. This was the case in the 1880s and 1890s when pesticides were first commercialized. It was the case in the 1920s and 1930s during a period of their widespread adoption. It was the case in the 1950s and 1960s when you were writing, and it is still the case today.[8] This fact is even more true once you realize that nonfood crops like cotton have always been some of the biggest consumers of pesticides or that much of our pesticide use continues to be for cosmetic reasons.[9] American agriculture's central problem has been and continues to be, as you pointed out, too much food, a problem that Henry A. Wallace once said has "as disastrous effects upon national well-being as crop shortages used to have on the isolated communities of a simpler age."[10]

You once wrote that our obligation to endure gives us the right to know, and one of the things we have the right to know is that the stories we are told about pesticides are not true. We have the right to know that pesticides have never been necessary for the United States to produce sufficient food. We have the right to know that pesticide use has been important to the production of other goods and services that are critical not to the survival of the population but to the survival of a particular form of political economy. We have the right to know that the regulatory systems we have can neither fully understand nor mitigate the impacts of our widespread use of toxic chemicals. We have the right to know that despite some laboratory testing, we are the real guinea pigs.[11] We have the right to know that our laws prioritize corporate well-being over human and environmental health. We have the right to know that ideologies of war and conquest still permeate our approaches to pest management.

But our obligation to endure, as you also wrote, entails more than just a right to know. It also requires us to develop a sense of humility in the face of the vast forces that we tamper with. It requires us to come to grips with the fact that technology will not create the utopian world that many of our technocrats envision. It requires that we learn one of the most difficult lessons of all: how to put people above profit. It requires that we rethink our relationship to each other and the nonhuman world. Raymond Williams and Clarence Glacken both wrote that how we talk about the environment reveals a great deal about who we are.[12] They said this because the metaphors and categories that we choose to describe our relationship to nature allow us to act in certain ways. You knew this, as your critique of the ideology of "pest control" made clear. This belief that we could actually control pests has long rested on the notion that "nature exists for the convenience of man," an idea that still pervades our agricultural and environmental policies and practices.[13]

It was your ability to tell an intimate story about a future without birdsong that drew readers to your book. But *Silent Spring*'s popular interpretations did not and still do not mention most of what is contained in it. For me, the most important and farseeing chapter that you wrote was "The Human Price." Reading that chapter, it becomes clear that your focus was not on birds, or even pesticides; rather, you were concerned with the massive influx of industrial chemicals into everyday life and how these chemicals were not only remaking the natural world but what it meant to be human. You wrote that "pesticides are just part of the chemicals now pervading the world in which we now live, acting upon us directly and indirectly, separately and collectively. Their presence casts a shadow that is no less ominous because it is formless and obscure, no less frightening because it is simply impossible to predict the effects of lifetime exposure to chemical and physical agents that are not part of the biological experience of man."[14] Perhaps nothing you wrote was more profound than this. Perhaps nothing you wrote better encapsulates what it means to be alive today.

But I also think your critique of agriculture did not go far enough. You repeatedly wrote that you were not averse to pesticides, just to their indiscriminate use. I understand why you said this. But your critique did not question why pesticides were used in the first place. It did not question the fundamental logic of growing food and fiber in a manner that demands a constant stream of industrial poisons. It did not question how even a discriminate use of pesticides can bring death and disease. It did not question our long history of exploiting people, particularly non-white bodies, in the production our food and fiber. You may have asked us to envision a world without birds, but you did not ask us to envision an agricultural system that begins to put people first; you simply asked us to stop using so many pesticides.

You once asked how intelligent beings could contaminate the world just to ward off a few insect species, but maybe that was the wrong question. Maybe the right question has nothing to do with pesticides, or contamination, but with the stories we keep telling ourselves and our inability to envision agriculture as anything else than a for-profit enterprise. Maybe the question we need to ask ourselves is why we continue to fear famine, despite abundance being our biggest problem.

Maybe the question we need to ask ourselves is how our arrogance still shapes how we cultivate food and fiber, or why we are waging an endless chemical war against nature and thus ourselves. Maybe, just maybe, we could begin by asking why those who harvest and process our agricultural abundance often cannot afford to eat it themselves, why they bear the brunt of our chemicalized agricultural policies and practices, or why millions of people are food insecure in a country that destroys and purposely wastes food to keep commodity prices high, rather than what pesticides are on our produce or whether our food is grown nearby. Maybe the question we need to ask is how we can create an agricultural movement that cares more about people than it does about what chemicals are on our food.

Yours truly,
Adam M. Romero

Acknowledgments

Like all books, this one was not a singular enterprise, and I am thankful to all who helped me throughout the process. I especially want to thank the librarians, archivists, and student library workers. None of this would have been possible without your expert advice, deep knowledge, resolute patience, and scanning skills. I also want to thank the institutions that provided funding. Funding came from the Geraldine R. Martin Foundation, the Science History Institute, the Bancroft Library at University of California (UC), Berkeley, the C3 Mellon Postdoctoral Fellowship, and the American Council of Learned Societies (ACLS). The ACLS fellowship in particular came at a crucial moment in the process and gave me the dedicated writing time needed to finish the book.

The Sayre Lab group at UC Berkeley read the earliest iterations of the manuscript. I miss those dinner discussions. Earlier drafts of chapter 2 first appeared in *Agricultural and Human Values* and of chapter 5 in *Agricultural History*, and I want to thank those reviewers for their insights. I also want to thank my colleagues in the School of Interdisciplinary Arts and Sciences at the University of Washington Bothell, especially the Geography Reading Group, for their comments on chapter drafts. I am lucky to teach at a school that has such caring, courageous, and creative colleagues.

Three manuscript reviewers provided me with discerning and invaluable comments and suggestions. Their insights improved the book immeasurably, and I hope to repay the favor someday. I also want to thank the series editors, Julie Guthman and Rebecca Lave, for their support throughout the publication process. Julie Guthman raised important concerns about the manuscript and provided invaluable feedback at crucial moments of the writing process. I also want to thank the editorial and production staff at UC Press, particularly Stacy Eisenstark. Her editorial guidance surpassed all of my expectations. Sharon Langworthy provided superb work during the copyediting phase. Nevertheless, all mistakes remain my own.

Last, I want to thank my partner Shannon Cram for her unwavering love and support. You continue to inspire me every day. Thank you for helping me turn our little piece of the Cascade foothills into a garden wonderland.

Introduction

This book began at a desk in the Suzzallo Library at the University of Washington. I had not planned on writing about the history of pesticides, but there I was, with a stack of old science journals in front of me. It had been a roundabout journey to get there. As an undergraduate I dreamed of becoming an environmental toxicologist and studying agricultural pollution. I wanted to be an environmental toxicologist because I thought it could be a way to help reduce the agrochemical burden that farmworkers live and die with. While I never had to pick crops for a living, my father did, and I grew up watching how a body burdened so young can respond. I naively thought the problem was that we just didn't know enough about agricultural pollution, and that once we did, practices would change. After undergrad I tried to get my PhD in environmental toxicology, but I quickly realized that it was not the right choice. On the surface, I left because I was flabbergasted that something as plastic as chemical risk assessment lies at the base of our regulatory regime. Deeper down, however, I left because I realized that toxicology could not answer the questions I was beginning to ask about why pesticides were used in the first place.

I ended up specifically at that desk in Suzzallo Library because my previous project on capitalism and midwestern agricultural pollution had fallen apart after a family health emergency, and I had moved from Berkeley, where I was still in grad school, to Seattle to be with my partner, who was doing research in Washington State. I tell you all this because I want you to know that when I picked up the first volume of the *Journal of Economic Entomology*, I did so not just as a geographer or a historian in need of a new project, but as someone who has always been keen to figure out why agriculture in the United States is so dependent on poisonous chemicals. I thought knowing more about the early history of pesticides would be a good place to start, and I chose the *Journal of Economic Entomology* because it was the flagship journal of the emerging science of pest control. Those who published in it were the scientists who had pioneered the interdisciplinary study of crop production, chemicals, and agricultural pests. I guessed they would have a lot to say.

When I began the project, I thought I would see, as I had already read so much about, a history of agroecological contradictions brought on by the industrialization of US agriculture. This would be followed by the growth and development of agrochemical firms to address these contradictions. That story was certainly there. Take for example the scientist John B. Smith, who stood before his peers at the first annual meeting of the American Association of Economic Entomologists in 1908 and argued that intensive fertilization made orchards prone to insect damage.[1] He believed that economic entomology should focus on growing healthy trees resistant to pests and disease, not only on better methods of chemical control. But J. B. was also quickly upbraided by his colleagues, who explained to him that his scientific heresy was antithetical to capitalist agriculture and mass production.

As I read on I could see that the growth of industrial chemicals on US farms, as the agrarian political economists David Goodman, Bernardo Sorj, and John Wilkinson argued so long ago, was clearly a history of capitalist appropriation and substitution.[2] I watched farmers become reliant on off-farm inputs and saw the founding, development, and rapid expansion of chemical firms that made and marketed these new inputs. I also saw, as the rural sociologist Susan Mann or the geographer George Henderson might have theorized, that early pesticide consumption was tied mainly to a few crops in a few geographic locations, and that pests were both obstacles and opportunities inherent in a new form of agriculture.[3]

But I also realized that I could see other patterns emerging, patterns that had nothing to do with agriculture at first glance but nevertheless connected on-the-ground impacts, like the skin cancer of a southern Black sharecropper in the 1920s, to the wastes of global industries like copper. I began to realize that industrial waste, at least prior to World War II, had played an oversized role as a raw material of agricultural toxicity.

That was the narrative that shouted from the pages as I turned them: that the transition to chemical agriculture was as much a story about trying to get rid of industrial waste as it was about using chemicals to mass produce food. By industrial waste I mean that the waste was coming from the production of commodities rather than from the commodities themselves. To make a modern analogy, it was not wasted plastic bottles that were made into pesticides; instead, it was the chemical wastes produced in the process of making the plastic bottles that became pesticides.

But if industrial waste did occupy such a central role as the material used to poison agriculture, it meant that as pesticide use spread across the United States, farms took on a new societal function. It meant that in addition to providing food, fiber, energy, and the properties of rural life, US agriculture also acted as a dumping ground for wastes of industrial production. The picture I saw emerging was a history of farming, farmlands, farm bodies, and farm communities acting as a sink for some of industrial society's most noxious wastes.

As agriculture industrialized, US farms became the type of ecosystems that could be used to launder industrial waste. But I could also see that farms were different than many places where society tried to hide its wastes. One key difference was that agriculture desired chemical toxicity; that these wastes were toxic was the point. As US agriculture industrialized, as farmers specialized and drove the land to produce more and more, crops were becoming, as J. B. Smith had warned, increasingly vulnerable to disease. Thus, as chemical toxicity became the cure to agriculture's new ailments, agriculture became a possible antidote to some of industry's toxic woes.

I want to back up for a second and briefly mention that agriculture has always been a place to recycle society's wastes: ashes from fires, crop residues, household wastes, human and animal excrement, even parts of animals themselves.[4] But this was different. The types of waste that scientists were experimenting with were not aimed at increasing fertility or improving the soil. These were toxic chemicals whose use-value came from the fact that they could kill. At the turn of the twentieth century, agriculture was certainly not the only industry that utilized the wastes of another; that is mostly what industrial chemistry does.[5] Agriculture's uniqueness comes from it being one of the few industries in which waste is valuable because it is toxic.

It took me three months and a lot of coffee to carefully read a half century of journal issues. I read not only the scientific papers but everything the journal contained, including editorials, minutes of annual and regional meetings, committee reports, and association business. After I finished, I reviewed my notes and decided on a handful of threads to follow. As I moved on from that library workstation, however, I quickly realized that researching the history of chemicals and chemical companies can be difficult. For one thing, archives of many pre–World War II agrochemical companies and the scientists they employed do not exist. For another, even for those that do exist, access can be restricted, as I found out at the Chevron corporate archive. In other cases, archival material was incomplete, like the labeled yet empty folders I encountered at the Chemical Heritage Foundation.[6] Nevertheless, these silences spoke volumes, not just about which narratives get to be written, but because they directed me to other source material like newspapers, industry and marketing journals, legal cases, and archives I had never considered.[7] In this book I offer a new interpretation of the chemicalization of American agriculture that considers the infrastructures that made agriculture a profitable sink for industrial waste and traces how toxicity became integral to industrial food and fiber production.

ECONOMIC POISONS AND INDUSTRIAL WASTE

You will likely notice in this book that I sometimes refer to pesticides as poisons and chemical pest control as the poisoning of crops. I am not doing this for shock value. I am purposely using the term *poison* because it better represents the pre-1945 history of chemical pest control than a term like *pesticide* does.[8] Prior to World War II, what we now call pesticides were often called economic poisons; thus to use them on a crop was to poison that crop.[9] What made a poison economic was that it had the characteristics to make it useful in agriculture. These characteristics were more than a poison's ability to kill. They included everything from how long a poison persisted in the environment to how well it stuck to a plant. Price, of course, also mattered, as the poison had to be cheap enough for farmers to afford to use it often multiple times a season, year after year, in an industry chronically plagued by low margins. In other words, lots of poisons existed, but only some had the potential to become economic.

I like the term *economic poison* because it calls our attention to both the materiality of pesticides and the act of using them. The title of this book comes from the dual nature of the term. It reminds us that these chemicals are poisons, just agriculturally useful ones. When a *Wall Street Journal* reporter wrote in 1924 that "good seed, plenty of fertilizer, and careful cultivation are necessary to produce a crop that is worth poisoning," that was what he meant.[10] In the late nineteenth and early twentieth centuries, crop poisoning required chemicals that were both deadly and cheap, and industrial waste was one of the few sources that met these criteria.

Since the turn of the twenty-first century, scholarship in the humanities and social sciences has delved deep into waste.[11] From e-waste to food waste to wastelands, this work has begun to pry apart the complex nature of waste and wasting. Yet aside from the nuclear industry, the meat industry, and energy production, industrial waste has not always been on scholars' radars. One reason for this, as the sociologist Zsuzsa Gille points out, is that "industrial and, in general, production wastes are rarely accessible to fieldwork methods."[12] Another is that because industrial waste is so often conflated with hazard and pollution, it is viewed as external to the production process rather than intrinsic to it. Conflating waste with pollution and calling waste an externality means that scholars have conceptually downplayed the role of industrial waste in the history of capitalism. Yet since the mid-nineteenth century, the production, utilization, and circulation of industrial wastes have been fundamental to capitalism's expanded reproduction despite the fact that many of these wastes go on to pollute and poison. Anyone who studies the chemical industry knows this to be the case. Thinking beyond industrial waste as an externality is crucial for imagining how commodity production itself can serve as a sink for industrial waste.

Sink is a term that environmental and ecological scholars now use to describe the ability of certain ecosystem processes, like the flow of a river or atmospheric circulation, to absorb, channel, and detoxify the wastes of production and consumption.[13] Sinks are often talked about in terms of their waste-assimilative capacity and commonly show up in discussions of climate change, wherein "carbon sinks" are often examined.[14] The term sink, however, has its origins in the fifteenth century, when it was used to describe a pool or pit formed by humans in the ground for the receipt of waste and sewage.[15] The sink in your house is derived from this very concept. But sinks are not simply places where filth is permanently swallowed up or lost.[16] Sinks are produced by humans first though the creation of waste and second through the creation of places to put it. For example, the use of rivers in the nineteenth century as sinks for industrial and urban wastes relied as much on the ability of rivers to dissolve and transport materials as on the scientific and discursive production of rivers as natural waste treatment systems.[17] Sinks are, as the sociologist Jennifer

Gabrys argued, a "complex set of natural-social processes always in the making" and are thus never permanent, but always provisional.[18]

More recently, economists and ecologists promulgating ideas of ecosystem services have also grabbed onto the concept of sinks. Ecosystem services, as proponents argue, are the free gifts of nature provided to humans by "properly functioning" ecosystems, including supporting, provisioning, regulating, and cultural services.[19] For them, sinks are the "waste disposal services of natural ecosystems" and should be monetarily valued as such. But this definition discounts the important waste disposal services of "properly functioning" ecosystems like high-input intensive agriculture. After all, it was the very ecological organization of a rapidly industrializing agriculture that made it such a good sink for certain types of industrial waste.

In the mid-nineteenth century, manufacturing firms across the world began viewing industrial waste in a new light as more and more of them successfully transformed their wastes into what came to be known as by-products.[20] Thus, it is not a coincidence that the term *by-product* emerged in the mid-nineteenth century.[21] As these new waste streams flooded society, so too did recognition of environmental harm as well as the idea that industrial waste could be put to work. Mid-nineteenth-century writers witnessed this waste–by-product nexus firsthand. For many, it wasn't cheap textiles, wage labor, or gargantuan machines that signaled the arrival of capitalist modernity. It was the mountains of waste that emerged from Europe's industrial centers that truly signaled the coming geological age of humans.

Even Charles Dickens, the keen observer and satirist of British society, couldn't escape from all the waste. His last novel, *Our Mutual Friend*, published in 1864, follows a nouveau riche protagonist who makes his money by gathering, sorting, and selling the wastes of industrial production and consumption. As Dickens wrote, "On his own small estate the growling old vagabond threw up his own mountain range, like an old volcano, and its geological formation was Dust."[22]

Political economists, geographers, industrialists, and scientists alike were also trying to come to terms with the emerging waste–by-product nexus. For example, as George Perkins Marsh observed the same year, "The utilization, or beworthing (*Verwentung*) of waste from metallurgical, chemical, and manufacturing establishments, is among the most important results of the application of science to industrial purposes."[23] What Marsh and others were witnessing was the creation of entirely new industries whose raw materials were the wastes of others. They were watching commodity production and consumption become profitable waste frontiers.

Karl Marx, in some of his unfinished writings, also examined the role of waste in the capitalist economy and laid out three conditions for the reuse of waste in a system of generalized commodity production.[24] First, there had to be massive amounts of waste produced commonly across industry.[25] Second, machines had to be improved to be able to handle refuse materials that were previously intractable. And third, scientific progress, especially in chemistry, was needed to turn production wastes into something that could possibly be exchanged. For Marx, however, the fact that capitalism, as Rebecca Altman has written, "wedded itself to the residues of industrialization" in the mid-nineteenth century, wasn't just a question of the nature of capitalism, but crucially also a question about how waste cum by-product altered the value and cost of the primary commodity.[26] Marx and other political economists were puzzled by how the industrial production process itself "without any previous outlay of capital, creates new matter for capital."[27]

The meat industry is perhaps the best example of this, an industry whose titans could claim that by the 1880s they were using every part of the hog but the squeal. In the late 1800s, Swift and Armour reconfigured meat production in the United States. But in the end what made the Chicago-based meat packers capable of outcompeting eastern abattoirs was not necessarily the new industrialized methods of slaughtering, dressing, preserving, transporting, and marketing that they had developed. Instead, the production of vast amounts of cheap meat was made possible by economies of scale in industrial waste production and the ability to turn that waste into the products of everyday life. As William Cronon wrote, "[Swift and Armour] earned their margin largely from things that butchers threw away."[28] The creation of an animal by-products industry not only expanded the sources and types of raw materials available for commodity production, but in doing so also subsidized the consumption of meat by reducing the cost of the primary product.[29] The fact that we now exist in a world dripping in nonfood commodities made from animal industry wastes highlights the role that waste utilization has played in the production of new material frontiers, as Marsh and Cronon observed, as well as its role in cheapening primary commodities, as Marx suggested.[30]

But as historians like Christine Rosen have repeatedly pointed out, turning wastes into by-products was not as easy as it sounds.[31] For one thing, the materiality of the waste itself really mattered. For another, how that waste's materiality intersected with environmental processes, politics, analytical chemistry, toxics regulation, and discourses of harm and pollution was also important. In other words, as the chemical engineer John Teeple argued in the 1920s, just because a waste *could* become a by-product did not mean that it *did*.[32] Capitalism, as Ester Leslie has written, eventually "raids everything for value," even the wastebaskets of industry.[33] But why industrialists and scientists go dumpster diving in the first place is more complicated than simply the idea that value can be extracted from industrial detritus. The stories in this book make this abundantly clear.

DISPLACEMENT AND PROLIFERATION

I want to be very explicit about something. I am not suggesting that industrial waste disposal caused the poisoning of agriculture. For starters, there are plenty of examples of pesticides that did not come from industrial waste, like pyrethrum, which was botanical in origin. An argument like that is much too simple, and scholars have already shown that this is not the case.[34] Further, that argument removes agency from the people who made the modern agricultural world, and I don't want to do that. What I am suggesting is that as American agriculture industrialized, it became a place to bury toxic waste. We could imagine this creating scenarios in which chemical salesmen cheered on and exploited insect outbreaks in order to offload more waste. Those situations actually happened.[35] But what is important about them was that they were part of larger industrial, cultural, and agricultural changes occurring at the time, changes often couched in a belief that chemistry was the solution to the world's problems and that humanity's domination of nature (using chemicals, of course) was just around the corner. The arrival of toxic chemicals at the farm gate was just part of the dramatic changes occurring in US agriculture, and it should never be separated from this context.

What I am arguing in this book is that industrial waste had an oversized role as a cheap source of agricultural toxicity, and that pre–World War II agriculture was a sink for toxic industrial waste. Where did pesticides and pesticide pollution during this period ultimately come from? Much flowed from industry's waste streams to a handful of chemical plants across the country and then on to millions of American farms. This waste not only provided agriculture with a cheap source of toxic raw materials; it provided the firms that happened to produce the right type of waste a profitable way to dispose of it.

But toxic waste never behaves. By its very nature it is unruly and hard to handle.[36] Even if we disguise it under a sheen of new use-value, we are not actually getting rid of it. We are using consumption as a way to dissipate it, to dilute it, and to displace it. "In the process of displacement," however, as the sociologist Z. Gille aptly put it, "waste proliferates."[37] Thus this book is also about how toxic industrial waste proliferated within agriculture. It proliferated into a toxicity-based pest control that allowed farmers to increase output even as pests became systemic and into new phenomenon like chemical foliage injury, insect resistance, consumer anxiety, and the contamination of land and people. It proliferated far and wide.

The geographer Julie Guthman gives us a good way to think about how toxic industrial waste could proliferate within agriculture.[38] In *Wilted*, Guthman conceptualizes agriculture not just as an industry that grows and processes food and fiber but instead as a more-than-human assemblage: a set of diverse elements and forces whose interactions are consequential. In an assemblage, "nonhumans play an active role in bringing phenomenon into being," "perturbations can reverberate throughout the whole," and everything is provisional.[39] I like to conceptualize agriculture as a more-than-human assemblage because it helps me explain what I first saw as I sat reading at that library desk. I observed how insects, soils, and weather weren't just obstacles for capitalism to overcome. They were active participants in the development of chemical pest control. For example, a shift in weather could quickly reverberate across the agrochemical assemblage, altering insect physiology, chemical markets, the amount of waste that industry gleaned from its streams, and farmer and farmworker health.

Guthman highlights two additional concepts that are important for thinking about agriculture and the proliferation of toxic waste: repair and iatrogenic harm. Since agricultural assemblages are always provisional, as any farmer would tell us, they need constant intervention to hold them together. Borrowing from the sociologist Christopher Henke, Guthman characterizes this human intervention as repair.[40] Repair can take many forms, from breeding new drought-resistant varieties to withstand climate change to devising new methods to dispose of surplus. The poisoning of agriculture was certainly an act of repair. As J. B. Smith foretold, chemical control evolved as a way to deal with the type of pest problems that come with growing crops in an industrially intensive manner. Indeed, as Leland O. Howard, head of the Bureau of Entomology in the 1920s and one of the early twentieth century's greatest pesticide champions, once said, it is the manner in which crops are grown that causes harm to agriculture.[41] Guthman conceptualizes this self-induced harm as iatrogenic. *Iatrogenic harm* is more commonly used in medicine to refer to a disease created by a medical treatment, but Guthman utilizes this concept to argue that strawberry growers' reliance on soil fumigation—a technology originally developed to heal sick soil—has created a new set of agriculturally-induced problems that now require their own repair.

A more-than-human assemblage that required repair, often due to problems that came from the repair itself, explained everything that I saw. I watched toxic waste become the cure to some of agriculture's pest problems, only to see how that cure proliferated into new problems, each of which then required its own repair. The story I tell in chapter 1 is a good example of this. Chapter 1 is a history of waste displacements and agricultural repair that stretches back to the earliest days of the Industrial Revolution. It follows arsenic waste from the excrement of British copper smelters to its pesticidal fate on US farms.

By 1945, arsenic waste had proliferated within agriculture for over seventy-five years. Arsenic-based pesticides were the most widely consumed agricultural poisons in the United States, and US farmers consumed most of the world's arsenic waste. This is an interesting bit of history, but that is not the point. The point is that the arsenic pollution problem was never solved; it was simply displaced. As arsenic waste proliferated within agriculture as a new type of repair, it contaminated everything it touched and caused harm at every step of the supply chain. By 1945, US farmers had helped arsenic become so ubiquitous an environmental contaminant that even forensic toxicologists had trouble distinguishing intentional arsenic poisoning from exposures in daily life.[42]

Arsenic's cheap toxicity gave some farmers the ability to achieve new feats of agricultural abundance. But it was this very abundance that then became the problem. This matters because the main justification for the widespread use of pesticides during this period was that they were necessary to prevent (impending) hunger and starvation. Yet I could see that this was clearly not the case, especially if we examine what crops consumed the most arsenic. Cotton growers, for example, became prodigious users of arsenic-based pesticides after World War I. While this cotton was fodder for the textile industry, it was not food.[43] As chemical pest control spread across the United States, abundance become the biggest problem in need of repair. When Rachel Carson wrote in *Silent Spring* that pesticide use was justified by "reasons that collapse the moment we examine them," this is what she meant.[44] Pesticides were helping to prop up a system whose "real problem" was overproduction. They were not necessary for the United States to produce sufficient food.

This rationale also matters because it became a key justification for chemical war. Before I opened that first journal, I had read Edmond's Russell *War and Nature*.[45] In that book Russell argues that chemical pest control and war coevolved. Thus, I had expected to see how metaphors, materials, techniques, and technologies moved back and forth between pest control and the military. I definitely saw that. But what I was not expecting to see was how integral war was to the very nature of industrial pest control and that chemical war stretched back even further into agricultural history than World War I, where Russell's story begins. At the time I had just come across an article in the journal about the history of cyanide fumigation in which the author argued that its development in the late 1880s was the first successful industry-wide use of toxicity to control insects.[46] I thought this moment would be a good case study to examine whether war had been integral to industrial chemical control and the movement of waste into agriculture since the beginning. I wanted to know, because I another question had been lingering in the back of mind: If industrial chemical control is a war on pests, then what kind of war is it? That is what chapter 2 is about.

Chapter 2 tells the story of cyanide fumigation's development among the capitalist citrus groves of late-nineteenth-century Los Angeles. It offers an alternative history of industrial chemical warfare, that began in 1887 as a way to repair a new type of agriculture, not on a European battlefield in 1915. More importantly, however, chapter 2 argues that as toxicity became integral to agriculture, so too did war. War became agriculture's normal state. This state of war not only expedited the movement and transformation of industrial waste into economic poisons; it was key to rationalizing away any collateral damage caused by agricultural chemical warfare. In this chapter I push the argument beyond the coevolution of war and agriculture and make the case that industrial chemical pest control has always been an act of war. For me what is important about examining this moment isn't how it shaped American democracy, as it was for Russell, but rather that in the late nineteenth century a state of war became a key part of agriculture's capitalist infrastructure.

I use *infrastructure* in the way that the anthropologist Barry Larkin would, as the people, pipelines, and buildings that moved and transformed chemical wastes into pesticides as well as the institutions, ideologies, and politics of pest control.[47] To believe that toxic chemicals are the only way to fight the pest war means that, as J. B. Smith argued, scientific research will focus on finding new poisons, to the detriment of alternative science never done. When we are at war, the infrastructure we build, whether experimental farms or bodies of knowledge, reflects that state. In chapter 3 we see this explicitly.

Chapter 3 examines the tandem formation of agricultural toxicology and the first generation of petroleum-based pesticides. At its simplest, agricultural toxicology is the study of the efficient use of poisons to kill agricultural pests, and it differed from other forms of human-centered toxicology in the first few decades of the twentieth century in that it was the study of poisons for their offensive use and not as a way to understand exposure or prevent disease. It was the science of chemical warfare and was a key ingredient in moving the oil industry's toxic leftovers into agriculture. To tell this story, I use the history of William Volck and the California Spray-Chemical Company's (Cal-Spray's) multidecadal quest to render agricultural toxicity from the physical properties of oil. But in making petrotoxicity reproducible, Volck also helped turn agriculture into a profitable sink for the oil industry's wastes. The growth of oil-based poisons in agriculture, however, didn't occur just because waste oil fractions were so much cheaper or the oil industry had found an outlet for its waste. In fact, their use also developed in response to reconfigurations in the agro-chemical assemblage that were caused by earlier toxicity-based repair technologies like arsenic, sulfur, and cyanide. Thus, in chapter 3 we also see how insect resistance was a crucial participant in the development of oil-based poisons.

The deeper I got into the business history of oil sprays, however, the clearer it became that research done at the University of California was integral to the success of Cal-Spray. By that time I had read Jack Kloppenburg's classic study of plant biotechnology, in which he delineates a pattern of research undertaken at public universities becoming the intellectual property of private companies.[48] This was clearly the case with oil-based poisons in California, and I wondered if was true for the rest of the country. Chapter 4 is my answer to that question.

Chapter 4 tells the story of an institution created in 1920 to grow and rationalize pesticide use across the United States by bringing chemical companies and public agricultural research together. The goal of the Crop Protection Institute (CPI) was to use the facilities and expertise of land grant universities and their agricultural experiment stations to assay the toxic materials spilling from a World War I–enlarged chemical industry. This would give experiment stations a source of private funding for pesticide research and give companies a way of determining whether any of their chemicals or industrial wastes had agricultural value. The CPI was a hybrid institution, meaning that it was neither public nor private. Its membership was composed of influential scientists interested in growing chemical control, chemical and mining companies interested in the potential of agriculture, and manufacturers of pesticide delivery equipment.

Throughout the interwar period, the CPI played a significant role in the rapid evolution and adoption of economic poisons. By the end of World War II, the CPI had funded more than 150 studies at more than fifty experiment stations across the United States. But it wasn't the pesticides that the CPI made possible or the toxic wastes it redirected into agriculture that were its biggest impacts. Instead, it was that the CPI helped build a chemical R&D infrastructure in which public agrotoxicological science was captured by private industry. This happened not only because individual companies so often directed and benefited from the research done at public universities, but also because during the interwar period toxicity-based repair became *the* solution to agriculture's pest problems. The CPI did not facilitate studies of biological or cultural control. It only funded studies that sought to annihilate humanity's nonhuman enemies with poisonous chemicals.

California's agriculture and its institutions also played a prominent role in the CPI's history. In the early 1930s, for example, the University of California at Davis and the University of California at Riverside emerged as leading destinations for CPI funds, particularly from those companies trying to develop the first generation of synthetic organic poisons. This coincided with an overall shift in the CPI's research agenda. While it was founded to provide knowledge that would benefit all of its members, by the 1930s it was more focused on testing proprietary chemicals for individual companies. This turn toward proprietary knowledge reflected similar changes occurring in the seed industry. Whereas hybrid-seed technology allowed companies to turn seeds into commodities, patented poisons gave companies toxic monopolies and the economic incentives that came with them.

In the late 1930s the CPI was ultimately undermined by its own success. Chemical companies began bypassing the CPI to work directly with agricultural experiment stations, as the Shell Chemical Corporation did, as we see in chapter 5, when it turned to UC Davis scientists in 1943 to help test its potentially revolutionary new poison. At the time

California's growers were facing the commercial loss of land due to soil-borne diseases. By planting the same crop in the same soil over and over, growers in places like the Central Coast and the Central Valley had created the types of novel ecosystems in which soil pests and disease flourished. As these iatrogenic problems multiplied, growers watched their fields become sicker and sicker. This soil disease–cropping pattern was also true for many other plantation types of agriculture across the world. By the early 1940s, the urgency of repair was never more apparent.

To call something revolutionary in agricultural history is surely cliché, but it also can be true, and in chapter 5 I make the case that the development of the petroleum-based soil fumigants revolutionized agriculture. They did so by severing the link between the intensive production of a single crop without rotation and the buildup of commercially destructive pests in the soil complex. The development of chemical fertilizers in the late nineteenth century had already removed the need for farmers to rotate crops as a way to manage soil fertility, but it did not overcome the need to rotate crops for pest management. Soil fumigants made it possible to chemically sterilize the soil and plant every year as if it were the first time the soil had been planted.

In chapter 5 I tell the story of Shell Chemical's commercialization of the soil fumigant DD, a mixture of two novel chlorinated chemicals that were produced as waste in some of Shell Chemical's groundbreaking petrochemistry. Shell had sent some of this waste to Hawaii at the request of Walter Carter, a university researcher who was searching for a chemical cure to the decline of pineapple yields across the islands. Like growers in California, pineapple companies watched their yields decline as continuous cropping facilitated the proliferation of destructive soil insects and pathogens. Yet in the fields that Carter treated with DD, he watched pineapples grow as though they had been planted in virgin soil. For Carter, salvation came in the shape of Shell's novel waste streams, and Shell saw an opportunity to spread this gospel far and wide.

Shell Chemical was in the perfect position to commercialize DD. In the late 1920s, scientists and engineers at the California-based Shell Development Company and Shell Chemical Company pioneered the first synthesis of ammonia using natural gas as a hydrogen source. In the 1930s, Shell's scientists developed a way to inject this ammonia into agricultural soils. I tell this story as well because these technologies were quickly adapted for use with soil fumigants. But I also tell this story because soil fumigants made from petroleum wastes were just part of the fully petrochemical agriculture that Shell's top brass envisioned when they set up their chemical shop in California in 1927. By the late 1930s, Shell Oil had helped turn California into the epicenter of petrochemical R&D, and agriculture was key to its plan to turn the waste gases of its oil wells and refineries into everything from fertilizer to soap to things not yet dreamed of.

In the fall of 1944, when the UC Davis scientist Walter Balch injected DD and ammonia into a disease-ridden Salinas lettuce field, petroleum-derived chemicals not only provided the motive and lubricative power but also the nutritive and killing power necessary to plant the same field with the same crop over and over and over. Growers did not need to change their practices; they just needed a new generation of chemical weapons that could penetrate the soil. The stories I tell in chapter 5 are all part of what I call the petrochemical turn in pest control. By the early 1940s, California agriculture had become fully integrated with its petroleum economy. Agriculture had become an important part of the oil industry's waste management infrastructure, while growers increasingly relied on petroleum to move their tractors, kill their insects, weed their crops, and fumigate and fertilize their soils.

It may seem that I am spending a lot of time focused on California for a book that is supposed to be about American agriculture. I did not set out to do this, but it quickly became clear that California agriculture and institutions like the University of California played a leading role in the development of chemical pest control. There were many other threads I could have followed, and I did follow many, but there was something about California agriculture that kept drawing me back. What made California and other Pacific states so different from other areas of the United States, especially at the turn of the twentieth century, was that they did not have farmers; they had growers.[49] These growers not only produced high-value crops like apples, oranges, and stone fruit, they did so by driving the land in new, intensive ways. They were not growing food; they were growing money, and lots of it. Indeed, it was in California, as the agricultural historian Deborah Fitzgerald has written, that "the earliest notions of industrial farming were first cultivated."[50] I turn to California as a leading center of pesticide development, just as economic entomologists and pesticide manufacturers did at the time.[51] California was not only a land of progressive farmers growing food as capitalism intended; it was often *the* key market for non-California-based pesticide manufacturers.

There is one critically important aspect of chemical control and waste proliferation missing from this book. It is the same feature missing from the history of chemical control found in the half century of journal issues that I read. What is apparent is how little human health and labor concerns came into play in the development of chemical pest control. When they did, it was usually white middle-class consumer health that was of concern, not the health of the those who applied the poisons or harvested the poisoned crops. There were certainly some who raised their voices for both people and the environment, but these were drowned out by the march of pesticide progress. Whether farmers' skin broke out in a debilitating rash after carrying hay in their arms or sharecroppers developed skin or liver cancer from chronic arsenic exposure did not matter.[52] They were simply collateral damage in the war on pests, a war that was considered right, necessary, and just.

Indeed, as the geographer Brian Williams has argued, agrochemical practices are always racialized practices.[53] This becomes especially clear when we zero in on the type of plantation style agriculture of early capitalism. These novel types of agricultural ecosystems were neither robust nor resilient. They were incredibly fragile environments that required constant repair. The way crops were grown—intensively, in "enormous fields"—made them more ecologically fragile.[54] Thus as you read the stories in this book, think about who paid the physical price of each new technology of repair and consider what sort of racialized agricultural practices these repairs perpetuated and intensified. One of the reasons I think it is important to know the early history of pesticides in the United States is that it demystifies why our current agricultural policies and pesticide practices prioritize profit and production over worker, consumer, and environmental health. Chemical pest control began solely as a way to kill pests, and nothing about this fact has changed despite laws intended to blunt the worst of these novel chemical harms.

Even the earliest production of the raw materials of capitalist agriculture are linked to racialized formations. For instance, the fertilizers that US citrus, apple, and cotton growers prodigiously consumed in the early part of the twentieth century required the creation of new racial categories. The historian Edward Melillo has shown how the creation of "workers who were neither chattel slavery nor wage laborers" was necessary for the British to extract nutrients from South America in order to repair soil fertility problems across the industrial world.[55] As both Williams and Melillo argue, questions about the chemicalization of agriculture are simultaneously always complex questions about the history of labor relations, racialized labor practices, and the government policies that support them. So despite this book's lack of focus on the impacts of these poisons on farmers, farm labor, and the environment, those questions are always there.

By 1945 the use of industrial waste as a material basis for toxicity-based repair had proliferated far and wide. Toxicity itself had become integral to the maintenance of the industrial agrarian assemblage. This toxicity caused extensive harm, even if this harm went unstudied or unacknowledged. After World War II, pesticide use expanded to new areas and new crops, and newer and newer poisons were introduced, but the logic never changed. In the end it did not matter whether that toxicity came from calcium arsenate, DDT, or chlorpyrifos; what mattered was that toxicity was the linchpin that held the assemblage together. This need for industrial-scale toxicity, in turn, made agriculture an ideal place for firms to bury their toxic waste.

CHAPTER I

Arsenic and Old Waste

Arsenic is mined from deep mines, for it is a material that
Nature hides from us, teaching us to leave it alone as harmful, but this does not cause the arrogant miners to leave it.

—Biringuccio, *The Pirotechnia*, 1540

The use of arsenic-based pesticides peaked in the United States in
1944.[1] That year American farmers spread them on 120 different types
of crops. Arsenic coated fruit trees and the soil below. It blanketed
cotton and the hands that picked it. By 1944, what began as a way to
kill potato bugs on the American frontier had evolved into the most
prominent weapon of chemical pest control. Arsenic's ability to kill
pests allowed farmers to reach new heights of abundance. But every
application also made arsenic pollution into more of a pervasive problem. By 1944, agriculture had helped make arsenic one of the most
ubiquitous contaminants.[2]

But arsenic pollution wasn't originally agriculture's problem. In fact,
agriculture's use of arsenic was a way for another industry to rid itself
of waste. This waste was produced by copper smelters, and it was
incredibly toxic. Thus, as US farmers covered those 120 different types
of crops with arsenic, they also consumed the majority of the world's
arsenic waste in the process. By 1944, what had once poisoned the land
near smelters was poisoning America's farms and fields. What was once
a point source pollution problem was a widely distributed agricultural
input. Agriculture, in other words, had become a place for copper companies to bury their toxic waste. Yet while spraying this waste onto
crops displaced it from the market sphere, it did not make it disappear. The transmutation of arsenic waste into economic poisons merely
redistributed it across the farms, fields, and bodies that comprised US

agriculture. The more farmers turned to arsenic's toxicity as a mechanism of repair, the more arsenic waste proliferated. That is what this chapter is about.

In this chapter I follow arsenic waste from its creation in the excrement of copper and tin smelters at the dawn of the Industrial Revolution to the peak of arsenic's use by American farmers. It is an interesting segment of history that explores the origins of arsenic waste, the creation of a significant technology of repair, and the production of agriculture as a waste sink. But more importantly, it shows that the arsenic waste problem was never solved; instead, copper companies just displaced it onto new lands and new bodies. As arsenic waste proliferated within agriculture, it created new problems in need of repair. Perhaps the most significant was that the use of arsenic was helping to support a system of massive overproduction. It is important to recognize that the development and growth of arsenic-based pesticides occurred when agriculture was in a constant state of surplus, in stark contrast to rationales for pesticide use at the time that invoked starvation and hunger as justifications for their use.

In fact, overproduction was so much of a problem that in the 1920s the chemical sciences were again called upon to fix agriculture.[3] By turning surplus food and fiber into new material desires, chemistry would alleviate the crushing effects of overproduction. Prices would rise even as yields grew. But *chemurgy*, as it came to be known, never lived up to expectations. Agriculture was not the ideal chemical factory that chemurgy's proponents said it was. Nor could chemistry overcome a fundamental symptom of American agriculture, what the historian Siegfried Giedion once called "surplus production and its artificial dissipation."[4] The upstream and downstream role of chemistry is important because it shows that while use of arsenic-based poisons was a key technology in a rapidly industrializing agricultural assemblage, their use was not necessary for the United States to produce sufficient food.

In ever-increasing amounts every year from the late 1860s to the mid-1940s, US farmers broadcasted arsenic-derived toxicity onto their crops. In the process they were consuming toxic waste pouring from copper smelters across the world, in a way that propped up an agricultural system whose real problem was overproduction. Agriculture's ability to internalize the toxic wastes of industry enabled mining and smelting companies not only to produce even more waste, but also to profit from its production.

INDUSTRIALIZING WASTE

Let's begin by taking a look at arsenic. Arsenic (As) is the twentieth most abundant element in the earth's crust, the fourteenth most abundant in seawater, and the twelfth most abundant in our bodies.[5] Throughout the earth's crust, arsenic is found as part of more than 250 mostly sulfur-containing minerals.[6] For thousands of years human cultures have exploited these naturally occurring arsenic sulfides as pigments, poisons, and medicines. But white arsenic (As_2O_3), the character at the center of our story, is an oxide, not a sulfide, and it has an entirely different biogeochemical history. For although white arsenic can occur naturally in small deposits, it is really an anthropogenic mineral, produced as waste during the smelting of metals like copper.[7] Humans have been synthesizing white arsenic in small quantities since the Bronze Age, but the scale of mineral production radically changed in the late seventeenth century as demand for metals like copper and tin surged in the early years of the Industrial Revolution.

Prior to the 1700s, the Prussians, French, and Swiss dominated nonferrous metallic capitalism.[8] However, in the late 1600s the British began building networks that linked their mines and smelters with their colonial and imperial interests across the world. By the turn of the century, the dominant economic geography of copper mining and smelting had shifted to the wet and windy landscapes of the British Southwest. Metals like copper enabled a vast political economy of empire: copper paid for slaves on the African coast; giant copper kettles distilled the products of slave labor and the plantation system into sweetness and power; copper-lined ship bottoms decreased the buildup of marine life and sped up the movement of people and products; and copper flowed to new industrial centers like London, Manchester, and Bombay, where laborers combined it with tin or other metals to make machines, bells, art, and coins.[9]

In the late eighteenth century, Welsh engineers revolutionized the British copper smelting industry. The "Welsh process" made possible the use of low-grade coal in the roasting ovens and expanded the types of ores that could be smelted. This new smelting technology not only bound Swansea's coal reserve to the industrialization of copper and tin mining in Cornwall and Devon, it also helped smelters there achieve the economies of scale, scope, and speed needed to command the world stage. Despite mediocre ore quality, by the turn of the century the Cornwall, Devon, and Swansea (CDS) mining and smelting complex had attained an unrivaled degree of industrial productivity.[10] However, an increase in smelting capacity demanded an increase in the availability of feedstocks, and miners went deeper in search of more ore.

In 1710, Huey Vor installed the second Newcomen engine built in Britain (the first was at a coal mine) at his Cornish tin mine, doing so in the hopes of pumping out the groundwater that was impeding labor's progress deeper into the bowels of the earth.[11] In the half century that followed, the Newcomen engine, although a prodigious consumer of coal, quickly spread across the CDS nonferrous mining industries. In the summer of 1777, James Watt arrived in Truro, the heart of Cornwall mining district, on his way to install one of his new pressurized engines at the Wheal Busy mine, a few miles to the south.[12] The next year, Watt returned to Cornwall, where he supervised the construction of an engine at a mine at Tregurtha Downs, perched on the cliffs overlooking the Celtic Sea. In the early 1780s, the CDS mining industry erected Watt engine after Watt engine.[13] By the turn of the century, in Cornwall alone, fifty-five Watt engines burning Welsh coal were actively pumping water out of copper and tin mines.[14]

By 1800, the pieces were in place for the coming British dominance in industrial copper, lead, and tin. Despite (or because of) ferocious competition and cutthroat cartelization, Britain's southwestern mining and smelting complex had attained an unrivaled degree of productivity.[15] Mining and smelting companies across the CDS region produced and refined more copper, tin, and lead than any other mining district around the world.[16] By 1820, the CDS region was mining and smelting three-quarters of global copper production.[17] Just a few years later, however, the eventual demise of the CDS complex appeared on the western horizon as the first ship loaded with foreign copper ore bound for a CDS smelter sailed up the Bristol Channel.[18] By the mid-1820s, the scene was commonplace, as ships with ores from Germany, Sweden, and Norway arrived at CDS ports. In the 1830s and 1840s, ships with ores from Chile, Cuba, Spain, Mexico, Australia, and the United States called at the same ports. Over the next decade, CDS smelters also processed ores from Portugal, Spain, Northern Rhodesia, and the Belgian Congo. Despite the costs involved in transportation, Britain's smelters remained the most lucrative option for foreign miners wishing to have their ores processed.[19] In addition, London was the center of finance and the main avenue of metallic exchange.

In 1850, British copper production hit an all-time high.[20] That year, however, the share of foreign ores consumed also hit an all-time high as two-thirds of copper that British smelters produced in 1850 arrived on foreign ships.[21] By midcentury, local ores could no longer compete, and ore production by the CDS region's nonferrous mines rapidly declined. The smelters and refiners, however, continued to expand their processing capacity to accommodate more foreign ores, increasing production until the early 1870s.[22] By the late 1870s, developments outside Britain, especially in the United States, began shifting the playing field. As a result, by the early 1880s the CDS smelting industry was nearing its end. Copper smelting's future was destined for a new industrial geography.

Between the late 1700s and the 1870s, CDS smelters had developed from small, open-pit roasting operations into high-technology, high-throughput, and high-finance operations. But these mid-nineteenth-century smelters, some with flues reaching 175 feet or more into the air, were the largest and most advanced smelters would ever get in the CDS region.[23] In 1890, copper production from CDS smelters fell to the lowest since 1800. Yet despite the rapid decline of the CDS copper complex in the face of the growing American juggernaut, many mining companies remained profitable.[24] They did so by turning to the waste streams that had been pooling across the region for the previous two hundred years.[25]

TRANSMUTING WASTE

Although examples can be found of the purposeful mining of arsenic, arsenic's industrial production should be considered solely a function of the desire for other more valuable metals, particularly copper. Over the last three hundred years, roughly 90 percent of global white arsenic synthesis has occurred during the smelting of copper.[26] It is also important to recognize that significant concentrations of arsenic are associated with specific copper ores, particular those in the enargite series, where it is found as part of larger copper-arsenic-sulfur minerals. Many copper ores, like the chalcopyrites, bornites, and chalcocites, do not contain significant concentrations of arsenic, although it can still be present. This matters because the smelting of some copper ores does not produce large amounts of arsenical waste. However, Britain's and many of the foreign ores that CDS smelters processed certainly did.

Arsenic is an impurity that poisons the quality of copper, and it has be separated in the smelting process.[27] In the smelter furnace, arsenic sublimates from red-hot ore and combines with oxygen in a distinctive blue flame to form various arsenic oxides; the trioxide (As_2O_3), the most toxic form arsenic takes, is the most commonly formed. Upon exit from the roasting oven, arsenic oxides rapidly cool, condensing into a heavy white cloud of poisonous dust that readily succumbs to gravity. Arsenic oxides tend to deposit near ore roasting operations in gradients of downwind concentration, or as one late-nineteenth-century reporter put it, smelters "deposit their soot as soon as they escape from the great heat of the furnace."[28]

Prior to 1800, the Prussians fulfilled the European world's limited demand for arsenic. In the late 1700s, most arsenic was commercially consumed as arsenic trisulfide (As_2S_3) in the manufacture of pigments like King's Yellow.[29] In the early 1800s, however, the rapidly growing synthesis of white arsenic by British smelters stimulated sporadic chemical exploration and industrial experimentation. For instance, British glass manufactures fused Venetian (Arab) clarification processes with industrial scale production and began using small amounts of white arsenic to clarify and decolorize glass.[30] White arsenic and its insidious derivatives also began seeping into the public sphere as the active ingredient in medicines, tonics, rat poisons, and eventually new lustrous green pigments.[31] By 1815, demand for the deadly white powder had grown considerably.[32]

In 1817, Dr. Richard Edwards and the Williams, Gregory, and Company partnership constructed the first dedicated white arsenic works in England.[33] Built in Perrenwell on the west coast of Cornwall, it immediately began producing a highly refined white arsenic product. The plant found its raw materials in the piles of crude arsenical wastes that had collected at nearby smelting operations. However, because they needed a steady supply of feedstock for the plant, the partners expanded their sourcing through informal partnerships with local copper smelters. They also encouraged them to build recovery flues onto their roasting ovens to collect and concentrate the arsenic oxides in their waste streams.

Seemingly overnight, white arsenic, a compound that once only the powerful had access to, had become accessible to even the poorest (see figure 1). By 1820, the deadly white powder could be found at any local pharmacist, and throughout the decades that followed white arsenic increasingly found itself in the small print below newspaper headlines like "Profligate Seduction and Suicide" and the "Melancholy of Poison."[34] Across Britain, white arsenic's new ubiquity, its utter cheapness, and its lack of odor and taste quickly earned it a reputation as a way for women to kill their husbands and a way to speed up getting one's inheritance.[35] By the 1830s, white-arsenic-derived pigments colored the

FATAL FACILITY; OR, POISONS FOR THE ASKING.

Child. "Please, Mister, will you be so good as to fill this bottle again with Lodnum, and let Mother have another pound and a half of Arsenic for the Rats (!)"
Duly Qualified Chemist. "Certainly, Ma'am. Is there any other article?"

FIGURE 1. "Fatal Facility; or, Poisons for the Asking," satirical cartoon highlighting the ease of acquiring white arsenic powder. Source: *Punch, or the London Chavirili,* September 8, 1849.

greenery of the imitation flower trade, much to the detriment of the girls and women who staffed it. Other manufactures began adding it to candy and foodstuffs to enhance their color. Together, these consumptive outlets served a greater and greater dissipative function for one of the early Industrial Revolution's most noxious industrial wastes. In other words, with each year that passed, the growth in commodity production expanded the commercial sink for white arsenic.

In 1835, Henry Conn and Company opened a second white arsenic plant near Truro in central Cornwall.[36] This plant's primary feedstock, like the Perrnewell plant's, was the wastes of previous mining and smelting processes. The presence of a second company seeking raw materials spurred competition, resulting in higher prices for crude arsenical wastes. Many nearby roasting operations responded to the market signal by installing recovery flues to concentrate the arsenic in their waste streams so they could sell it to refiners. In the early 1840s, a third Cornwall-based arsenic plant came online, and more white arsenic flowed from these plants into new forms of dissipative consumption.[37] For example, white arsenic found new uses in the manufacture of lead shot; as the basis for soaps for the taxidermy industry; and as the chemical basis for new colors for enamels, fireworks, and prints. Importantly, it also emerged as a principal chemical agent to deal with "pests" like mice, sheep parasites, and even Australian aboriginals.[38]

In the early 1850s, the three arsenic plants in Cornwall were joined by three recently built plants in Swansea. Together these plants accounted for the vast majority of global arsenic manufacture. In the late 1850s, industrial and consumer demand for white arsenic surged and higher prices, like the discovery of a new continent, instigated new quests for deposits of the anthropogenic mineral that dotted the CDS region. Small-scale entrepreneurs, including impoverished women and children, joined the hunt.

Working at a white arsenic refinery in the mid-nineteenth century was one of the most toxic occupations of the time. In addition to being horrific places to work, these arsenic plants were also technologically rudimentary.[39] Since the white arsenic industry was an industry whose feedstock was the waste of another, it only became possible in the nineteenth century as the smelting of primary metals like copper soared. As such, it lacked a history of scientific and technological development and capital investment. In the early 1860s, British mining companies finally brought new technology and economies of scale to white arsenic's manufacture.[40] Faced with rapid decline in the quality and profitability of British copper ores and the looming passage of the Alkali Acts, these companies built arsenic works with larger, more efficient, purpose-designed ovens.[41] The new plants could produce a much higher purity of white arsenic at a much faster rate than all previous methods.[42] These state-of-the-art plants produced the first "Cornish white," the high-purity white powder that quickly became the standard bearer of quality and price the world over.

The rationalization of the white arsenic industry in the early 1860s could not have been better timed, as only a few years later a farmer on the American frontier found that the arsenic-based pigment known as Paris Green could kill insects on his potato plants.[43] By the late 1870s, the CDS region was producing more than five thousand tons of refined

FIGURE 2. Copper and tin mines and arsenic plants dot "the Centre of the Cornish Mining Industry," Cornwall, UK, 1897. Source: *Pictorial England and Wales with upwards of Three Hundred and Twenty Copyright Illustrations* (London: Cassell & Co., 1897).

white arsenic per year, more than 80 percent of global production, or as one mine commission put it in 1875: "Stored in the warehouses of the [CDS] mines, ready packed for sale, [is] a quantity of white arsenic sufficient to destroy every living animal upon the face of the earth."[44] By 1880, mining industrial waste deposits had become the "chief source of profit" for the skeletal remains of the once magnificent CDS mining complex.[45]

At its peak in the early 1890s, eighty-five arsenic plants were active across the CDS region, producing over eight thousand tons of white arsenic per year from old industrial wastes (see figure 2).[46] At the time, the British held such a monopoly on arsenic that a reporter could hyperbolically state that the owner of the Devon Great Consols mine, the largest refiner of white arsenic, held "all the arsenic in the world in his hands."[47] But by the turn of the century, low arsenic prices caused by a vastly oversupplied market had laid waste to the industry, and all but the largest and most profitable arsenic works had been shuttered. The chemical horrors of World War I briefly revived the Cornish arsenic industry as wartime demand brought a new generation of prospectors to the defunct smelters of CDS region in search of the "white stones that yield poison."[48] And even though the global demand for white arsenic exploded after the war, the CDS region's old waste streams could not compete with the rivers of industrial waste flowing from foreign copper smelters.[49]

SMELTER TO THE WORLD

In the late 1870s, copper smelters in places like Sweden and Germany moved on from the midcentury designs of CDS plants.[50] As Swedish and German companies sank more and more capital into smelter design and construction, plants got bigger and more efficient, and their capacity increased. Despite this growth of copper smelting in continental Europe, it was the United States that replaced Britain as the copper smelter to the world. In the last quarter of the nineteenth century, US mining companies brought vast ore deposits and new mining and smelting technologies in line with the rapid expansion of the US rail network, waves of immigrant labor, and vertical integration to create the largest and most productive copper mining and smelting industry in the world.[51] With a bonanza of US smelter construction throughout the 1880s and 1890s, the flow of American ores to the ports of Cornwall, Devon, and Swansea ceased.

Historians usually label 1845 as the beginning of the American copper industry.[52] That year investors formed the Pittsburgh and Boston Mining Company to exploit copper deposits on the southern shores of Lake Superior.[53] Miners first applied crude milling and concentration methods on site, then loaded these ores onto ships bound for the British southwest. By 1865, 78 percent of US copper ores came from the Upper Peninsula of Michigan. Many of the ores mined in Michigan contained significant levels of arsenic, particularly Mohawkite, a copper-nickel-arsenic mineral.[54] However, because most of these ores were shipped to CDS smelters to be refined, much of the arsenic they contained was exported as well, although it is likely that some arsenic made its way back to the United States as new commodities. "Lake copper" continued to be the dominant source of American copper ore until the early 1880s.

The discovery of rich copper deposits in Montana in the 1870s ultimately persuaded American mining companies to build their own smelters. Titans of the copper industry argued that instead of being held hostage by the ore buyers of the CDS complex, they could produce finished copper cheaper than CDS smelters and profit handsomely at both ends of the red metal industry. In 1879, at its mine near Butte, Montana, the Colorado Smelting and Refining Company began construction on the first commercial copper smelter in the American West.[55] Two years later the plant came online just as the Utah Northern Railroad reached Butte from Salt Lake City.

Two other significant events occurred in 1881.[56] The first was the commencement of large-scale mining in southern Arizona at the Globe Mine and the Copper Queen Mine, mines eventually linked with the Southern Pacific and the rapidly expanding US rail and port network in 1898.[57] The second, and more important for our story, was the purchase of the Anaconda mine northwest of Butte by the partners Daly, Haggin, Tevis, and Hearst. They paid $30,000 for the claim, which was a small silver mine at the time. In the process of expanding the mine in search of silver deposits, miners cut across seam after seam of rich copper ore. Importantly, many of Montana's deposits consisted of enargite (Cu_3AsS_4), a mineral rich in both copper and arsenic. And it was the waste streams produced by smelting deposits like these that would eventually become the major feedstock of the American arsenic industry and the major source of arsenic-based toxicity for US agriculture.[58]

In 1882, the Anaconda Mining Company turned its focus from silver to copper. Soon after loads of concentrated copper ores began flowing from the mountains of Montana to CDS smelters.[59] For the owners of Anaconda, this situation was untenable. That is why in 1883, the Anaconda mining company began construction of its own smelter complex in the Deer Lodge Valley, not far from the mine. In 1885, for the first time, US exports of finished copper to Britain surpassed the exports of concentrated ore. By 1890, the Anaconda mine was the largest producer of copper in the United States, and US copper production was seven times its 1870 levels. American ore exports to CDS smelters had all but ceased.[60]

Over the next two decades, US mining companies erected state-of-the-art smelting complexes in Montana, Arizona, Utah, and Washington State.[61] During this period the copper industry was also the subject of increasingly vicious financial battles. Trusts formed and crumbled, companies grew larger and more vertically integrated, mines and smelters repeatedly changed hands, and red metal production soared.[62] In the 1890s, American mining engineers introduced two new technologies to the smelter industry—the Bessemer process and electrolytic refining—that enabled a qualitative shift in copper smelting capacity and efficiency, in turn enabling the expansion of copper mining via the ability to profitably smelt ores formerly considered unprofitable.[63] These major

American developments in metallurgy foretold the coming dominant American position in the world copper industry. Or as the economic historian Frederic Richter put it, "The years from 1895 to 1901, inclusive, were in certain respects among the most spectacular that the American copper industry has ever known."[64]

In the spring of 1902, Anaconda finished construction of a new smelter in the Deer Lodge Valley.[65] This new machine was the largest and most technologically advanced smelter in the world. But because it was processing copper ores with high arsenic concentrations, it immediately became the world's largest producer of arsenic waste. For example, by 1903, in addition to large sulfur emissions, the smelter's stack was releasing more than twenty-nine thousand pounds per day of crude arsenical waste downwind into the surrounding forest.[66]

By the outbreak of World War I, the handful of smelters across the US West—Montana, Arizona, Utah, Colorado, and Washington—produced 60 percent of the world's finished copper. The US smelting industry, like the CDS complex before it, had become the copper smelter to the world. Many of these ores, particularly the Japanese and Swedish ores shipped to American Smelting and Refining Company's (ASARCO) Tacoma, Washington, smelter contained high levels of arsenic.[67] Unlike many US smelters at the time, ASARCO's Tacoma smelter actively sought out and specialized in processing arsenic-laden ores.

In the face of low copper prices after World War I, mining companies went through further rounds of consolidation, and companies ventured abroad into places like Mexico.[68] By 1929, the maelstrom of merger and acquisition upon merger and acquisition had coalesced into four large US companies that controlled more than half of the world's copper production. The smelters of Anaconda, ASARCO, Kennecott Copper, and Phelps Dodge produced all but a small portion of US copper.[69] But as US copper smelting soared, so too did the domestic production of the early one of Industrial Revolution's most toxic industrial wastes.

FROM SOURCE TO SINK

In 1901 the Puget Sound Reduction Company launched the American arsenic industry when it constructed the first US white arsenic plant at its Everett, Washington, smelter just north of Seattle (see figure 3).[70] Refining arsenic-heavy copper, silver, and gold ores originally from California, Washington, British Columbia, and Japan, the plant made about three hundred tons of white arsenic its first year, about 10 percent of the

FIGURE 3. ASARCO (formerly Puget Sound Reduction Company) smelter, Everett, WA, ca. 1910. Arsenic mill and kitchens are in the left foreground, beneath the stacks. Dust-collecting chambers proceed from each smokestack. Source: Everett Smelter Site History, Washington State Department of Ecology, Seattle.

white arsenic consumed by US industries in 1901. Plagued by low arsenic prices and a lack of direct access to the necessary feedstocks, over the next few years the plant produced an average of about six hundred tons per year while never running at full capacity.

In 1905, the Anaconda Mining Company began construction of an arsenic plant adjacent to its immense Washoe smelter.[71] The impetus for its construction, as we will see, was not that the market demanded it. The arsenic market was already vastly oversupplied, and capturing more waste would only make it worse.[72] Low prices and cheap foreign imports kept the plant idle most of the next few years year. Low prices meant that the nearby forest remained the company's preferred sink for the smelter's arsenic waste.

It is important to understand that white arsenic supply was not determined by its demand.[73] Rather, the amount of arsenic waste produced by US smelters and thus its price was a function of copper production.[74] What this meant in practice was that the arsenic market operated from a basis of surplus; it was chronically oversupplied and thus prices remained low. During the first decade of the US arsenic industry this meant that the desire to recover arsenic from smelter effluent shifted with movements in price. Thus, it would not be the market that eventually persuaded smelting companies to install better pollution-scrubbing technology to capture more of the arsenic in their smelter effluent. Instead, it would be public responses to arsenic pollution, what the chemical engineer John Teeple called "chemical progress by injunction," that eventually pressured smelting companies to constrain their waste streams and try their hand at manufacturing more refined white arsenic.[75]

For example, in 1903, shortly after Anaconda fired up the colossal ovens at its new smelter, downwind farmers, foresters, and residents who suffered from the smelter's toxic excretions appealed to state and federal officials. Anaconda responded by compensating some of the farmers whose crops and livestock had been poisoned and sought to remedy the problem by increasing the height of its stack. Shortly thereafter, the Theodore Roosevelt administration, emboldened by a growing conservation movement, began pressuring smelter companies to install pollution-scrubbing technology. By the end of Roosevelt's tenure this pressure had turned toward the power of legal edict.[76]

This situation wasn't unique to Anaconda. It was symptomatic of a larger pollution problem plaguing the US smelter industry. Nor was it only arsenic pollution that was causing forest damage. The sulfur that was liberated with arsenic in the roasting oven was returning to the surface of the earth as acid rain, causing its own set of issues. The Roosevelt administration had informed several other mining and smelting companies that the wanton and wholesale destruction of American forests from arsenic and sulfur pollution would not be tolerated.[77] Many of these smelting companies responded, as Anaconda did, that the only way they could operate their plants profitably was by using the current highly polluting method, and that even though the technology existed to better capture smelter effluent, it was too expensive to install. The companies argued that the proposed regulations would shutter mines and smelters, resulting in job and economic losses.

In 1909, George Wickersham, President William Howard Taft's attorney general, filed a lawsuit against the Anaconda Mining Company seeking a permanent cessation of all mining activities.[78] Anaconda and other companies eventually bowed to the power of the state and installed better scrubbing flues that captured more, though definitely not all, of the white arsenic that flowed up their stacks. For the Taft administration this proved a successful and symbiotic outcome. In the government's eyes, the "the companies spent the money necessary to convert their harmful fumes to a valuable product and many additional men got work."[79] But whereas the forests gained, the problem of toxic waste

FIGURE 4. Anaconda Mining Company parade wagon advertising 99.90% pure white arsenic for sale by the train-car load, ca. 1915. Courtesy of the Montana Historical Society Research Center Photograph Archives, Helena.

remained.[80] Although better scrubbers stopped some of the waste from escaping the flue, they did not eliminate the waste. Capturing a greater share of arsenic in the effluents meant that crude white arsenic increasingly piled up at the smelters.

By 1910, US consumption of arsenic had reached more than five thousand tons per year, yet the market supply still vastly superseded demand. In practice this meant that, as the mining engineer Albert Fay observed at the time, "smelter companies only make it [white arsenic] to prevent its escape to the atmosphere" and not because the market demanded it.[81] Thus, mining companies were constantly looking for places to put their growing piles of toxic waste, and they could be creative in how they went about it (see figure 4). For instance, one of the strategies employed by Anaconda and other companies in the early 1910s was to price their white arsenic at the cost of transportation. Trying to rid themselves of their accumulating toxic waste, these companies gave their arsenic away for free to those who would pay to have it shipped. Fortunately for Anaconda and other smelting companies, agricultural demand for arsenic surged in the lead-up to World War I.

By the outbreak of the war, the poisoning of crops had become the largest consumer of white arsenic in the United States. As we will see in the next section, much of this new demand came from western apple and pear growers who had developed capital-intensive export-oriented industries in coastal central California, eastern Washington, and the Hood River valley of Oregon.[82] Wartime demand for white arsenic was also a function of its use in the manufacture of lead shot, as a substitute for antimony oxide (Sb_2O_3) in glass manufacture, and its secret incorporation into chemical weapons like Lewisite and Adamsite. Demand also came from the expanded use of pesticides during the war.[83] With higher food prices, more farmers could afford the fertilizers, machines, and pesticides they needed to specialize and intensify their production. As war raged in Europe, more and more arsenic waste found its way onto farms and fields across the United States.

US industries consumed more than ten thousand tons of white arsenic in 1915, most of it by agriculture, but at a price of three cents a pound it was still not profitable for many US companies to capture and refine more of their waste.[84] Even though US smelters synthesized more than double the domestic demand, most of it was not captured or refined.[85] That year 90 percent of the white arsenic that US manufactures consumed was still imported from Mexico, Japan, Spain, and Germany. In 1916, soaring prices finally enticed some mining companies to capture more of their arsenical wastes.[86] For example, in 1916, ASARCO installed a state-of-the-art Cottrell electrical precipitator at its Tacoma smelter to capture more white arsenic in its waste stream.[87] With wartime demand, for the first time US white arsenic plants operated at full capacity.[88]

In 1917, the Anaconda Mining Company enlarged its arsenic plant at Great Falls, Montana, to treat more "accumulated flue dusts."[89] Strong demand and a constrained foreign supply drove the price of white arsenic in the United States to five times its prewar levels, and by the end of the year seven US plants were refining approximately 80 percent of domestic white arsenic demand. Earlier that spring, the Food Administration (FA) Division of the War Industries Board brought arsenic under its control.[90] It banned all exports and began regulating its price and uses.[91] The war came to an abrupt end in the fall of 1918. Even so, in 1919, expanded agricultural use caused US demand for white arsenic to remain at wartime levels.

Shortly after the war drew to a close, the Anaconda Mining Company fired up the ovens on its new copper smelter. The smelter's design

FIGURE 5. Electrostatic plates used to precipitate arsenic in flue dust, 1919. Courtesy of the Montana Historical Society Research Center Photograph Archives, Helena.

reflected Anaconda's response to government pressure to reduce the toxic waste spewing from its effluent stacks (see figure 5).[92] But while new pollution abatement technology again reduced the fraction of arsenic waste released into the surrounding environment, it created another problem.[93] That is why in addition to a new smelter with its state-of-the-art pollution-scrubbing technology, Anaconda also built two massive "arsenic kitchens" to refine its growing share of arsenical waste into something the company could sell (see figure 6).

In the early 1920s, agricultural commodity prices collapsed as farmers confronted severe agricultural depression. White arsenic production and prices also fell sharply. But unlike US agriculture in general, the production and consumption of refined arsenic quickly recovered as more and more farmers began poisoning their fields.[94]

In 1922, ASARCO built a new and larger smelter and arsenic plant at Tacoma, Washington. That same year the US Smelting, Refining, and Milling Company, at its Midvale, Utah, arsenic plant, became the first mining company to directly manufacture insecticides (calcium arsenate

FIGURE 6. White arsenic barreled for sale. Courtesy of the Montana Historical Society Research Center Photograph Archives, Helena.

$[Ca_3(AsO_4)_2])$ for agricultural use.[95] By this time, three companies at five plants controlled the US arsenic market. ASARCO operated arsenic plants in Denver, Colorado, Tacoma, Washington, and New Jersey. The Anaconda Mining Company operated twin plants at its Washoe, Montana, smelter, and the US Smelting, Refining, and Milling Company operated a plant at Midvale in Utah. In the mid-1920s, the refined white arsenic market was again vastly oversupplied. This caused some mining companies to simply bury their "ore" and wait for higher prices. It also led chemical salesmen to pray for large pest outbreaks that would increase demand.[96] Others looked offshore for new sinks. For example, in 1926 US mining and chemical companies began exporting both white arsenic and arsenical insecticides in significant quantities to places like the West Indies and South America, especially to the cotton-producing areas of Peru.[97]

By the mid-1920s, arsenic-based pesticides had generalized across the intensive pome-fruit-growing regions of the US West.[98] However, reflecting the state of agricultural development at the time, agricultural consumption east of the Rockies was less consistent.[99] For example, less than 20 percent of southern cotton farmers used arsenical poisons on a regular basis.[100] As more than one observer noted at the time, an expansion of pest control across the entire southern cotton-growing region would create "a potential outlet for practically all the arsenic now produced in the United States."[101] This potential expansion was aided a few years later with the introduction of the crop-dusting airplane (see figure 8, later in the chapter).

The year 1929 was a good one for the white arsenic industry. That year US companies refined more than sixteen thousand tons of white arsenic, while US industries consumed more than twenty-seven thousand tons, or more than two-thirds of global production. The difference between production and consumption was largely made up by imports from American-owned refineries in Mexico.[102] Arsenic demand in the United States dropped sharply following the stock market crashes of late 1929. However, it quickly rebounded over the next few years, not only because of growing farmer demand but also because of large purchases by the United States Department of Agriculture (USDA) to poison grasshoppers that were adding insult to injury across dust bowl country.

In the early 1940s, US production and consumption of white arsenic peaked.[103] With more than two-thirds of it used to poison crops, agriculture remained the largest disposal site for this toxic industrial waste. The historian Joel Tarr has written that the "history of industrial waste disposal . . . involves the search for a sink in which wastes could be disposed of in the cheapest and most convenient way possible."[104] But cheapness and convenience must also be read as shorthand for the messy, contested, and transformational history of industrial waste disposal.[105] In the early twentieth century, economic entomologists, policy makers, and farmers rebranded arsenic waste as the active ingredient in nonhuman mass death, in turn making US agriculture the largest market and the largest sink for the streams of toxic waste flowing from the world's copper smelters. In the next section I turn to how that transformation happened.

ARSENIC-BASED REPAIR

During the early 1860s, as the US military and colonists pushed farther west of the Mississippi, the Colorado potato beetle (*Leptinotarsa decemlineata*) began the inverse trek.[106] By the mid-1860s, the beetle had spread from Colorado to states like Missouri and Wisconsin via the logistics networks built to supply these new outposts and settlements. The beetle immediately found that the new territory was ripe for colonization. Legend suggests that in 1867 a Missouri farmer first successfully "controlled" the Colorado potato beetle by throwing some leftover green paint colored with the arsenic-based pigment Paris Green onto his infested potato plants. Other evidence suggests that Paris Green was used as a poison in Colorado as early as 1862.[107] Either way, in 1868 Edwin Reynolds, a Wisconsin farmer, published the first report of an experiment using Paris Green. Mixing Paris Green, wood ashes, and water into a spreadable paste, he applied it to his potato plants.[108] By the mid-1870s, despite a growing concern over foliage injury, farmers across the United States were experimenting with Paris Green on a variety of crops.

Paris Green, a copper-arsenic-based compound named for the doctor who developed it, not the French city, was a brilliant and unnatural derivative of Scheele's green. It had been used extensively across the European color industries since the early 1850s, and by the 1860s paints colored with arsenic-based green pigments were common in the United States.[109] These green paints could be found even in many small frontier settlements. In the mid-1870s, a cheap industrial waste product called London Purple joined Paris Green in US wholesale chemical markets.

London Purple consisted of a mixture of calcium arsenate ($Ca_3(AsO_4)_2$), calcium arsenite ($CaHAs_3O_3$), aniline ($C_6H_5NH_2$), and organic matter.[110] The rivers, creeks, and canals near British dyeworks had been the first disposal site for this purple-tinged industrial waste. However, with the discovery of Paris Green's agricultural worth in the United States, British dye companies had found a new sink.[111] London Purple's physical properties, such as its ability to be easily emulsified in a paste or a spray, made it easier to apply than Paris Green.[112] Plus, as a rapidly growing waste product lacking a nonagricultural utility, it was also cheaper than Paris Green. London Purple made significant inroads into the eastern US economic poison market in the 1870s and 1880s. However, its inconsistent chemical composition and its readily apparent damage to crops limited widespread acceptance. Paris Green's spread across US agriculture was also quite limited. Progressive farmers and agricultural scientists had tried it on many other crops besides potatoes, but its tendency to be toxic to plants limited its uptake.

In the early 1880s, the major concern of economic entomologists turned from potato bugs to the spread of the European gypsy moth (*Lymantria dispar*) in northeastern forests.[113] A decade prior, the entrepreneurial Frenchman Etienne Leopold Trouvelout had imported the gypsy moth into Boston in the hopes of spawning an American "silk" industry. However, this scheme quickly collapsed, and the moths escaped and rapidly spread. Throughout the 1880s, economic entomologists repeatedly foretold the ecological and economic collapse of northeastern forests unless they intervened chemically.

In 1892, F. C. Moulton developed (hydrogen) lead arsenate ($PbHAsO_4$) as an alternative to Paris Green and London Purple in the hope of annihilating the gypsy moth.[114] What made lead arsenate different was that it was not immediately soluble in water, and thus it could be sprayed onto the delicate foliage of shade and forest trees.[115] Lead arsenate quickly became the chief weapon during the ensuing and ultimately unsuccessful "gypsy moth wars" that took place across northeastern forests over the next decade. However, it was on the farm that lead arsenate ultimately found its home. By the turn of the century, the use of arsenicals in agriculture, particularly lead arsenate, was rapidly expanding. Yet they were still used by only a small fraction of US farmers.

Many American farmers were hesitant to coat their crops with poisons. Some had observed firsthand or heard secondhand stories of significant crop damage caused by these new chemicals. Newspapers at the time also began reporting the mass die-offs of fish and fowl caused by arsenical pesticides running off a farmer's fields into lakes and rivers.[116] Other farmers resisted the use of poisons on the farm indirectly by opposing the industrialization of US agriculture that was well underway.[117] The situation, however, was vastly different on the West Coast, where intensive export-driven commercial agriculture was booming.[118]

As we will see in the next chapter, turn-of-the-century California agriculture is perhaps best remembered for the citrus empire of Southern

California. By 1900, the citrus industry was the pinnacle of agroindustrial progress. Yet the citrus industry is only one example of the dramatic changes that came to the fertile valleys of California during the last quarter of the nineteenth century as growers shifted out of expansive wheat production and into intensive horticulture.[119] For instance, in the late 1890s, growers began turning the coastal valleys of the Monterey Bay area, especially the Pájaro Valley, into a major apple-producing region. As the industry developed, the codling moth (*Cydia pomonella*), the proverbial worm in the apple, first introduced to the eastern United States sometime in the late 1700s, quickly merged its life cycle with the industrial apple tree. In other words, as the industry grew and intensified, the codling moth began to cause more extensive commercial damage.[120]

Pájaro Valley apple growers first used lead arsenate to combat the codling moth in 1902.[121] Right away, though, growers noticed that spraying resulted in extensive foliage injury. First thinking it was caused by impurities in their poisons, growers tried switching brands, but all of them caused significant harm. In 1905, growers finally appealed to Charles Woodworth, professor of entomology and head of the UC Agricultural Extension, for a remedy to the situation. In the spring of 1906, Woodworth sent two UC Berkeley researchers, William Volck and Ellerslie Luther, south to Watsonville to appraise the situation and come up with a diagnosis and a possible solution (see figure 7).[122]

Apple trees in the coastal valleys of California were subject to different climatic regimes than East Coast or Midwest orchards. California had a Mediterranean climate, meaning that there was no summer rain. What the central coast did have, especially during the height of the arsenical spraying season in May and June, were nightly fogs that closed off the valleys, as John Steinbeck put it, "from the sky and from all the rest of the world."[123] Unlike the Midwest's and East Coast's rains, these Steinbeckian fogs that enveloped the apple trees wet the lead arsenate dust without washing it off. Volck and Luther quickly determined that the lead arsenate dusts were reacting with the water in nighttime fogs, and therefore they needed a new insoluble poison.

During the fall and winter of 1906–1907, Volck and Luther discovered two things that dramatically increased the consumption of lead arsenate. The first was the successful development of a nonsoluble lead arsenate known as "basic" lead arsenate that could be used successfully in the foggy coastal valleys of California. As the central coast's apple trees sat dormant following the 1906 growing season, Luther and Volck worked furiously to develop a lead arsenate compound that would resist

FIGURE 7. Mr. Volck and Mr. Luther experimenting with economic poisons on the Charles Rodgers Ranch, Watsonville, CA, ca. 1910. Courtesy of the Pajaro Valley Historical Society, Watsonville, CA.

the dense coastal fogs. By the early spring of 1907, they concluded that one of their four hundred newly synthesized lead arsenate compounds $(Pb_5OH(AsO_4)_3)$ had the necessary properties to successfully kill the codling moth without injuring the foliage or damaging the fruit.[124] After bud break they returned to Watsonville to conduct field tests. These tests proved that basic lead arsenate was extremely effective in killing the codling moth and did not harm the trees as the hydrogen form did. Importantly, though, not only was their new product effective, it was much cheaper to make than all other lead arsenates on the market.

The second improvement came in the production of compounds for their experiments. Luther and Volck figured out that they could replace the expensive lead acetate catalyst with cheap lead oxide and acetic acid (vinegar), significantly decreasing the cost of production. This reagent change also dramatically increased reaction yields and reaction velocity. Thus, in the process of searching for an insoluble poison, Luther and Volck developed a commercial method of quickly making cheap, high-purity lead arsenate. In the fall of 1907, Luther and Volck

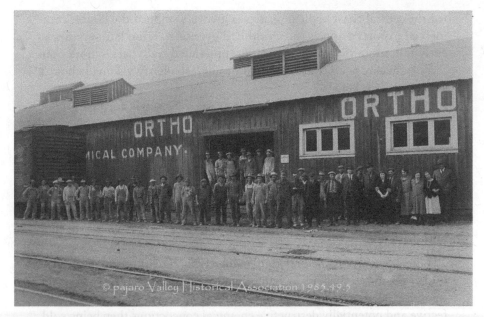

FIGURE 8. California Spray-Chemical Company manufacturing plant, Watsonville, CA, ca. 1915. Courtesy of the Pajaro Valley Historical Society, Watsonville, CA.

dispatched patent applications for both discoveries to the US Patent Office.[125]

Early the next year, they resigned their positions at the University of California and spun off the Berkeley-based company California Spray Chemical Company (Cal-Spray) to manufacture and sell basic and hydrogen lead arsenate under the Ortho brand (see figure 8). By the end of the year, the two entrepreneurs had built a pesticide plant in Watsonville to manufacture both types of poisons as well as lime-sulfur, a commonly used dormant spray among the stone fruit growers in the Santa Clara, San Joaquin, and Sacramento Valleys. In 1909, Luther and Volck incorporated their company in California and brought in the grower-shippers Siliman and Rodgers as well as the Bean Spray Pump Company as major investors.[126] They also began licensing their patents to other chemical companies in the United States and Europe.[127]

Between the discovery of basic lead arsenate in 1907 and the end of the 1910 apple-growing season, economic poison consumption rose dramatically among Pájaro Valley apple growers as the use of lead arsenate became a necessary input of industrial apple production.[128] The close of the 1910 growing season also marked a significant milestone for the central coast apple industry as growers shipped the largest commercial export of apples the world had ever seen. From late summer to early fall, more than four thousand apple-filled train cars—more than sixty train cars per day at the height of harvest—left Watsonville bound for eastern markets.[129]

Making this harvest possible, of course, were newly formed private spraying companies that consumed the entire stock of Cal-Spray's novel poison to coat 95 percent of the apple orchards within ten miles of Watsonville. And more would have been sprayed if more of the poison had been available. During the 1911 spray season, these private spray companies in the Watsonville area doubled their consumption of lead arsenate. This new poison was so effective that in 1912, in a show of confidence, Luther offered growers one dollar for every worm they found in orchards sprayed with Ortho brand lead arsenate.[130]

On July 1, 1911, the first significant US insecticide regulation went into effect in California.[131] Championed by California agribusiness, the Insecticide Law was aimed at protecting California growers from ineffective and potentially destructive chemical concoctions then being sold. The law stipulated that all products sold as economic poisons must have their composition registered with the state. It also required that companies affix a label on the product stating the true chemical composition. The law gave UC Extension agents the power to regulate, test, and levy fines on incorrectly or falsely labeled insecticides, which stimulated the development of the Insecticide and Fungicide at UC Berkeley. California pesticide manufacturers benefited from the law because it stamped out the sale of low-quality and fraudulent imports while also providing the legal basis needed to rationalize California's economic poison industry.

By this time California growers stood foremost among all users of economic poisons across the world, and the production of pesticides within California was rapidly growing.[132] In 1912, Cal-Spray began shipping lead arsenates to apple and pear growers in eastern Washington, where they quickly displaced many of the lower quality lead arsenates that growers had been using. In 1916, Cal-Spray opened multiple sales branches in Oregon and Washington, and in 1919, they consciously became the first provider of "scientific pest control."[133] This meant that all of its salesmen would have to undergo scientific training in entomology and chemistry before they could sell economic poisons to farmers.[134]

After World War I, arsenic consumption by southern cotton farmers began to rival that of western apple and pear growers. Although calcium arsenate was first discovered in 1906, it wasn't until wartime

FIGURE 9. "[Calcium arsenate] dust settling over cotton plants in the wake of the airplane, November 28, 1925." Courtesy of the Special Collections Research Center, North Carolina State University Libraries, Raleigh.

demands intersected with an explosion of the boll weevil across the South that cotton growers first embraced the killing power of arsenic. By 1919, a small number of scientifically minded cotton growers were poisoning their crops on a regular basis. The consumption of calcium arsenate grew slowly over the next few years. However, poison consumption spiked alongside the introduction of the crop-dusting airplane (see figure 9). Suddenly, as the president of the Association of Economic Entomologists put it, "an airplane [could] poison an acre of cotton thoroughly in less than two seconds," doing more and far better work over a season "than 4000 laborers applying calcium arsenate spray by means of knapsack pumps."[135] The rapid expansion of calcium arsenate among southern cotton growers would also make cotton gins into one of the most potent point sources of arsenic into the environment in the interwar era.

As the use of arsenic-based poisons spread to more farms and more crops, arsenic residues on fruits and vegetables became the subject of increased governmental and public scrutiny.[136] Since the late 1910s there had been a growing public discomfort with arsenic-laden produce, especially among East Coast health and pure food activists.[137] Concern over arsenic was not limited to the United States. British consumers and health officials had been wary of some US agricultural goods since the late 1890s.[138] This was easy to understand, as produce sprayed with arsenic-based poisons was often coated with a whitish film that was hard to wash off. The very same properties that kept lead arsenate from causing foliage injury made it difficult to remove post-harvest. In the early 1920s, city inspectors in places like Boston began seizing and analyzing produce they deemed a public hazard. The USDA responded by launching scientific studies into spraying practices and the human toxicity of arsenic residues even as political battles raged over the power of the USDA to regulate arsenic (and eventually lead) on produce.[139] At the time, the Bureau of Chemistry, via the Food and Drug Act of 1906, had the power to seize hazardous produce that crossed state lines. Yet it remained reluctant to do so.[140]

In April 1925 Florida celery growers finally forced the Bureau of Chemistry's regulatory hand. Earlier that spring, growers began using lead arsenate to try to exterminate the false celery leaftier caterpillar (*Udea profundalis*). Despite its lack of efficacy, they repeatedly doused their celery with lead arsenate, many of them doing so right up until the day of harvest.[141] A Bureau of Chemistry inspector tested some of the celery and found that a single celery stalk contained upwards of 9 mg of arsenic.

Later that year Washington apples made international headlines, and not for their taste. Beginning in October, English newspapers began reporting people falling ill after consuming Washington-grown apples.[142] Washington growers by this time were spraying hundreds of pounds of lead arsenate per acre on their apples throughout the growing season.[143] As a result, the next year the USDA finally began enforcing the tolerance—the maximum amount of arsenic residue allowed on produce—originally set as part of the Pure Food and Drug Act. Bureau of Chemistry inspectors began seizing interstate fruit and vegetables that were found to contain more arsenic than allowed. For growers, what had once been the key to bringing an unblemished crop to market had become a potentially ruinous problem in need of a solution. Not only could it cause immediate harm to growers in places like the Pacific Northwest, but shippers were wary of losing the lucrative British market share to Australian apple growers over the long term.[144]

By the late 1920s, after fierce political skirmishes between the USDA, Congress, and the pome-fruit industry, western growers, packers, and shippers had adapted their spraying and post-harvest practices to meet the new regulatory climate. Growers started allowing for more time between the last spray and day of harvest, while shippers built chemical washing houses to clean their apples in order to meet federal tolerances.[145] These repairs in no way fixed the problem; in fact lead arsenate residues remained a contentious issue until they were replaced by newer poisons after World War II. Regulation also stimulated investigation into arsenical substitutes, like the fluoride wastes of the American phosphate industries or oil sprays made from California petroleum industry wastes.[146] And although it originally appeared that fluoride-based poisons would replace arsenic-based ones, their readily apparent human toxicity and lack of effectiveness limited their experimentation and use.[147] Oil-based poisons would not end up replacing lead arsenate; instead, as we see in chapter 3, they eventually became an additional component of pome-fruit growers' arsenal in the lead-up to World War II.

By 1927, nineteen companies were operating twenty-two arsenical pesticide plants across the United States.[148] Many different types of chemical firms produced these poisons. Large chemical companies like Sherwin-Williams, the Grasselli Chemical Company, and the DOW Chemical Company produced arsenical poisons as part of a suite of early nineteenth-century chemical products. Some companies, like Cal-Spray, specialized in economic poisons, while numerous smaller chemical firms specialized in making a single product. Unlike the bigger chemical firms, these smaller companies often built their factories near copper smelters or near agricultural markets with high demand. For example, in 1927 the Latimer-Goodwin Chemical Company opened a second lead arsenate plant on the tide flats near ASARCO's Tacoma, Washington, smelter, which specialized in processing high-arsenic-content copper ores from the United States and abroad. With cheap access to raw materials and a steadily growing market among eastern Washington apple growers, the Latimer-Goodwin company saw a bright future ahead as "fruit protection becomes more universal on part of all growers."[149] In the interwar period, poison consumption by farmers did just that.

Between 1919 and 1929, the on-farm use of lead arsenate more than doubled, while calcium arsenate consumption grew an order of magnitude. In the late 1920s, sodium arsenite and crude arsenical wastes gained popularity among railroad companies as herbicides along rights of way and as bait for grasshoppers.[150] With these poisons what once required teams of men to clear the tracks of weeds now required a couple of men with a pressurized spray machine. Despite the global economic malaise during the 1930s, arsenical poison consumption by US farmers continued to increase rapidly.[151] With every growing season that passed, more and more arsenic flowed from the waste streams of the smelter industry to a small number of chemical plants and then on to the farms and fields of the United States. In 1934, arsenic consumption spiked, due in part to large purchases by the USDA's Bureau of Entomology for its fight against grasshoppers that had descended upon the dust bowl West.[152] Government purchases of arsenical poisons for grasshopper control continued to be significant until the early 1940s.[153]

By that time, the American home had also become a steady market for arsenic-based poisons, particularly Paris Green and lead arsenate, where they were used to poison rodents and flies and helped make the perfect American lawn possible. At the outbreak of World War II, about one-third of all the Paris Green sold in the United States poisoned urban lawns and golf courses.[154] So much arsenic was moving into the household by this time that when asked to convert their lawns to victory gardens, many home gardeners expressed concern over potential arsenic toxicity from the food that they would produce. In May 1942, the US War Production Board classified arsenic as a Group 1 material, regulating its use and price.[155] And just as during World War I, US smelters captured more white arsenic in their waste streams, and once again arsenic refineries ran at full capacity. In 1943, despite rationing, American farmers consumed even more arsenic.

Both the domestic production and consumption of white arsenic peaked in the early 1940s.[156] Agricultural use of arsenic-based poisons peaked shortly thereafter.[157] After World War II, inorganic arsenicals like lead arsenate quickly fell out of favor with farmers as new organic poisons like DDT and 2,4-D gained in popularity. The production of domestically refined white arsenic also rapidly fell, reflecting both a decline in demand as well as the restructuring of the US copper industry.[158] In 1985, US production of refined white arsenic ceased for good with the closing of ASARCO's arsenic plant adjacent to its Tacoma, Washington, smelter that had been shuttered the previous year.[159] US industrial consumption, however, did not follow the same pattern, especially as arsenic's use as a wood preservative became more popular during the 1970s and 1980s.

Another significant reason for the continued industrial use of white arsenic after World War II was that new arsenic-based organic poisons began to be used in the poultry and cotton industries.[160] After World War II arseno-organic compounds became a standard component of poultry feed, where they were used to rid the industrial chicken of the parasites that robbed growers of their maximum yield.[161] Although this practice is mostly banned across the United States today, many chicken growers still feed their chickens similar compounds. In addition, despite the rapid growth of organochlorine-based pesticides and herbicides after the war, pesticide companies also introduced arsenic-containing synthetic compounds such as cacodylic acid for use as nonselective herbicides. Shortly after its introduction, the US military began spreading cacodylic acid as a main component of the chemical weapon Agent Blue across the rice-growing regions of Vietnam.[162] By the early 1980s, organic arsenicals like monosodium methyl arsenate (MMSA), disodium methyl arsenate (DSMA), arsenic acid (H_3AsO_4), and cacodylic acid (($CH_3)_2AsO_2H$) were some of the most used herbicides by volume in the United States. For example, throughout the 1980s as fall approached, cotton farmers coated about fifteen million acres with these organic arsenicals to defoliate their cotton plants and make possible large-scale mechanical harvest.[163] Despite being accompanied by carbon and chlorine instead of lead or calcium, the poisoning of US agriculture remained a profitable disposal site for one of the copper industry's most noxious wastes.

WASTE DISPLACEMENT, ARSENIC-BASED REPAIR, AND THE PROLIFERATION OF SURPLUS

By 1945, the transformation of arsenic waste into economic poisons had allowed American farmers to reach new heights of abundance. But it was this very abundance, to borrow a phrase from the historian Frederick Davis, that became a "tragic irony" of pesticide use.[164] This tragic irony was that pesticides helped exacerbate the overproduction of agricultural commodities, meaning that they were not helping to save the nation's farmers but instead undermining their ability to make ends meet. I bring this up now because the history related here, as well as the other stories I tell in this book, all took place in an era of agricultural surplus. For far too long pesticide proponents have used the specter of starvation and hunger to justify their use. But if we, as Rachel Carson suggested, take a look at the historical development of pesticides, we can see that they had nothing to do with feeding the nation or supporting America's farmers. Instead their use was about maintaining a particular type of agricultural political economy. This is best exemplified by the development of chemurgy in the interwar years. Chemurgy was as much a political movement as it was a way to reduce farm surplus. What is important about it is that chemistry was again called in to repair agriculture by turning this surplus into the products of everyday life.

After World War I, US farmers were confronted by what the agricultural economist and economic historian William Cochrane has called the "curse of agricultural abundance."[165] By this he simply meant the pattern of farm output exceeding demand, a pattern that has plagued American agriculture since its inception. This chronic condition, as Henry A. Wallace once argued, has a "disastrous effect upon national well-being as crop shortages used to have on the isolated communities of a simpler age."[166] In the interwar phase of this recurring problem, chemists and government officials believed that they had finally found a solution that would allow the system to continue without any significant changes. If chemistry could remove surplus goods from the market, prices would rise even as farmers produced more. If chemistry could turn that surplus into new material desires, consumers would get better things and live better lives. If only.[167]

I don't want to get into the nitty gritty of chemurgy here; there is already excellent scholarship on the topic.[168] What is important about it is that it is a prime example of how toxic mining waste proliferated far and wide within agriculture. The use of arsenic as a technology of repair not only led to the poisoning of US agriculture and to new problems that needed to be repaired; its use also propped up a system whose actual problem was overproduction. A letter to the *Washington Post* in 1933 spoke to this very contradiction. "It is rather inconsistent" wrote Robert A. Mullen, "with enormous crop surpluses and the Government preparing to subsidize the farmers of this country with taxpayers' money in return for a reduction of acreage and production, that farmers are spending money on poison to kill the very solution to the perplexing overproduction problem—namely Nature herself."[169] What Robert Mullen was getting at was that it might be okay if insects ate some of the nation's crops. This would not only help reduce farm surplus and make farmers more prosperous; it would also mean that farmers would not have to poison their crops and contaminate themselves, their workers, and the environment. It would mean, as Robert Mullen also pointed out, that the great national experiment of chronic arsenic poisoning via agriculture would not be necessary.

But the type of solution that Robert Mullen described would never have worked within the ideological, political, and economic context of interwar agriculture. By the interwar period there were already vested interests aimed at maintaining the chemical status quo, in both industry and government. We can also imagine that the copper mining industry would not have been pleased by a precipitous drop in agricultural arsenic consumption. They were already dealing with considerable localized pollution problems, and having to hold onto vastly greater amounts of arsenic waste would only have exacerbated them.[170] Nor would government agencies do an about face on their policies aimed at increasing pesticide use among American famers. By the mid-1930s chemistry and chemicals were viewed as the ultimate solution to many of the nation's problems. Agriculture didn't need to change; in fact, surplus production could be turned into a benefit if only chemists could figure things out. Therefore, that pesticides were helping to exacerbate overproduction was a good thing because it eventually meant more prosperity for everyone.

The type of solution that Robert Mullen outlined would also not have worked because he did not recognize that for economic entomologists, chemical pest control was about more than simply warding off future starvation or developing a new agricultural science. For many, the deployment of toxic chemicals in agriculture was the last battle in humanity's war with pestilent life. It took me a while to recognize how important this war to end all wars was in the development of chemical pest control. It would be clear to anyone studying the history of pre–World War II pesticides that war metaphors and wartime technology moved back and forth between the military and agriculture, but I didn't expect war to be so fundamental to the developmental of toxicity-based repair. I did not expect it to be a key infrastructural development of an agroindustrial waste regime that transformed the toxic wastes of industry into agricultural inputs. In the next chapter I zero in on a critical moment in the development of pest control, one in which chemical war became just another input.

CHAPTER 2

Commercializing Chemical Warfare

In times of peace and prosperity, states and individuals alike
follow higher standards. . . . But war is a stern teacher.

—Thucydides, *History of the Peloponnesian War,* ~400 BCE

In 2014 I became a master gardener. Master gardeners are trained volun-
teers who provide research-based advice to home gardeners.[1] Individual
Master Gardener programs are a part of the cooperative extension of
the land grant university (LGU) in the state in which they operate, and
specialists from these universities lead the training. Thus, as part of my
education, in the spring of 2014 an internationally renowned expert
from the University of California lectured the class on the science of
pest control. The speaker began by emphasizing that extension agents
were shifting away from a nomenclature of pest control and into one
of pest management. The speaker noted that they were doing this as a
way to broaden the idea of pest control to include biological, cultural,
and physical methods. But the speaker also emphasized the negative
connotation that comes with the idea of control, specifically the notion
that toxic chemicals can actually be used to battle agricultural pests into
submission.

I found this proviso particular engrossing because at the time I was
researching the history of cyanide fumigation, the first industry-wide use
of toxic chemicals to control insects, and thus I was quite sensitive to
the language that economic entomologists and other pest control scientists used to describe their practices. For me what was fascinating about
this presentation was not the material that the speaker covered; rather,
it was that they kept reverting to language of dominance and warfare
despite the reference to rebranding pest control as pest management. In

one instance the speaker caught themselves using this type of language to describe how growers had to "attack" pests at particular stages of development, yet that did not stop the rest of the lecture from continuing in the same manner.

I found it fascinating that the speaker could not get away from references to a war on pests despite beginning the talk with acknowledging the need for change. They could not escape the pest war because, as I argue in this chapter, in the late 1880s war itself became just another input of a rapidly industrializing agrarian assemblage. Thus, to truly get away from a war on pests would mean more than just a change of names or an increased emphasis on nonchemical methods of pest control. It would require a fundamental transformation of agriculture away from an infrastructure of chemical war.

You may be asking yourself what war has to do with the transformation of waste into agricultural inputs. When I first began this project, I was not sure that it had anything to do with it. I was already familiar with Edmond Russell's classic book *War and Nature*, in which he describes the coevolution of agriculture and war since World War I.[2] But as I read the *Journal of Economic Entomology* cover to cover, I could also see that agriculture's chemical war stretched back beyond the Ypres front in the spring of 1915, where Russell begins his story. I could see how integral war was to the development of chemical pest control since the very beginning. In other words, in the late 1880s chemical war became a key part of the very same infrastructure that moved industrial waste from factory to field. It not only expedited the movement and transformation of this waste; it was key to rationalizing any collateral damage caused by waste's transmutation into economic poisons. What I began to realize was that war served as the ultimate justification for the poisoning of agriculture. That humans were at war with pests and that pests were at war with humans was fundamental to the development of chemical pest control, and it remains so today. That is why the pest control specialist I sat listening to in 2014 had such a hard time distancing themselves from the pest war, because no matter what they said or what they called it, industrial chemical pest control has always been an act of war.

War theorists and war historians have long observed that in times of war societal values often go by the wayside, so what does it mean that industrial agriculture has been at war for over one hundred years? It means that agriculture has been allowed to behave in ways that would never be tolerated in times of peace. If you are fighting the war to end all wars, then something like environmental contamination or damage to worker health becomes trivial. Both become just inadvertent consequences of a necessary war. But as war became increasingly integral to the poisoning of agriculture and the transformation of agriculture into a sink for toxic waste, justifications for the war became increasingly fraught. As war spread across agriculture, growers' biggest problem became too much food, meaning that the pest war was not being fought to make sure we had enough to eat. Instead, it was being waged in the name of agroindustrial accumulation and to maintain a particular type of agrarian political economy that cared more about short-term profit than it did about feeding the nation or worker or environmental health.

In this chapter I use the development of cyanide fumigation in the late 1880s to argue that war has always been a critical part of the infrastructure of chemical pest control. I want to push the argument beyond the coevolution of war and agriculture and refocus it back onto the pest war itself. I do this because I've had a lingering question in the back of my mind ever since I first read Edmond Russell's book. While Russell is more interested in examining how the control of nature can increase military power and vice versa, I am more concerned with whether the pest war is a just war. I want to examine the pest war outside of its relationship to technology or the spread of democracy, as Russell did. It is true that cyanide fumigation eventually became a weapon of human war and a tool of genocide, but that is not my focus.[3] What matters to me is that industrial pest control has always been an act of war, no matter what we call it. Thus, my concern is whether that war was just when it started and whether it continues to be so today. As such, in addition to the narrative that follows, I also consider the pest war within a framework of just war theory.

The origin story I tell in this chapter highlights how both toxicity and warfare became foundational agricultural inputs. I offer an alternative history of the origins of industrial chemical warfare that began on the western floodplain of the Los Angeles River in 1886, not on a European battlefield in 1915.[4] Cyanide fumigation—the practice of releasing hydrogen cyanide gas under a tented tree—discovered in Los Angeles in the fall of 1886, bought a temporary reprieve from the ravages of insects that had aligned their life histories with intensive monoculture. But the rapid development of toxicant-based repair also tied the efficient production of high-quality citrus fruit to endless chemical war. In the story that follows I have expressly used the language of pest control scientists at the time. I do this not only to highlight how important a state of war was to these growers and scientists, but also to convey how they perceived of the intention of pests to cause harm. I want you to think beyond the metaphorical use of war language. I want you to literally take them at their word.

CAN INSECTS WAGE WAR?

In the conclusion of this chapter I turn to the question of whether the pest war is a just war. But to do that we have to first consider whether an insect intends to commit harm when it eats a farmer's crop. To begin with, no insect is born a pest; they are made into pests by humans calling them pests.[5] To call something a pest is to set certain forms of life in opposition to economic, social, and political order. It is always a moral and political act that subjects certain forms of life to possible eradication. Calling something a pest means that it intends to harm, and thus the question becomes not whether to eradicate the danger, but how and when. Further, by linking pests with dirt, disease, and ideas of purity, pests become "matter out of place" that demands to be "cleansed" to maintain social order.[6]

The history of the animal trials in western Europe offers us a way to think about how calling something a pest provides justification for waging war against it.[7] These cases, though few and far between, put animals on trial for their crimes against humans and property. These were more than show trials. The accused had representation, plus real harm had been done. What is important about them for the story that follows is that by the seventeenth century legal arguments coalesced around intent as a central theme. Intent was paramount, for instance, to whether insects could be guilty of harming farmers by eating their crops or whether they were unconscious automatons and thus could not be held accountable. By the seventeenth century, as the historian E. P. Evans argued, most courts maintained that "the overt act alone [of causing harm] was assumed to constitute a crime."[8] In other words, the fact that insects committed harm meant that they intended to commit harm. The intent of insects to commit harm even shows up in the definition of pest that arose during this time, as in the late eighteenth and early nineteenth centuries the term *pest* took on a new meaning as a way to describe an insect that "attacks" crops.[9]

I am not suggesting that these trials are representative of how all Europeans and eventually Americans viewed insects or other animals that caused them harm. There were certainly some who did not view insects as an enemy with fell intent.[10] But what is important to note from these trials is how insects were given a particular type of agency in order to justify eradicating them. This type of agency is fundamental to whether waging war against insects is just or not and is different than modern social science approaches that would, for instance, view insects as active participants in the creation of a pest control assemblage.[11] My concern in this chapter is not, as Timothy Mitchell put it, whether a mosquito can speak.[12] Instead, my concern is what it would say if it could. By threatening humanity's domination of the earth, insects brought the war upon themselves.[13] Or as a pest war reporter put it in the 1930s: "The war is by no means one sided."[14]

By the nineteenth century the conception of insects as moral enemies was widespread.[15] Such conceptions were often exacerbated by social Darwinist concerns about population growth and feeding the civilized world.[16] In the United States, these ideologies were also wrapped around nativist identities that often saw agricultural pests as invasive, dirty immigrants (and vice versa) pent on destroying the nation.[17] Indeed, what changed in Los Angeles in the late nineteenth century was not necessarily how Americans conceived of pests or the fact that many of them wanted to wage war against them. What changed was that these particular ideologies were fused with, as Rachel Carson pointed out, "the most modern and terrible weapons."[18] Evans also makes the same point, highlighting the fusion of medieval ideologies with late nineteenth-century scientific pest control through what he called the "impious and atheistic substation of Paris green and the chlorate of lime for prayer and fasting as exterminators of potato bugs."[19] Since pests by definition intend to cause harm, substituting science for theology did not change the nature of an insect's guilt; it only changed the nature of their punishment. In the late nineteenth century, it suddenly became possible to use industrial poisons instead of a papal decree to banish pests, even human ones.

A WAR ON PESTS

Throughout the 1870s and 1880s the valleys of Southern California were inundated with immigrants. From all corners of the earth they came, at first just a trickle, but soon a flood, seeking opportunities among the sun-drenched landscapes of the Golden State.[20] These immigrants came in many forms, including people, insects, plants, and even chemicals. At the turn of the twentieth century, as the semitropical pot of gold on the western shores of manifest destiny, Southern California began producing something golden in color yet far sweeter than precious metals.[21] Beginning in the 1850s and rapidly accelerating as the turn of the century approached, the flooding of the promised land's valleys with homogenous citrus trees sparked a radical reorganization in the life histories of California's insects and the historical trajectories of California's ecologies. By the early 1880s, as the nonlinear population dynamics of native and introduced insects began to realign with an emerging industrial citrus biome, the economic pest problem grew exponentially.[22]

The number of citrus trees offers a quantitative proxy for the radical social and ecological change that came to the valleys of Southern California. In 1870, there were fewer than 35,000 citrus trees in the entire state, with only 8,000 of them in Los Angeles (LA) county.[23] By the mid-1880s, there were more than 500,000 citrus trees on 13,000 acres in LA County alone. By 1900, there were over 3 million citrus trees of only a few varieties bearing fruit across Southern California, with millions more coming into production over the next decade (see figure 10).[24] The winter-ripening navel orange, which emigrated from Brazil via Washington, D.C., in 1873, dominated the arid inland "citrus belt" that ran along the eastbound line of the Southern Pacific Railroad from Pasadena to Riverside. The summer-ripening Valencia orange, imported from the Azores in 1876, was grown in the coastal valleys from San Diego to Santa Barbara, and the ever-bearing Eureka lemon, originating in Los Angeles from Italian seed stock in the late 1850s, was grown in both regions.

In 1841, William Wolfskill planted the first commercial orange grove in Los Angeles, at what is now the corner of 4th and Alameda Streets (see figures 11 and 12).[25] Securing trees from the San Gabriel Mission, he planted two acres of oranges. Wolfskill, a trapper (of both animals and Native Americans) who arrived in Los Angeles from Kentucky after a brief detour into Mexico, was a founding member of the city of Los Angeles and perhaps California's first agrocapitalist.[26] On his extensive lands, which he had received from the Mexican government in 1836 (hence the detour), he planted vineyards and fruit trees, made wine, and grazed sheep.[27] He even planted a banana grove.

By the 1850s, with the help of his neighbor, Jean-Louis Vignes—also known as the father of California wine and the first to import French varieties into California—William Wolfskill and other growers had turned the fertile lands near the Los Angeles River into a major wine-producing region.[28] By the mid-1850s, he had over forty thousand grape vines in production, and cuttings from his "celebrated vineyards" were sold across California.[29] In 1870, these floodplain vineyards produced

FIGURE 10. Orange groves of various ages, Redlands, CA, ca. 1880. Courtesy of the USC Digital Archive, Los Angeles.

FIGURE 11. The Wolfskill grove, Los Angeles, CA, ca. 1885. Courtesy of the Bancroft Library, UC Berkeley.

FIGURE 12. Artist's representation of the Wolfskill property, ca. 1882. Courtesy of the USC Digital Archive, Los Angeles.

almost 20 percent of the wine made in the United States.[30] Thus, it was not preordained that citrus would come to dominate the agricultural production of Southern California.

By the mid-1850s, Wolfskill had added more than two thousand more citrus trees to his LA groves; by 1860, he had over seventy acres of citrus, mostly orange, but also lemon, lime, and citron. He also had extensive lands and plantings in the San Gabriel Valley and southern Los Angeles near what is now the city of Vernon. Upon his passing in 1866, his land—the richest agricultural property in LA County—was divided, with most of it deeded to his two sons, Louis, and J. W.[31] Louis received his father's holdings in the San Gabriel Valley, and J. W. received his father's LA groves, as well as large swaths of land east of the LA River.[32] J. W. would take up where his father left off, expanding and intensifying citrus production, as well as becoming the first local producer of cut flowers.[33] In the early 1870s, in conjunction with a grape disease outbreak (*phylloxera*), J. W. turned away from grapes, razing his vineyards and planting more citrus.[34]

In 1877, J. W. Wolfskill loaded a carload of his oranges onto a Southern Pacific train bound for St. Louis in what was the first commercial interstate export of oranges from Los Angeles.[35] By the early 1880s, J. W. Wolfskill's LA grove, a product of his father's initiative, his business acumen, and the sweat of countless laborers, was the pinnacle of capitalist agriculture.[36] The arrival of the Santa Fe Railroad in 1885 and the subsequent decline in shipping costs that resulted from its competition with the Southern Pacific meant that by 1886 East Coast markets were becoming more lucrative.[37] On February 4, 1886, the first special train loaded only with citrus left Los Angeles bound for St. Louis.

Since the Wolfskill groves were the first commercial citrus groves planted in California, it was not a coincidence that by the mid-1880s they were some of the most "dirty" groves in Los Angeles.[38] The intensive production of a single crop over a large geographic area created a historically novel set of socio-ecological environments for insects to colonize. Attracted by the irrigated, highly fertilized, and repetitious flesh of citrus, insects quickly adapted to these new ecological niches, integrating their life histories with the rapidly expanding industrial citrus biome.

The creation of intensive monocultural agriculture in the second half of the nineteenth century was increasingly complicated by insects and pathogens that rode piggyback on the rapid expansion of the transportation and communication networks developed throughout the first half of that century. Sometimes these introductions were intentional, sometimes not. The white or cotton cushiony scale (*Icerya purchasi*) was inadvertently introduced into California from Australia on nursery stock that arrived at the port of San Francisco sometime in the late 1860s. It was first identified in Southern California in 1872, again, on nursery stock. By the late 1870s, white scale had spread throughout the established groves in Los Angeles.[39] By 1884, white scale, along with red (*Aonidiella aurantii*) and black scale (*Saissetia oleae*) (also foreign invaders), was causing serious commercial damage to citrus in many Southern California locations. In 1885, much of the orange crop failed "because of the ravages of insects."[40] Even the Wolfskill groves—"the pride of Southern California"—were reduced to fields of stubs alive with pests.[41] Without any effective recourse, many growers burned their trees. Many others simply abandoned their groves. Growers, politicians, horticultural commissioners, and local businessmen foresaw a complete collapse of commercial citrus.[42]

In 1885, Charles Riley, chief entomologist of the USDA Division of Entomology, after years of persistent appeals from growers, finally recognized the magnitude of the citrus scale problem and deputized Daniel Coquillet, a trained entomologist and Southern California resident originally from Illinois, to investigate the scale problem and to devise a way to repair the industry.[43] Asked about the pest situation by a *Los Angeles Times* reporter shortly after his appointment, Coquillet lamented, "Only a few years ago it was one of the boasts of California that we had no fruit pests—or scarcely any. They have been brought in, however, and the climate of this State seems to suit them as well as it suits other animate beings, for they have increased and multiplied at an alarming rate, and are now more destructive than in the East. By far the most dangerous to citrus fruit trees is the white cotton cushiony scale."[44]

For Coquillet, scale infestation was more than a scientific problem to decipher.[45] It was foremost a commercial problem. In 1886, he approached the most progressive grower in Los Angles, J. W. Wolfskill, and his orchard manager, Alexander Craw, wanting to couple their resources in the hopes of finding a solution to the plague that was descending upon Southern California. Because the Wolfskill groves were the pinnacle of intensive horticulture, yielding more than $1,000 per acre in profit in the late 1880s, J. W. Wolfskill had both more to lose and more to gain than others if a repair could be worked out, and he had made the research and development of citrus pest control a commercial priority.[46]

Two years earlier, growers had declared war on the unwanted occupants of the rapidly expanding industrial citrus biome. Skirmishes with soaps and other sprays had flared between growers and citrus pests across Southern California since the late 1870s, but in 1884, these battles escalated into full-fledged war.[47] Craw, manager of the Wolfskill orchards during the 1880s and 1890s, recalled, "Previous to the year 1884, we had only black scale (*Saissetia oleae*) to contend with and only in the Wolfskill orange groves, and these were kept in check by application of whale-oil soap in the form of a spray; one application every two years was sufficient. In the fall of the year 1884 we found a few trees on the south side of the large grove infested with the Cottony Cushion-scale (*Icerya purchasi*). They became infested from an adjoining grove. We prepared for war."[48] Indeed they did.

Throughout late 1884 and 1885, they threw every weapon in their arsenal at the scale. In recalling the events of 1885, Craw wrote that no matter what weapon they used, it "would not check this prolific creeping curse."[49] The following year, the cottony front advanced across Los Angeles so that many trees were, as a horticultural commissioner quoted in the *Los Angeles Times* put it, "literally white with the voracious and virile insects in all stages of development, every leaf, limb and twig being coated completely."[50]

In the early summer of 1886, Wolfskill and Craw undertook what can be considered the most sophisticated scientific experiments to date for the chemical control of citrus pests.[51] The fact that they were using a canvas tent bathed in linseed (flax) oil to enclose a tree and introduce a gas produced in situ was more than cutting edge. Previous experiments with greenhouse and tent fumigation can be found. But none of these were done with the determination that came from the expansive disquiet of unrealized value among California's late nineteenth-century agroindustrial landscapes.[52]

Wolfskill and Craw first used stoves to raise the temperature inside a tented tree, but while this appeared effective against black scale, cotton cushiony scale, the Aussie emigrant, seemed to thrive on the heat. Then they tried steam, tobacco, sulfur, muriatic acid, chloroform, arsenic fumes, and carbon disulfide. The only promising experiment involved carbon disulfide (CS_2), but this required fumigation with noneconomic concentrations of highly explosive CS_2 for at least three hours.

By late summer, Dr. Coquillet of the USDA had joined their research. He was so impressed with the carbon disulfide fumigation results that he decided to lead the USDA-mandated "crusade" on scale the following month in the Wolfskill groves.[53] Enlarging the extent of their "science in the orchard," Coquillet first tried a strong solution of whale-soap, but it was so strong that while it appeared to remove the scale, all the trees used in the experiment were defoliated.[54] Although the insects appeared to be wiped out, the treated trees were soon covered again. During September 1886, Coquillet performed 163 experiments with soaps, sprays, and fumigants, including caustic soda, caustic potash, chloride of lime, chloroform, muriatic acid, methyl alcohol, whale-soap, sheep-dip, vinegar, Paris Green, and carbon disulfide. But when Coquillet and his team removed the tent after the hydrogen cyanide experiment, they witnessed the selective annihilation that would become the biochemical future of industrial pest control.[55] For the first time in the Wolfskill groves the chemical gas "mode of warfare" was "extended to trees and plants growing in the open air."[56] The machine in the garden now had offensive capabilities.

Immediately recognizing cyanide's potential, they set out to remedy its only flaw, foliage injury. They found that by removing the water from the reaction, a pure stream of hydrogen cyanide could be produced, killing the scale "without even injuring a blossom."[57] After a bit of practice with the dry technique, the team of Coquillet, Wolfskill, and Craw could kill black scale, red scale, San Jose Scale (*Aspidiotus perniciosus*),

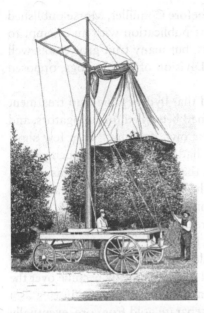

FIGURE 13. The Wolkskill fumigator. Source: R. Wallace, *Farming Industries of the Cape Colony* (Johannesburg, South Africa: J. C. Juta, 1896).

and their eggs in ten minutes, and cotton cushiony scale and its eggs in thirty minutes. Upon realizing that hydrocyanic acid was an effective economic poison, Wolfskill and Craw rapidly developed an apparatus for faster deployment of tents on tall trees (see figure 13).

Coquillet did not immediately publish his findings, partly because in late fall 1886, after only a year of work, he was dropped from the USDA payroll due to funding problems. Coquillet's first publication followed his reinstatement with the USDA in July 1887.[58] However, even without publication, rumors began to spread of Coquillet's success with the gas method.[59] With no official reports published, Alfred Chapman and Luther Titus, two prominent San Gabriel growers desperately seeking a fix of their own, became impatient at the slow appearance of progress. Impatience turned to imposition, and they appealed to Eugene Hilgard, head of the UC Agricultural Experiment Station, to send them a chemist, whose salary and expenses they would provide. In April 1887, Hilgard sent the UC scientist Mr. Frederick Morse to San Gabriel to investigate and determine the efficacy of certain gases as economic poisons for control of citrus pests.[60]

By the end of April, Morse had also discovered the cyanide fumigation method in the San Gabriel groves of one of Wolfskill's main rivals.[61] A witness at one of these trials said that it was the "best killing" they had ever seen.[62] In June 1887, one month before Coquillet, Morse published his findings.[63] Morse followed his first publication with an attempt to patent the cyanide fumigation process, but many fruit growers as well as Charles Riley, head of the USDA Division of Entomology, opposed this. Morse never filed the patent.[64]

In spring 1888, Coquillet observed that hydrocyanic acid treatment was coming into general use. Patents had been filed for fumigators, and others began using fumigators of their own devising.[65] In a few short years, the cyanide fumigation process had been brought to such perfection that a reporter could claim "that the application of the gas is safe, sure, and easy. The only drawback is the cost of the gas."[66] It wasn't just the cost of the gas, however, that limited fumigation's spread. Impure potassium cyanide was also causing tree injury, some serious enough to question whether fumigation had any benefits.

At the time, potassium cyanide, while not a new chemical, was not the widespread industrially made chemical it would quickly become over the next decade. Synthetic cyanide didn't arrive in Southern California as a pesticide.[67] It was cyanide's ability to separate gold from ore, eventually perfected by the John Stewart MacArthur and brothers Robert and William Forrest in Scotland in 1887, that originally brought large quantities of cyanide to the mineral-rich West.[68] The subsequent boom in industrial cyanide production in Scotland, Germany, and New Jersey to meet the mining demand in Southern Africa, Australia, and the United States was critical in making potassium cyanide available for a rapidly industrializing citrus industry.[69] The companies that synthesized cyanide employed the use of the vast industrial and consumer waste recycling networks to make it.[70] In the United States, potassium cyanide manufacturing relied on the wastes of Philadelphia slaughterhouses, tanning factories, and the worn-out leather shoes of its residents. While the type of cyanide use by citrus growers went through multiple iterations over the course of its use in agriculture, at all points it came from some type of waste. For example, in the mid-1910s, the much cheaper sodium cyanide, produced as waste in coking ovens, replaced potassium cyanide as the weapon of choice for citrus growers.[71]

The mining cyanide first used by Coquillet and Morse was only about 30 percent pure potassium cyanide. During separate experiments in 1887, among rival growers' trees, Coquillet and Morse introduced various gases, such as carbon dioxide, into the tents along with the potassium cyanide and sulfuric acid to see if they would help prevent foliage damage.[72] These protective measures all failed, but from their failure and the results from a chemical assay of the brands of potassium cyanide available in Los Angeles, both Coquillet and Morse concluded that the problem of foliage damage came from impurities in the cyanide. Protectant gases were unnecessary; only better quality cyanide was needed.[73]

As cyanide fumigation shifted from scientific experiment to standard grower practice, three LA growers tried to profit from its spread by patenting the fumigation of citrus trees at night. Growers, especially in Orange County, had noticed that every fumigation technique they tried produced poor results. (Unbeknownst to them, the humidity levels of the coastal valleys of Southern California created complications for potassium cyanide fumigation.) But some fumigators, like William Wall and Amos Bishop, found that with dark tents they could achieve a sufficient level of commercial control. These painted tents were cumbersome and much more expensive than the oiled canvas tents that other fumigators were using. "Then came the woman on the scene," Charles Woodworth later recalled, "and Mrs. Bishop asked why, instead of going to the expense of making opaque tents, they did[n't do] their work at night."[74] With that the practice of nighttime fumigation was born. Less than two months later, on December 10, 1889, Wall, Bishop, and Moses Jones filed for a patent for the night process of citrus fumigation.[75] Though their patent was granted on January 27, 1891, no grower, county official, or government scientist paid any heed to it. By the end of the 1891 fumigation season, daytime fumigators had metamorphosed into nocturnal executioners, their deeds now hidden in the darkest shadows of the citrus-scented killing fields.

Chemical warfare was not the only solution that growers sought. In 1888, again after persistent appeals from growers, Riley sent Alfred Koeble to Australia to look for parasites of the white cotton cushiony scale.[76] Koeble, a naturalized German immigrant and an "enthusiastic and comical bug hunter," was a USDA scientist first sent by Riley to Alameda, California, in 1885 to investigate the life histories of California's insects.[77] Two important discoveries came from Koeble's first trip to Australia, and these arrived as several packages from December 1888 to February 1889.

In December 1888, Coquillet received Koeble's first shipment of the fly *Cryptochaetum iceruae,* a parasite of the white cotton cushiony scale, discovered a few years earlier in a garden in Adelaide, Southern Australia.[78] Coquillet released this parasite under a tented orange tree in Wolfskill's LA groves. The following month, after receiving another package, and again in the Wolfskill grove, Coquillet released the Vedalia beetle

(*Rodolia cardinalis*) under another tented orange tree that was thickly covered with white scale. The discovery of the Vedalia beetle was pure coincidence and came from Koeble's perceptive eye. Sent to Adaleide to find a parasitic fly, Koeble found the now familiar beetle "feeding upon a large female Icerya" in a garden in Northern Adelaide.[79]

By the end of 1889, the "blessed bugs," the 129 beetles sent in four shipments, had multiplied to tens of millions by swarming from one infested orchard to another.[80] The effectiveness that the dipterus parasite and the Vedalia beetle had in controlling cotton cushiony scale still stands as the one of the hallmarks of biological control success in California.[81] Even so, both the beetle and the parasitic fly could not check the prolific creeping curse of red, brown, black, and purple scale that by 1890 had launched a sinister counterattack.

With the discovery of cyanide fumigation, a suite of private fumigation companies quickly formed. Some tried to develop and sell new fumigating machines for practical use, some to organize outfits to fumigate groves, and others to provide the necessary chemical inputs and fumigation supplies. Fumigation equipment was very expensive and out of the reach of most growers, making fumigation prohibitively expensive. But by using fumigation outfits, growers were only liable for the cost of chemicals and the labor of the outfit, not the large upfront capital outlay needed to buy fumigation equipment. Designs for fumigators and tent enclosures varied widely, but by 1890, most fumigation outfits had settled on the generation of hydrocyanic gas using the dry pot method and the use of oiled No. 2 Duck (linseed oil and often the juice of the prickly pear cactus) tents rigged to a cumbersome system of pulleys (see figures 14 and 15).[82]

For the first three years of use, citrus fumigation was commercially haphazard and driven by the desire to rid citrus trees of the white cottony masses that collected on the branches of infested groves. By 1890, most scientists and growers working to perfect citrus fumigation had turned to trying to control red scale.[83] As the Vedalia beetle "phalanx" advanced, white scale exponentially declined, and the red scale, an immigrant from southern China and first recognized more than a decade earlier on citrus trees in Los Angeles, was taking its turn as the apex predator of the industrial citrus tree, exploding as a commercial pest across Southern California. This pattern would repeat, and still repeats to this day. With the control of one pest, others realigned their life histories to fill the abruptly vacant niches that chemical war continuously brought to the industrial citrus ecosystem. Control of the

FIGURE 14. Crew with fumigating derricks and tents, Chino Valley, CA, ca. 1893.
Source: *Popular Science Monthly* 44 (1893).

FIGURE 15. Fumigation derricks and tents, ca. 1895. Courtesy of the USC Digital
Archive, Los Angeles.

red scale menace was followed by black scale outbreak, the purple scale problem, the Argentine ant invasion, the yellow scale question, the red spider threat, and then red scale again, but now resistant to hydrogen cyanide gas.[84] And all of this took place before the outbreak of World War I.

Between 1887 and 1893, cyanide fumigation expanded from Los Angeles to all of the satellite citrus-growing regions—the counties of Riverside, Orange, San Diego, Santa Barbara, and San Bernardino—and to all varieties of citrus. As it spread, the three men who had patented the nighttime fumigation process grew increasingly frustrated with the fact that they had not received any royalties, nor had they profited in any way from its rapid growth. In the late summer of 1893, Wall and Jones tested the validity of their patent by getting the police to arrest two growers who had recently fumigated and charge them with patent infringement. They sought to redress their lack of compensation by suing W. L. Adams and H. N. Kellum in LA circuit court, seeking license fees and any profit that resulted from using their invention.[85]

News of the arrest of Adams and Kellum spread rapidly throughout the citrus-growing regions. If Wall and Jones were successful with their lawsuit, the rapid expansion of fumigation would slow, and perhaps stop in many areas. It would also open up the possibility of taking the citrus-growing counties to court, seeking compensation for use of the nighttime process. Because of the high initial cost of fumigation equipment, counties would often buy equipment and then rent it out to the growers in their district at nominal cost. It was in the counties' best interests to maintain groves free of infestation, and thus they made sure that as many growers had access to fumigation as wanted it.

On October 15, 1893, the district attorney (DA) of LA County called an emergency meeting in San Bernardino to address the fumigation situation and devise an organized approach. Present at the meeting were the DAs of all the citrus-growing regions, as well as legal advisers and some prominent growers. The legal position that emerged from discussions was that the fumigation process was public property and thus nonpatentable. The LA DA took this same legal position in court, arguing that the process was general knowledge. Then the DA called Coquillet to the stand. Coquillet not only explained that he was the first to discover cyanide fumigation, but he also brought plenty of evidence to prove that the plaintiff's lawsuit was meritless. Two items in particular were quite damming.[86] The first was that Coquillet had the paperwork to prove that Bishop, who was listed on the patent but not on the lawsuit, had participated in some of the first fumigation experiments in the fall of 1886 at the Wolfskill grove. On September 26, 1886, Bishop was part of the fumigation team when Coquillet, Wolfskill, and Craw fumigated seven lemon trees at night, with much success.

The most incriminating evidence, however, was a personal letter that Coquillet provided. In the letter, dated November 12, 1889, a month before the patent was filed, Wall pleaded for Coquillet to give him "the formulas you used, and the length [of] time the tent remained over the tree. Was the tent dark enough to exclude the light to any great extent? Did you dilute the acid at all? I know you are busy but I would really like to know the particulars of your first work in the Wolfskill Orchards."[87] To close out his testimony, Coquillet echoed the DA's argument that the lawsuit was fallacious "since the Patent Office decided a few years ago, before any of these persons had obtained a patent, that the Hatch patent referred to in my former report covers this process, and as the patent has expired the process becomes public property, and cannot again be patented."[88] On April 9, 1894, Judge Erskine Ross of the Federal Court of Southern California invalidated the patent on the night process. The basis for his decision was twofold: (1) doing something at night does not make it novel and (2) the original discovery was made by the USDA, and the Patent Office's interpretation of the Hatch Act provisions made sure the discoveries of the USDA and the state agricultural experiment stations remained public property.[89]

Between 1895 and the early 1900s, millions of citrus trees across Southern California were in production, millions more reached commercial age, and millions of others were recently planted. Every tree planted was another tree to be infested, and scale infestation became the multicolored silhouette draped on the contours of citrus expansion. As the industrial citrus ecosystem matured, the infection became more systemic, and the demand for fumigation grew with it. By the late 1890s, county fumigation outfits of the early 1890s gave way to outfits organized by cooperative associations. This change magnified the expansion of fumigation through multiple means, but the most basic reason was a decrease in the cost of fumigation per tree by tapping into the economies of scale that resulted from the formation of citrus cooperatives. By buying chemical inputs in large lots, especially potassium cyanide, the unit price of cyanide fumigation per tree rapidly fell. And by coordinating fumigation labor, cooperatives were able to streamline fumigation practices, fumigating more trees per person-hour. Taken together, cooperatives were often able to cut the cost of fumigation per tree in half.[90]

In 1896, the Covina association of the Southern California Fruit Exchange was the first branch to undertake the general fumigation of all its "stockholders through the cooperative plan."[91] However, recognizing the need to inaugurate a "general crusade" against red and black scale, which was causing increased commercial damage, they also offered their services to nonmembers in the hope of cleansing as much of the district as possible. Leaving pockets of uncleansed groves meant cooperative groves would be more easily reinfested. With fumigation's high costs and without the ability to do it themselves, not all growers were convinced of its promise, and many growers turned to sprays as their weapon of choice.

In the first two decades of chemical control in California, there were no state or federal statutes regulating anything about economic poisons, which meant there were as many brands of citrus treatment for sale as there were brands of citrus. These concoctions often contained plant extracts, coal-tar compounds, soaps, acids, caustic sodas, and arsenic, but the only group of possible poisons that showed any promise were the various waste fractions of crude oil that were available in increasing amounts from Southern California's oil wells and refineries (see chapter 3).[92] These crude distillates were usually emulsified in water with soap, glue, blood, or another binder, then sprayed under pressure onto trees, in the hope that they would coat the trees with a deadly film.[93] Other growers tried resin washes and arsenic-based sprays, which although much cheaper than fumigation, did not provide the killing power needed and damaged foliage and fruit. Responding to a promoter of distillate spays, one fumigation operator quipped that the "answer to all this is seen in the endless array of fumigation tents now in operation in the orchards of Southern California." These tents "make no mistake in summing up the impotency of all other methods."[94]

What began to convince growers of the value of clean orchards, more than the sight of tents extending to the horizon, was the higher price that growers received for their fumigated fruit. No one wanted to have to fumigate; "few citrus growers look[ed] with favor upon any tree wash or spray."[95] Economic poisons like cyanide were not only highly toxic; they were also very expensive and labor intensive to apply. However, as the markets for Southern California's citrus moved east, progressive growers began to rethink the way they envisioned loss from pests. Wholesalers began looking for citrus with the best carrying quality, that is, citrus that would arrive unspoiled, in prime eating condition, a week or more later in cities across the Midwest and East Coast.

Throughout the 1890s, oranges from groves where fumigation wasn't practiced often had to be scrubbed to make them sellable to eastern markets. The honeydew excrement of scale insects that rained down from the encrusted branches above led to "black smut," a sooty mold, on the fruit. Consumers could be picky, and any blemishes on the skin of the fruit would ruin the consumer's increasingly constructed conception of the orange as a condensed nugget of California's healing sunshine.[96]

Since eastern buyers did not want fruit with black smut, cooperatives and their subsidiary branches organized washing houses as end-of-pipe solutions to dirty fruit. The presence of smut and the rudimentary practices and technology of early washing houses (which spread decay-causing organisms) would decrease the carrying quality of citrus by inducing the rapid onset of decay.[97] This fruit had to be sold and shipped east immediately.[98] Sellers had to take the first offer; they could not wait for another. When fumigation was done effectively, the fruit harvested on the cleaned trees usually did not have to be scrubbed and was of prime quality for shipping east. Now blessed with first-rate produce not prone to decay, wholesalers had the upper hand; they could sit on the boxes until their price was met. By the turn of the century, as scale pests became generalized throughout Southern California, the difference between a carload of prime shipping citrus and one that lacked any carrying quality was the difference between fumigated and nonfumigated fruit.[99]

A *Popular Science Monthly* writer summed up the new agricultural market conditions best. "How goes the fight?" he asked rhetorically. "The statistics of the fruit industry answer this question. The cost of destroying insect pests has become a permanent item of expense, the results of which are increased profits. Care and management of orchards now include preparation of the soil; selection of varieties adapted to the place; planting and culture of the trees; pruning, according to different systems for different species and localities; the use of special fertilizers, *and the destruction of noxious insect life*" (emphasis added).[100] These new practices signaled a new era in agriculture, one in which toxic chemicals became necessary for industrial agriculture and in which industrially organized agriculture became enmeshed in an accelerating and endless war (see figure 16).[101]

By 1900, the Faustian bargain that had allowed industrial citrus to flourish in the face of relentless attack was more than a decade removed and rapidly spreading.[102] In the process, toxicity and chemical warfare became fundamental inputs of industrial citriculture.[103] A *Los Angeles Times* reporter, after spending a week shadowing fumigation crews,

FIGURE 16. Fumigating cart with cyanide generator, ca. 1920. Source: Pacific R&H Chemical Corporation sales booklet, 1923.

summed it up best: "Perhaps never in the history of the world have there been so many specimens of animal life slaughtered by artificial means as are now succumbing to the cyanide process. As the shades of night fall upon the orange groves, one hundred, five hundred large sheets of canvas enshroud the trees, and when they are drawn away death has claimed every living thing within them."[104] This chemically derived industrial death saved an industry from pest-induced collapse and made possible the industrial production of commercial quality citrus fruit.

IS CHEMICAL PEST CONTROL A JUST WAR?

Poison has long been considered an illegitimate weapon of war. I have never understood why. Perhaps the use of "asphyxiating or deleterious gases" terrifies the psyche more than using chemicals to make explosives or launch projectiles that kill and maim.[105] Maybe it is because the use of poisons has often been viewed as sneaky, uncivilized, and effeminate.[106] Whatever the reason, the use of industrial chemicals to poison soldiers and civilians has been a part of every international convention on the

Laws of War since 1899.[107] To think there could be treaties governing how countries act in war may seem laughable to some people, but ideas and practices of restraint in war have played an increasingly important role in both how wars are fought and how the public conceives of war. For example, international conventions state that hospitals should not be bombed and that prisoners of war cannot be tortured even if those acts may hasten the war's end. In the Western tradition, what is and what is not considered the right conduct in war has occupied thinkers since at least the Middle Ages. This type of thinking, however, really got a jump start in the latter half of the nineteenth century with the understanding that the horrors of war, like the manufacture of textiles, could be industrialized. It continues to inform how modern wars are practiced and prosecuted, and it is part of scholarship known as "just war theory." In essence, just war theory is the study of the moral limits of war as well as war's moral justifications. As such, justice in war (*jus in bello*) must always be considered at the same time as justice of war (*jus ad bellum*).[108]

I want to briefly consider industrial chemical pest control from the standpoint of the just war tradition. I argued earlier that in the late nineteenth century chemical war became just another input of a rapidly industrializing and specializing US agrarian assemblage. But here I want to consider whether the war that started among the citrus trees of Los Angeles was just in purpose and in practice. According to the just war tradition, the right to make just war has always rested on questions of intent, authority, proportionality, and whether war was a first or last resort. It is not my aim to cover each of these aspects in exhaustive detail, but I do want to examine the pest war in this light.

To begin with, we have to consider first the question of intent, as it is the crucial distinction needed to parse whether mass death is considered just or not. Did insects intend to commit harm when they ate growers' crops? Did they purposely and malevolently intend to form phalanxes and armies, as economic entomologists said they did? Did they see humans as the ultimate rivals for dominion over earth? There is, of course, no way to understand an insect's intent. But that did not stop economic entomologists and pest war protagonists from ascribing intent to them. As in the animal trials in western Europe, these soldiers assumed that because insects committed harm, they intended to commit harm. In other words, calling insects pests gave them just enough agency to justify a war against them. In grappling with issues of insect intention, the geographer Jake Kosek has noted that the way humans ascribe agency to nonhuman life is often reflective of a "politics simply animated by human practice," and that clearly is the case with the early history of chemical pest control.[109] It is impossible to know whether pest war protagonists actually believed that it was the insects' goal to destroy human civilization, but their practices clearly reflected that they did.

Even if we decide to leave the question of intent aside, the just war tradition compels us to ask why the war is being fought. In other words, why do we poison crops? Hunger and starvation are usually the reasons trotted out to justify it. But are potential hunger and starvation adequate reasons for waging a pest war? Pesticides have never been necessary for the United States to produce sufficient food, and when taking a look at some of the earliest uses of economic poisons, it is clear that pesticides were first used most extensively on industrially grown crops like apples, citrus, and cotton, meaning that in the beginning waging chemical war was more about agroeconomic accumulation rather than starvation or hunger. Indeed, as I argued in the last chapter, the rapid growth of pesticides in the interwar era exacerbated the overproduction of food and fiber. And as I mentioned in the introduction, that is what Rachel Carson meant when she said that justifications for the use of pesticides broke down under scrutiny. For Carson, the "staggering excess of crops" served as the most substantial counterpoint to claims that pesticides are necessary to feed the nation.[110] Hunger and starvation have never been morally just arguments for the widespread poisoning of US agriculture, and therefore they cannot be used to justify why the chemical war began.

Finally, I want to turn to proportionality, and I want to use the environmental movement's response to *Silent Spring* to do so. *Silent Spring* is filled with literal and metaphorical allusions to wartime chemical technologies and Cold War rhetoric.[111] These references to war were more than literary technique; they were also part of how Carson interpreted the morality of the war against pests. For instance, it is clear that Rachel Carson thought that the chemical war on nature (*jus ad bellum*) was being fought for unjust reasons. For her, the fact that the war was being waged in the name of the "gods of profit and production" and not to help farmers or save us from impending starvation made it an unjust war.[112] But Carson also reserved a forceful critique for those who practiced the chemical war (*jus in bello*).[113] It was the indiscriminate use of poisons and those that poisoned indiscriminately that became the object of her criticism.[114] Despite Carson's belief that the war was unjust in reason and in practice, many of her supporters came away with conviction only about the latter. Because it was the practice of war that was unjust, what needed to change was the way the war was fought. What was needed was a more proportionate response.

I understand the political practicality of this position, but I also believe that this political practicality has enabled Carson's supporters to champion the types of chemical reform, like banning DDT, that had little to no impact on the structure of agriculture or on how chemical companies profited from manufacturing weapons of war.[115] Indeed, the historian Fredrick Davis has argued that a focus on the weapons of war has resulted in a "tragic irony" wherein agricultural workers suffered increased harm by banning DDT in the name of saving the environment. At the time, William Ruckehaus, the head of the Environmental Protection Agency, said the same thing, but that did not stop him from banning the chemical.[116] In addition, Davis also notes that this ban actually benefited large chemical companies because it forced growers to move from generic DDT to newer patented poisons. The geographer Brian Williams put more it forcefully when he wrote that the environmental movement's myopic focus on pesticides following the publication of *Silent Spring* meant that they remained "silent to the violence of agro-environmental racism which *enabled* pesticide-intensive production" (emphasis in original).[117]

A focus on proportionality and justice in war is still how many activists approach harm from pesticides. Better regulation of the weapons and conduct of war is viewed as the solution to problems of worker and environmental health. What is needed is cleaner, more precise, and safer war. Make no doubt, I think this is crucial work. But I also think it allows us to sidestep the larger issue of whether the pest war was just when it began and whether it remains so today. It allows us to evade the larger question about what types of racialized practices the chemical war perpetuates. Focusing on the morality of the practices of war makes it easy not to question how even a discriminate and more proportionate use of poisons still harms, and in particular, whom it harms. Focusing on justice in war does not force us to question whether nonhuman organisms that eat our crops are really at war with us. It does not ask us to imagine a just agricultural system; it only asks us to imagine one that is practiced in a less harmful manner.

The war on pests is still such a fundamental part of agriculture's infrastructure that the pest control specialist I sat listening to in 2014 could not escape from it. One of the first things that cyanide fumigators learned early on was the that once the war began, there could be no end to it. An "endless," "ceaseless," and "unending" war was often how they described it.[118] The weapons may change, but the war will continue. So despite an individual's or an institution's desire to move beyond the war, without a fundamental restructuring of agriculture, the unjust war will continue to be waged. In the late nineteenth century, chemical warfare became fundamental to the spread of economic poisons, and it became a critical part of the infrastructure that moved industrial waste into agriculture. In the next chapter I explore how the development of the science of agricultural chemical warfare was key to the transformation of petroleum wastes into economic poisons and the production of agriculture as a sink for oil wastes.

CHAPTER 3

Manufacturing Petrotoxicity

All substances are poisons; there is none which
is not a poison.

—Paracelsus, *Dritte Defensio*, 1538

Despite my best efforts, I don't know much about the early life of William Hunter Volck. I know he was born in Riverside, California, in 1879, making him one of the first white children conceived in the newly founded citrus colony.[1] I know his father was a Protestant minister, that his mother's name was Ella, and that they had emigrated from the Midwest a year earlier to start a new life conjuring Eden from the arid highlands east of Los Angeles. Maybe it was a fortuitous act of predestination then that brought William into the world only a few years after the Bahia orange (Washington navel) arrived in Riverside (see chapter 2). Perhaps William came into this world already destined to change agriculture. I may never know how William spent his early years, but I am certain that whatever he was doing, he witnessed firsthand the rapid development of the citrus industry and the growth of Riverside from a desert outpost into a leading center of national commerce.[2]

While I don't know the source of Volck's agricultural calling, I do know that he enrolled at the University of California (UC) at Berkeley in 1897, where he studied entomology, chemistry, and agriculture under the tutelage of the eminent entomologist and polymath Charles W. Woodworth.[3] Volck was not a "teacher's pet."[4] He was a child of industrial citrus, and thus his impulses to think about agriculture differently than his professors often left him at odds with their "prescribed courses of study." Volck's need to tackle pressing agricultural problems sometimes led him to do his own unsanctioned experiments, which of course didn't always succeed and sometimes led to stern words from his teachers.[5] Nevertheless, his experimental skill, original thinking, and deep understanding of the new agriculture rapidly spreading across California must have impressed Woodworth, who offered him a job with the UC Agriculture Experiment Station upon graduation.[6] In early 1902, citrus growers lobbied Eugene Hilgard, the station's head, to send a researcher to Southern California to figure out what was causing "spotting" and the commercial loss of citrus fruit. Answering their call, Woodworth, the station's second in command, sent the new hire back home.

I like to imagine William Volck feeling awe on his train ride south as he surveyed the rapid afforestation of the southern Central Valley and the Los Angeles Basin, not this time with the citrus or shade trees as he had witnessed in his youth, but with the oil derricks then sprouting from the soil like weeds after fall rain. In just the few years that Volck was away at college, oil output from California had exploded. In 1903, California became the largest producer of oil in the United States, and with the exception of a few years, it remained so for the next three decades.[7] The rapid growth of petroleum from the Los Angeles Basin and the southern Central Valley must have been a magnificent sight to behold.[8] Even by 1903, one could see how California would quickly become, to paraphrase the historian Paul Sabin, a place where both landscape and culture were intertwined with oil (see figures 17 and 18).[9] But Californians were not just swimming in "oceans of oil," as reporters at the time liked to put it.[10] As Volck quickly found out, they were also drowning in seas of oil well and refinery wastes.[11]

Volck traversed the southland's major citrus-growing regions off and on for eighteen months, searching for the cause of citrus "spotting." He published his report shortly before he left Los Angeles to return to Berkeley in the fall of 1903.[12] Volck concluded what many citrus growers already knew from experience: that spotting was caused by spraying crude oil, kerosene, and refinery wastes (often referred to as *distillates*) onto trees.[13] Despite the proven efficacy of cyanide fumigation, some citrus growers had turned to oil because it was so incredibly cheap.[14] With cheap petroleum-based poisons, a grower could potentially rid an orchard of its pestilent life at a fraction of the cost of cyanide fumigation.

Volck observed that some of these sprays could be incredibly effective at killing pests, but he also saw that some could be so thoroughly ineffective that they did nothing at all to abate pest damage. In addition, Volck also saw that these oil-based sprays could cause commercial loss through aesthetic or taste problems or could defoliate trees, cause

FIGURE 17. Oil derricks among citrus groves, Santa Fe Springs, CA, ca. 1920. Courtesy of the Santa Fe Springs, CA, Public Library on Behalf of Hathaway Ranch.

FIGURE 18. Standard Oil of California refinery, Richmond, CA, 1920. Courtesy of the Richmond, CA, Public Library.

the blossoms and fruit to drop, or at worst, outright kill them. He surmised that while petroleum had the potential to be an ideal economic poison, oil's compositional and toxicological uncertainty meant that growers should be wary of using it. Nevertheless, he concluded that in the future it might still be "possible to arrive at a point where all insects will be killed" using oil without injuring the tree or commercially damaging the fruit.[15]

In 1903, not only was there no standard type of oil used as an economic poison, there was very little about oil that was standard at all. The chemical composition of petroleum still remained largely unexplored, and oil refiners lacked the technology to abstract oil and oil products from the landscapes of their formation. Each barrel of crude pumped from the ground or barrel of refined product—even the waste—still retained a particular biogeochemical terroir.[16] The inability to technologically abstract petroleum from earth's long-term biogeochemical processes meant that oil sprays, despite being made from physically similar refinery fractions, often varied tremendously in their toxicity to plants and animals.[17] Both petroleum's chemically complex nature and a lack of knowledge about it stood in the way of the potential widespread use of oil as an economic poison and the creation of the first agricultural sink for oil refinery wastes.

AGRICULTURAL TOXICOLOGY

Contemporary scholarship on the history and politics of toxicology has advanced significantly in the twenty-first century.[18] This scholarship shares a focus on what I call *defensive toxicology*, science and policy conducted under the auspices of keeping people from harm.[19] Indeed, this is pivotal scholarship, yet the history of toxicology is also more expansive than these works reveal.

I point this out because the development of agricultural toxicology was not about protecting people but about creating knowledge specifically for offensive purposes. It was the science of poisons that supported an endless chemical war. As such, it focused on making mass nonhuman death as reproducible and efficient as possible. That is why some of agricultural toxicology's earliest pioneers, like George Gray, argued that the agricultural study of poisons should be called *economic toxicology* as a way to distinguish it from the studies that aim to prevent unreasonable human harm. In 1918 Gray wrote in *Science* that "this science [industrial hygiene/forensic toxicology], however, has been developed largely among men of the medical profession and deals with the poisons in respect to their harmfulness to man and their use with criminal intent. As undertaken by this laboratory, poisons are studied *for an altogether different purpose*" (emphasis added).[20]

By the time Gray wrote those words, agricultural toxicology had advanced significantly from its earliest days. Much of the early foundation came from the citrus industry and its intensive history of cyanide fumigation. For example, between 1905 and 1915, UC and USDA scientists developed an extensive set of research-based dose-response theories and practices that tied the war on citrus pests explicitly to the notion of efficient death.[21] But toxicological knowledge was also fundamental to industrial pest control's growth outside its role in developing new poisons. In particular, its development was central to recognizing and responding to the problem of pesticide resistance that began to appear alongside the rapid expansion and scientific rationalization of pest control.[22] A scientific understanding of the relationship between the dose of poison and an insect's response was necessary to determine if insects were becoming resistant to that poison.

In this chapter I argue that the development of agricultural toxicology played a dual role in the commercialization of oil-based sprays: first, through the development of physical proxies for oil's toxicity, and second, through the creation of demand for oil-based sprays via recognition of insect resistance.[23] To explore this argument I use the history of Volck and Cal-Spray's multidecadal quest to manufacture petrotoxicity from the physical properties of oil. By the late 1910s it was clear to pest control scientists like Volck that the first round of toxicity-based repair needed to be repaired itself, and they believed that petroleum was going to be the remedy. But in making petrotoxicity reproducible, Volck and Cal-Spray also helped turn agriculture into a profitable sink for the oil industry. Agriculture became more than just an industry that needed fuel for trucks and tractors; it became a sink that could absorb low-value or worthless fractions of oil. As toxic oil became part of the pest war, agriculture became an important part of the California oil industry's waste disposal infrastructure.

I want to be clear that when I use the term agricultural toxicology, I am lumping together an assortment of toxicological research that entangled both the public and private spheres. Agricultural toxicology was not a singular discipline. It was informed by research in economic entomology, crop science, and plant pathology, as well as agricultural and analytical chemistry. Some of this research took place in laboratories at LGUs, and some of it took place at private research institutions. Some of it was done by chemical company scientists and some on the farm by private spraying companies. But no matter who did it or where it took place, all of this research shared a commitment to the pest war. For Volck and Cal-Spray this commitment meant using toxic oils to make nonhuman mass death as efficient as possible.

TOXIC OIL

Elementally, all oil is fairly simple, with carbon and hydrogen making up more than 90 percent of its composition by weight and the remainder composed of nitrogen, oxygen, sulfur, and trace metals.[24] Compositionally, however, oil is complex, mysterious, and fluid, and it is imprinted with the geochemical processes that created it.[25] As the geographers Gavin Bridge and Phillipe Le Billon have written, "Oil takes on the characteristics of time and place."[26] Oil also behaves differently than coal tar, the main feedstock for the organic chemical industry in the early twentieth century. Organic chemists had developed significant skill in analytically probing coal tar, but petroleum resisted their techniques.[27] Chemists did not have the ability to separate and isolate petroleum molecules. Further, the complexity of oil meant that hydrocarbon molecules with the same molecular weight could vary significantly in their molecular structure.[28] Importantly, these elementally identical yet structurally dissimilar molecules can exhibit vastly different physical, chemical, and toxicological properties.

When California exploded onto the oil scene in the late 1890s, kerosene was still the oil industry's main product. But California oil did not yield much kerosene. What it did yield was large amounts of the heavier and more viscous collection of hydrocarbon molecules now known as *fuel oil*. "The biophysical world does indeed present all sorts of obstacles to accumulation," wrote the geographers William Boyd, W. Scott Prudham, and Rachel Schurman, and this was certainly true for California petroleum.[29] But the biophysical world also presents opportunities, and for California oil producers and consumers, opportunity took the form of fuel oil.[30]

A surplus of fuel oil permeated deep into California's industrial landscapes.[31] California's factories were the first to burn oil to power their boilers. Trains that crisscrossed California were the first to turn toward the energy-dense liquid fuel, and oceangoing ships that called at California ports were also the first to replace coal with oil.[32] That California oil refiners produced so much fuel oil, of course, was not due just to their having the types of oil that could be cheaply refined. It was also a function of California's land use politics, which drove the overproduction of oil as well as structure of the oil industry at the time. As a result there was way more oil coming out of the ground than there were uses for it, and people experimented with using crude oil and oil refinery wastes for everything under the sun.[33]

Farmers and agricultural scientists across the United States had been experimenting with oil as a poison since the late 1870s, but it was in California at the turn of the century that petroleum-derived economic poisons experienced commercial growth and development.[34] For example, by the time Woodworth sent Volck to Los Angeles to study the citrus-spotting problem, the use of oil-based sprays had expanded so much among citrus growers that it was causing significant enough commercial loss for growers to appeal to UC for help in remedying the situation.

Shortly after the turn of the century, Santa Clara Valley stone-fruit growers became the first to use oil-based sprays on a regular commercial basis.[35] These sprays were made from eastern kerosene, California crude oil with the asphalt extracted, or various other California distillates.[36] Growers sprayed these poisons on dormant fruit trees in late winter to kill insects such as San Jose scale (*Aspidiotus perniciosus*). These sprays were most commonly applied in the form of an emulsion, meaning that they were mixed with a number of other ingredients like water and soap and then mechanically agitated to create a suspension of oil at ~3–12 percent concentration.[37] The major concern about oil sprays was that they harmed trees, especially the foliage. But since deciduous fruit growers sprayed their trees prior to leaf emergence, they had a much wider range of toxicological error than citrus growers did with their with evergreen trees. The introduction of winter oils also was also key to fighting back new predators of the industrial fruit tree. For instance, the recently introduced Italian pear scale (*Epidiaspis leperii*) was not harmed by the lime-sulfur treatment then common as a winter spray.

In the mid-1910s, LA citrus growers increasingly turned to oil as the efficacy of cyanide fumigation decreased. Inklings of insects becoming resistant to the poisons that had once killed them date back to the late 1890s, but the earliest recorded accounts begin after the turn of the century in places with long histories of intensive poison use. Economic entomologists, farmers, and spray crews first found these new resistant populations on fruit trees in the San Jose and Santa Clara Valleys, the Los Angeles Basin, and Central Washington. For example, in 1908 the Washington State University economic entomologist A. Leonard Melander published an account of San Jose scale resistant to lime-sulfur sprays even at ten times the normal concentration.[38] To deal with resistant populations, Melander recommended oil-based poisons despite their phytotoxic potential.

About the same time, citrus growers and fumigating outfits began noticing exceptionally poor fumigation results in two Southern California citrus districts.[39] Across these districts, fumigation failed to kill both the black scale (*Saissetia oleae*) and red scale (*Aonidiella aurantii*), which it had always eliminated in the past. Growers and scientists originally dismissed these results as a fault of poor technique, but the USDA scientist Russell Woglum proved that the problem was not careless fumigation. Instead, it was that two subpopulations of black and red scale had become resistant to cyanide fumigation.[40]

Oil use by citrus growers also increased as a way to control new pests, like the citrus red spider mite (*Panonychus citri*), which had arrived in California on Florida nursery stock sometime in the early 1890s and by 1895 had established itself as a pest in a few citrus districts.[41] The mite's spread was tied to the fact that cyanide fumigation did not kill the mite but did remove all other competition. In other words, the foreign arachnids thrived under the grower's industrial pest control practices, and they certainly wouldn't be the last to do so. By the mid-1910s, the mite was causing significant damage to citrus trees and other important California crops, such as almonds, and oil sprays were called upon to repair a new problem that resulted from cyanide fumigation.[42]

The historian John Ceccatti has written that in the decades preceding World War II "insect resistance to insecticides posed significant economic problems in the affected areas and also challenged scientists, notably entomologists working at agricultural research stations, to provide a coherent scientific explanation of the phenomenon and to develop practical solutions."[43] It is true that resistance caused significant economic problems for growers, including having to spray or fumigate multiple times a year or having to use multiple poisons, but it also provided significant economic opportunities for both oil refiners and manufacturers of oil sprays.[44] In a pattern that continues to this day, the need to repair the harm caused by the original repairs created new sites of accumulation for agrochemical companies.

One such manufacturer was Cal-Spray, which had Volck as its head of research and development. When Volck and Luther first spun off the company from UC in 1907, it was to manufacture lead arsenates and

lime-sulfur under the Ortho brand. Despite the growth of the company's new lead arsenates, Volck never let the potential of oil-based poisons lie fallow. By the early 1910s he had returned to his quest to render an effective and tree-safe poison from oil. In 1914, Cal-Spray introduced a new "winter oil" emulsion that had a higher margin of safety than other commercial poisons on the market.[45] Cal-Spray introduced the poison across California, Oregon, and Washington over the next few years. It was not the only company selling oil-based sprays, as any farm journal from the time makes clear, but Volck and his company were the only ones that commanded the most sophisticated private research laboratory in the world dedicated to the production of ever-newer economic poisons (see figure 19).[46] In addition, they made superb use of public agricultural research and the US patent system.

What Volck and other scientists began to figure out in the early 1910s was that certain narrower cuts of refinery fractions in the light lubricating or "white oil" range offered both the necessary killing power and protection against tree injury.[47] *Narrow cut* refers to oil fractions that contain less variation and more uniformity in molecular weight than so-called wider cut oils. At the refinery, narrow cuts were volatized under a smaller temperature window and thus more expensive to produce. But even with the ability to cut petroleum better, considerable compositional variation existed between oils used as poisons, even those made by the same manufacturer and sold under the same brand.

This happened because the only analytical methods available for determining if one had similar refinery fractions were based on oil's physical properties, not its chemical composition. Without a way to determine the chemical composition of oil, agricultural toxicologists were stuck using analytical methods developed and commonly used by refiners to, for example, determine the illuminating power of kerosene or the ability of certain oil fractions to behave as good lubricants.

In fact, the expansion of fuel oil and the development of lubricants gave scientists like Volck the raw materials they needed to manufacture petrotoxicity in the first place. The rapid growth of automobile use in the 1910s drove oil refiners to produce more gasoline and other "engine distillates," but this demand also increased the consumption of lubricants that could withstand the frictional demands of internal combustion. In 1911 the US Justice Department broke Standard Oil apart. One of the resulting pieces, Standard Oil Company of California, began manufacturing nonenergy oil products they once were not allowed to make.[48] By 1915, Standard Oil of California was producing industrial lubricants from California's heavy oils that for some uses rivaled if not surpassed the quality of lubricants coming from midwestern and eastern oils.[49] The concurrent growth in lubricants and the technology to make uniform lubricants became critical for the development of oil sprays. It was the low value and waste lubricant fractions, with twenty to forty carbon atoms per molecule, that agricultural scientists like William Volck eventually rendered into economic poisons.

By the early 1920s, refiners, their chemists, and their marketers had been steadily introducing a wide variety of new petroleum-derived commodities into industry and consumer markets. "Uses for these by-products," as a *Los Angeles Times* reporter wrote in 1925, "have only been found within the last score or more years."[50] For example, in the early 1920s Standard Oil of California began marketing the low-value lubricant fractions also known as white oil, the same oils that eventually found their main outlet as economic poisons, home dry-spot cleaning fluids, and a component of new skin treatments for women and polishes for automobiles.[51]

In the early 1910s, Volck and other agricultural scientists began systematically probing the toxicity of oil by using oil's physical properties. The earliest physical proxies they used for the right type of toxicity were specific gravity (the density of oil relative to water) and flashpoint (the temperature at which vapors of the oil will ignite).[52] The problem was that it was possible to have two oil fractions or mixtures of different fractions with the same specific density and flashpoint that differed widely in their chemical composition and toxicological properties.[53] In the mid-1910s, distillation temperature (the temperature at which the fraction evaporates) and viscosity (the magnitude of internal friction) were added as two additional physical parameters. These proxies helped scientists like Volck close in on the collection of hydrocarbons that would provide the bioselective toxicity necessary for agriculture.[54] But something more was needed. "Toxicology is fundamentally a chemical study," wrote the Cal-Spray scientist Robret Vickery in 1920, "and little is gained by testing the insecticidal values of different oils distinguished from one another by their physical properties. We must go deeper and study the oils as chemicals if we are to improve our present knowledge."[55]

Those digging deeper included scientists at UC, especially Elmer de Ong, Department of Entomology researcher and instructor, and Gray, then an experiment station and Insecticide and Fungicide Laboratory scientist.[56] By 1915, Gray and de Ong had deduced that unsaturated hydrocarbons were a main culprit for foliage injury.[57] Unsaturated hydrocarbons like propene or benzene contain at least one double carbon bond and are more biologically and chemically reactive than saturated hydrocarbons like propane and cyclohexane. To solve this issue, Gray and de Ong used sulfuric acid to scrub a large proportion of these unsaturated molecules from the narrow cuts. Then they adapted US Forest Service experiments with coal tar creosote to develop a "sulfonation residue" test that would potentially allow them to predict the phytotoxicity of oils used as economic poisons. Both their laboratory and field experiments the following year showed that removing unsaturated hydrocarbons decreased foliage injury, yet the results were not published at the time. Nevertheless, word of their success got around.

I do not know how Volck came upon the information, nor does it really matter. Cal-Spray had its main office directly across the street from UC Berkeley, and Cal-Spray scientists like Volck had close relationships with many UC scientists, including his mentor, Woodworth, who participated in Gray and de Ong's field trials in 1916. In fact, Volck had remained an employee of Woodworth and the UC experiment station until 1913 despite being the chief chemist at Cal-Spray. What is clear is that by the late 1910s Volck had heard of Gray and de Ong's success with chemical refining and was pursuing it in his own research on oil sprays. Volck patented the first phytonomic oil sprays in 1922, which Cal-Spray introduced into the California and Pacific Coast pesticide markets the following year.[58]

Volck coined the term *phytonomic* to describe the ability of an oil to kill the target species while allowing the plant to live up to its full photosynthetic potential. Volck came up with the term because it allowed room for oil sprays to have positive effects as well, such as increased plant vigor or staggered fruit set. It is likely that as early as 1903, when Woodworth sent him home to Southern California to solve the citrus-spotting problem, Volck had observed that oil sprays could cause fruit trees to exhibit abnormal yet commercially promising behavior like elongated shoots, larger buds, and early fruit set. Imagine being a grower who could use oil to not only kill pests but also have your trees reach maturity faster, produce more fruit, or break dormancy weeks early. Imagine that you could spray a chemical on your trees that would increase their "virility" far beyond what nature could conjure up.[59]

Historians of science have argued that in the United States, plant hormone research arose in the late 1920s and 1930s at plant physiology laboratories at elite universities and private research institutes.[60] But Volck wasn't a plant physiologist at one of those elite universities. In the mid-1920s, he was the chief chemist at a cutting-edge agrochemical company that was increasingly focused on developing oil-based poisons. He had shown a practical interest in stimulating plants with chemicals as early as the 1910s.[61] In 1913, Volck became the horticultural commissioner of Santa Cruz County, and as part of this work he often spoke to public audiences about the possibility of plant stimulation. On occasion, he outlined the results of his experiments, for example, with foliar applications of Chilean sodium nitrate or crude oil mixtures on fruit trees.[62]

By the mid-1920s, Volck was certain that some petroleum hydrocarbons had analogous effects to compounds that promote the growth of hair in humans when applied to the skin.[63] "The action of substances upon plant life and animal life," Volck wrote "is much more widespread than has been supposed." It is not surprising that Volck turned to animal hormones as an analogy for the endocrine-disrupting substances he discovered. Even by the late 1920s, most of the fundamental research on plant hormones had not been done yet. Nor is it clear that Volck knew of any of the research that had been done. Nevertheless, he was able to manufacture and patent oils that could consistently result in trees "overbearing."[64]

Volck, however, wasn't the only scientist to realize that certain oils could be used to bend tree physiology in potentially profitable ways.[65] Cal-Spray was an agrochemical company that manufactured and sold poisons; it did not operate crews that sprayed trees. That responsibility was left up to either the individual grower or the firm that growers or their cooperative hired to spray for them. As with cyanide fumigation, it was often easier for growers to hire out the poisoning of their trees than to have to buy their own spray machines. There were many firms that did this, but one of the earliest and largest was Balfour, Guthrie & Co. (BGC). BGC was a British firm involved in numerous ventures on the US West Coast, including oil and the transportation and storage of agricultural goods.[66] By 1915, BGC crews were spraying winter oils on more than twenty-five thousand acres of California's industrial fruit trees every year. Since BGC had business ventures in oil refining, the oils it used were its own, not Cal-Spray's.

By the early 1920s, some of BGC's scientists had also noticed that many of the deciduous orchards that the company sprayed with certain "heavy oils" exhibited "stimulation."[67] They too had realized that particular oils caused trees to behave in new and potentially profitable ways. BGC's spray scientists investigated tree stimulation, especially its relation to the timing of spray. However, unlike Volck, they likened the effect of oil to the use of stimulating salts in humans and not to the disruption of a tree's endocrine system. BGC scientists thought that in the future these oil-based stimulants would finally allow "fruit trees to function properly," and that they could be used to help growers deal with harvest labor demands by staggering the harvest over a longer period.

Using oil to manipulate tree physiology, however, never became commercially viable. Despite rapid progress in oil refining technology, oil sprays retained the material shadows of their formation, and thus just like acute toxicity, hormonal action varied widely between batches of oil, even those with the same physical characteristics. As the energy historian Harold Williamson and his colleagues have written, it wasn't until the introduction of new refining technology in the lead-up to World War II that refining was able to "free itself from the natural characteristics of crude oil."[68]

Even so, Cal-Spray's new phytonomic oils, named in honor of their creator, sold widely (see figure 20). They were vastly safer than other oil sprays on the market, which meant that they could be used on a wider variety of crops. Most importantly, they could also be used during the summer without significant harm to trees. By the mid-1920s, these "summer oils" had made significant inroads not only among California and Pacific slope growers but also among tree-fruit growers in New York, New Jersey, Michigan, and Florida.

Consistent Production
follows the Use of VOLCK

How about production? What kind of a crop do the trees mature?

What are the results of your spraying — in dollars received when the crop is picked?

Here's the real test of effective pest control.

Dirty scale-infested trees can't produce clean fancy fruit.

Trees properly sprayed with VOLCK quickly show decided improvement. When freed from the devitalizing effects of scale, they soon take on a cleaner, finer color and a more thrifty appearance.

Clean Trees Produce Best

This improvement becomes more evident as groves are sprayed with VOLCK for several successive years—and groves that have been so treated stand out noticeably from trees that have been neglected or where control has been attempted with other methods or materials.

The improvement is marked not only in appearance, but in *production.*

Ask any grower who has adopted the VOLCK program of scale control, and who has sprayed his grove with VOLCK for several years, and he will tell you that he is getting consistent production of fancy fruit season in and season out. The cost of the spraying is saved many times over by the increased production and the improved quality of the fruit.

This steady improvement in the general health of the trees and in

the production of quality fruit is the result of the liberation of the trees from the devitalizing effects of the pests.

Scale robs the tree of the necessary sugars and starches—and starved trees can't produce big crops of fancy fruit.

VOLCK Gives Clean Trees

VOLCK is the first and only spray material to produce results like these. Ordinary sprays have never been satisfactory. If effective against the pests they have carried high hazard to the tree. If safe for the tree they have not been very effective against the pests. For years the grower eagerly awaited a material that would combine real killing effectiveness with safety for fruit and foliage.

After an extended period of intensive work in the laboratory and in the field, our Research Department succeeded in producing such a material—deadly to scale and other insect pests, yet safe to apply any time of year and under almost any conditions—named VOLCK in honor of its inventor, Mr. Wm. H. Volck—and widely used for the past several years with the most astonishing and satisfying results.

A Highly Improved Spray

VOLCK is a highly improved contact spray of the "quick breaking" type. It "breaks" as it passes thru the spray nozzles and quickly covers the entire sprayed surface with a uniform protective film of oil which penetrates and saturates both egg and adult with deadly effectiveness.

It continues to spread for some time after application so that very complete coverage is assured. Moreover, VOLCK retains its active oiliness for an extended period, so that any young which may escape temporarily are brought into contact with the spray on emergence and are either killed at once or prevented from settling down.

This same oily film which protects the tree from the pests also shields the leaves from the blighting effects of the occasional hot winds. Trees sprayed with VOLCK come thru these winds little the worse for the experience—while the trees not VOLCK-sprayed are often severely injured.

Eradicates Red Spider

VOLCK also offers highly effective control over Red Spider, killing both spider and scale in the same application. It kills the pest in all stages of development from the egg to the adult and retards reinfestation over a surprisingly long time.

Now is the time to spray your grove—kill the scale while the hatch is young and most easily and economically controlled. See our nearest representative at once.

California Spray-Chemical Company

734 Standard Oil Building
Los Angeles

Lindsay   Watsonville   Fresno   Sacramento

The California Spray-Chemical Company maintains the following staff of trained entomologists in Southern California, who are at your service always. Call them in to help you with your pest control problems.

EARL MORRIS
812 East First, Santa Ana

DONALD PENNY
423 Beverly Square, Ontario

HUGH KNIGHT
Southern Research Laboratory
San Dimas

R. W. HUNT
1000 Second Street, Porterville

VOLCK
~for real citrus pest control

FIGURE 20. Cal-Spray advertisement for Volck oil, 1926.
Courtesy of the *Los Angeles Times*, August 22, 1926.

In 1925, Volck and Cal-Spray developed quick-breaking emulsions.[69] A quick-breaking emulsion allows water and other "inert" ingredients like soap or calcium caseinate to separate out immediately on contact with the tree, leaving a pure film of oil on leaves, stems, and branches while the rest drips off. The development of quick-breaking emulsions was important because they allowed the active ingredient, in this case the toxic oil, to come into direct contact with the insect without it being diluted by water and emulsification chemicals. Cal-Spray normally manufactured highly refined oil spray emulsions at up to 13 percent final oil concentration, but with the development of quick-breaking emulsions, the oil's concentration in the spray mix could be reduced to ~2 percent.[70] Not only did this make the oil in oil sprays more toxic to insects, it significantly reduced the cost of the active ingredient per gallon of spray mix and further decreased the acute phytotoxicity of oil sprays. Cal-Spray also saved on manufacturing costs by moving away from more expensive "stable emulsions" that had grown in popularity.

But in this case as well, I am not sure that Volck actually discovered quick-breaking emulsions on his own, despite only his name being listed on the patent. The study of quick-breaking emulsions began in 1924 as a cooperative study involving scientists at UC Berkeley and UC Riverside Citrus Experiment Station in partnership with the Standard Oil Company of California.[71] Yet by the fall of 1925, when the patent was filed, one of those citrus experiment station scientists, Hugh Knight, was employed by Cal-Spray. The historian Steven Stoll has argued that UC and California's pesticide corporations occupied two distinct yet complementary niches in the emerging pesticide research-manufacturing-sales ecosystem. This resulted in a "revolving door connecting college and company."[72] This was certainly the case for Volck and Cal-Spray, who somehow managed to turn research done by UC scientists into new patents and new poisons.

In late 1925, manufacturers of oil sprays found a helping hand from across the pond as newspaper reports began circulating of British children being sickened by eating apples sprayed with lead arsenate.[73] These apples were grown in Washington State, where each year more and more lead arsenate was needed to control the codling moth. As discussed in chapter 1, by the mid-1920s growers were using an "almost continual application of lead arsenate" throughout the growing season, which resulted in high lead and arsenic residues on fruit.[74] In fact, the international arsenic problem brought so much attention to lead arsenate residues that Washington growers considered it "the most serious event that has ever occurred, affecting apple production in the Northwest."[75] The scale of public attention also forced the Bureau of Chemistry, under the authority vested in it by the 1906 Food and Drug Act, to start enforcing its own tolerances.[76]

After much consternation, the apple industry responded in a few ways. The first was building washing houses as end-of-pipe fixes to clean apples prior to interstate and international export.[77] The second was to get farmers to stop using arsenicals a few weeks prior to harvest to allow time for a natural decrease in residue levels. The third was to develop substitutes for lead arsenate. Pest-control scientists thought that fluoride-based compounds, nicotine extracts, and oil sprays might be up to the task. Although fluorides showed promise in laboratory and field trials, and although some were commercialized, they were much less effective in controlling the codling moth than a continuous coating of lead arsenate. Most of the fluoride compounds used were mined from the waste piles of the aluminum and phosphate fertilizer industries, although a few, like cryolite, were geological in origin. Unfortunately for apple growers, these fluorides were clearly toxic to humans, and thus they too fell prey to government regulation.[78] Nicotine extracted from tobacco sweepings also fell short of its toxic promise.[79]

Volck's new summer oils, however, seemed to work well. In addition, oil sprays didn't have a government-set tolerance, nor did apples sprayed with oil look like they had been poisoned.[80] Cal-Spray's marketers and salesmen leaned heavily into this regulatory and aesthetic opportunity. By the fall of 1926, Cal-Spray was using the lead arsenate residue problem to advertise its newer and safer oil sprays, asking growers to "note the difference in residue" between the apples sprayed with lead arsenate and those sprayed with its oils.[81]

In response to the residue crisis, Montana Agricultural College scientist John Parker organized the Western Co-Operative Oil Spray Project.[82] As highlighted in the next chapter, the project epitomized the cooperative capitalist spirit that permeated US industry following World War I. It included scientists from agricultural colleges in Washington, Idaho, Montana, Oregon, and California as well as representatives from the USDA and the Canadian Department of Agriculture. The project brought them together with representatives of dusting and spray equipment, manufacturers of economic poisons, and prominent western oil companies like Standard Oil of California, Shell Oil Company, Union Oil Company, and the Associated Oil Company (see figure 21). The goal of the project was fairly straightforward: (1) to determine and develop the right oil sprays for deciduous fruit growers across the West; (2) to study the physiological effects that oils have on trees; and (3) to share this knowledge in a cooperative fashion among investigators, companies, and growers.[83]

The group issued a report outlining the best practices for oil sprays following their first official meeting at Tacoma, Washington, in 1927.[84] But by the time this first report was released, UC was no longer a part of the project, as its representative, the scientist de Ong, was disinvited because he was already working directly with Standard Oil of California researching oil sprays in a noncooperative manner.[85] But that certainly didn't stop Standard Oil of California from participating.[86] The first report noted that one of the major problems to overcome was Volck

FIGURE 21. Oil-spraying rig from the experiments of the Western Co-Operative Oil Spray Project, Wenatchee, WA, ca. 1930. Courtesy of Washington State University Manuscripts, Archives, and Special Collections, Pullman.

himself. "It would not be amiss at this time to mention a series of patents recently granted," the authors wrote, "to Mr. Volck of the California Spray-Chemical Company. From these it appears that he has patented all the important features of summer oil sprays, and all those making or selling them will have to come to some agreement with him."[87]

But any sort of cooperative agreement was never developed. Cal-Spray had a tremendous market advantage and was not going to give it up, especially because the western United States was not the only market for Volck's new poisons. By the late 1920s, tree-fruit growers in New Jersey, New York, Florida, Missouri, and Michigan also used oil sprays on a regular basis. So too do did many international growers in South Africa, Australia, New Zealand, Egypt, France, England, Italy, North Africa, India, and Palestine.[88]

The use of oil sprays grew rapidly in the late 1920s and early 1930s, yet they did not end up substituting for lead arsenate or cyanide fumigation in the way that growers and scientists thought they would.[89] Instead, oil became a complementary poison used in conjunction with other pesticides to provide the killing power necessary to produce blemish-free fruit and vegetables. After World War I, the "battle that never ends" had grown bigger and the enemies more numerous and more experienced, and newer weapons were always needed.[90] Volck and Cal-Spray believed that future fights would be waged with oil, and they were not alone.[91]

In 1931, Standard Oil Company of California (SOC), along with Standard Oil Company (New Jersey), bought half of a newly reorganized company called the California Spray-Chemical Corporation, with SOC taking over operations.[92] The reorganization and takeover of the company was instigated by Cal-Spray's inability to pay its debts.[93] The Great Depression caught Cal-Spray off guard and overextended. Farmers were unable to sell their crops, meaning that they could not pay for the pesticides they bought on credit, which meant that Cal-Spray could not pay for its oil supplies. By early 1931, Cal-Spray found itself more than a million dollars in debt to SOC and almost a million dollars in debt to Standard Oil Company (New Jersey).

Cal-Spray had also been spending large amounts of money on attorney's fees and patent litigation, which also may have contributed to its debt load but was nevertheless key to the company's success after recapitalization in 1931. Although debt may have instigated the purchase, SOC and Standard Oil Company (New Jersey) bought an exceptional research and manufacturing company at the forefront of the rapidly expanding agricultural poisons industry. Standard Oil of California's statement to shareholders in the fall of 1931 summed up the purchase well:

> In the last seven years its business has increased rapidly, until today the reorganized company is one of the world's largest manufacturers of products used for the control of tree and plant pests. Its business centers around the marketing of oil sprays which consists principally of petroleum oils. The higher relative efficiency of California Spray-Chemical Corporation's patented oil sprays as agricultural and horticultural insecticides that can safely be applied to trees and plants, compared to other kinds of products used for this purpose, is now well established. The patents of the corporation give it a very strong position in this growing field.[94]

With this purchase, SOC became the owner/operator of one of the world's largest agrochemical companies and perhaps the only chemical company with an experienced research, sales, marketing, and manufacturing staff dedicated to the production and commercialization of ever newer economic poisons.[95] In addition to Volck's toxic genius, the company also acquired extensive national and international distribution, sales, and research networks, which it immediately put to use.

At the time of purchase, Cal-Spray had three operational oil spray plants. The largest was in Richmond, California, but it also had chemical factories in Bayway, New Jersey, and East St. Louis, Missouri.[96] The company was also just finishing construction of a fourth plant in Australia. In 1932, Cal-Spray opened its fifth plant on the River Thames near Purfleet, England, to supply the British market, and the following year it built a sixth plant at La Mailleroye-Sur-Seine in France to supply the French and North African markets. In 1934, the company opened a seventh plant in Italy at Trieste to supply the Italian market, and in 1935 it opened an eighth plant in Spain near Barcelona to manufacture oil sprays and other poisons for Spanish fruit and vegetable growers. Unfortunately, the Barcelona plant became an early casualty of the Spanish Civil War. In 1936, Cal-Spray built a second oil spray plant adjacent to its plant at Richmond, California, and completed construction of a second research laboratory in Haddonfield, New Jersey, to develop the best practices and best poisons for eastern fruit and vegetable growers.

In 1936, Volck stepped down as the chief chemist of Cal-Spray, although he remained a research scientist until shortly before his death in 1943. During this time he focused on Cal-Spray's new line of oil-based poisons for livestock and home use. In the thirty years since he and Luther had spun off a pesticide start-up company from UC, it had become one of the largest agrochemical companies in the world, producing a variety of high-quality economic poisons for a wide range of crops. Volck passed away before the end of the war, but the work he had accomplished, as the Cal-Spray scientist Leo Gardener put it, "laid the foundation for the growth [of pesticide production and consumption] that was to occur after WWII."[97]

The consumption of oil-based sprays exploded with the entry of US agriculture into World War II.[98] But one growth area was particularly novel. In the late 1930s and early 1940s, scientists turned to oil to create the first generation of broad-spectrum and selective herbicides. This first generation of herbicides, as the weed scientist Alden Crafts wrote, "were by-products of the chemical industry or compounds of very low value. Examples are arsenic trioxide, a smelter waste, iron-sulfate, a by-product of the steel industry, and waste oils of low value."[99] As you can probably guess, Volck, Cal-Spray, and SOC were at the forefront of herbicidal oils as well.

These oils had outsized effects. They not only killed weeds; they were also a critical part of the mechanization of agriculture, first in California, then across the United States and the world. For example, in the late 1930s "oil sprays [herbicides] allowed complete mechanization" of guayule production in the Salinas Valley of California, which was by then the epicenter of both herbicide research and consumption.[100] What Volck and others had figured out was that the same molecules in petroleum that had once made them harmful to fruit trees also made them effective herbicides, especially against weeds in the grass family.[101] By the late 1940s, in California alone more than ten million gallons of "cracked gas oils" were used each year as an active ingredient to poison canal banks, roadsides, farms, and orchards.[102] And even more was used as preemergence weed control on lettuce, beets, and onions and as a selective postemergence herbicide on flax, carrots, celery, and parsnips (see figure 22). These oils were also used, as herbicides are today, as desiccants for crops like flax, clover, and alfalfa.[103]

During World War II, Cal-Spray's chemical plants could not keep up with the insatiable demand for its poisons.[104] The situation was exacerbated in 1943 when the creation of the US Victory Garden program led to a huge spike in demand for Cal-Spray's home and garden products, which by then were rapidly expanding into a major part of its business.

After World War II, oil's active toxicity took a back seat to new chlorinated poisons like DDT, 2,4-D, and DD, but not immediately.[105] Industries like citrus continued to use them for their toxic activity well into the 1950s despite it being abundantly clear that while phytonomic oils sprays did not have the acute toxicity they once did, their chronic use certainly harmed trees. Charles Teague, president of the California Fruit Growers Exchange, made this clear to a *Wall Street Journal* reporter shortly after the war ended. "There is no question in my mind that oil sprays hurt [trees]," he said, "but we're all using them, because that's all we've got. Our growers are tired of winning victories that cost too much. Too many times they've been able to keep the upper hand at enormous expense and by using methods which harm many of their trees."[106] Even after demand for oil's acute toxicity waned, the sprays did not disappear. Many became the solvents, adjuvants, spreaders, and stickers used with newer synthetic poisons, and some, including the eponymous Volck®, are still used today, often as an alternative to the synthetic insecticides that once replaced them.[107]

FIGURE 22. "Oil Sprays for Weeding Carrots and Related Crops," cover of California Agricultural Extension Service circular, 1947.

RESEARCH AND DEVELOPMENT

The world is now so overflowing in petrochemicals that it is difficult to imagine a time before them.[108] Of course this wasn't always the case. William Volck was born into a time before the building blocks of society were made from the collection of hydrocarbons known as petroleum.[109] Yet by the time he died in 1943, his life's work had helped set in motion the post–World War II marriage of agriculture, chemistry, and the oil industry. These first-generation petrochemicals were not the synthetic molecules that growers turned to after World War II. They were collections of hydrocarbons whose toxicity was identified via their physical properties and not their chemical structure. Nevertheless, they set the stage for the growth of petroleum-based poisons across agriculture and wetted the appetites of oil companies.

As we will see in chapter 5, in the late 1920s California and its agriculture became a leading center of petrochemical development. Throughout the 1920s, oil companies began to view oil and oil wastes in a new light, though not always because they wanted to. Their sales of non-energy oil commodities had grown substantially, but oil companies and refineries had yet to become, as the meat industry had in the late nineteenth century, users of every part of the hog but the squeal. What these companies began to recognize was that all parts of oil could be put to use if only a use for them could be found. In particular, these oil companies envisioned agriculture as a major user of their chemical progress, and they saw California's agrarian infrastructure as the scaffold on which to build a petrochemical future. California not only had the type of growers that were scientifically and capitalistically minded and ones already consuming the most oil-based poisons; it had abundant oil supplies and an emerging public-private R&D infrastructure to help make this petrochemical future possible.

One of the most critical parts of that R&D infrastructure was the ability to evaluate, test, and compare poisons to each other as well as to determine commercially efficient dosages across space and time. It seems mundane now, but the development and standardization of scientific practices for agricultural toxicology was pivotal to the growth of economic poisons, especially during the interwar period. These dose-response criteria would eventually become the toxic rules that guided the discriminate poisoning of the world, and without them, as I discuss in the next chapter, it would be difficult for pesticide companies to maximize manufacturing efficiencies and for farmers to know when and how to use poisons. The creation of agricultural toxicology was just as fundamental to the mass production and mass consumption of economic poisons as the discovery of new toxic chemicals was. The history of Volck and oil sprays is a prime example. Underlying the growth of toxic oil was the ability to evaluate, test, and compare poisons to each other, which required the development of standardized dose-response practices in the laboratory and the field. These practices were critical to both manufacturing oils with the same toxicological profiles as well as recognizing and responding to the rise of insect resistance.

But this history also highlights how important public agricultural research was to the commercialization of oil-based poisons and to the success of Cal-Spray. Scientists at UC, many of whom went on to work under Volck, played an important part of an emerging public-private division of labor for economic poison development. This was not surprising, as UC had been at the forefront of toxicity-based repair since the late nineteenth century. By the early 1920s there was already an established symbiosis between the direction and funding of UC's agricultural research, agribusiness interests, legislation, and the needs and lobbying efforts of California's most powerful grower organizations.[110] In some cases, grower organizations supported research directly through grants to the university or through scientific research fellowships directed at specific needs. In others, agribusiness lobbied to pass specific legislation, like the 1911 California Insecticide Law, which drove fraudulent sales of poisons from the market and established the UC Insecticide and Fungicide Laboratory, bestowing on it regulatory power.[111] But not all states were like California. Land grant institutions in other states often lacked any direct relationship with pesticide or chemical companies, nor did farmers in these states have the intensive relationship to poisons that California's growers did. Their LGUs did not have the regulatory power that UC did, nor did they have publicly funded laboratories dedicated to studying agricultural toxicology and evaluating new potential economic poisons. California's atypical situation was not lost on economic entomologists and government officials at the time. But those circumstances were about to change.

After World War I, powerful scientists, government officials, and chemical companies wanted to scientifically rationalize and grow the use of economic poisons across the entire United States, and these pesticidal visionaries saw this coming from collaboration between public research and private industry. It was in publicly funded laboratories and on publicly funded research fields that new poisons would be discovered and where the toxicological rules for the widespread poisoning of agriculture would be developed. In the next chapter I explore the creation of an institution shortly after World War I to link public agricultural science with the chemical industry, as well as how it facilitated the development of a public-private pesticide R&D infrastructure that became commonplace across the United States after World War II, an infrastructure that was necessary for production of ever newer economic poisons.

CHAPTER 4

Public-Private Partnerships

The problem of the manufactures is one of tonnage.
The solution of problems which will extend the use
of fungicides and insecticides will make for
cheaper production.

—G. R. Cushman, General Chemical Company, 1920

This chapter tells the story of an institution created in 1920 to grow and rationalize pesticide use across the United States by linking the capital and toxic materials of the US chemical industry with the nation's LGUs. In the last chapter I explored the role of UC in the development of oil sprays and how public agricultural research played a fundamental part in the toxicological knowledge that companies like Cal-Spray needed to manufacture and patent new economic poisons. What was emerging in California in the first two decades of the twentieth century was the type of public-private partnership that came to dominate pesticide research and development (R&D) after World War II. This social division of labor was fundamental to the ability of pesticide companies to ensure a more systematic search for newer and newer economic poisons. But I also argued that the type of relationships that California agribusiness had with UC was atypical and not the case for most LGUs at the time. The goal of the Crop Protection Institute (CPI) was to change this and make explicit connections between US chemical companies and agricultural experiment stations across the United States.

The CPI was designed to coordinate the use of facilities and expertise of LGUs to assay the toxic materials spilling from a chemical industry enlarged by World War I. This would give experiment stations a source of private funding for pesticide research and give chemical companies a way of determining whether any of their chemicals or wastes had agricultural value. Throughout the interwar period, the CPI played a significant role in the rapid evolution of agricultural toxicology and the growth of pesticides. But the biggest impact of the CPI was not the pesticides that it made possible or the industrial wastes it redirected into agriculture. Instead, it was that the CPI helped build a pesticide R&D infrastructure in which public agrotoxicological science was captured by private industry. This was so not only because individual companies often directed and benefited from the research done at public universities, but also because during the interwar period the CPI helped make toxicity-based repair *the* solution to agriculture's pest problems.

A CHEMICAL LARGESSE

The United States emerged from World War I as a dominant player in industrial chemistry.[1] The chemical industry historian Lutz Haber called the Great War a technological "forcing house" for applied chemistry and the chemical industry.[2] Not only did the war raise chemistry to the forefront of military imaginaries; it also reshaped the landscapes of the chemical industry and how people conceived of chemicals.[3] During the war, as the chemical industry historian William Haynes remarked, "For the first time chemicals became news. Strange words—benzene, phenol, Salvarsan, salicylates—flashed in the headlines."[4] Although chemicals entered warfare and industry through almost every conceivable channel, the manufacture of explosives and the manufacture of poisons and protective gear were the most prominent facilitators of applied chemistry and the growth of industrial chemical capacity during the war.[5]

The dramatic growth of the US chemical industry and the rapid chemicalization of US industries during the war, however, could not have been accomplished without large-scale coordination between the US government and the chemical industry.[6] Industrial chemical development by US companies in the early years of the war was hesitant and haphazard, due in part to promises of a speedy war and resumption of trade with Germany, then the world's largest producer of coal-tar-based organic chemicals like dyes and pharmaceuticals. By the end of 1915, however, as the war ground to an attritional halt, the industrial picture had recrystallized, and the chemical industries had begun responding to the materials demands of US allies. In early 1916, the United States established the Council on National Defense, legislatively burdening it with the complex task of turning the resources and industries of the United States toward the trenches of the first major industrialized war. Later that year, at the request of Woodrow Wilson's administration, the

National Academy of Sciences (NAS) formed the National Research Council (NRC) to function as the clearinghouse for wartime scientific activity.[7] Immediately following the US declaration of war in April 1917, the Council on National Defense formed multiple divisions and tasked each one with a specific set of responsibilities.

The Munitions Standards Board, for example, collaborated with the War and Navy Departments and with chemical and ordinance companies to grow, standardize, and streamline munitions manufacture across the United States. The newly minted NRC became the acting Department of Science and Research for the Council of National Defense.[8] By the end of the war the NRC was occupied in every branch of wartime R&D and had helped American science and industry attain heights unimaginable only a few years earlier.[9] Even so, the NRC's direct wartime influence can be difficult to gauge.

While the NRC was directly involved in the development of sonar and chemical warfare technologies, most of the research that it coordinated took place within the confines of industrial laboratories and universities across the United States.[10] Furthermore, the NRC did not fund any of the research directly, nor was it a government organization despite being formed by and sometimes funded by the federal government. The NRC was a private body composed of the nation's most influential scientists, prominent military and government officials, and representatives of the most powerful industrial and financial interests in the country. It was the liaison between government and industry when it came to questions of science and technology fundamental to a nation at war.[11] The NRC's most important impact, therefore, was that as the coordinator of industrial and scientific activity during World War I, it was at the same time a de facto body making US industrial and scientific policy, which it would continue to do throughout the interwar period.[12] Shortly after the war, President Wilson directed the NAS to enlarge and reorganize the NRC as a permanent body that would be devoted to "stimulating and organizing scientific research" that bears "directly on the promotion of the national strength and well-being."[13]

By virtue of serving a common cause, the first major industrial war brought together formerly competing companies with the anti-free-enterprise despotism that is government oversight. The resulting rapid increase in scientific and industrial capacity during the war, along with the recognition of Germany's research and industrial prowess prior to the war's outbreak, demonstrated to many scientists, industrialists, and government officials that large-scale coordination between industry and government on fundamental scientific and technological problems was necessary for national security.[14] Many of these same interests also believed that the NRC should play a major role in cultivating the spirit of capitalist cooperation and industrial scientific progress that had grown so quickly in the hothouse of war.

AGRICULTURE, WORLD WAR I, AND ECONOMIC POISONS

American agriculture was also profoundly affected by World War I. European demand for food and fiber drove US farmers to invest more capital in new inputs like machines, mortgages, chemical fertilizers, and economic poisons.[15] However, soon after the bombs stopped falling, a thick malaise descended upon US agriculture. Between the war's end and the 1920 harvest season, the price of wheat fell over 50 percent.[16] The values of US farmland followed this same pattern. By 1921, national farm income had dropped from a war-driven high of $16.9 billion in 1919 to less than $9 billion.[17] After the war, US farmers confronted an entirely different agricultural reality, as many began returning home from the market each year with less money than they had spent to raise their crops.[18] There was simply way too much product and not enough places to put it.

But as US farmers confronted this postwar curse of abundance, government officials, pest control scientists, and chemical companies saw different agricultural problems emerging. Farmers faced grave problems, they said, but none more serious than the insect menace, which never stopped waging its war against humans.[19] It was now time, these voices chanted, to summon the spirit of the Great War to aid in the country's counterattack.[20] The prevention of mass famine and societal collapse was a task that could only be accomplished by expanding and rationalizing the poisoning of agriculture.[21] In other words, the war to maintain Western civilization would no longer be fought in the trenches of Europe. Instead, it would be fought on the farms and fields of the United States.

By the end of World War I, although many firms were directly involved in the manufacture of economic poisons, there were very few agroindustrial concerns operating outside California that had dedicated R&D departments or that maintained close connections to public agricultural science (see chapter 3).[22] Very few chemical companies were attempting to produce economic poisons in a modern industrial-scientific manner with staff and laboratories dedicated to the production of ever newer toxic chemicals.

At the time, chemical, mining, or other companies which thought they had a promising new poison had three choices to get their materials tested. The could hire scientists and build a laboratory, certainly an expensive endeavor for something that might never pay off. They could send their promising chemicals directly to experiment stations and/or private researchers in the hope that they would test it in the lab or on a crop.[23] Or they could place it on the market with grand claims about its usefulness and see whether it actually worked.[24] Without access to expert knowledge and the ability to field test their poisons, these companies had no way of knowing what they possessed and thus could not recognize the potential promise of their new chemicals and new toxic wastes, nor could they develop the toxicological knowledge needed to spread their poisons far and wide.

In early 1920, the distinguished entomologist Vernon Kellogg became the permanent secretary of the NRC and the head of the Division of Education Relations. He believed he could solve agriculture's grave problems by melding the needs of public agricultural research with the toxic materials and desires of "forward-thinking" chemical companies. Before Dr. Kellogg became the permanent secretary of the NRC, he was a professor of economic entomology at Stanford University. During World War I, Kellogg worked alongside Herbert Hoover on relief work in Belgium, and by the time he returned home, he was sure that food, not fighting, would be *the* critical component of any future war.[25] Kellogg fundamentally believed that a "starving world cannot be made safe for democracy," and thus the development of pesticide science and the spread of pesticides to all US farms was fundamental to national security.[26] Kellogg also believed that to do this the NRC had to help transform the country's farmers into the type of "intelligent growers" who would view the poisoning of their crops as just another required input.[27]

One of Kellogg's first major initiatives at the NRC was to push for the scientific rationalization of the US pesticide industry while helping to enlarge the agrotoxicological research capacity of the nation's LGUs and agricultural experiment stations. Kellogg believed that newer and better economic poisons already existed, especially in the waste piles of chemical companies. The development of the chemical industry during the Great War had happened at such a pace that these companies did not know what they possessed. Without a systematic process of getting these chemicals tested, Kellogg believed that promising new poisons scattered across the United States might simply be wasted.

Shortly after arriving at the NRC, Kellogg tasked the chemical engineer Harrison Howe, vice chairman of the NRC's Division of Research Extension, with enacting his vision. The NRC had created the Division of Research Extension to serve as its industrial relations arm with the goal of promoting, developing, and disseminating applied science across US industry.[28] Kellogg and Howe spent the spring of 1920 lobbying key representatives from chemical companies as well as prominent LGU and USDA scientists. In the early summer of 1920, Kellogg and Howe put their plan into action.[29]

THE CROP PROTECTION INSTITUTE

Rochester, New York, June 23, 1920, the Seneca Hotel: NRC's Division of Biology and Agriculture Conference of Plant Pathologists, Entomologists, and Manufactures of Fungicides and Pesticides. I like to imagine what it would have been like to be there, sitting in the lobby with its grand columns, potted palms, and yellow and red decor, watching prominent East Coast and midwestern scientists, NRC officials, and representatives of chemical and spray companies make their way to the conference room. I wonder what it would have been like to be filled with the optimistic spirit of cooperative capitalism that infused the immediate postwar era. After all, US agriculture and the US chemical industry had just helped win the Great War, and it must have seemed that with the right coordination, anything was possible. Kellogg, Howe, and the proponents of the CPI certainly thought so.

Howe opened the meeting by extolling the virtues of the NRC. He highlighted its role as a clearinghouse for the natural sciences as well as its role in advancing the technical capabilities of the United States during the Great War. Howe explained that the peacetime goal of the NRC was to continue the work done in the war and extend scientific research into all facets of industry. Capitalism was about competition among firms, he said, but as the Great War showed, competitors could also unite to attack common problems. The main problem facing the United States was the most fundamental national security issue of all. The greatest threat facing civilized humanity was no longer other countries; instead, it was the relentless attacks by insects and pathogens that led to crop loss.

Professor Percival Parrot followed Howe and spoke on behalf of economic entomologists. Dr. Parrot had previously served as the president of the Association of Economic Entomology and was the director of the Geneva, New York, agricultural experiment station. He had been a persistent advocate for the expansion of chemical control and was an avid early promoter of the CPI. He began by outlining the key reasons chemical pest control work was restricted in its attempts to develop a sounder scientific basis. In particular, he cited the lack of cooperation between agricultural experiment station workers, farmers, the chemical industry, and university scientists. He emphasized that the prevailing policies of most state experiment stations and the USDA either confined the station entomologists to their home states and/or limited the use of private money for experiment station research. Parrot stressed that the complexity of effectively poisoning crops over time and space provided the clearest example of why research must reach across state lines. After all, as a *New York Times* reporter put it, "Insects do not stop at state lines."[30] Without the ability to coordinate spray materials, spray schedules, and delivery methods, scientific results would continue to vary from place to place and from year to year.

The influential USDA scientist Dr. George Lyman then spoke on behalf of plant pathologists. He echoed what Dr. Parrot had said and added that there was a need to harmonize crop protection science across states "so that manufacturers can intelligently push for the sale of their product." G. R. Cushman of the General Chemical Company followed and spoke on behalf of chemical manufacturers. He passionately argued that past antagonisms between chemical companies and government officials must be forgotten. The war had clearly shown how industrial and scientific cooperation could result in rapid scientific and technological progress. Without this type of coordination, chemical pest control would continue to fall short of its promise. Like Dr. Lyman, Cushman saw cooperation between industry and government as the only way to develop the standardized poisons needed to achieve the economies of scale that pesticide manufacturers needed to spread chemical control. Once scientists agreed on the composition of poisons that were effective across different regions, it would lower the cost of marketing and make sales easier and more consistent, ultimately resulting in cheaper food for American consumers.

Howe and Cushman then presented conference members with a draft constitution for an independent nongovernmental organization to be known as the Plant Protection Institute, whose membership would be composed of crop protection scientists, chemical companies, and manufacturers of pesticide spray and delivery equipment. The goal of the Plant

Protection Institute would be to promote the general welfare of US consumers through the efficient control of crop pests and diseases. Money for scientific research, as well as for the institute's expenses, would come from the annual dues of member companies, which would fulfill the NRC's mission to create a self-supporting organization. In addition, to prevent any undue influence, a board of governors composed of six scientists and three industrial members would select research projects and determine where they would take place. Howe then adjourned the meeting and tasked Cushman and the organizing committee with drafting the institute's constitution and bylaws to be presented to the NRC for ratification.

Washington, D.C., September 28, 1920, National Academy of Sciences Building: NRC's Division of Research Extension Meeting. Kellogg called the meeting of the NRC because the Plant Protection Institute needed its approval before it could proceed. Present at the meeting were members of the NRC's Division of Research Extension, members of the Division of Biology and Agriculture, prominent Midwest and eastern crop protection scientists, representatives from Midwest and East Coast chemical companies, and the upper echelons of the USDA and its bureaus.[31]

Dr. Henry Bumstead, chairman of the NRC, began the meeting by outlining the ways in which the proposed institute would be an example of activity that the NRC was anxious to foster. He said that because there were no existing organizations that would bring the chemical industry and public agricultural science together, the NRC would fully support the formation of the CPI.[32] (After the Rochester meeting part of the name of the institute was changed from *Plant* to *Crop* to highlight its commercially oriented nature.) Dr. Elmer Ball, assistant secretary of the USDA, spoke next. The country's agriculture was faced with terrible economic problems, he argued, and crop protection occupied a fundamental position in dealing with these concerns. It was only with increased cooperation between government, industry, crop protection scientists, and pesticide companies, Ball insisted, that a sounder scientific basis for chemical pest control could be developed.

But not everyone at the NRC and the USDA was satisfied with the CPI and its initial structure. For instance, Dr. Carl Alsberg from the Bureau of Chemistry forcefully criticized the composition of the board of governors. Because all crop protection required industrially manufactured chemicals, Alsberg thought that there should be more representation from chemical organizations on the board. Others, like Dr. Karl Kellerman from the Bureau of Plant Industry, skeptically questioned Kellogg and the rest of the institute's promoters about whether the CPI would operate as a commercial enterprise or for the public welfare. Dr. William Taylor, chief of the Bureau of Plant Industry, also questioned the ultimate purpose of the CPI and whether government employees should participate in an organization financed by private money. In fact, Taylor was so skeptical of the institute that he prepared written remarks questioning its very nature. "The public is entitled to the full service of the public servant and the to the results of his work," he read to the audience. "The investigator can not, in fairness to the public, be in partnership with the manufacturer, nor make over to him for monopolistic or restrained use the results of his work or his suggestions."

Taylor believed that an organization such as the CPI would ultimately undermine the public's trust in government science and pesticide regulation. Taylor even went so far as to argue that something like the CPI could ultimately undermine democracy itself, a system of governance that requires public employees to be free of manipulation by commercial interests. Taylor argued that the CPI as proposed would eventually lead to the "interlocking" of private interests and public agricultural science. But Taylor's denunciation of the CPI's purpose was met with assurances that the CPI would lead to no such outcome. Kellogg himself pushed back against Taylor's suggestions that "a fusion or cooperation between scientific men in pure and applied science and industrial men is necessarily wrong." He argued that Dr. Taylor's denunciation of the CPI was irresponsible and used the example of Germany's technological, scientific, and industrial advantage at the outbreak of World War I as his cudgel. Because the greatest threat that civilized humanity faces is insects, not other countries, the development of pesticide science is a national security issue, and if commercial interests benefit at the same time that the public does, then all the better.

Howe then submitted a revised constitution and bylaws for the CPI to the NRC for approval. The only major revision was to expand the board of governors to include two representatives of the Association of Official Agricultural Chemists as well as one representative from the NRC and one representative from companies that manufacture pesticide delivery equipment. The meeting concluded with a general vote of the NRC's Division of Research Extension to affirm the proposed bylaws, the first board of governors, and the continued role of Howe as CPI secretary and NRC liaison.

The CPI's mandate inscribed in the constitution consisted of the following:

1) To promote the efficient control of injurious insects, plant diseases, and toxic substances affecting economic and ornamental plants and their products

2) To promote efficient control of insects and plants injurious to man, domestic animals and animal products, and for that purpose to hold patents, copyright, or to take other suitable measures;

3) To support and direct research upon these and other problems of a similar nature

4) To further cooperation between scientific workers and the producers of chemicals; the manufacturers of insecticides, fungicides and other similar materials; the manufacturers of appliances required for their use; and the manufacturers, growers, packers and shippers of the foregoing and of plant, animal, and other products

5) To assist in the dissemination of scientifically correct information regarding the control of injurious insects, plant diseases, and toxic substances.[33]

With the formation of the CPI, the NRC initiated a "get-together movement on the part of three groups–the intelligent grower, the scientist, and the business man."[34] Using the post–World War I needs of public agricultural institutions for research funding and chemical companies' desires to access public agrotoxicological science, the NRC, despite strong reservations by some in the USDA, purposely initiated the private capture of public agrotoxicological science.[35] For example, shortly after the NRC's ratification of the CPI, the board of governors modified the institute's constitution and bylaws to allow for an expansion of its industrial membership. This decision was made in response to the surprising growth of the CPI's industrial member base as well as legal advice from NRC attorneys.[36] The changes revised the structure of the board of governors and how they chose research projects. But most importantly, these changes also gave industrial trustees more power and allowed individual companies to fund specific projects rather than just relying on the board to choose research applicable to them.[37] The board justified these changes by asserting that they would still choose the LGUs where the research was done and that all members would have access to the results. Nevertheless, these changes also began the "interlocking" of public agricultural science and the chemical industry that Dr. Taylor had warned would happen.

Between 1920 and 1945, the CPI coordinated more than 150 research projects that linked the capital and toxic materials of US chemical companies with the expertise and infrastructure of LGUs and agricultural experiment stations across the country. This research was aimed at developing a science of industrial pest control to stave off the collapse of Western civilization and deliver cheap food to American consumers. In the process, the CPI also facilitated the transformation of the growing mass of organic and inorganic wastes of industrial manufacture into the by-products that made toxicity-based repair possible.[38] But perhaps most importantly, because the CPI was a part of the NRC's peacetime mission to expand scientific research into all facets of industry, it was also an institution that helped set national scientific and industrial policy during the interwar years. The CPI played a major role in making agrotoxicological R&D and the utilization of public agricultural infrastructures a critical component of any successful post–World War II agrochemical company. In other words, during the interwar era, the CPI helped make publicly subsidized agrochemical innovation a fundamental part of pesticide development.

COOPERATIVE CPI PROJECTS

To get into the nuts and bolts of each CPI project is beyond the scope of this chapter. Between 1920 and 1945, more than one hundred companies and more than fifty state agricultural experiment stations, botanical gardens, and private laboratories participated in the CPI's projects.[39] I use a small subset of these projects to highlight the role that the CPI played in mediating the chemicalization of US agriculture in the interwar years. The first project was a cooperative dusting experiment undertaken in 1921 and deals with the homogenization and standardization of pesticides and toxicological science. The second project was an expansive study to develop chemical control of smut in stored grains, while the third project investigated the toxic properties of sulfur as an insecticide. These earlier projects sought to fulfill the cooperative mandate of the CPI.

I describe the fourth and fifth projects in the most detail. I do this because it was from these studies and others like them that the first organo-chlorine pesticides and bioselective organic poisons emerged. These latter projects not only demonstrated the complications of bringing a promising poison to market; they are also both prime examples of the noncooperative type of agrochemical R&D that became commonplace after World War II.

In the early 1920s, two main issues confronted non-California-based chemical companies and pest control researchers. The most pressing was the lack of standardized toxicological research. There were only a few ways to attempt scientifically comparative agrotoxicology, and none of these were widely used outside of California. Some theoretical work on chemical toxicity had been done, but again, most of that research came out of California as well.[40] Without the development of methods and standards for comparative toxicology, a science of industrial pest control was impossible. The second problem was directly related to the first, namely the standardization of a poison's composition and dosage over time and space. A pesticide's success often varied dramatically from place to place and from year to year, and scientists wanted to know why. At the same time, chemical companies wanted to create one standardized product that they could sell across diverse geographies in order to help them achieve the economies of scale they needed to maximize production. That is why one of the first major projects undertaken by the CPI was to attempt to standardize dose, composition, and delivery of poisons for apple, pear, and peach pests across multiple northeastern states.

In 1921, the board of directors selected Dr. N. J. Geddings at the University of West Virginia Experiment Station as the project's primary investigator.[41] He was tasked with coordinating research at experimental stations across Connecticut, West Virginia, New York, and Pennsylvania. While Dr. Geddings oversaw the project, scientists at the individual experiment stations were responsible for securing nearby commercial orchards in which to conduct the tests. The commercial growers and extension agents provided the labor for the tests, and the CPI made sure that the industrial members supplied the participating scientists with the spraying and dusting materials at no cost. For these experiments, this included a cornucopia of sulfurs, arsenates, coppers, and nicotines emulsified in various soaps, spreaders, and stickers.[42] These materials were furnished by the Sherman-Williams Company, the General Chemical Company, the National Sulfur Company, the Tobacco By-Products Company, and the Niagara Sprayer Company.

Some interesting results were obtained from these trials, but the timing and extent of insect damage and a lack of standardization of data collection, including how to determine and report foliage injury, made scientific generalizations difficult. Furthermore, the lack of material consistency between supposedly equivalent sprays and dusts made any general conclusion problematic. The following season, the CPI's board of governors expanded the experimental trials to two more states— Virginia and Minnesota—and asked F. D. Fromme at the University of Virginia Agricultural Extension to join Dr. Geddings in coordinating the experiments and analyzing the results. Unfortunately, the 1922 poisoning season did not bring about a more promising outcome.

The cooperative dusting experiment failed to live up to expectations, but that did not diminish the resolve of the CPI. In fact, it demonstrated the importance of standardized approaches to toxicological research and the "feasibility of looking to the Crop Protection Institute as an available means of bringing about a profitable and desirable cooperation among investigators."[43] Questions about standardized laboratory and field-based toxicological research and the composition and delivery of economic poisons were at the forefront of pest control research throughout the early 1920s, and many of the CPI's early projects attempted to answer them with multiple-year studies across multiple states.[44]

For example, in another early project the CPI coordinated research across ten states and four Canadian provinces: Washington, Delaware, Minnesota, Pennsylvania, New York, Idaho, Ohio, North Dakota, Illinois, South Dakota, Quebec, Ontario, Manitoba, and Saskatchewan. This massive study, funded by the Cereal Manufacturers' Association and the American Phytopathological Society, was aimed at developing better chemical control of grain smut (fungus) in stored wheat, oats, and barley.[45] The problem was twofold: to find a poison that could control smut in stored grain and to find a poison that could control smut while not hindering the grains' germination potential. The project, unlike the dusting experiments, delivered usable results for cereal companies. Researchers concluded that copper dusts controlled smut in wheat and hulled oats and that formaldehyde did so for barley and nonhulled oats.

In 1922, the CPI launched another large-scale research project. This study was organized to investigate the toxic properties of sulfur, and it was funded by the three largest US sulfur producers: Texas Gulf Sulfur Company, Union Sulphur Company, and Freeport Sulfur Company.[46] The board of governors of the CPI divided the research across five experiment stations and three research labs. The field studies were conducted at the agricultural experiment stations of Michigan, Colorado, Pennsylvania, New York, and Missouri, while the laboratory studies were conducted at the Missouri Botanical Gardens, the Boyce Thompson Institute for Plant Research in New York, and the New York State Agricultural Experiment Station. The board of the CPI distributed the scientific labor in this manner to try to overcome one of the most critical issues confronting companies that wanted to develop new pesticides, namely, the cost and complexity of moving a potential poison from the laboratory to the commercial field.

The most important finding of the sulfur project was that the physical size of sulfur particles influenced their ability to kill fungi; essentially, the smaller the better.[47] The research also demonstrated new ways to produce extremely fine sulfur particles, which led to new methods of processing sulfur for use in fungicides.[48] Interestingly, following some back and forth with the NRC's lawyers, the CPI patented the discovery (via assignees), meaning that the patent was available to any of the industrial members of the institute.[49] But these were the only cooperative patents of the CPI, as intellectual property rights to the next discoveries would go to the individual companies that funded the research.

The three projects just described are a good proxy for the types of research that the CPI coordinated during its first few years. Most projects lived up to the cooperative spirit that Kellogg and Howe had originally sought for the institute. However, cracks in the CPI's cooperative structure quickly appeared. For example, in 1925 the Standard Oil Company of Indiana contracted the CPI to research Flit, its new proprietary oil-based poison.[50] The contract stipulated that Standard Oil retained the exclusive right to any knowledge produced by the study. It also provided Standard Oil the right to withhold publication of the research. The contract alarmed lawyers at the NRC because it went against the idea that the results of the institute's research would be available to all its members. For example, Gano Dunn, chairman of the NRC, said that the they could not approve of the patent clause in the Flit contract. However, he also stated that because the contract was between the CPI and Standard Oil of Indiana, the NRC had no grounds to contest it despite its variance from NRC policy.[51]

By the late 1920s the CPI was evolving into an organization at which individual companies could get their poisons tested without having to give up proprietary rights, which reflected a general shift by the economic poisons industry into proprietary chemicals. The CPI was quickly becoming an appendage of the rapidly developing chemical industry, which at the time, as Walter O'Kane, chairman of the CPI's board of governors throughout the 1920s, wrote, found itself increasingly "long in product and short of market."[52]

CHLORINATED NAPHTHALENES

The fourth project requires greater examination, as it represents US chemical companies' first push into the type of chlorinated organic pesticides that became prominent after World War II. Following World

War I, US chemical manufactures were awash in organic compounds from coal tar. They were also drowning in an abundance of chlorine wastes from the explosive growth of the chlor-alkali industry and the collapse in demand for chlorine needed for chemical weapons manufacture.[53] Chemical companies began exploring newer ways of reacting these wastes-cum-by-products together in the hope that they might yield fruitful compounds.[54]

Prior to World War I, the German chemical industry had been pushing the bounds of organic chemistry by chlorinating naphthalene to produce synthetic waxes and other novel materials. Materials made from these novel chemicals had physical properties that made them waterproof, gas tight, rat proof, and resistant to physical abrasion and chemical corrosion. During World War I, German manufacturers had incorporated them into gas masks and other protective clothing. But they also quickly found out that that these types of chemicals could be quite toxic to humans, as workers developed chloracne, a telltale sign of being poisoned with chlorinated organic chemicals.[55]

After the war, US companies too came to recognize the futuristic properties of chlorinated naphthalenes. One company in particular, the Halowax Corporation, began experimenting with polychlorinated naphthalenes as insulators and began manufacturing them as coatings for electrical cables.[56] Using high-pressure synthesis techniques introduced after the war, Halowax's chemists were able to exercise significant control over reaction yields, meaning that they could manufacture naphthalene molecules with varying numbers of chlorine atoms. This allowed them to manipulate the physical properties of their novel waxes, with harder halowaxes, their trademarked term, produced from more highly chlorinated molecules.[57] The Halowax Corporation, however, was not the only chemical company to see the promise of chlorinated naphthalenes.[58]

Scientists at the Monsanto Chemical Works had also been experimenting with these novel chemicals, and Monsanto's chemists thought that these compounds might have a range of toxicity that could make them useful to agriculture. At the time Monsanto was purely a chemical company. It did not have any agrotoxicological laboratories and was not going to build any just to test one compound.[59] That is why in 1928 the Monsanto Chemical Works funded a CPI study into the agrotoxicological properties of its experimental naphthalene mixtures. The CPI chose scientists at the University of Illinois to conduct the study. The year of tests showed the potential of these new chemicals, but the CPI-funded scientists also concluded that the commercialization of Monsanto's poisons would need further study, in particular the need to develop new standardized and comparative laboratory methods. Monsanto did not pursue this agricultural research any further, but the Halowax Corporation picked up where Monsanto left off.

In 1932, the Halowax Corporation funded a much larger study of chlorinated naphthalenes. The CPI split the work between the Ohio State University, the University of New Hampshire, and the University of Florida.[60] These three agricultural colleges were chosen for both their expertise and, perhaps more importantly, their locations. They were places where experiment station scientists could test halowaxes against a variety of insects on a variety of crops under different environmental conditions. These experiments, like the cooperative dusting study, demonstrated the need to be able to manufacture and formulate materially consistent economic poisons. For example, in the first series of experiments, agricultural experiment station workers mixed the halowaxes with white oil and other emulsifiers just prior to spraying. In the second round of experiments, the Halowax Corporation's own chemists mixed the sprays, which were then shipped to participating experiment stations. This resulted in a situation in which despite supposedly containing the same chemical mixture, the poisons mixed by Halowax's chemists (0.5% Halowax and 0.5% light-medium mineral oil) were much more toxic than those made by extension scientists. Nevertheless, the experiments demonstrated the ability of chlorinated naphthalenes to kill the eggs of insects like the codling moth when emulsified with white oil. Based on these results, the following year, the Halowax Corporation extended and enlarged the original project.[61]

But before Halowax could think about moving toward commercialization, it had to confront the agrotoxicological dilemma that still plagued the pesticide industry. Thus, part of Halowax's new round of funding paid two scientists at Ohio State University, E. P. Brekey and A. C. Miller, to develop a quantitative method of comparing the ovicidal properties of Halowax emulsions to the ovicidal properties of widely used economic poisons such as lead arsenate.[62] To move toward commercialization, Brekey and Miller needed to develop standardized laboratory procedures that would also consider practical and environmental considerations when testing new poisons. For example, in previous experiments they had dosed codling moth eggs attached to plates of glass, but for these they dosed eggs on live foliage. The halowaxes again showed toxicological promise, but significant obstacles still existed in trying to turn them into commercially viable poisons. These chlorinated compounds had physical and chemical properties unlike any chemicals before them. This made them economically useful in some ways, but it also made them incredibly difficult to handle and thus to use practically as a pesticide. After all, toxicity to insects was just one of the characteristics that made a poison economic. The two scientists concluded that despite their potential toxicity, more research was needed before any attempts could be made to commercialize their halowaxes as pesticides.[63]

By the early 1930s, the Halowax Corporation's hopes of developing commercially viable chlorinated naphthalene-based poisons was further complicated by the growth of industrial hygiene. As had happened to German manufacturers during World War I, severe health problems were occurring among workers who handled these novel materials, particularly electricians.[64] In addition, some of Halowax's own workers had died following exposure to chlorinated naphthalene fumes.[65] Thus, even as these companies were denying the toxicity of these chemicals to humans, they were trying to develop them into poisons for agricultural use.[66] Despite the toxic potential of chlorinated naphthalenes, the project wound down at the end of the 1935 season without Halowax having a clear path to commercialization.

DINITROPHENOL

The fifth project involves the Dow Chemical Company and the development of one of the first series of synthetic organic insecticides and herbicides. Dow emerged from World War I a world leader in industrial phenol chemistry.[67] During the war Dow became the largest US producer of trinitrophenol (TNP), the favorite explosive of French and British forces. But this also meant that Dow became one of the largest manufacturers of chemical wastes produced during trinitrophenol synthesis, especially dinitrophenol (DNP).[68] In the mid-1920s Dow's scientists became interested in DNP's agrotoxicological potential when the German company Bayer began selling a DNP derivative known as dinitro-ortho-cresol (DNOC) as an economic poison in Europe. Dow's research scientists had originally dismissed DNOC as much too phytotoxic, but Bayer's introduction of DNOC into Europe pushed Dow's chemists to reconsider its potential. In the late 1920s, Dow's chemists synthesized new derivatives of DNP at its Organic Research Laboratory in Michigan. The lab was headed by the prominent industrial chemist and future chemurgy evangelist William Hale, and he thought one compound in particular, dinitro-ortho-cyclo-hexyl-phenol (DNOCHP), had the potential to be an economic poison. Like Monsanto, Dow also lacked the infrastructure to conduct agrotoxicological research, so the company turned to the CPI to explore the toxic potential of Hale's new phenolic concoctions.[69]

In 1931, Dow and the CPI arranged a preliminary laboratory study to analyze the toxicity of these new dinitrophenols.[70] The CPI chose Iowa State University and tasked the graduate student John Kagy with toxicologically surveying Dow's novel poisons.[71] In his doctoral thesis, completed in 1937, Kagy demonstrated the potential of DNOCHP in the lab.[72] To accomplish this, Kagy spent most of his time developing new standardized screening techniques to compare the toxicity of synthetic organic chemicals in agricultural settings.

However, even before Kagy finished, Dow Chemical had used his preliminary results as the basis for expanded trials of DNOCHP. In 1935, the CPI arranged for Dow to send DNOCHP to key economic entomologists across the United States for further research.[73] One of the scientists who received Dow's new poisons was the economic entomologist Alfred Boyce, director of the University of California Citrus Experiment Station in Riverside and a future member of the CPI's board of governors.[74] Boyce was conducting an expert on the control of citrus pests, and he thought the compound might have potential against the red spider mite. As discussed in chapter 3, the red spider mite was an invasive species that had become economically destructive to citrus growers in the late 1910s and the spread of which was aided by cyanide fumigation.[75] After graduating, Dow paid for Kagy (via a CPI fellowship) to join Boyce in Riverside.[76]

Both Dow and Kagy recognized the potential of this new synthetic organic compound, but bringing it to commercialization still required significant work, particularly overcoming the problem of DNOCHP's oil-adjuvated phytotoxicity. In other words, DNOCHP became more toxic to trees after emulsification than it was on its own. Yet over the next year, Boyce and Kagy overcame this problem and developed a DNOCHP dust formulation that could kill the red spider mite without causing significant foliage injury.[77] In 1938, Dow commercialized DNOCHP as DN-Dust and began manufacturing a poisonous dust comprised of 1 percent DNOCHP and 99 percent California walnut shell flour at its chemical plant in Long Beach, California.[78]

DN-Dust was an instant commercial success, especially among citrus growers. As a result, in 1940 Dow built a new chemical plant at Seal

Beach, California, specifically to manufacture "DN" insecticides for the California agricultural market.[79] But Dow's chemists also thought that DN could be reformulated to work with a wider range of crops. For example, in 1940 Dow bypassed the CPI and directly contracted with the University of Oregon Experiment Station to evaluate DNOCHP's efficacy on hops and similar row crops.[80]

Dow's organic chemists had also been busy. While Boyce and Kagy were performing their first set of experiments in Southern California, Dow's Michigan-based scientists had synthesized an amine salt of DNOCHP and preliminarily tested it in their recently built experimental farm near their Michigan headquarters.[81] Dow then sent this new derivative to Boyce and Kagy, who field tested the compound in oil at the UC Citrus Experiment Station as well as on numerous nearby commercial fields. Based on these trials, in 1941 Dow launched "DN-111," an oil-based amine salt of DNOCHP, which could be used effectively and profitably as a dormant spray for the broad-spectrum control of pests across a wide variety of deciduous tree crops. DN-111, like DN-Dust, was immediately successful upon introduction, and it remained so throughout the agricultural production environment of World War II. After the war DN-Dust and DN-111 consumption by California growers exploded as a result of the introduction of DDT. DDT, like cyanide fumigation, was not effective against the red spider mite. This meant that with every application of DDT, red spider mite populations grew. As mite populations soared, so did the demand for an effective acaricide.[82]

In 1941, Kagy left his Dow-funded post at the UC Citrus Experiment Station to head up Dow's new agricultural chemical research facility at Seal Beach and to focus on the commercialization of other DNOCHP derivatives.[83] DNOCHP was not the only promising dinitrophenol derivative that Kagy had identified in his dissertation research. Dow had originally presented him with a smorgasbord of synthetic novelties based around the dinitro-orthro-cresol molecule, and Kagy screened many. The other main potential compound was dinitro-o-sec-butyl-phenol (DNOSBP), which Kagy thought had potential not just as an insecticide but also as an herbicide.[84]

A few years before Kagy joined Dow, it had already used his preliminary research to expand research into DNOSBP. In 1936 Dow bypassed the CPI and directly approached the scientists and experiment stations that it thought were necessary to commercialize DNOSBP as an herbicide. Specifically, Dow sought out the weed expert Alden Crafts at UC Davis for research and development of DNOSBP. Crafts was a world expert on

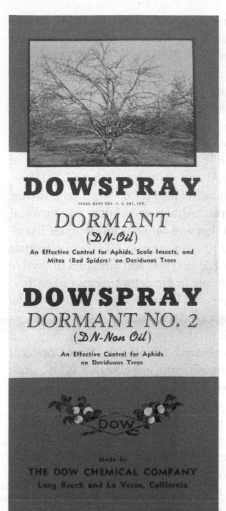

DOWSPRAY

TRADE MARK REG. U. S. PAT. OFF.

DORMANT
(DN-Oil)

An Effective Control for Aphids, Scale Insects, and
Mites (Red Spiders) on Deciduous Trees

DOWSPRAY
DORMANT NO. 2
(DN-Non Oil)

An Effective Control for Aphids
on Deciduous Trees

Made by
THE DOW CHEMICAL COMPANY
Long Beach and La Verne, California

FIGURE 23. "Dowspray Dormant No. 2" herbicide pamphlet, 1944. One of the many dintro compounds Dow commercialized in the 1940s. Courtesy of the University of California, Davis, Special Collections.

weeds and plant physiology and one of the few experts at the time on the herbicidal action of synthetic compounds. Dow and Crafts's team at UC Davis built on Kagy's preliminary work and demonstrated that DNOSBP was an effective contact herbicide. In 1942, Kagy, now with Dow, introduced "Dinoseb" as a general herbicide into the California market, making it the first "synthetic" herbicide used in the United States.[85] That same year, Kagy's team also introduced DN-289 (DOWSPRAY) as a new dormant poison for orchard tree pests (see figure 23). Dow manufactured both Dinoseb and DN-289 at its new Seal Beach plant.[86]

But Dow was not the only chemical company interested in the toxicity of dinitrophenols. For example, in 1936 the Standard Agricultural Chemical Company had contracted the CPI to study "Sinox" as an herbicide. Sinox was the brand name for Standard's DNOC compound, and the company's scientists thought that its phytotoxicity might exhibit biological selectivity. The CPI's board of governors chose the University of New Hampshire and UC Davis as sites for a series of experiments that explored the use of Sinox as a selective herbicide. Sinox was initially screened at the New Hampshire Agricultural Experiment Station, but the project was quickly enlarged and shifted entirely to UC Davis. In the spring of 1938, UC Davis scientists field tested Sinox on a variety of crops near the UC Davis campus. Almost incredibly, the chemical seemed to kill broad-leaf weeds in flax and other grains without harming the crop. By the end of the next growing season, UC Davis scientists had field tested Sinox with mechanized sprayers and airplanes on twelve thousand acres of flax and other grains in the delta regions of San Joaquin as well as Contra Costa County.[87] The results were as clear as the ground between rows after being sprayed with Sinox.

It was not the Standard Agricultural Chemical Company, however, that ultimately benefited from this research.[88] It was the Dow Chemical Company. Dow chemists had been experimenting with DNOC since they first heard of Bayer's plan to sell it as an economic poison in Europe, and it was also one of the compounds screened by Kagy in his doctoral studies.[89] In 1939, shortly after the Standard Agricultural Chemical Company's contract with the CPI ended, Dow contracted directly with UC Davis scientists to help commercialize DNOC as the first synthetic selective herbicide for the control of broad-leaf annual weeds in cereals, flax, alfalfa, and corn.[90] In 1942, Dow introduced DNOC to California growers as the world's first selective synthetic herbicide.[91] Throughout World War II, it was used most extensively in the Salinas Valley, where it facilitated the rapid mechanization of agriculture already underway.[92]

CAPTURE

In 1942 the NRC's Division of Biology took over and enlarged the functions of the CPI as part of the War Industries Board's wartime planning.[93] As in World War I, the NRC became the coordinator of scientific and technological research involving agriculture and chemicals across the United States. It became the liaison between chemical companies and university research. Nevertheless the CPI was quickly becoming obsolete. By the early 1940s the bonds that Kellogg had envisioned between public agricultural research and pesticide companies had solidified. Pesticide R&D had become a priority for many chemical firms, and these companies began bypassing the CPI to work directly with LGUs.[94] After World War II, the CPI remained a coordinator of scientific activity at some LGUs, particularly projects at the University of New Hampshire and in surrounding states.[95] This was because Walter O'Kane, a founding board member, kept the CPI going at his home institution, reincarnated as the CPI Biological Research Center.[96] Nevertheless, by the early 1950s, its role as the mediator between chemical companies and agricultural experiment stations had waned.

Despite its radically reduced role in the decades after World War II, the CPI fundamentally changed the way that pesticide R&D was done in the United States and thus continued to impact how chemical companies developed new economic poisons. "The institute has played an important role in pioneering the way for new type of collaboration between scientific institutions and industrial organizations," wrote the crop scientist Milton Farrar in the late 1940s, "which has had the most significant consequences."[97] "From these programs of research have come new organic insecticides and fungicides whose performance has been *so* outstanding that the field for new and better agricultural chemicals appears almost limitless" (emphasis in original).[98]

In the 1930s two things became clear to chemical companies. The first was that they needed an agrotoxicological research infrastructure to get poisons scientifically to market. Gone were the days of chance discovery and trial by fire. It took time, money, and expertise to make a poison economic. The second was that public agricultural science had an important role to play in this infrastructure. In the late 1930s and 1940s pesticide firms across the United States began building their own agricultural labs and research farms, but LGUs still had a fundamental role to play. LGUs were becoming *the* place for chemical companies to get their promising and proprietary chemicals tested, particularly in the types of field settings that companies needed to determine and standardize dose-response criteria.

Years later, the Dow Chemical Company highlighted how its experience working with institutes like the CPI not only taught the company the importance of field-based R&D but also confirmed the benefit of maintaining close relationships with state, federal, and university scientists. It was one thing to demonstrate efficacy in the lab; it was an entirely different proposition to bring a potential product to market, and Dow recognized that public-private partnerships were critical in bridging the gap between the laboratory and field.[99] That is what Kellogg and the NRC had in mind when they first conceived of the CPI. Chemical firms could turn to the network of LGUs and agricultural experiment stations across the United States to assay the toxic largesse of a post–World War I chemical industry. This would not only provide funds for agrotoxicological research and help develop a science of pest control; it would also help chemical companies achieve new economies of scale and lead to widespread use of pesticides by farmers.

The CPI's mission was to link the chemical industry to public science, and that it was it did. Through the industrial, scientific, and political networks of the CPI, chemical manufacturers, agricultural producers, and crop protection scientists collaborated to develop new outlets for primary chemical products and new methods to transmute the growing masses of toxic industrial wastes from costs of production into valuable and effective agricultural poisons. In the process, however, the CPI facilitated what Dr. Taylor warned they would, namely the private capture of public agrotoxicological science and the undermining of public faith in chemical regulators to keep people safe.[100]

In the 1960s and 1970s, environmental activists echoed Dr. Taylor's prescient words and began to question the role of LGUs in the development of pesticides, going as far as to accuse LGU administrators and scientists of conspiring with chemical companies at the expense of the public welfare.[101] But what this chapter has shown is that it was not a conspiracy that first brought chemical companies and public agricultural research together. In fact, the opposite is true. It was the direct policies of the NRC and the CPI that brought chemical firms in contact with public agricultural science. During the interwar period, the CPI helped chemical firms build a pesticide R&D infrastructure that ensured a more systematic search for newer economic poisons, one that implicated LGUs and their scientists in the process.

Throughout the interwar era the CPI helped make toxicity-based repair *the* solution to agriculture's pest problems. In the end this may have been the biggest impact that it had. The CPI did not facilitate the development of biological control science, nor did it push for breeding disease-resistant varieties or rethinking how crops are grown. It did not coordinate the growth of firms dedicated to producing "good" insects or try to link these firms with the nation's LGUs. That is not to say that biological and other methods of pest control were not explored during the interwar period. But I am arguing that the CPI played an important role in making toxicity-based repair *the* form of repair after World War II.[102]

The historian Margaret Weber has called the type of public-private infrastructural arrangements that the CPI fostered a "hybridization of scientific knowledge."[103] Though true, this begs the question of who ultimately benefits from this web of expertise.[104] The NRC decided in 1920 that helping chemical companies find new outlets for their chemicals and toxic wastes by developing a public-private agrotoxicological infrastructure was akin to helping the American farmer and thus the American consumer. One of the most telling things about the history of the CPI is that there was not a single farmer in any of the meetings or on the board. Farmers were only talked about in the abstract, as operators of biological food factories that would always benefit from more pesticides and larger yields. It was the chemical companies and food processors that held sway among people like Kellogg and Howe. After all, their ultimate goal was not to help the American farmer; it was to make sure that the United States and the civilized world had enough food to win the next war. For them, this required the expansive use of pesticides and the development of public-private partnerships that allowed chemical companies to benefit from publicly subsidized research.

Who should benefit from public agricultural research has long been a controversial topic. But what the history of the CPI shows is that, aside from a few voices, by the 1930s it was not controversial that LGUs should be used for the benefit of the pesticide manufacturers and food processors. During the interwar era, the relationships that Kellogg first envisioned between chemical companies and public agricultural science became just part of the way that pesticides are made.

CHAPTER 5

From Oil Well to Farm

The use of pest control underground is a new field for chemical industry development.

—"Shell Oil Testing Soil Fumigants," *New York Times*, 1950

California is often imagined to be a land without seasons. For California agriculture, however, those seasons are as distinct as the return of cold temperatures and the changes in leaf color in other parts of the United States. Every fall, as the first rains (hopefully) return to California's parched landscapes, fumigation crews stir from their commercial slumber, dust off their gear, gather their chemicals, and mobilize for the soil fumigation season that lies ahead. Whether under the cool fogs of America's "Salad Bowl," the high clouds of the great Central Valley, or the winter sun of the desert counties, these fumigation crews migrate from field to field, introducing a variety of toxic chemicals into the subsoil of much of California's incredibly productive farmland. These toxic gases move through the soil complex like an army of insidious assassins, temporarily cleansing the soil of commercially destructive organisms. Without the ability for growers to chemically disinfect the soil of nematodes and other soil-dwelling pathogens, the fertile valleys of California and much of the world's industrial agriculture would look radically different.

I used to spend countless hours watching these crews operate. At the time I was working for a laboratory that was monitoring nutrient runoff from central coast agriculture. Since I was in charge of sampling the water from the ditches and streams that drained these fields, I often found myself in ankle-deep water as the intricate dance of soil fumigation went on around me. What first caught my attention was how humans, machines, and chemicals blurred together in the process of fumigating the soil. I used to marvel at how quickly a field could be stripped of its end-of-season chaff, fumigated, and replanted. And it is that latter term that is the focus of this chapter and what soil fumigants truly accomplished: the ability to replant the same crop in the same soil year after year. But the discovery of soil fumigants did something else as well. They were an important part of what I call the petrochemical turn in the history of pesticides. Soil fumigants marked the rise of petroleum waste gases as a major source of toxicity for agriculture and opened up the subsoil as a vast new market for the petrochemical industry.

Despite their fundamental importance to the organization of modern industrial agriculture, soil fumigants have received scant historical attention.[1] But as I argue in this chapter, in the early 1940s these toxic chemicals revolutionized agriculture by giving growers the tools to temporarily conquer "replant disease." Replant disease was not caused by a singular pest, but rather by the way that crops were grown. Petroleum-based soil fumigants gave growers the ability to overcome the buildup of soil-borne pests and diseases that resulted from growers planting the same crop over and over and over. By the 1930s, the types of novel ecosystems that growers had produced and reproduced had led to a buildup of soil-borne organisms that began to render farmland commercially unproductive for that crop. These iatrogenic problems were increasingly common for many types of agriculture across the world, especially in places that had a long history of intensive monoculture.[2]

The discovery of inorganic fertilizer sources in the mid-nineteenth century and the development of commercial fertilizers removed the need for farmers to rotate crops as a way to manage soil fertility.[3] Fertilizers did not, however, overcome the need to rotate crops for pest management. Rather, it was the discovery of cheap and effective petroleum-based soil fumigants in the early 1940s that severed the link between the intensive production of a single crop without rotation and the buildup of commercially destructive pests in the soil complex. With soil fumigants, growers did not have to change their practices; instead, all they needed was a new generation of chemical weapons that could penetrate the soil. The ability to chemically sterilize soil, as Dr. Robert Salter, chief of the USDA's Bureau of Plant industry, put it in 1947, was "one of the greatest boons to agriculture since the development of fertilizer."[4] If inorganic and synthetic fertilizers first revolutionized the organizational possibilities of agriculture, then these new soil fumigants did it again by making it possible to plant every year as if it were the first time the soil had been planted.

In this chapter I tell the origin story of the soil fumigant DD, a mixture of two novel chlorinated chemicals (1,3-dicloroproene and 1,2-dicloropropane) that were produced as waste in some of Shell Chemical Company's groundbreaking petrochemistry. Shell Chemical had sent some of this waste to Hawaii at the request of Walter Carter, a university researcher who was searching for a chemical cure to the decline of pineapple yields across the islands. Like growers in California, pineapple companies watched their yields decline as continuous cropping facilitated the proliferation of destructive soil insects and pathogens. Yet in the fields that Carter treated with DD, he watched pineapples grow like they were planted in virgin soil. For Carter, salvation came in the shape of Shell's novel waste streams, and Shell saw an opportunity to spread this gospel far and wide.

Shell Chemical was in the perfect position to commercialize DD. In the late 1920s, scientists and engineers at the California-based Shell Development Company and Shell Chemical Company pioneered the first synthesis of ammonia using waste natural gas as a hydrogen source. In the mid-1930s, Shell's scientists developed a way to inject this ammonia first into irrigation water and then directly into agricultural soils. I tell this story as well because these fertilizer technologies were quickly adapted for use with soil fumigants. But I also tell this story because soil fumigants made from petroleum wastes were just part of the fully petrochemical agriculture that Shell's top brass envisioned when they set up their chemical shop in California in 1928. During the 1930s, the Shell Oil Company and their subsidiaries helped turn California into the epicenter of petrochemical R&D, and agriculture was key to their plan to turn the waste gases of their oil wells and refineries into everything from fertilizer to soap to things not yet dreamed of.[5] By the early 1940s, California agriculture had become fully integrated with its petroleum economy. Its agriculture had become an important part of the oil industry's waste management infrastructure, while its growers increasingly relied on petroleum to move their tractors, kill their insects, weed their crops, and fumigate and fertilize their soils.

The two stories in this chapter have a common origin in the post–World War I mind of J. B. August Kessler, head of operations for Royal Dutch/Shell. Prior to the 1920s, the notion that a chemical industry could be based on petroleum was, for many, incomprehensible. However, with the rapid expansion of new refining technology for the production of gasoline during and following World War I and the dramatic increase in oil production, the scale of wastes from petroleum extraction and refining increasingly abutted potential waste-value thresholds.[6] But industrial chemistry needed more than a new source of raw material. New industrial sciences, new industrial apparatuses, and large amounts of capital were also required to aid chemistry's transmutation of gaseous petroleum wastes into the petrochemicals that remade the world.

In October 1917, Kessler laid out the guiding principles of the Royal Dutch/Shell Group's proposed approach to making chemicals from petroleum at the Royal Dutch/Shell board meeting in Amsterdam.[7] Beginning by appealing to the chemical industry's inherently revolutionary nature, Kessler described his vision for the future: imagining the transformation of Shell's petroleum extraction and refining wastes into the chemical products of tomorrow. The oil business and the chemical business were rapidly approaching each other, he said, and it was inevitable that they would one day overlap. Thus, without an organized approach to their integration, capital, time, and raw materials would be wasted. Believing that the very happiness of humankind was at stake, Kessler argued that it was only through the development of petrochemistry that better things for better living could be made, that Shell's petroleum wastes could simultaneously enrich *both* oil companies and humanity. In his proposal to Shell's board, Kessler presciently envisioned a fertile marriage of agriculture, petroleum, and the chemical industries and foresaw the establishment of an entirely new chemical industry based on the materiality of petroleum.

AMMONIA FROM OIL

In 1913, the German scientists Fritz Haber and Carl Bosch, along with engineers at BASF, were the first to transform nitrogen gas into ammonia fertilizer on an industrial scale.[8] To do this Haber and Bosch passed nitrogen and hydrogen gas over a catalyst under high pressure. In this reaction, however, it was hydrogen and not nitrogen that was the limiting factor. BASF produced this hydrogen from coal. Bosch had originally wanted to use natural gas (methane) as a source of hydrogen, but Germany had no access to natural gas. He had wanted to use methane because it has the highest hydrogen-to-carbon ratio, which made it cheaper to use than any coal-based source.

After World War I, industrial nitrogen fixation grew slowly but steadily. In the United States, the first commercial nitrogen fixation plant was built in 1921 by the Atmospheric Nitrogen Corporation at Syracuse, New York. This small plant also relied on coal as its source of hydrogen.

So too did the subsequent plants built in the United States in the following years.[9] But unlike Germany in the first few decades of the twentieth century, the United States was blessed with abundant reserves of natural gas. California, in particular, had lots of it. In fact, its oil companies were dumping hundreds of millions of cubic feet of natural gas into the air every day.[10]

In the early 1910s, Royal Dutch/Shell stormed into the California oil market. In 1914 its subsidiary, Shell Oil Company of California, completed a state-of-the-art refinery at Martinez, and by 1916 Shell's West Coast operations had become fully integrated from well to consumer. In 1922 Shell bought most of the Union Oil company as a way to Americanize Royal/Dutch Shell's California operations and protect Shell from the political harassment that it suffered as a "foreign" company during World War I.[11] By the mid-1920s, an average Shell Union Oil Company well in the Central Valley produced a million cubic feet of dry gas and 250,000 cubic feet of wet gas per day, all of which was simply vented to the atmosphere.[12]

In the early 1920s the chemical engineer John Teeple said that one of the biggest factors influencing the transmutation of waste into valuable products was what he called "chemical progress by injunction."[13] By this he meant that laws aimed at preventing pollution and encouraging conservation often prodded chemical companies to rethink their wastes. Thus, we can read Shell's push to turn oil well gases into ammonia fertilizer and other chemical products not only as a way to turn waste into value but also as a method to continue to produce as much oil as the company wanted in the face of impending regulation. Indeed, as the historian Paul Sabin has noted, by the mid-1920s it was clear that a natural gas conservation law would eventually be passed in California as an indirect way to regulate the overproduction of oil. However, if a company could capture its oil well gases and turn them into something to sell, then it could "produce oil at will."[14] Some oil companies, like Standard Oil of California, turned toward developing residential markets for natural gas to get rid of their oil well gases, but Shell was determined that petrochemicals would be the largest sink for both the oil well and refinery waste gases.

As part of its push to make chemicals from petroleum, Shell wanted to build an ammonia plant as well as a petrochemical research facility. Royal Dutch/Shell was a globally dispersed company. The problem was that its main research hub in Amsterdam lacked access to oil well and refinery waste gases, while key production sites like Romania lacked access to the agricultural markets the company needed. But Shell's rapidly growing California operations had both of these. Not only would the company have access to an abundance of waste gases, it might also gain access to California's agrochemical markets. In early 1928, the Shell Union Oil Company of California, a subsidiary of the Royal Dutch/Shell Group, floated $50 million in bonds to help finance the development of a chemical and petrochemical research subsidiary and the construction of the world's first ammonia plant using natural gas for its hydrogen feedstock.[15] In June of that same year, Royal Dutch/Shell and the Shell Union Oil Company of California formed the Shell Development Company, a subsidiary tasked with R&D of petroleum-based chemicals.[16] By early 1929, Shell had broken ground at two California locations: an industrial research lab in Emeryville on the sunny side of San Francisco Bay and an ammonia plant on 640 acres of estuary shoreline near Pittsburg.[17] In February 1929, Royal Dutch/Shell and the Shell Union Oil Company formed the Shell Chemical Company to produce ammonium sulfate fertilizer for the California market.[18]

The previous year Royal Dutch/Shell had begun construction of a pilot nitrogen fixation plant at its Amsterdam site to use for R&D into the design of the California plant.[19] But Shell was still in need of a method of making ammonia. The German chemical consortium I. G. Farben held the patent on the Haber-Bosch route to fixed nitrogen, and Shell believed that I. G. Farben would never consider licensing the process in Europe. Instead, Shell turned to a German mining group that had funded the development of a novel lower-pressure process of ammonia synthesis in the mid-1920s, known as the Mont-Cenis process.[20] The Mont-Cenis process was one of many nitrogen fixation processes—Casale, Fauser, Nitrogen Engineering, Claude—developed in the interwar period that grew out of the Haber-Bosch method.[21] Despite similar chemistry, each of them modified the original design just enough to not run afoul of I.G. Farben's patents.

In September 1928 Royal Dutch/Shell was granted worldwide rights to the Mont-Cenis process.[22] Shell's chemical engineers, known as technologists, set immediately to work ironing out the industrial kinks that accompanied the license and remedying issues associated with poisoned catalysts, insufficient compressors, and defective heat exchangers. In fact, Shell's technologists improved and modified the process so much from the original patent that they were able to patent many new inventions and break from the Mont-Cenis group in 1934.[23]

With the problem of its nitrogen fixation reaction solved, Royal/ Dutch Shell proceeded with the design and construction of the California plant. Shell assembled parts for two ammonia plants at its Amsterdam research site, which were then shipped to California for assembly. But Shell still had to devise a way to extract hydrogen from the methane pouring from California's oil wells before it could start fixing atmospheric nitrogen.[24] Kessler had considered using steam to reform natural gas in order to produce hydrogen and carbon dioxide. This was the method that Bosch originally proposed and studied in the early 1910s.[25] (The first ammonia plant to use steam reforming was built in California in 1939 by the Hercules Powder Company.) But as this process had never been applied on an industrial scale, he considered it too expensive an investment at the time.[26] Instead, the plant design, an amalgam of US and European chemical technology, proceeded with a hydrogen stream derived from the direct cracking of natural gas.[27]

The thermal decomposition of natural gas at extreme temperatures disintegrates methane into hydrogen and carbon black.[28] But at these extreme temperatures, hydrogen yields are low and are thus economically inefficient. By decreasing the intensity of decomposition, however, Shell's technologists were able to substantially increase hydrogen yield. Unfortunately, this also resulted in increased impurities in the hydrogen stream.[29] Shell's technologists then turned to what was to become one of their early industrial petrochemical advantages, the efficient purification and separation of mixed gases. In conjunction with the Southern California Gas Company of Los Angeles, Shell's technologists developed a commercial scale system of high-temperature reforming units that relied on purification and separation of mixed yields to economically produce the necessary hydrogen stream for the world's first natural gas–based ammonia plant.

In April 1931, the reforming units were installed at Shell Point in Pittsburg, California, and on July 20 of that same year, the first ammonia dribbled from the plant though a pipeline that "had been optimistically marked with a dollar sign."[30] However, in the interim between Shell's initial decision to enter the ammonia sulfate fertilizer market in 1927 and its construction and operation of the Shell Point plant in 1931, the world economy crashed, and with it the price of fertilizer. In 1927 ammonium sulfate was selling for $40–46 a ton. By 1931 the price had dropped as low as $16.50 per ton.[31] The world's descent into economic depression left Shell without profitable outlets for its ammonia, and most of the ten thousand tons of ammonia it produced in the first year was sold directly to the chemical industry, where it was converted to nitric acid and used to manufacture explosives.[32]

While Kessler and other senior management in California were convinced that chemicals derived from extraction and refinery gases would eventually be very profitable and thus would justify a loss for a period of time, others were not so sure. The need to economize inspired Shell's technologists to assess and develop the potential for profit in other wastes like sulfuric acid, which was being thrown away by the ton on a daily basis and yet was also one of the fertilizer plant's main operating costs.[33] Indeed, it was the high cost of sulfuric acid, freight charges, and seasonal demand that prompted Shell's technologists in the closing months of 1931 to first seriously consider the use of anhydrous ammonia (pure NH_3) as fertilizer. Because ammonia would be much cheaper to produce per unit of fixed nitrogen and cheaper to ship and eventually store, and because so much of California agriculture was irrigated, Shell's technologists hypothesized they could simply add anhydrous or aqua ammonia directly to irrigation water instead of first converting it to ammonium sulfate.[34]

Before venturing down this road, however, Ludwig Rosenstein, the chief chemist at Shell Development, approached his friend Dennis Hoagland at the University of California, Davis, to ask whether the application of anhydrous ammonia to irrigation water was even possible.[35] Hoagland's reply was optimistic, and he advised Rosenstein to contact Dean Waynick and Floyd Leavitt at the Association Laboratory in Southern California to undertake the necessary experimental work. The selection of Waynick's lab was important because he had previously worked with the Prizer brothers, who had patented the idea of fertilization via irrigation water.[36] In 1928, John and Eugene Prizer, concerned with the availability and cost of labor on large citrus groves, had built an applicator that would dissolve soluble fertilizers into irrigation water, thus doing away with the labor needed to fertilize by hand or spreader. In early 1932, the Shell Development Company secured the full rights to the patent with the help of the Association Laboratory. Waynick and Leavitt immediately commenced their experimental work.

A year and a half later, after preliminary lab experiments showed no lasting deleterious effects of anhydrous ammonia on soils, and after Shell engineers had worked out an effective metering device, they conducted the first experimental field applications in several orange groves near their Alhambra lab.[37] These experiments and subsequent analyses showed that if accurate and precise irrigation practices and ammonia flow rates were maintained, ammonia could be distributed evenly along furrows. In 1934, buoyed by these and other experimental field results, Shell patented the process and moved toward commercialization.[38]

That same year, Shell appointed the Greening-Smith Company of Norwalk as the first commercial distributor of anhydrous ammonia for Central and Southern California. This decision was critical because the Greening-Smith Company was both a large owner of citrus groves and at the same time engaged in the sale of fertilizer to other growers.[39] The appointment of the Greening-Smith Company as distributor brought, along with its transportation and storage infrastructure, an aggressive sales company with vast knowledge of Southern California growers and fertilizer sales. In 1935, Shell appointed the James Mill Orchards Company of Hamilton City as its Northern California distributor.[40]

The Greening-Smith company began commercial "nitrogation"— Shell's trademarked term for the process of introducing anhydrous ammonia into irrigation water—in the fall of 1934.[41] However, even with the established sales networks of the Greening-Smith Company, the growth of nitrogation in Depression era California was slower than Shell would have liked.[42] One of the biggest initial unknowns was how much ammonia to use and at what concentrations for different crops. For Shell, the commercialization of nitrogation was both a profit-making venture and a way to conduct the series of large-scale field experiments needed to refine the technique and begin to develop dosage recommendations.[43] By 1936, Shell technologists had demonstrated nitrogation's efficacy on over twenty crops across California, and by 1937, 16 percent of the ammonia that Shell produced was introduced into irrigation water, with the majority of this used by Southern California citrus growers.[44] Shell's salesmen faced opposition from some growers across the state who believed anhydrous ammonia was a poor fertilizer. However, with the help of UC, the University of Arizona, and state extension scientists, demand for the product kept growing.[45]

As the growing season wound down in late 1939, Shell's board and its senior scientists decided that if they wanted to expand the market for anhydrous ammonia, they needed to figure out how to apply it to soils that were not irrigated, or when irrigation and fertilization timing or methods were mismatched.[46] After all, while California had almost five million irrigated acres, the rest of the country did not have equally large irrigated acreage. Earlier that year Leavitt, now a senior agricultural technologist for Shell Chemical, had conceived of injecting anhydrous ammonia directly into the soil after watching a telephone company lay cable underground in a new housing development outside Sacramento. What Leavitt observed was essentially an oversized subsoiler with a tube down the back attached to a trailing spool of cable that unwound as the machine moved forward, thus laying the cable at depth. In place of the trailing spool of cable, however, Leavitt envisioned an ammonia tank, and in place of the large subsoiler shank he pictured multiple cultivator shanks that released ammonia from their tips deep within the soil.

Shell technologists put Leavitt's vision into action in the beginning of 1940. In a Santa Paula blacksmith's shop, Shell technologists forged the first injection shank by modifying a ⅝-inch John Deere spear point shank blade.[47] They then outfitted an off-the-shelf Killifer cultivator with their new injection shanks and one of their ammonia meters and started field testing their new method of ammonia application across the Oxnard plain. Leavitt's vision had come true. Instead of laying phone cables, these new injection shanks were capable of laying cables of ammonia gas in the subsoil. Further experimental work showed that the distribution of ammonia could be manipulated through depth, flow rate, and spacing for maximum nitrogen stimulation.[48]

Limited commercial applications began in the spring of 1942 across a wide variety of California crops and soils.[49] Later that year, Leavitt and others began a larger set of field and lab experiments to study the effects of anhydrous ammonia on the chemistry of various soils. In May of that year, the US War Production Board suspended agricultural sales and began diverting Shell's ammonia into explosive manufacture.[50] On January 1, 1943, the sales ban was lifted, and full-scale commercial field applications got underway across California. By 1945, with the development of Shell's injection applicator, the method was on its way to being fully commercialized.[51] Shell had spread its technique to Washington state's apple orchards and to the citrus groves of southern Arizona.[52] By the late 1940s, in collaboration with the USDA, the Tennessee Valley Authority, and scientists at the University of Mississippi Experiment Station, Shell had spread the method east of the Rockies.[53]

INTO THE SUBSOIL

In the spring of 1940, Walter Carter, lead scientist at the University of Hawaii's Pineapple Research Institute, conducted a series of soil fumigation experiments with a recently acquired batch of petrochemical waste. The Pineapple Research Institute was affiliated with University of Hawaii's agricultural extension, and Carter's work was sponsored by the three main Hawaiian Pineapple companies: the Maui Pineapple Company, Dole, and Del Monte. In these chemical trials, Carter was trying to solve a problem common to all three major companies: dramatic declines in yields as continuous cropping led to accumulation of deleterious organisms in the soil. Soil pests had become so problematic that some even predicted the end of the Hawaiian pineapple industry.[54] It was well known to Carter and others that pineapples planted in virgin soil did not have the same pest issues as those on older plantations. "Nematodes are least damaging in virgin soil" Carter once said.[55] Thus, in the mid-1930s Carter initiated a research agenda to see if he could "do the impossible" and "restore [the] virginity" of the soil.[56]

In 1936, he tried ammonium thiocyanate as a soil fumigant, along with a suite of other common pre–World War II economic poisons such as sodium cyanide, sodium cyanamide, formaldehyde, paradichlorobenzene, and carbon disulfide. However, he found that these economic poisons either caused severe growth problems or were not effective against soil-dwelling organisms. He then tried chloropicrin, the World War I chemical weapon cum pesticide, and was impressed by the initial results. However, while chloropicrin showed promise, Carter worried that it was much too expensive for use in commercial control, that it presented practical difficulties in handling and application, and that it might have deleterious impacts on long-term pineapple growth.[57]

Carter continued his studies over the next few years, eager to pursue any promising lead and writing numerous companies asking for samples of their toxic chemicals in the hopes that one of them would work. Indeed, his requests were met by "bottles, drums, cans, and steel cylinders" that spilled in from across the United States from "synthetic rubber, petroleum, coal tar, and gasoline" companies.[58] Carter and his assistants systematically tested each new chemical on infested pineapple fields near Wahiawa, in the fertile highland valley of Oahu, but none of them showed any promise.

Then, in late 1939, Carter received a shipment of fifty-five-gallon drums filled to the brim with synthetic organic chemicals from Shell Oil's Emeryville-based petrochemical R&D subsidiary. These chemicals—allyl alcohol, allyl chloride, methallyl alcohol, methallyl chloride, and a mixture of 1,3-dichlororopropene and 1,2-dichloropropane (DD)—were the waste products of Shell's groundbreaking industrial synthesis of glycerol from propylene and consisted mostly of novel compounds, particularly the chlorinated ones.[59] Propylene and gases like ethylene and the butylenes make up a significant proportion of the by-product gases that occur during the cracking of crude oil.[60] They are also present in the wet gases that are released from oil wells during extraction. These compounds—known as *olefins*—are highly reactive and can be turned into an endless variety of products and still serve as one of the main feedstocks of the petrochemical industry. During the 1930s, Shell scientists developed techniques to add halogens like chlorine and bromine to these unsaturated olefins while retaining their unsaturated nature, a process that came to be known as *high temperature substitution*.[61] But with Shell's cutting-edge chemical synthesis also came state of the art toxic waste.

Promising preliminary tests with Shell's wastes in late 1939 demanded further trials, especially with the DD mixture. Carter initially tested DD on a pineapple field heavily infested with destructive nematodes. He and his assistants punched holes in the soil every fifteen inches and poured in the dark, pernicious liquid, covered the holes, and allowed the chemicals to do their work. The effects were dramatic. "[DD] spread through the soil like a lump of sugar. Fumes shot out in a circle, killing every worm they reached."[62] It was almost as if the chemicals actively sought out the microscopic worms. Encouraged by these results, Carter and his associates spread out across the Hawaiian Islands throughout the early months of 1941, hand injecting DD in 840 plots in every major pineapple-growing region. These experimental fields were then replanted with pineapple.

In the closing days of 1941, Carter walked among some of the experimental plots near Wahiawa. As he did, he noticed that the pineapples in the DD test plots had grown significantly. A few months later he concluded that the pineapple plants in the DD plots were behaving as if there were no nematodes in the soil at all. By harvest time, the evidence of DD's subterranean killing power was unmistakable. The plants on untreated plots were stunted and diseased, while the "treated plots were covered with healthy plants of towering broad, live-green leaves from the center of which grew giant-sized, golden yellow pineapples."[63] These infested soils, from which pineapple companies had previously harvested fifteen tons of fruit per acre, now yielded an average of forty tons. DD had allowed Carter to do the impossible and restore the virginity of the soil, temporarily cleansing it of nematodes and other destructive soil-dwelling organisms.

DD had the potential to reshape world agriculture. Not only it was incredibly effective; as a waste product of the synthesis of glycerol from propylene, it had the potential to be commercially affordable.[64] Carter went public with his discovery in the April 1943 edition of *Science Magazine*. Although his results were preliminary, he felt it was necessary to communicate their revolutionary nature. DD, Carter wrote, "has such great potential usefulness for other more rapidly maturing crops in a great many agricultural areas, it seems advisable to present the preliminary results at this time so that these potentialities can be fully explored."[65] With the ability to chemically disinfect the soil, growers all over the world could expect bigger and better crops in areas where continuous cropping caused the proliferation of damaging soil organisms.[66]

Before Carter's publication in *Science*, however, Shell's technologists, USDA scientists, the US War Production Board, and UC Agricultural Experiment Station scientists had been informed of its success and were actively exploring its utility in California.[67] By the 1940s, more than 60 percent of California's arable farmland was heavily infested with destructive organisms, including key areas like the central coast and Central Valley.[68] At that time, California's pesticide industry was the most sophisticated in the world, and soil fumigants had been experimented with extensively in California, yet a commercial solution to subsoil control still remained elusive.[69] But not for long.

Shell and UC Davis scientists hand injected DD into a Central Valley bean field in the spring of 1943.[70] These preliminary trials in the heavily infested sandy soils of Merced County proved successful beyond anyone's expectations. In the treated plots, beans and tomatoes grew like there were no destructive organisms in the soil at all (see figure 24). In the fall of 1943 Shell scientists partnered with UC Davis and the scientist Henry Lange Jr. to undertake full-scale field tests.[71] Lange played a critical role in DD's commercialization. He not only coordinated lab experiments at UC Davis; he oversaw field experiments and found growers who would allow Shell to inject their fields with an experimental poison as well as linking large commercial growers, like the Speckles Sugar Company, directly to scientists and salesmen at Shell. The tests that Lange oversaw were different than Carter's in one important way. Since Shell had been in the process of developing equipment for the injection of anhydrous ammonia into the subsoil, the company was able to quickly convert its equipment for use with DD, immediately mechanizing the process.[72]

Supplied with chemicals directly from Shell, Lange continued laboratory experiments with DD over the first half of 1944. Throughout the late summer and early fall, he and Walter Balch, the Shell technologist leading the commercialization of DD, traversed the Salinas Valley and

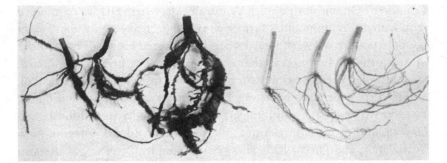

FIGURE 24. Bean roots showing effects of nematodes in soil (left) versus soil fumigation with DD mixture (right). Courtesy of the University of California, Davis, Special Collections.

injected DD into as many "sick" fields as possible, using growers' desperation for profitable healing as a way to turn semicommercial applications into the field experiments needed to fully commercialize the poison. As fall turned to winter, the rapidly maturing crops replanted after these semicommercial soil disinfection experiments showed immediately identifiable results. On December 10, 1944, using a modified Shell experimental cultivator attached to a small John Deere tractor modified to carry tanks of DD as well as anhydrous ammonia, Lange and Balch applied DD in simultaneous combination with anhydrous ammonia into the subsoil of a heavily infested Salinas Valley lettuce field. On that field, in the late autumn of 1944, Shell's transmuted waste products quietly met for the first time.[73]

Early the next year, Lange and Balch ran the experiments again on a larger scale, selecting fields so sick that commercial production was no longer possible. One such experiment took place on June 4, 1945, when they injected fertilizer and fumigant in continuous streams into the subsoil of a Salinas Valley farm. Ten days later, on June 14, lettuce was planted. When yields were checked the following September, the fields treated with DD and anhydrous ammonia yielded eight times more trimmed lettuce than control fields. The yields were not just back to normal; *they were better than they had ever been*. Later that year, Lange and Balch conducted more commercial field trials in the Sacramento Valley, this time hoping to determine dosages, to test efficacy, and to study the synergistic effects of ammonia and DD.[74]

In the fall of 1945, two private companies began commercial application of DD in Los Angeles, Ventura, Monterey, Merced, and Sacramento

Counties.[75] On one of those sick Ventura fields, where DD was combined with anhydrous ammonia, a farmer who had been averaging about eight hundred pounds of sweet potatoes per acre boosted his yields by an order of magnitude.[76] In 1945, at the request of the War Production Board, Shell installed specialized units for the production of DD, allyl alcohol, and allyl chloride at its Houston, Texas, refinery complex.[77] During the 1946 growing season, soil fumigation spread rapidly in California and Hawaii, and growers in Georgia, Florida, Texas, Idaho, Oregon, New York, Utah, and Puerto Rico also began using it. Commercial use also spread internationally to parts of Southern Africa and New Zealand.[78] By 1947, the poison had spread to most of the southern United States, where millions of acres of sick land were in desperate need of Shell's chemical healing. Shell and the US government also spread it to allied Europe, where its use led to a 75 percent increase in potato yields per acre.[79] For the 1948 growing season, many southern farmers who had applied DD prior to planting heavily infested tobacco fields saw yields that were better than if the tobacco had been planted in virgin soil.[80]

The active ingredient in DD is now sold under multiple brands and remains one of the most consumed economic poisons in the United States. It is used to ensure the "clean fields" needed for the industrial production of many of our most important commercial crops.[81] Without it and the other toxic gases used to temporarily rid the soil of destructive organisms, the continuous production of a single crop without rotation would not be possible. These petroleum-based soil fumigants not only transformed the practice of crop rotation and how industrial agriculture came to be organized; they also marked the ascendency of petroleum-based chemicals in the chemicalization of agriculture and opened up the subsoil as a sink for petroleum wastes.

MONOCULTURES OF TIME

In late 1945, spurred on by the outstanding success and rapid adoption of anhydrous ammonia and DD across the West, Shell broke ground on an agricultural experiment station in the heart of California's Central Valley.[82] Spread across 142 acres of prime farmland just outside Modesto, Shell established its private experimental farm to extend the use of petrochemicals in agriculture. Its goal was to use the experimental farm and its laboratories as a scientific proving ground for potential economic poisons overflowing in abundance from Shell's cutting-edge petrochemical R&D facility eighty miles to the west.[83] DD, by opening up the subsoil to economic poisons, created entirely new agricultural markets for toxic chemicals.[84] Shell and other petrochemical companies believed that this was just the beginning, and they were certain that the material basis of these new poisons would be oil well and petroleum refinery by-products, or what they called "one of the largest sources of raw material" for the development of poisonous gases, sprays, and dusts.[85]

After 1945, chemical pest control entered a new and expanded phase, one in which synthetic organic chemicals replaced older poisons like sodium cyanide, lead arsenate, and white oil. Some of these were more effective and cheaper than those in the past, at least for a while. Others, particularly herbicides, displaced the labor needed to weed fields and sped up the mechanization of agriculture. But it was soil fumigants and underground chemical warfare that revolutionized agriculture by giving growers the ability to produce not only monocultures of space but also monocultures of time.

Imagine an industrial agricultural production system in which soil fumigants were never discovered. How would replant disease have been dealt with? It is impossible to know what would have happened, but we can still venture a few guesses, as there really were only two possible answers at the time.[86] The first is that crop scientists could have developed plant varieties resistant to the populations of soil organisms built up by growing the same thing in the same soil over and over. While the development of disease-resistant crops may have resulted in a system that looks similar to the one we have now, with geographic and infrastructural crop specialization, it would not have resulted in the collateral damage that comes from soil fumigation, particularly the impacts on worker and environmental health.[87]

The second possibility is that crop rotation schemes could have been developed to minimize the impacts and likelihood of iatrogenic soil diseases.[88] Prior to the development of soil fumigants, some soil scientists had already begun working on rotational schemes that dealt with issues of replant disease. The development of a system of widespread and intensive crop rotation would have resulted in an agricultural system radically different from today's. For example, regions that now specialize in strawberry, potato, tobacco, cotton, and tree fruit would have to produce other crops as well. This would mean that the physical and economic infrastructures developed in these places would also have had to be more flexible. While there would likely still be monocultures of space each year, the diversity of crops over time would have changed.

I bring up these counterfactuals not to long for a future that never happened or to pine for science that was never done (although I do), but instead to emphasize how critical soil fumigants became to both agriculture and the petrochemical industry after World War II. Soil fumigants not only penetrated the subsoil and created entirely new markets for the chemical industry; they also radically recast the organizational possibilities of agriculture and allowed growers to achieve the monocultures of time necessary to make today's agriculture possible.

Conclusion

It is unscientific to devote ourselves merely to securing and testing spray mixtures, however necessary these may be for immediate results.

—J. B. Smith, "Cultivation and Susceptibility to Insect Attack," 1908

I began this project as a way to better understand the history of chemical-intensive agriculture. I did not expect to focus so much on California in a book that was supposed to be about American agriculture, but since California's input-intensive growers developed commercial crop protection before farmers in other states, its agricultural and chemical industries pioneered the models of toxicity-based repair that became integral to all of US agriculture after World War II. As the historian Edward Melillo has suggested about alfalfa, commercial pest control should be considered one of the "eastward moving [agroindustiral] trends that began on the North America's Pacific coast."[1] Yet while California and Pacific slope growers may have led the way, they were certainly not alone. By the end of World War II economic poisons had become integral to the industrial production of hundreds of crops across the United States.

I also did not set out to focus so much on the role of industrial waste in the chemicalization of American agriculture. While I was familiar with the role of industrial waste in the history of the chemical industry, I did not know the extent of the role that it played as the raw material for so many pre-1945 economic poisons. As agriculture industrialized, growers needed cheap and effective poisons to repair the fragile ecosystems they created, and industrial waste was a key source of that cheap toxicity. But as growers transformed their farms into the types of ecosystems that required toxic chemicals to remain productive, they also turned them into the types of ecosystems that some firms could use to bury their toxic waste. But that waste never disappeared, and its proliferation has had profound effects on the structures of agriculture and the development of the chemical industry. "Our industrial waste tinkers with the chemistry of our bodies and the chemistry of our climate," writes the interdisciplinary scholar Rebecca Altman.[2] Indeed, it has even remade who we are and how we relate to the world.

There are a few things that I will take away from being immersed for so long in the pre-1945 history of American agriculture. The first has to do with expanding the functions that agriculture plays in industrial society. What I mean by this is that in addition to agriculture as a source of food, fiber, and the properties of rural life, in the late nineteenth and early twentieth centuries, growers, scientists, and government officials transformed agriculture into a sink for some of society's most toxic industrial wastes. While agriculture was certainly not the only place that society tried to bury its waste during this period, it was one of the few places where the toxicity of the waste gave it a potential value.

One of the major issues of writing a book like this, and a major historiographical concern about the whiggish history of science and technology in general, is that scholarship tends be about the successes and not the countless failures that informed those successes. As you have read, I succumbed to this predicament as I wrote mostly about the industrial wastes that became important economic poisons and the conditions that made that possible. With the exception of a few examples, I did not write about the endless stream of industrial wastes that were thrown at agriculture in the hopes that something would stick. I also did not write much about the critically important nonactive ingredients of the pesticide mixtures, many of which also came from industrial waste. After all, a rapidly industrializing agriculture gave producers of industrial waste not just a potential place to bury it but also a way to profit from the act of burial.

That is why I still prefer the term *economic poison* over the term *pesticide*, because it speaks to the relational and historical aspects of these chemicals. The term embodies the material and societal transformations that turned a specific waste into a by-product that was used to poison crops. It also captures the fact that what makes a poison economic is not just its efficacy. For example, while calcium arsenate and DDT could still be considered pesticides, agricultural and societal changes mean that they are no longer economic poisons. The industrial poisons that became economic not only had to have the right kind of toxicity, they also had to have a broader set of characteristics that made them useful in agriculture. In the late nineteenth and early twentieth centuries, industrial wastes often fit these criteria and thus were an important source of the raw materials that agricultural chemists, economic entomologists, and growers across the United States used to poison agriculture. Not all pesticides came from industrial waste, yet industrial waste was fundamental to the making of American agriculture.

My second takeaway is that the development of chemical-intensive agriculture was not inevitable. If we examine the early history of commercial pesticide use, it is readily apparent that the development of toxicity-based repair was not about producing sufficient food. Chemical control first developed around industrial crops like oranges, apples, and cotton, none of which were necessary to feed the nation. Furthermore, the development of a science of chemical control did not protect American farmers from the destitution caused by producing too much. Instead, chemical control protected a particular logic of agriculture, as it still does today, one in which productivity and cheap food are the ultimate goals and an imagined future of scarcity is used to justify practices that continue to pollute the world, harm workers, and drive overproduction.[3] What I mean by this is that the proponents of chemical control often turned to a future of more people and less food to justify the use of toxic chemicals in agriculture. This appeal to future scarcity not only belied the curse of abundance that afflicted so many US farmers, it ultimately served to justify what the historian Siegfried Gideon called the "idolatry of production" and the necessity and collateral damage of the accompanying chemical war.[4] Don't get me wrong; feeding people will always be a challenge. But those who continue to go hungry, especially in countries like the United States, do so not because there is not enough food to eat; they do so because they are poor.

I am hopeful that once we take the history of agricultural abundance seriously, a shift away from a future of imagined scarcity is possible. Rachel Carson once wrote that any sort of "control must be geared to realities, not to mythical situations," and I think that is still the issue today.[5] Since the very beginning of industrial pest control we have geared our policies to the mythical situations that our fears so readily accept, like the idea that we are running out of food or that insects are intent on attacking us. But if we see the history of US agriculture as one of abundance and the constant struggle to develop new ways to dissipate that abundance, then we can also read the history of pesticides as not a way to protect crops from insect attack but instead as a way for farmers to try to outrun the pressure to produce ever cheaper food as their neighbors do the same.

Embracing a history of abundance would also mean that justifications for an endless chemical war would lose their purchase. Then perhaps, as Robert Mullen posited in 1933, it would be okay for insects to eat or blemish some of the nation's crops without our declaring war on them.[6] Maybe then we could rethink the notions of harm and intent that are embedded in our discourse about pests and pesticides. Of course, that would mean remaking much of the nation's agriculture and the infrastructures that support it. Nevertheless, a reality of too much food still means that it is possible.[7] As the agricultural historian Deborah Fitzgerald has said, "It might behoove us to think of agricultural transformation as a set of possibilities, rather than inevitabilities, for change."[8]

My last major takeaway is that the infrastructures of chemical pest control had already solidified prior to the end of World War II. Pesticide use spread rapidly to most crops in the years after 1945; however, the post–World War II history of pesticides is one of substitution, wherein one pesticide replaces another after a cheaper alternative is found, the pesticide no longer works, or it is deemed too toxic for humans or the environment. In the early twentieth century toxicity-based repair became the lynchpin that held the assemblage together. It did not matter what chemical that toxicity came from; what mattered was that it was always there.

I have to admit that this conclusion makes me less hopeful, because it means that the agricultural assemblage appears locked into a logic of toxicity-based repair that is resulting in industrial agroecosystems growing more precarious at a time when we need ones with larger margins of error. In *Silent Spring*, Rachel Carson invoked Robert Frost's image of two roads diverging in the woods to call for a new approach to pest control.[9] One of these roads was wide and deceptively easy, while the other was narrow and filled with obstacles. What worries me is that we have taken that easy road and really never looked back. I am afraid that we have gotten farther and farther away from the possibility of an agricultural system not built on the assumption of widespread chemical control. That chemical control came to dominate agriculture's approach to dealing with insects and pathogens was not inevitable, yet I worry that it is now because we have bred it into agriculture, which in turn has made us scientifically and imaginatively ignorant of other possible futures. Some of those futures may entail the use of toxic chemicals in agriculture, but that decision should not be foreclosed, as it is now.

One thing that helps me to remain open to the possibility of a different future is that the type of agricultural assemblage that we have now resulted from a series of choices that powerful people made, and thus it can be remade again with a collection of new decisions. But it also means that any agricultural transformation to deal with a future of increased environmental and economic change must occur in many other realms than the farm itself. It must include changes to everything from the public university system to the laws that weigh workers' lives against food prices. It must also include the radical idea that maybe the market is not the ultimate decider of what is good for America's farmers and farmworkers. American agriculture has always relied on massive government subsidies to function. Whether seed collection, dams and irrigation canals, publicly funded science, rural electrification, lax immigration and occupational health laws, marketing campaigns, food assistance programs, inadequate chemical regulation, or direct subsidies, the US government has always had its hand in agriculture, and it will do so in the future. What matters then is who guides that hand.

Change must come from the top, and it must be so systemic that it begins to reform the entire assemblage. I spent many of my formative years working in the agricultural space at the Center for Sustainable Food Systems at University of California, Santa Cruz, where I helped researchers design alternatives to chemical-intensive agriculture. I still remember coming to terms with the fact that creating an alternative to the dominant food system was just that, an alternative, when what was needed was systemic change. I remember realizing that voting with our forks would not bring about the reform that is needed to face a future of climatic, environmental, and iatrogenic change. Changing what we buy will not give agricultural workers a living wage and the protection from toxic chemicals that they deserve, nor will it stop farmers from living under a mountain of debt or decrease the number of farmer suicides each year. "To alter these logics," writes the geographer Julie Guthman, "takes political will, not will power."[10] The road not taken will be hard and filled with obstacles.

Notes

PREFACE

1. R. Carson, *Silent Spring* (1962; repr. New York: Mariner Books, 2002), 8.

2. L. Lear, "Rachel Carson's Silent Spring." *Environmental History Review* 17, no. 2 (1993): 23–48; and E. Griswold, "How 'Silent Spring' Ignited the Environmental Movement," *New York Times*, September 21, 2012.

3. F. R. Davis, *Banned: A History of Pesticides and the Science of Toxicology* (New Haven, CT: Yale University Press, 2014).

4. J. Beard, "DDT and Human Health," *Science of the Total Environment* 355 (2006): 78–89; R. Altman, "On What We Bury," *Interdisciplinary Studies in Literature and the Environment* 21, no. 1 (2014): 85–95; and S. A. Mackintosh et al., "Newly Identified DDT-Related Compounds Accumulating in Southern California Bottlenose Dolphins," *Environmental Science and Technology* 50, no. 22 (2016): 12129–37.

5. H. G. Lawson, "Death in the Fields: Phosphate Pesticides Suspected in Poisoning of Some Farmhands." *Wall Street Journal*, July 16, 1971; and R. Carson, "Women's National Press Club Speech," in *Lost Woods: The Discovered Writing of Rachel Carson*, ed. L. Lear (1962; repr. Boston: Beacon Press, 2002); and Davis, *Banned*, 2014.

6. J. Guthman, *Agrarian Dreams: The Paradox of Organic Farming in California* (Berkeley: University of California Press, 2004); and J. Guthman, *Weighing In: Obesity, Food Justice, and the Limits of Capitalism* (Berkeley: University of California Press, 2011).

7. C. Gundersen, B. Kreider, and J. Pepper, "The Economics of Food Insecurity in the United States," *Applied Economic Perspectives and Policy* 33, no. 3

(2011): 281–303; and L. A. Minkoff-Zern, "Hunger Amidst Plenty: Farmworker Food Insecurity and Coping Strategies in California," *Local Environments* 19, no. 2 (2014): 204–19.

8. W. W. Cochrane, "Farm Technology, Foreign Surplus Disposal and Domestic Supply Control," *Journal of Farm Economics* 41, no. 5 (1959): 885–89; J. H. Perkins, "Insects, Food, and Hunger: The Paradox of Plenty for Us Entomology, 1920–1970," *Environmental History Review* 7, no. 1 (1983): 71–96; J. Poppenndick, *Breadlines Knee-Deep in Wheat: Food Assistance in the Great Depression* (Berkeley: University of California Press, 2014); and K. Gee, "America's Dairy Farmers Dump 43 Million Gallons of Excess Milk," *Wall Street Journal*, October 13, 2016.

9. National Research Council, "Report of the Committee on Persistent Pesticides, Division of Biology and Agriculture, National Research Council to U. S. Department of Agriculture" (Washington, DC: National Academy of Sciences, 1969); T. D. Eichers, R. Jenkins, and A. Fox, "DDT Used in Farm Production" (Washington, DC: USDA Economic Research Service , 1971); and D. Pementel, C. Kirby, and A Shroff, "The Relationship between 'Cosmetic Standards' for Foods and Pesticide Use," in *The Pesticide Question: Environment, Economics, and Ethics*, ed. D. Pimentel and H. Lehman (New York: Chapman and Hall, 1993), 85–105.

10. H. A. Wallace, "Extension Service Review—May" (Washington, DC: USDA, 1933).

11. A. Kallet and F. J. Schlink. *100,000,000 Guinea Pigs: Dangers in Everyday Foods, Drugs, and Cosmetics* (New York: Vanguard Press, 1933); and J. Whorton, *Before Silent Spring: Pesticides and Public Health in Pre-DDT America* (Princeton, NJ: Princeton University Press, 1974).

12. G. J. Glacken, "Reflections on the Man-Nature Theme as a Subject for Study," in *Future Environments of North America*, ed. F. F. Darling and J. P. Milton (Garden City, NY: Natural History Press, 1966), 355–71; R. Williams, *Key Words: A Vocabulary of Culture and Society*, 2nd ed. (Oxford: Oxford University Press, 1983); and C. Merchant, *The Death of Nature: Women, Ecology, and the Scientific Revolution* (New York: HarperCollins, 1990).

13. Carson, *Silent Spring*, 2002, 297.

14. Carson, *Silent Spring*, 2002, 188.

INTRODUCTION

1. J. B. Smith, "Cultivation and Susceptibility to Insect Attack," *Journal of Economic Entomology* 1, no. 1 (1908): 15.

2. D. Goodman, B. Sorj, and J. Wilkinson, *From Farming to Biotechnology: A Theory of Agro-Industrial Development* (Oxford: Basil Blackwell, 1987).

3. S. A. Mann, *Agrarian Capitalism in Theory and Practice* (Chapel Hill: University of North Carolina Press, 1990); and G. Henderson, *California and the Fictions of Capital* (Oxford: Oxford University Press, 1999).

4. J. Tarr, "From City to Farm: Urban Wastes and the American Farmer," *Agricultural History* 49, no. 4 (1975): 598–612; R. Wines, *Fertilizer in America: From Waste Recycling to Resource Exploitation* (Philadelphia: Temple University

Press, 1985); J. von Driel, "Ashes to Ashes: The Stewardship of Waste and Oeco-
nomic Cycles of Agricultural and Industrial Improvement, 1750–1800," *History and Technology* 30, no. 3 (2014): 177–206; and S. Barles, "History of
Waste Management and the Social and Cultural Representations of Waste," in
The Basic Environmental History, ed. M. Agnoletti and S. Serneri (New York:
Springer, 2014), 199–226.

5. L. F. Haber, *The Chemical Industry during the Nineteenth Century: A
Study of the Economic Aspect of Applied Chemistry in Europe and North
America* (Oxford: Oxford University Press, 1958); D. Landes, *The Unbound
Prometheus: Technological Change and Industrial Development in Western
Europe from 1750 to the Present* (New York: Cambridge University Press,
1969); K. Warren, *Chemical Foundations: The Alkali Industry in Britain to
1926* (Oxford: Clarendon Press, 1980); and R. U. Ayres, "Industrial Metabo-
lism," in *Technology and Environment*, ed. J. H. Ausubel and H. E. Sladovich
(Washington, DC: National Academy Press, 1989), 23–49.

6. Now the Science History Institute.

7. D. Thomas, S. Fowler, and V. Johnson, *The Silence of the Archive* (London: Facet Publishing, 2017).

8. For example, G. P. Gray, "The Consumption and Cost of Economic Poisons in California in 1916," *Industrial & Engineering Chemistry* 10, no. 4
(1918): 301–2.

9. E. R. De Ong, *Chemistry and Uses of Insecticides* (New York: Reinhold,
1948).

10. "Increasing Use Calcium Arsenate," *Wall Street Journal*, January 28, 1924.

11. For recent reviews of the waste literature, see T. Cooper, "Recycling
Modernity: Waste and Environmental History," *History Compass* 8, no. 9
(2010): 1114–25; N. Gregson and M. Crang, "Materiality and Waste: Inorganic Vitality in a Networked World," *Environment and Planning A* 42, no. 5
(2010): 1026–32; S. A. Moore, "Garbage Matters: Concepts in New Geographies of Waste," *Progress in Human Geography* 36, no. 6 (2012): 780–99; and
J. Reno, "Waste and Waste Management," *Annual Review of Anthropology* 44
(2015): 557–72.

12. Z. Gille, "Actor Networks, Modes of Production, and Waste Regimes:
Reassembling the Macro-Social," *Environment and Planning A: Economy and
Space* 42, no. 5 (2010): 1049.

13. G. C. Daily, ed., *Nature's Services: Societal Dependence on Natural
Ecosystems* (Washington, DC: Island Press, 1997); and J. Gabrys, "Sink: The
Dirt of Systems," *Environment and Planning D: Society and Space* 27, no. 4
(2009): 666–81.

14. For example, S. Luyssaert et al., "Old-Growth Forests as Global Carbon
Sinks," *Nature* 455, no. 7210 (2008): 213–15.

15. *Oxford English Dictionary* (Oxford: Oxford University Press, 2018).

16. J. Tarr, "The Search for the Ultimate Sink: Urban Air, Land, and Water
Pollution in Historical Perspective," *Records of the Columbia Historical
Society* 51 (1984): 1–29.

17. A. Keeling, "Urban Wastes Sinks as a Natural Resource: The Case of
the Fraser River," *Urban History Review* 34, no. 1 (2005): 57–70. The STS

scholar Max Liboiron makes a similar point about how the "logic of assimilative capacity" has informed the development of environmental regulation since the 1930s. M. Liboiron, *Pollution Is Colonialism* (Durham, NC: Duke University Press, 2021).

18. Gabrys, "Sink," 2009, p. 668.

19. G. C. Daily and K. Ellison, *The New Economy of Nature* (New York: Island Press, 2002); and Millennium Ecosystem Assessment, *Ecosystems and Human Well-Being* (Washington, DC: Island Press, 2005).

20. Landes, *Unbound Prometheus*, 1969.

21. *Oxford English Dictionary* (Oxford: Oxford University Press, 2018).

22. C. Dickens, *Our Mutual Friend: Book the First* (1865; repr., New York: Charles Scribner's Sons, 1901), 12.

23. G. P. Marsh, *Man and Nature, or, Physical Geography Modified by Human Action*, ed. D. Lowenthal (1864; repr., Seattle: University of Washington Press, 2003), 37n5.

24. K. Marx, *Capital: A Critique of Political Economy*, vol. 3 (New York: Penguin Books, 1981).

25. Christine Rosen makes the inverse point about scale of waste production and why certain firms didn't attempt to utilize industrial wastes. C. M. Rosen, "Fact versus Conjecture in the History of Industrial Waste Utilization," *Econ Journal Watch* 9, no. 2 (2012): 112–21.

26. R. Altman, "How the Benzene Tree Polluted the World," *Atlantic*, October 4, 2017, www.theatlantic.com/science/archive/2017/10/benzene-tree-organic-compounds/530655/.

27. K. Marx, *Capital: A Critique of Political Economy*, vol. 1 (New York: Penguin Books, 1976), 663.

28. W. Cronon, *Nature's Metropolis: Chicago and the Great West* (New York: W. W. Norton, 1992), 251.

29. J. Teeple, "Economic Factors in the Chemical Industry," *Industrial and Chemical Engineering* 19, no. 10 (1927): 1085–87; T. J. Kreps, "Joint Costs in the Chemical Industry," *Quarterly Journal of Economics* 44, no. 3 (1930): 416–61; W. Haynes, *Chemical Economics* (New York: D. Van Nostrand, 1933); and Marx, *Capital*, 1981, vol. 3.

30. H. Kurz, "Classical and Early Neoclassical Economists on Joint Production," *Metroeconomica* 38, no. 1 (1986): 1–37; and A. Blanchette, *Porkopolis: American Animality, Standardized Life, and the Factory Farm* (Durham, NC: Duke University Press, 2020).

31. Christine Rosen often points outs how this transition to by-product utilization was driven by regulation and litigation and that it did not fully solve the pollution problems. C. M. Rosen, "'Knowing' Industrial Pollution: Nuisance Law and the Power of Tradition in a Time of Rapid Economic Change," *Environmental History* 8, no. 4 (2003): 565–97; P. Thorsheim, *Inventing Pollution: Coal, Smoke and Culture in Britain since 1800* (Athens: Ohio University Press, 2006); and P. Reed, *Acid Rain and the Rise of the Environmental Chemist in Nineteenth-Century Britain: The Life and Work of Robert Angus Smith* (New York: Routledge, 2014).

32. J. Teeple, "Waste Pine Wood Utilization," *Journal of Industrial and Engineering Chemistry* 7, no. 11 (1913): 929–30; and J. Teeple, "Raw

Materials—Waste and By-Products," *Industrial and Engineering Chemistry* 8, no. 11 (1926): 1187–90.

33. E. Leslie, *Synthetic Worlds: Nature, Art, and the Chemical Industry* (London: Reaktion Books, 2005), 14.

34. For example, J. E. McWilliams, *American Pests: Losing the War on Insects from Colonial Times to DDT* (New York: Columbia University Press, 2008).

35. "Is Arsenic Down to Stay? Demoralization of Present Market Had Driven Prices to Lowest Level of the Last Ten Years," *Drug & Chemical Markets* 27, no. 2 (1925): 77–78; and "Just So Long as the Weather Holds the Boll Weevil in Check, the Calcium Arsenate Is a Drug on the Market, but the Potential Demand Is 100,000,000 Lbs.," *Chemical Markets* 19, no. 13 (1926): 517–18, 564.

36. Tarr, "Search for the Ultimate Sink," 1984.

37. Z. Gille, *From the Cult of Waste to the Trash Heap of History: The Politics of Waste in Socialist and Postsocialist Hungary* (Bloomington: Indiana University Press, 2007), 35.

38. J. Guthman, *Wilted: Pathogens, Chemicals, and the Fragile Future of the Strawberry Industry* (Berkeley: University of California Press, 2019).

39. Guthman, *Wilted*, 2019, 18–20.

40. C. R. Henke, *Cultivating Science, Harvesting Power: Science and Industrial Agriculture in California* (Cambridge, MA: MIT Press, 2008).

41. L. O. Howard, *The Insect Menace* (New York: D. Appleton-Century, 1933).

42. For example, J. Fordyce, I. Rosen, and C. Myers, "Quantitative Studies in Syphilis from a Clinical and Biologic Point of View II: Normal Arsenic," *Archives of Internal Medicine* 31, no. 5 (1923): 739–57.

43. Cotton seed eventually became feed for animals, but it was first used to make soaps and other oil-based goods. J. Murray, "The Once Despised Cottonseed Now Gives Cottonseed Oil to Make Soap and Many Other Products," *Chemical Markets* 19, no. 33 (1926): 1361–62.

44. R. Carson, *Silent Spring* (1962; repr., New York: Mariner Books, 2002), 9.

45. E. Russell, *War and Nature: Fighting Humans and Insects with Chemicals from World War I to Silent Spring* (Cambridge: Cambridge University Press, 2001).

46. R. S. Woglum, "The History of Hydrocyanic Acid Gas Fumigation as an Index to Progress in Economic Entomology," *Journal of Economic Entomology* 16, no. 6 (1923): 518–21.

47. B. Larkin, "The Politics and Poetics of Infrastructure," *Annual Review of Anthropology* 42 (2013): 327–43.

48. J. R. Kloppenburg, *First the Seed: The Political Economy of Plant Biotechnology* (Madison: University of Wisconsin Press, 2004.)

49. H. V. Moses, "'The Orange-Grower Is Not a Farmer': G. Harold Powell, Riverside Orchardists, and the Coming of Industrial Agriculture 1893–1930," *California History* 74, no. 1 (1995): 22–37.

50. D. Fitzgerald, *Every Farm a Factory: The Industrial Ideal in American Agriculture* (New Haven, CT: Yale University Press, 2005), 16.

51. L. O. Howard, "Progress in Economic Entomology in the United States," in *Yearbook of the United States Department of Agriculture for 1899*, 135–56

(Washington, DC: US Government Printing Office, 1900); C. W. Woodworth, "The Insecticide Industries in California," *Journal of Economic Entomology* 5, no. 5 (1912): 358–64; C. C. McDonnell, "Recent Progress in Insecticides and Fungicides," *Industrial and Engineering Chemistry* 16, no. 10 (1924): 1007–13; and R. C. Roark, "Insecticides and Fungicides," *Industrial and Engineering Chemistry* 27, no. 5 (1935): 530–33.

52. R. T. Legge, "Occupational Hazards in the Agricultural Industries," *American Journal of Public Health* 25, no. 4 (1935): 457–62.

53. B. Williams, "'That We May Live': Pesticides, Plantations, and Environmental Racism in the United States South," *Environment and Planning E: Nature and Space* 1–2 (2018): 243–67.

54. "Calls Man to War on Insect Pests: Entomologist Pictures Bugs as Driving Humanity Off the Planet Unless Halted," *New York Times*, September 10, 1931.

55. E. D. Melillo, "The First Green Revolution: Debt Peonage and the Making of the Fertilizer Trade, 1840-1930," *American Historical Review* 117, no. 4 (2012): 1028–60.

CHAPTER 1. ARSENIC AND OLD WASTE

V. Biringuccio, *The Pirotechnia*, trans. C. Smith and M. Gnudi (1540; New York: American Institute of Mining and Metallurgical Engineers, 1942), 106.

1. J. C. Alden, "The Continuing Need for Inorganic Arsenical Pesticides," in *Arsenic: Industrial, Biomedical, Environmental Perspectives*, ed. W. H. Lederer and R. J. Fensterheim, 63–70 (New York: Van Nostrand Reinhold, 1983).

2. K. Vogel, "The Significance of Arsenic in the Excretions," *American Journal of the Medical Sciences* 176, no. 2 (1928): 215–a24; J. O. Nriagu and J. M. Azcue, "Food Contamination with Arsenic in the Environment," in *Food Contamination from Environmental Sources*, ed. J. O. Nriagu and M. S. Simmons, Advances in Environmental Science and Technology (New York: John Wiley and Sons, 1990); and H. Garelick et al., "Arsenic Pollution Sources," in *Reviews of Environmental Contamination and Toxicology: Arsenic, Pollution and Remediation, an International Perspective*, ed. D. M. Whitacre (New York: Springer, 2008).

3. R. Beeman, "'Chemivisions': The Forgotten Promises of the Chemurgy Movement," *Agricultural History* 68, no. 4 (1994): 23–45.

4. S. Giedion, *Mechanization Takes Command: A Contribution to Anonymous History* (New York: Oxford University Press, 1948), 215.

5. W. T. Frankenberger, ed., *The Environmental Chemistry of Arsenic* (New York: Marcel Decker, 2002).

6. B. K. Mandal and K. T. Suzuki, "Arsenic Round the World: A Review," *Talanta* 58, no. 1 (2002): 201–35.

7. K. Nelson, "Industrial Contributions of Arsenic to the Environment," *Environmental Health Perspectives* 19 (1977): 31–34; and J. O. Nriagu, "Arsenic Poisoning through the Ages," in *Environmental Chemistry of Arsenic*, ed. W. T. Frankenberger (New York: Marcel Dekker, 2002), 2.

8. J. W. Moore, *Capitalism in the Web of Life: Ecology and the Accumulation of Capital* (New York: Verso, 2015).

9. J. R. Harris, "Copper and Shipping in the Eighteenth Century," *Economic History Review* 19, no. 3 (1966): 550–68; S. W. Mintz, *Sweetness and Power: The Place of Sugar in Modern History* (New York: Penguin Books, 1986); and J. Day, "Copper, Zinc, and Brass Production," in *The Industrial Revolution in Metals*, ed. J. Day and R. F. Tylecote (London: Institute of Metals, 1991), 131–99.

10. R. Tredinnick, *A Review of Cornish Copper Mining Enterprise, with a Description of the Most Important Dividend and Progressive Copper and Tin Mines of Cornwall and Devon, and Detailed Account of the Buller and Bassest District*, 2nd ed. (London: Thompson and Vincent, 1858); R. O. Robert, "The Development and Decline of the Non-ferrous Metal Smelting Industries in South Wales," in *Industrial South Wales, 1750–1914* (London: Frank Cass and Company, 1969), 264; H. G. Dines, *The Metalliferous Mining Region of South-West England*, Memoirs of Geological Survey of Great Britain, vol. 1 (London: Her Majesty's Stationary Office, 1956); D. B. Barton, *A History of Tin Mining in Devon and Cornwall* (Cornwall, UK: Truro Bookshop, 1967); and D. B. Barton, *A History of Copper Mining in Cornwall and Devon* (Cornwall, UK: Truro Bookshop, 1968).

11. H. Jones, *Steam Engines: An International History* (London: Ernest Benn Limited, 1973); and M. Lynch, *Mining in World History* (London: Reakton Books, 2002).

12. Jones, *Steam Engines*, 1973, 34–35; and Lynch, *Mining in World History*, 2002.

13. I refer to the mining and smelting industries of Cornwall, Devon, and Swansea as the CDS complex. Although certain activities agglomerated in certain geographic areas—coal mining in Swansea, copper ore mining in Cornwall, copper smelting in Swansea, arsenic smelting in Cornwall and Devon—I argue that they must be viewed together as pieces of a larger industrial complex.

14. Robert, "Development and Decline," 1969.

15. Tredinnick, *Review of Cornish Copper Mining*, 1858; G. G. Francis, *The Smelting in the Copper in the Swansea District of South Wales, from the Time of Elizabeth to the Present Day*, 2nd ed. (London: Henry Southern, 1881); and Robert, "Development and Decline," 1969.

16. Dines, *Metalliferous Mining Region of South-West England*, 1956; W. H. Dennis, *A Hundred Years of Metallurgy* (Chicago: Aldine, 1964); Barton, *History of Copper Mining in Cornwall and Devon*, 1968; Robert, " Development and Decline," 1969; and Day, "Copper, Zinc, and Brass" 1991.

17. Bureau of the Census, *Historical Statistics of the United States, 1789–1945, a Supplement to the Statistical Abstract of the United States* (Washington, DC: US Department of Commerce, 1949); and W. H. Weed, *The Copper Mines of the World* (New York: Hill Publishing, 1907).

18. Tredinnick, *Review of Cornish Copper Mining*, 1858; Francis, *Smelting in the Copper*, 1881; Robert, "Development and Decline," 1969; and Lynch, *Mining in World History*, 2002.

19. Redgrave's Report in *Reports of Inspectors of Factories*, October 1852, outlines the productive advantages of Cornwall mines, especially in terms of energy use per unit of output. Duplicated in K. Marx, *Capital: A Critique of Political Economy*, vol. 3 (New York: Penguin Books, 1981), 193.

20. 154,299 tons. Tredinnick, *Review of Cornish Copper Mining*, 1858.

21. S. G. Checkland, *The Mines of Tharsis: Roman, French and British Enterprise in Spain* (London: George Allen & Unwin, 1967).

22. Robert, "Development and Decline," 1969.

23. B. Earl, *Cornish Mining: The Techniques of Metal Mining in the West of England, Past and Present* (Cornwall, UK: D. Bradford Barton, 1968).

24. R. P. Rothwell, ed., *The Mineral Industry: Its Statistics, Technology, and Trade in the United States and Other Countries to the End of 1897*, vol. 6 (New York: Scientific Press, 1898); B. Earl, "Arsenic Winning and Refining Methods in the West of England," *Journal of the Trevithick Society* 10 (1983): 9–29; and B. Earl, *The Cornish Arsenic Industry* (Cornwall, UK: Penhellick Publications, 1996).

25. "In an Arsenic Mine," *Los Angeles Times*, July 4, 1894; "Gleaners of Poison: Arsenic Picked Up by the Roadside and Made by the Ton in Cornwall," *Los Angeles Times*, September 5, 1897, 16; and P. Ball, *Bright Earth: Art and the Invention of Color* (Chicago: University of Chicago Press, 2003).

26. Frankenberger, *Environmental Chemistry of Arsenic*, 2002.

27. Arsenic's content is about 1% in concentrated copper ore, but can range considerably depending on the type of ore. H. O. Hofman, *Metallurgy of Copper* (New York: McGraw-Hill, 1914).

28. "Gleaners of Poison," *Los Angeles Times*, 1897, 16; Francis, *Smelting in the Copper*, 1881; and Earl, "Arsenic Winning," 1983. Arsenic, is of course, just one of the major wastes of smelting. Besides the waste rock known as gangue, many smelters also emit sulfur oxides. These sulfur oxides can remain aloft for great distances, eventually returning to the land as sulfurous dusts or acid rain.

29. Earl, "Arsenic Winning," 1983; Earl, *Cornish Arsenic Industry*, 1996; and Ball, *Bright Earth*, 2001.

30. P. Hills, *Venetian Colour: Marble Mosaic, Painting and Glass, 1250–1550* (New Haven, CT: Yale University Press, 1999).

31. Arsenic's use as medicine was likely encouraged by the fact that because the hair (keratin) and skin are physiographical fates of biological detoxification; that is, sublethal arsenic intoxication often causes the skin and hair to appear shiny and lustrous. The hair is a main exit route of metabolic arsenic detoxification in humans and other animals. "Crazed by the Use of Arsenic," *Washington Post*, July 11, 1878; and X. C. Le, "Arsenic Speciation in the Environment and Humans," in *The Environmental Chemistry of Arsenic*, ed. W. T. Frankenberger (New York: Marcel Dekker, 2002), 95–116. Arsenic is still added to makeup, particularly lipstick. N. M. Hepp et al., "Survey of Cosmetics for Arsenic, Cadmium, Chromium, Cobalt, Lead, Mercury, and Nickel Content," *Journal of Cosmetic Science* 65 (May/June 2014): 125–45.

32. J. Whorton, *The Arsenic Century: How Victorian Britain Was Poisoned at Home, Work, and Play* (Oxford: Oxford University Press, 2010).

33. Earl, *Cornish Arsenic Industry*, 1996.

34. "Melancholy Effects of Poison," *Sunday Times*, March 30, 1823; and "Profligate Seduction and Suicide," *Sunday Times*, December 26, 1824.

35. S. Hempel, *The Inheritor's Powder: A Tale of Arsenic, Murder, and the New Forensic Science* (New York: W. W. Norton, 2013).

36. Earl, *Cornish Arsenic Industry*, 1996.

37. P. W. Bartrip, "How Green Was My Valence? Environmental Arsenic Poisoning and the Victorian Domestic Ideal," *English History Review* 109, no. 433 (1994): 891–913; and Whorton, *Arsenic Century*, 2010.

38. "Sheep Dipping, and Sheep Killing, with Corrosive Sublimate of Arsenic," *Sunday Times*, September 12, 1858; C. Mattingley, *Survival in Our Own Land: "Aboriginal" Experiences in "South Australia" since 1836* (Adelaide, Australia: Wakefield Press, 1988); and T. Barta, "Discourses of Genocide in Germany and Australia: A Linked History," *Aboriginal History* 25, no. 1 (2001): 37–57.

39. Earl, *Cornish Arsenic Industry*, 1996.

40. Earl, "Arsenic Winning," 1983; and Earl, *Cornish Arsenic Industry*, 1996.

41. A. E. Dingle, "'The Monster Nuisance of All': Landowners, Alkali Manufacturers, and Air Pollution, 1828–1864," *Economic History Review* 35, no. 4 (1982): 529–48.

42. Earl, "Arsenic Winning," 1983; and Earl, *Cornish Arsenic Industry*, 1996.

43. J. Whorton, "Insecticide Residue of Foods as a Public Health Problem: 1865–1938" (PhD thesis, University of Wisconsin, 1969).

44. Quoted in "Arsenic: Devon, England," *Daily Constitution*, February 2, 1875.

45. "Arsenic," *Daily Constitution*,1875.

46. "Poison by the Ton," *Los Angeles Times*, December 24, 1893; "In an Arsenic Mine," *Los Angeles Times*, 1894; "Arsenic Factories: Habits Acquired by People Who Work in Them," *Atlanta Constitution*, January 24, 1902, 10; Barton, *History of Copper Mining in Cornwall and Devon*, 1968; and Earl, *Cornish Arsenic Industry*, 1996.

47. Quoted in "Gleaners," *Los An geles Times*, 1897; A. A. Meharg, *Venomous Earth: How Arsenic Caused the World's Worst Mass Poisoning* (New York: Macmillan, 2005).

48. "Gleaners of Poison," *Los Angeles Times*, 1897; "Dust Is Worth Millions: Fortunes Now Obtained from What Formerly Waste Matter," *Washington Post*, August 17, 1913; and "Our Super-Poison Gas: First Story of Compound 72 Times Deadlier Than 'Mustard,' Manufactured Secretly by the Thousands of Tons," *New York Times*, April 20, 1919.

49. Imperial Mineral Resources Bureau, *The Mineral Industry of the British Empire and Foreign Countries: War Period; Arsenic (1913–1919).* (London: His Majesty's Stationery Office, 1920).

50. Dennis, *Hundred Years of Metallurgy*, 1964.

51. F. E. Richter, "The Copper-Mining Industry in the United States, 1845–1925," *Quarterly Journal of Economics* 41, no. 2 (1927): 236–91; and T. A. Rickard, *A History of American Mining* (New York: McGraw-Hill, 1932).

52. F. W. Paine, "Copper," in *Political and Commercial Geology and the World's Mineral Resources*, ed. J. E. Spurr, 223–60 (New York: McGraw-Hill, 1920).

53. Richter, " Copper-Mining Industry," 1927.

54. P. B. Moore, "Copper Arsenides at Mohawk, Michigan," *Rocks & Minerals* 27, nos. 1/2 (1962): 24–26.

55. Rickard, *History of American Mining*, 1932.

56. W. H. Weed, "Copper Deposits of the United States," in *The Copper Mines of World* (New York: Hill Publishing, 1908), 253–367.

57. Richter, "Copper-Mining Industry," 1927; and R. G. Raymer, "Early Copper Mining in Arizona," *Pacific Historical Review* 4, no. 2 (1935): 123–30.

58. J. R. Browne and J. W. Taylor, *Reports upon the Mineral Resources of the United States* (Washington, DC: US Government Printing Office, 1867).

59. Rickard, *History of American Mining*, 1932.

60. Rothwell, *Mineral Industry*, 1898.

61. Richter, "Copper-Mining Industry," 1927; and Dennis, *Hundred Years of Metallurgy*, 1964.

62. R. B. Pettengill, "The United States Copper Industry and the Tariff," *Quarterly Journal of Economics* (1931): 141–57; C. Schmitz, "The Rise of Big Business in the World Copper Industry 1870–1930," *Economic History Review* 39, no. 3 (1986): 392–410; and K. D. Underwood, "Mining Wars: Corporate Expansion and Labor Violence in the Western Desert, 1876–1920" (PhD diss., University of Nevada, Las Vegas, 2009).

63. This is especially true for sulfur-based ores like energite.

64. Richter, "Copper-Mining Industry," 1927, 264.

65. Richter, " Copper-Mining Industry," 1927.

66. W. R Ingallis, ed., *The Mineral Industry: Its Statistics, Technology, and Trade during 1905*, vol. 14 (New York: Engineering and Mining Journal, 1906); J. K. Haywood, "Injury to Vegetation and Animal Life by Smelter Fumes," *Journal of the American Chemical Society* 29, no. 7 (1907): 998–1009; and D. MacMillan, *Smoke Wars: Anaconda Copper, Montana Air Pollution, and the Courts, 1890–1924* (Helena: Montana Historical Society Press, 2000).

67. Paine, "Copper," 1920; Bureau of the Census, *Historical Statistics of the United States*, 1949; and I. F. Marcosson, *Metal Magic: The Story of the American Smelting and Refining Company* (New York: Farrar, Straus, 1949).

68. V. C. Heikes, "Arsenic," in *The Mineral Industry: Its Statistics, Technology and Trade during 1924*, ed. A. B. Butts and G. A. Roush (New York: McGraw-Hill, 1925), 63–70. Legal/political wrangling by mining companies allowed for Mexican imports to often be classified as American production, making some of the statistics of American production less reliable.

69. United States Geological Survey, "Historical Statistics for Mineral and Material Commodities in the United States" (Department of the Interior, 2019), http://minerals.usgs.gov/minerals/pubs/historical-statistics.

70. R. P. Rothwell and J. Struthers, eds., *The Mineral Industry: Its Statistics, Technology, and Trade in the United States and Other Countries to the End of 1901* (New York: Engineering and Mining Journal, 1902). Purchased by Guggenheim/ASARCO in 1903.

71. Ingallis, *Mineral Industry*.

72. W. R. Ingallis, ed., *The Mineral Industry: Its Statistics, Technology, and Trade during 1909*, vol. 18 (New York: Engineering and Mining Journal, 1910).

73. W. Haynes, "The Chemical Era of Modern Industry," *Chemical Markets* 21, no. 2 (1927): 43–44; L. W. Bass, "Chemical Economics," in *Annual Survey of American Chemistry*, ed. C. J. West (New York: National Research Council, Chemical Catalog Company, 1931), 582–600; and W. Haynes, *Chemical Economics* (New York: D. Van Nostrand, 1933).

74. G. A. Roush and A. B. Butts, eds., *The Mineral Industry: Its Statistics, Technology, and Trade during 1920*, vol. 29 (New York: McGraw-Hill, 1921); and C. C. McDonnell, "Recent Progress in Insecticides and Fungicides," *Industrial & Engineering Chemistry* 16, no. 10 (1924): 1007–13.

75. Haywood, "Injury to Vegetation," 1907; R. E. Swain, "Atmospheric Pollution by Industrial Wastes," *Industrial & Engineering Chemistry* 15, no. 3 (1923): 296–301; J. Teeple, "Raw Materials–Waste and By-Products," *Industrial & Engineering Chemistry* 8, no. 11 (1926): 1187–90; and MacMillan, *Smoke Wars*, 2000.

76. "May Sue Copper Company: President Will Learn If Poisonous Fumes Can Be Prevented," *New York Times*, December 6, 1908; "The Washoe Smelter: Believed That There Is Not Danger of the Plant Being Closed," *Wall Street Journal*, December 21, 1908, 3; and S. Norman, "Problem Solved: Smelting Process Kills All Fumes," *New York Times*, February 16, 1908, II13.

77. "Montana Smelters Sued: Government Action against Anaconda Company to Protect Forests," *New York Times*, March 17, 1910.

78. "Montana Smelters Sued," *New York Times*, 1910.

79. "Montana Smelters Sued," *New York Times*, 1910.

80. Forest damage was also caused by high-sulfur-content coal used in the smelters.

81. A. H. Fay, ed., *The Mineral Industry, Its Technology and Trade during 1910*, vol. 19 (New York: McGraw-Hill, 1911).

82. C. W. Woodworth, "Codling Moth Control in California," *Journal of Economic Entomology* 3, no. 6 (1910): 470–73; J. J. Davis, "The Value of Crude Arsenious Oxide in Poison Bait for Cutworms and Grasshoppers," *Journal of Economic Entomology* 12, no. 2 (1919): 200–203; "Wide Use of Arsenic: Is Principally Employed in Glass Making and in Insecticides, as Well as Paints and Medicines," *Los Angeles Times*, May 10, 1914; and "Arsenic Poison Spray Used to Destroy Weeds," *San Francisco Chronicle*, November 15, 1915.

83. "Our Super-Poison Gas," *New York Times*, 1919; and J. A. Vilensky, *Dew of Death: The Story of Lewisite, America's World War I Weapon of Mass Destruction* (Bloomington: Indiana University Press, 2005).

84. Haynes, *Chemical Economics*, 1933.

85. "Domestic Arsenic," *Los Angeles Herald*, December 15, 1907; "Wide Use of Arsenic," *Los Angeles Times*, 1914; and C. L. Parsons, "Miscellaneous Mineral Wastes," *Industrial & Engineering Chemistry* 4, no. 3 (1912): 185–88.

86. T. LeCain, "The Limits of 'Eco-Efficiency': Arsenic Pollution and the Cottrell Electrical Precipitator in the U.S. Copper Smelting Industry," *Environmental History* 5, no. 3 (2000): 336–51.

87. Marcosson, *Metal Magic*, 1949; and L. Tepper and J. H. Tepper, "The Rise and Fall of the Tacoma Arsenic Industry," *Journal of the Society of Industrial Archeology* 39, nos. 1/2 (2013): 65–78.

88. G. A. Roush, ed., *The Mineral Industry: Its Statistics, Technology, and Trade during 1915*, vol. 24 (New York: McGraw-Hill, 1916).

89. G. A. Roush and A. B. Butts, eds., *The Mineral Industry: Its Statistics, Technology, and Trade during 1918*, vol. 27 (New York: McGraw-Hill, 1919).

90. B. M. Baruch, *American Industry in the War: A Report of the War Industries Board* (New York: Prentice-Hall, 1921).

91. Vilensky, *Dew of Death*, 2005.

92. Teeple, "Raw Materials," 1926, 1187; F. C. Cottrell, "Progress Report to Anaconda Smelter Commission," 1913, Anaconda Copper Mining Company Records, Collection no. 169, box 261-2, 1–7, Montana Historical Society Research Center, Helena; and J. Elton, W. Welch, and E. Dunn, "Blueprints of Proposed New Arsenic Plant Design, Recommendations for Improved Arsenic Plant Operation at the Washoe Reduction Works of the Anaconda Copper Mining Company," 1913, Anaconda Copper Mining Company Records, Collection no. 169, box 261-6, 1–7, Montana Historical Society Research Center, Helena.

93. Anaconda Mining Company, "Arsenic Daily Report, Year-to-Date," 1920, Anaconda Copper Mining Company Records, Collection no. 169, box 265-2, 1–7, Montana Historical Society Research Center, Helena.

94. R. R. Henderson, "Agricultural Insecticides: Raw Materials and Methods of Manufacture," *Chemical Age* 29, no. 257–60 (1921): 167–69; J. J. Brown, R. C. Berckmans, and T. G Hudson, "Georgia Refuses to Buy Arsenate at Present Price: Situation Declared by Entomology Board to Be the Result of Manipulation of the Market," *Atlanta Constitution*, December 14, 1922, 1; R. R. Henderson, "Arsenic, Calcium Arsenate, and the Boll-Weevil," *Chemical Age* 31, no. 12 (1923): 547–48; "May Be Shortage in Arsenate," *Drug & Chemical Markets* 14, no. 3 (1924): 167; "Just So Long as the Weather Holds the Boll Weevil in Check, the Calcium Arsenate Is a Drug on the Market, but the Potential Demand Is 100,000,000 Lbs," *Chemical Markets* 19, no. 13 (1926): 517–18, 564; "Where Arsenic Is Produced," *Chemical Markets* 19, no. 33 (1926): 1364; "Weevil Causing Some Concern in Texas," *Chemical Markets* 21, no. 2 (1927): 58; "Is Arsenic Down to Stay? Demoralization of Present Market Had Driven Prices to Lowest Level of the Last Ten Years," *Drug & Chemical Markets* 27, no. 2 (1925): 77–78; and "Chemical Costs," *Chemical Markets* 19, no. 23 (1926): 933.

95. Davis, "Value of Crude Arsenious Oxide," 1919; G. A. Roush and A. B. Butts, eds., *The Mineral Industry: Its Statistics, Technology, and Trade during 1921*, vol. 30 (New York: McGraw-Hill, 1922); and "Arsenic in 1924," *Los Angeles Times*, June 5, 1925.

96. "Is Arsenic Down," *Drug & Chemical Markets*, 1925.

97. H. W. Ambruster, "Arsenic," in *The Mineral Industry: Its Statistics, Technology and Trade during 1926*, ed. A. B. Butts and G. A. Roush (New York: McGraw-Hill, 1927), 54–65; R C. Roark, "United States Insecticide Statistics for 1928," *Journal of Economic Entomology* 22, no. 4 (1929): 699–701; and G. N. Wolcott, "The Status of Economic Entomology in Peru," *Bulletin of Entomological Research* 20, no. 2 (1929): 225–31.

98. Roark, "United States Insecticide Statistics for 1928," 1929.

99. "Farms and Farmers: Don't Believe in Scientific Farming," *Atlanta Constitution*, April 14, 1913; National Research Council, Minutes of the Conference of Plant Pathologists, Entomologists, and Manufacturers of Insecticides and Fungicides at the National Academy of Sciences, Washington, DC, September 28, 1920, National Research Council, Institutions: Associations, Individuals, Archive of the National Academy of Sciences, Washington, DC.

100. B. R. Coad, "Killing Boll Weevils with Poison Dust," in *Yearbook for 1920* (Washington, DC: USDA, 1921), 241–52; and D. Helms, "Technological

Methods for Boll Weevil Control," *Agricultural History* 53, no. 1 (1979): 286–99.

101. O. Bowles, "Arsenic," in *The Mineral Industry: Its Statistics, Technology and Trade during 1929*, ed. A. B. Butts and G. A. Roush (New York: McGraw-Hill, 1930), 36.

102. A. Renick, "Arsenic," in *Minerals Resources of the United States* (Washington, DC: US Bureau of Mines, Geological Survey, 1931), 162–66.

103. United States Geological Survey, "Historical Statistics," 2019.

104. J. A. Tarr, "Searching for a 'Sink' for an Industrial Waste: Iron Making Fuels and the Environment," *Environmental History Review* 18, no. 1 (1994): 9.

105. Teeple, "Raw Materials," 1926; D. Landes, *The Unbound Prometheus: Technological Change and Industrial Development in Western Europe from 1750 to the Present* (New York: Cambridge University Press, 1969); R. U. Ayres, "Industrial Metabolism," in *Technology and Environment*, ed. J. H. Ausubel and H. E. Sladovich (Washington, DC: National Academy Press, 1989), 23–49; and E. Leslie, *Synthetic Worlds: Nature, Art, and the Chemical Industry* (London: Reaktion Books, 2005).

106. C. V. Riley, *The Colorado Potato Beetle: With Suggestions for Its Repression and Methods of Destruction* (London: George Routledge and Sons, 1877); and R. A. Casagrande, "The Colorado Potato Beetle: 125 Years of Mismanagement," *American Entomologist* 33, no. 3 (1987): 142–50.

107. E. G. Lodeman, *The Spraying of Plants: A Succinct Account of the History, Principles and Practice of the Application of Liquids and Powders to Plants for the Purpose of Destroying Insects and Fungi* (London: Macmillan, 1909).

108. Whorton, "Insecticide Residue of Foods," 1969.

109. Ball, *Bright Earth*, 2001; and Whorton, *Arsenic Century*, 2010.

110. A. J. Cook, "Bulletin No. 58—Insecticides" (Ann Arbor: University of Michigan Agricultural Experiment Station, 1890); J. K. Haywood, "The Composition and Analysis of London Purple," *Journal of the American Chemical Society* 22, no. 12 (1900): 800–809; C. A. Browne, "Chronological Table of Some Leading Events in the History of Industrial Chemistry in America from the Earliest Colonial Settlements until the Outbreak of the World War," *Industrial & Engineering Chemistry* 18, no. 9 (1926): 884–93; and E. O. Essig, *A History of Entomology* (New York: Hafner, 1931).

111. "The Cotton Worm in the South," *Manchester Guardian*, August 9, 1880; and S. W. Lanman, "Colour in the Garden: 'Malignant Magenta,'" *Garden History* 28, no. 2 (2000): 209–21.

112. C. V. Riley, "Insecticides: Summer and Spring Washes and Remedies against Pests," *Los Angeles Times*, May 3, 1887.

113. J. E. McWilliams, *American Pests: Losing the War on Insects from Colonial Times to DDT* (New York: Columbia University Press, 2008); and R. Spear, *The Great Gypsy Moth War: A History of the First Campaign in Massachusetts to Eradicate the Gypsy Moth, 1890–1901* (Boston: University of Massachusetts Press, 2005).

114. L. O. Howard, *A History of Applied Entomology (Somewhat Anecdotal)* (Washington, DC: Smithsonian Institution, 1930).

115. C. V. Riley, "Bulletin No. 10—Our Shade Trees and Their Insect Defoliators" (Washington, DC: Government Printing Office, 1887).

116. For example, "Millions of Fish and Fowl Dying, Results of the Use of Paris Green," *New York Times*, August 9, 1878; and "Pheasants Die by Poison," *Washington Post*, August 26 1897, 3.

117. J. B. Smitch, "Cultivation and Susceptibility to Insect Attack," *Journal of Economic Entomology* 1, no. 1 (1908): 15–17; T. B. Symons, "Should State Departments Conduct Public Sprayers?" *Journal of Economic Entomology* 1, no. 2 (1908): 106–10; and D. Danbom, *The Resisted Revolution: Urban American and the Industrialization of Agriculture, 1900–1930* (Ames: Iowa State University Press, 1979).

118. "Paris Green," *Los Angeles Times*, November 2, 1895, 12; "The Codling Moth Work at Watsonville," *Pacific Rural Press*, August 6, 1904; C. W. Woodworth, "The Battle of the Arsenicals," *Pacific Rural Press*, November 26, 1910; H. V. Moses, "'The Orange-Grower Is Not a Farmer': G. Harold Powell, Riverside Orchardists, and the Coming of Industrial Agriculture, 1893–1930," *California History* 74, no. 1 (1995): 22–37; and R. Walker, *The Conquest of Bread: 150 Years of Agribusiness in California* (New York: New Press, 2004).

119. G. Henderson, *California and the Fictions of Capital* (Oxford: Oxford University Press, 1999).

120. Smith, "Cultivation," 1908; "Tacoma's Poison Factory Is Interesting Industry," *Tacoma News Tribune*, April 6, 1927, 13; and Essig, *History of Entomology*, 1931.

121. "Codling Moth Crusade," *Los Angeles Herald*, December 23, 1903; "Codling Moth Work," *Pacific Rural Press*, 1904; and Woodworth, "Codling Moth Control," 1910.

122. Woodworth, "Codling Moth Control," 1910; Essig, *History of Entomology*, 1931; and Chevron Chemical Company, "A Brief Chronological History of the Ortho Division, Chevron Spray Company," 1964, California Spray Chemical Company, Chevron Chemical Company, Chevron Corporate Archive, Concord, CA, 29.

123. J. Steinbeck, *The Chrysanthemums and Other Stories* (New York: Penguin Books, 1996), 1.

124. W. H. Volck, "The Significance of Lead Arsenate Composition," *Science* 33, no. 857 (1911): 866–70.

125. E. E. Luther and W. H. Volck, "Process of Making Lead Arsenate," Patent #892,603, US Patent Office, 1908; E. E. Luther and W. H. Volck, "Process of Making Arsenate of Lead," Patent #903,389, US Patent Office, 1908; and E. E. Luther and W. H. Volck, "Manufacture of Lead Arsenate," Patent #929,962, US Patent Office, 1909.

126. Woodworth, "Codling Moth Control," 1910.

127. Chevron Chemical Company, "Brief Chronological History of the Ortho Division," 1965.

128. Essig, *History of Entomology*, 1931.

129. Woodworth, "Codling Moth Control," 1910.

130. Chevron Chemical Company, "Brief Chronological History of the Ortho Division," 1965.

131. G. P. Gray, "The Workings of the California Insecticide Law," *Journal of Industrial and Engineering Chemistry* 6, no. 7 (1914): 590–94; and G. P. Gray, "Economic Toxicology," *Science* 48, no. 12 (1918): 329–32.

132. "The Wide Use of Arsenic," *Journal of Industrial and Engineering Chemistry* 4, no. 9 (1912): 696–97; "Wide Use of Arsenic," *Los Angeles Times*, 1914; and C. W. Woodworth, "The Insecticide Industries in California," *Journal of Economic Entomology* 5, no. 4 (1912): 358–64.

133. G. P. Gray, "The Consumption and Cost of Economic Poisons in California in 1916," *Industrial & Engineering Chemistry* 10, no. 4 (1918): 301–2; and L. R. Gardner, *The First Thirty Years: The Early History of the Company Now Known as Ortho Division, Chevron Chemical Company* (San Francisco: Chevron Chemical Company, 1978).

134. Chevron Chemical Company, "Brief Chronological History of the Ortho Division," 1965.

135. W. E. Hinds, "Presidential Address: Some Achievements in Economic Entomology," *Journal of Economic Entomology* 27, no. 1 (1934): 37–52.

136. W. D. Lynch et al., "Bulletin 127—Poisonous Metals on Sprayed Fruits and Vegetables" (Washington, DC: USDA, 1922); C. N. Myers et al., "Significance and Danger of Spray Residue," *Industrial & Engineering Chemistry* 25, no. 6 (1933): 624–29; and M. J. Reuter, "The Arsenic Problem: Report of a Case of Arsenic Dermatitis from Wearing Apparel," *Archives of Dermatology and Syphilology* 31, no. 6 (1935): 811–18.

137. A. Kallet and F. J. Schlink, *100,000,000 Guinea Pigs: Dangers in Everyday Foods, Drugs, and Cosmetics* (New York: Vanguard Press, 1933); and R. Lamb, *The American Chamber of Horrors: The Truth about Food and Drugs* (New York: Farrar & Rinehart, 1936).

138. J. Whorton, *Before Silent Spring: Pesticides and Public Health in Pre-DDT America* (Princeton, NJ: Princeton University Press, 1974).

139. Whorton, *Before Silent Spring*, 1974.

140. H. W. Wiley, *The History of a Crime against the Food Law: The Amazing Story of the National Food and Drugs Law Intended to Protect the Health of the People, Perverted to Protect the Adulteration of Foods and Drugs* (Washington, DC: Self-published, 1929); and Whorton, *Before Silent Spring*, 1974.

141. Lamb, *American Chamber of Horrors*, 1936.

142. Whorton, *Before Silent Spring*, 1974.

143. A. L. Quaintance, P. B. Dunbar, and L. S. Tenny, "Confidential Minutes of Conference between Representatives of the US Department of Agriculture, the Insecticide and Fruit Industries and Others Relative to Arsenical Spray Residues of Fruits," 1926, Western Cooperative Spray Project Records, 1921–1952, US Department of Agriculture, Washington State University Manuscripts, Archives, & Special Collections, Pullman; and R. L. Webster, "Insecticide Situation in the Pacific Northwest," *Journal of Economic Entomology* 37, no. 6 (1944): 818–21.

144. "40 Ships Carrying Australian Apples to British Market: Dominion Taking Advantage of Disfavor American Fruit Has Met," *Washington Post*, May 2, 1926.

145. R. H. Robinson, "New Solvents for the Removal of Arsenical Spray Residue," *Industrial & Engineering Chemistry* 21, no. 11 (1929): 1132–36; and D. F. Fisher, "Arsenical and Other Fruit Injuries of Apples Resulting from Washing Operations," in *Technical Bulletin* 12 (Washington, DC: USDA, 1931).

146. W. E. Fleming, "Fluorosilicates as Insecticides for the Japanese Beetle," *Journal of Economic Entomology* 20, no. 5 (1927): 685–91; and R. H. Carter and R. C. Roark, "Composition of Fluorides and Fluorosilicates Sold as Insecticides," *Journal of Economic Entomology* 21, no. 5 (1928): 762–73.

147. H. A. Wallace, "Notice to Producers and Consumer of Apples and Pears," 1935, Western Cooperative Spray Project Records, 1921–1952, US Department of Agriculture, Washington State University Manuscripts, Archives, & Special Collections, Pullman, WA.

148. Roark, "United States Insecticide Statistics," 1929.

149. Quoted in "Tacoma's Poison Factory Is Interesting Industry," 1927.

150. McDonnell, "Recent Progress in Insecticides and Fungicides," 1924; "Mass Attack of Worms Stopped at Trenches," *Los Angeles Times*, August 16, 1925; P. M. Tyler and C. N. Gerry, "Arsenic," in *Minerals Resources of the United States* (Washington, DC: US Bureau of Mines, Geological Survey, 1931–1932), 319–27; E. O. Essig, "Farm Machinery in Relation to Insect Pest Control," *Journal of Economic Entomology* 26, no. 4 (1933): 864–68; A. P. van Siclen and C. N. Gerry, "Arsenic," in *Minerals Resources of the United States* (Washington, DC: US Bureau of Mines, Geological Survey, 1935), 496–501; and H. W. Ambruster, "Arsenic," in *The Mineral Industry: Its Statistics, Technology and Trade during 1937*, ed. G. A. Roush (New York: McGraw Hill Book Company, 1938), 63–66.

151. Van Siclen and Gerry, "Arsenic," 1935.

152. E. Douglas, "Millions Are Slain. Farmers Turn on Grasshopper Horde," *Los Angeles Times*, July 2 1933; R. C. Roark, "Insecticides and Fungicides," *Industrial & Engineering Chemistry* 27, no. 5 (1935): 530–32; and H. S. Siverson, "Arsenic Breakfasts Ready for 'Hoppers': Middle West Preparing for Grasshopper Swarms Predicted by Experts to Be Greatest in Many Years of Farm History," *Washington Post*, May 16, 1937.

153. C. E. Nighman, "Arsenic," in *Minerals Resources of the United States* (Washington, DC: US Bureau of Mines, Geological Survey, 1944), 743–51.

154. H. C. McLean, A. L. Weber, and J. S. Joffe, "Arsenic Content of Vegetables Grown in Soils Treated with Lead Arsenate," *Journal of Economic Entomology* 37, no. 2 (1944): 315–18.

155. Nighman, "Arsenic," 1944.

156. Nighman, "Arsenic," 1944.

157 Alden, "Continuing Need for Inorganic Arsenical Pesticides," 1983; and Nriagu and Azcue, "Food Contamination," 1990.

158. C. K. Hyde, *Copper for America: The United States Copper Industry from Colonial Times to the 1990s* (Tucson: University of Arizona Press, 1998).

159. Tepper and Tepper, "Rise and Fall," 2013.

160. Alden, "Continuing Need for Inorganic Arsenical Pesticides," 1983.

161. In the 1930s, USDA scientists discovered that the addition of organic arsenical acids like aminophenyl arsenic acid to feed stimulated the growth of chickens. H. F. Wilson and C. E. Holmes, "Little Danger in Eating Arsenic-Fed Chickens," *Journal of Economic Entomology* 29, no. 5 (1936): 1008–14; and C. C. Calvert, "Arsenicals in Animal Feeds and Wastes," in *Arsenical Pesticides*, ed. E. A. Woolson (Washington, DC: American Chemical Society, 1975).

162. A. H. Westing, "Agent Blue in Vietnam," *New York Times*, July 12, 1971; P. F. Cecil, *Herbicidal Warfare: The Ranch Hand Project in Vietnam* (New York: Praeger, 1986); and J. M. Stellman et al., "The Extent and Patterns of Usage of Agent Orange and Other Herbicides in Vietnam," *Nature* 422, no. 6933 (2003): 681–87.

163. J. R. Abernathy, "Role of Arsenical Chemicals in Agriculture," in *Arsenic: Industrial, Biomedical, Environmental Perspectives*, ed. W. H. Lederer and R. J. Fensterheim (New York: Van Nostrand Reinhold, 1983), 57–62.

164. F. Davis, *Banned: A History of Pesticides and the Science of Toxicology* (New Haven, CT: Yale University Press, 2014), xii.

165. W. W. Cochrane, *The Curse of Agricultural Abundance: A Sustainable Solution* (Lincoln: University of Nebraska Press, 2003).

166. H. A. Wallace, "Extension Service Review—May" (Washington, DC: USDA, 1933).

167. Beeman, "Chemivisions," 1994; and M. Finlay, "The Failure of Chemurgy in Depression-Era South: The Case of Jesse F. Jackson and the Central of Georgia Railroad," *Georgia Historical Quarterly* 81, no. 1 (1997): 78–102.

168. A. B. Effland, "'New Riches from the Soil': The Chemurgic Ideas of Wheeler McMillen," *Agricultural History* 69, no. 2 (1995): 288–97; and M. Finlay, "Old Efforts at New Uses: A Brief History of Chemurgy and the American Search for Biobased Materials," *Journal of Industrial Ecology* 7, nos. 3–4 (2008): 33–46.

169. R. A. Mullen, "Why Poison Bugs, Foes or Surpluses?" *Washington Post*, June 25, 1933.

170. B. M. Morin, *The Legacy of American Copper Smelting: Industrial Heritage versus Environmental Policy* (Knoxville: University of Tennessee Press, 2013); and LeCain, "Limits of 'Eco-Efficiency,'" 2000.

CHAPTER 2. COMMERCIALIZING CHEMICAL WARFARE

Thucydides, *History of the Peloponnesian War*, trans. R. Crawley (New York: E. P. Dutton, 1910).

1. D. Gibby et al., "The Master Gardener Program: A WSU Extension Success Story, Early History from 1973" (Pullman: Washington State University Extension, 2008).

2. E. Russell, *War and Nature: Fighting Humans and Insects with Chemicals from World War I to Silent Spring* (Cambridge: Cambridge University Press, 2001).

3. H. Friedlander, *The Origins of Nazi Genocide: From Euthanasia to the Final Solution* (Chapel Hill: University of North Carolina Press, 1995).

4. J. B. Tucker, *War of Nerves: Chemical Warfare from World War I to Al-Qaeda* (New York: Pantheon Books, 2006).

5. A. Leopold, "What Is a Weed?," in *The River of the Mother of God and Other Essays*, ed. B. Callicott and S. Flader (1943; repr., Madison: University of Wisconsin Press, 1992), 306–9.

6. M. Douglas, *Purity and Danger: An Analysis of the Concepts of Pollution and Taboo* (1966; repr., New York: Ark Paperbacks, 1988); and H. Raffles, "Jews, Lice, and History," *Public Culture* 19, no. 3 (2007): 521–66.

7. E. P. Evans, *The Criminal Prosecution and Punishment of Animals: The Lost History of Europe's Animals Trials* (1906; repr., London: Faber and Faber, 1987); and D. Dinzelbacher, "Animal Trials: A Multidisciplinary Approach," *Journal of Interdisciplinary History* 32, no. 3 (2002): 405–21.

8. Evans, *Criminal Prosecution*, 1987, 200.

9. *Oxford English Dictionary* (Oxford: Oxford University Press, 2005).

10. "Slandered Insects," *Constitution*, August 1, 1876.

11. P. Howell, "Animals, Agency, and History," in *The Routledge Companion to Animal-Human History*, ed. H. Kean and O. Howell (New York: Taylor & Francis, 2018), 197–221.

12. T. Mitchell, *Rule of Experts: Egypt, Techno-Politics, Modernity* (Berkeley: University of California Press, 2002).

13. "Humans Face Insect War," *New York Times*, June 20, 1926.

14. "War on Insect Pests. Poison, Petrol, and 'Planes," *Observer*, September 22, 1935.

15. Anonymous, "Fighting Our Insect Enemies: Achievement of Professional Entomology," in *Agriculture Information Bulletin* no. 121 (Washington, DC: USDA, Agricultural Research Service, 1954).

16. E. Russell, "War on Insects: Warfare, Insecticides, and Environmental Change in the United States, 1870–1945" (PhD diss., University of Michigan, 1993); and R. Bannister, *Social Darwinism: Science and Myth in Anglo-American Social Thought* (Atlanta, GA: Temple University Press, 2010).

17. G. A. Fine and L. Christoforides, "Dirty Birds, Filthy Immigrants, and the English Sparrow War: Metaphorical Linkage in Constructing Social Problems," *Symbolic Interaction* 14, no. 4 (1991): 375–93; P. Coates, *American Perceptions of Immigrant and Invasive Species: Strangers on the Land* (Berkeley: University of California Press, 2006); and J. N. Shinozuka, "Deadly Perils: Japanese Beetles and the Pestilent Immigrant, 1920s–1930s," *American Quarterly* 65, no. 4 (2013): 831–52.

18. R. Carson, *Silent Spring* (1962; repr., New York: Mariner Books, 2002), 297.

19. Evans, *Criminal Prosecution*, 1906, 53.

20. C. McWilliams, *Factories in the Field*, vol. 342 (Berkeley: University of California Press, 1935); C. McWilliams, *Southern California: An Island on the Land* (Salt Lake City, UT: Gibbs Smith, 1946); R. S. Street, *Beasts of the Field: A Narrative History of California Farmworkers, 1769-1913* (Stanford, CA: Stanford University Press, 2004); and D. C. Sackman, *Orange Empire: California and the Fruits of Eden* (Berkeley: University of California Press, 2005).

21. J. M. Guinn, "From Cattle Ranch to Orange Grove," *Annual Publication of the Historical Society of Southern California* 8, no. 3 (1912): 145–57; W. A. Spalding, "Early Chapters in the History of California Citrus Culture," *California Citrograph* 7, no. 4 (1922): 94–95, 122–24, 150–51; and H. J. Webber and L. D. Batchelor, *The Citrus Industry*, vol. I, *History, Botany and Breeding* (Berkeley: University of California Press, 1943).

22. L. M. Holt, "Orange Tree Diseases," *Southern California Horticulturist* 1, no. 2 (1877): 61–62; S. Bristol, "The Oleander and Orange Scale-Bug," *Southern California Horticulturist* 1, no. 12: 374–75; "The Red Scale,"

Southern California Horticulturist 2, no. 9 (1879): 280; and L. M. Holt, "The Red Scale on Citrus Trees," *Pacific Rural Press* 19, no. 5 (1880): 67.

23. California State Agricultural Society, *Table of Statistics: Transactions of the California State Agricultural Society* (Sacramento: California State Agricultural Society, 1872).

24. W. Spalding, *The Orange: Its Culture in California: With a Brief Discussion of the Lemon* (Riverside, CA: Press and Horticulturist Steam Press, 1885); Webber and Batchelor, *Citrus Industry*, 1943; and Sackman, *Orange Empire*, 2005.

25. J. E. Coit, *Citrus Fruits: An Account of the Citrus Industry with Special Reference to California Requirement and Practices and Similar Conditions* (New York: Macmillan, 1915).

26. "Wolfskill of Los Angeles and His Vineyard," *Daily Alta California*, December 20, 1858; "History of the Orange in Los Angeles," *Los Angeles Herald*, April 5, 1882; H. D. Barrows, "William Wolfskill, the Pioneer," *Annual Publication of the Historical Society of Southern California and of the Pioneers of Los Angeles County* (1902): 287–94; and I. H. Wilson, *William Wolfskill, 1798–1866: Frontier Trapper to California Ranchero* (Glendale, CA: Arthur H. Clark, 1965).

27. W. Wolfskill, "Petition for Guillermo Wolfskill for Grant of Agricultural Parcel," 1836, Los Angeles City Archives, 1836–1872, USC Digital Archive; and "Wolfskill of Los Angeles," *Daily Alta California*, 1858.

28. "California Wine-Growers Association: Secretary's Report," *Daily Alta California*, June 25, 1863.

29. "Advertisement: Grape Cuttings: Grape Cuttings," *Sacramento Daily Union*, April 9, 1851; and "Later from the South: Arrival of the Southerner," *Daily Alta California*, September 5, 1854.

30. I. A. Wilson, "Early Southern California Viniculture, 1830–1865," *Historical Society of Southern California Quarterly* 39, no. 3 (1957): 242–50; and Spalding, *The Orange*, 1885.

31. "Death of William Wolfskill," *Daily Alta California*, October 5, 1866; J. J. Wolfskill, "William Wolkskill, the Pioneer," *Daily Alta California*, October 12, 1866; and A. Solano, "Land of L. Wolfskill in the Rancho Santa Anita," 1871, Maps, Huntington Digital Library, San Marino, CA.

32. G. C. Knox, "Map of the Wolfskill Orchard," 1886, Maps, Huntington Digital Library, San Marino, CA; and Hansen and Solano Co., "Moulton Crystal Springs Property of J. W. Wolfskill on the East Side of the Los Angeles River," 1888, Maps, Huntington Digital Library, San Marino, CA.

33. "Agricultural Notes: California—Los Angeles," *Pacific Rural Press* 3, no. 14 (April 6, 1872): 213.

34. "Pacific Coast Items," *Sacramento Daily Union*, March 18, 1874.

35. "Orange Culture," *California Farmer and Journal of Useful Sciences* 49, no. 4 (September 5, 1878); and "Practical Agriculture: Orange Culture in California," *Sacramento Daily Union*, January 3, 1880.

36. "Horticulture: Los Angeles Fruit Growers Association," *Pacific Rural Press* 13, no. 20 (May 19, 1877): 307; "Agricultural Notes: California—Los Angeles," *Pacific Rural Press* 13, no. 9 (March 3, 1877): 133; "Growing

Interest—the Money in Raising Oranges," *Los Angeles Herald*, August 25, 1878; and Street, *Beasts of the Field*, 2004.

37. "Agricultural Notes," *Daily Alta California*, February 28, 1885.

38. "Entomological: Citrus Scale and Their Foes," *Pacific Rural Press*, March 10, 1883.

39. D. W. Coquillet, "Talks with Citizens," *Los Angeles Times*, May 27, 1888.

40. A. F. Kercheval, "What Shall We Do about the Scale?," *Los Angeles Times*, March 22, 1885.

41. "Agricultural Notes," *Daily Alta California*, 1885.

42. A. F. Kercheval, "What Shall We Do about the Scale?," *Los Angeles Times*, March 22, 1885; A. F. Kercheval, "Shall the White Scale Go, or Shall We?," *Los Angeles Times*, July 11, 1886; D. W. Coquillet, "Farm and Range: Cotton Cushiony Scale, Experiments with Remedies for Their Destruction," *Los Angeles Times*, July 18, 1886; D. W. Coquillet, "Insect Killing by Fumigation: An Essay Read at the Santa Barbara Convention of Fruit Growers," *Pacific Rural Press* 35, no. 18 (May 5, 1888): 404; D. W. Coquillet, "Report on the Gas Treatment for Scale Insects," in *Agriculture Yearbook for 1887* (Washington, DC: USDA, 1888), 123–42; D. W. Coquillet, "Entomological: Origin of the Gas Treatment for Scale Insect," *Pacific Rural Press* 35, no. 18 (September 5, 1891): 193; and "The White Scale: Some Terribly Infested Orange Groves; Where Are the Inspectors?," *Los Angeles Herald*, June 12, 1886.

43. W. A. Henry, "Pacific Coast Work of the Division of Entomology," *Insect Life* 2, no. 5 (1889): 141–44; D. W. Coquillet, "Another Foe for Icerya," *Pacific Rural Press* 40, no. 26 (December 27, 1890): 551; and Coquillet, "Entomological: Origin of the Gas Treatment," 1891.

44. Coquillet, "Talks with Citizens," 1888.

45. D. W. Coquillet, "US Department of Agriculture Report for 1886" (Washington, DC: USDA, 1887).

46. "State Notes," *Daily Alta California*, June 30, 1886; and E. O. Essig, *A History of Entomology* (New York: Hafner Publishing, 1931).

47. "Entomological: Citrus Scale and Their Foes," 1883, 205.

48. A. Craw quoted in Coquillet, "Insect Killing," 1888.

49. A. Craw quoted in Coquillet, "Insect Killing," 1888.

50. A. F. Kercheval, "Letters to the Times: Are the Bugs Sick?," *Los Angeles Times*, October 4, 1888.

51. Coquillet, "USDA Report for 1886," 1887; and A. Koebele, "US Department of Agriculture Report for 1886" (Washington, DC: USDA, 1887), 558–69.

52. For example, G. Dimmock, "The Effect of a Few Common Gases on Arthropods," *Psyche: A Journal of Entomology* 2, nos. 35–36 (1877): 19–22.

53. "The Gas Treatment for Scales," *Pacific Rural Press* 33, no. 21 (July 30, 1887): 85; Coquillet, "Insect Killing," 1888; and Coquillet, "Report on Gas Treatment," 1888.

54. E. Hilgard, "Science in the Orchard," *Riverside Daily Press* (Riverside, CA), April 16, 1895.

55. Coquillet, "Insect Killing," 1888; and Coquillet, "Report on Gas Treatment," 1888.

56. Coquillet, "Report on the Gas Treatment for Scale Insects," 1888, 123–42.

57. Coquillet, "Insect Killing," 1888.

58. Coquillet, "Insect Killing," 1888.

59. Coquillet, "Entomological: Origin of the Gas Treatment," 1891; C. W. Woodworth and M. B. Messenger, "Introductory Lecture: School of Fumigation" (paper presented at the School of Fumigation, Conducted by C. W. Woodworth, University of California, Pomona, 1915).

60. F. W. Morse, "The Uses of Gases against Scale Insects," *California Agricultural Experiment Station Bulletin* 71 (1887); F. W. Morse, "Use of Hydrocyanic Acid against Scale Insects," *California Agricultural Experiment Station Bulletin* 73 (1887); and "Gas Treatment for Scales," *Pacific Rural Press*, 1887.

61. Morse, "Use of Hydrocyanic Acid," 1887; and F. W. Morse, "Entomological: Comments by Mr. Morse," *Pacific Rural Press* 42, no. 10 (September 5, 1891): 193.

62. A. C. Chapman, "Letter to the Editor," *Pacific Rural Press* 33, no. 25 (June 18, 1887): 539.

63. Morse, "Use of Hydrocyanic Acid," 1887.

64. Essig, *History of Entomology*, 1931.

65. J. P. Culver, "Tree Cover and Fumigator," Patent #367,134, US Patent Office, 1887.

66. "Entomological: More Foes of Icerya," *Pacific Rural Press* 36, no. 26 (December 29, 1888): 556.

67. A. Romero, "Beyond the Mother Lode: Synthetic Cyanide and the Chemicalization of California Gold Mining (1885–1905)," *California History* 95, no. 1 (2018): 2–24.

68. E. M. Scheidel, "The Cyanide Process: Its Practical Application and Economical Results," in *California State Mining Bureau Bulletin*, ed. J. J. Crawford (Sacramento, 1894); J. S. MacArthur, "Gold Extraction by Cyanide: A Retrospective," *Journal of the Society of Chemical Industry* 24, no. 7 (1905): 311–15.

69. "Financial Records 2297–2299," 1900, Yellow Aster Mining and Milling Company Records, 1898–1918, California State Library, Sacramento; F. W. Braun, "The Manufacture of Sodium Cyanide" (paper presented at the School of Fumigation, Conducted by C. W. Woodworth, University of California, Pomona, 1915); M. Wolf, *It All Began in Frankfurt: Landmarks in the History of Degussa Ag* (Frankfurt am Maim, Germany: Degussa AG, 1985); A. L. Loughheed, "The Anatomy of an International Cyanide Cartel: Cyanide, 1897–1927," *Prometheus* 19, no. 1 (2001): 1–10; and Romero, "Beyond the Mother Lode," 2018.

70. J. E. Carter and G. E. Scattergood, "Transfer Ledger Binder," 1913, Carter and Scattergood Business Records, Hagley Library and Archive, Wilmington, DE; J. E. Carter and G. E. Scattergood, "Agreement of Sale to the Henry Bower Chemical Manufacturing Company," 1911, Carter and Scattergood Business Records, Hagley Library and Archive, Wilmington, DE; S. P. Sadtler,"Early Chemical Manufacture in Philadelphia," *Journal of Industrial and Engineering Chemistry* 8, no. 12 (1916): 1153–57; "History of American Chemical Industries: Roessler and Hasslacher–Partners," *Industrial & Engineering Chemistry* 21, no. 10 (1929): 989–91; DuPont, "Digest, R&H Chemical Company,

Subsidiaries and Affiliates," 1930, Absorbed Companies, Records of E. I. du Pont de Nemours, Hagley Library and Archive, Wilmington, DE; and Wolf, *It All Began in Frankfurt*, 1985.

71. Braun, "Manufacture of Sodium Cyanide," 1915.

72. F. W. Morse, "Doses of Acids of Different Strengths," *Pacific Rural Press* 34, no. 10 (September 3, 1887): 182; and F. W. Morse, "Scale Insects. The Use of Hydrocyanic Acid to Exterminate Them," *Sacramento Daily Union*, September 3, 1887.

73. "Horticulture: The Fumigation of Trees without the Use of Carbonate of Soda," *Daily Alta California*, December 9, 1887; Coquillet, "Another Foe," 1890; and Coquillet, "Entomological: Origin of the Gas Treatment," 1891.

74. Woodworth and Messenger, "Introductory Lecture," 1915.

75. W. B. Wall, M. S. Jones, and A. D. Bishop, "Process of Fumigating Trees and Other Plants," Patent #445,342, US Patent Office, 1891; and "Patent Twilight: The Orange Tree Fumigator Patent to Be Bought," *Los Angeles Herald*, May 30, 1891.

76. C. V. Riley, "Importation of Icerya Enemies from Australia," *Pacific Rural Press* 38, no. 25 (December 21, 1889): 570; and R. L. Doutt, "Vice, Virtue, and Vedalia," *Bulletin of the Entomological Society of America* 4, no. 4 (1958): 119–23.

77. "Chasing a Beetle: Our Foreign Relations with the Icerya Purchase, an Enthusiastic Entomologist, Surprising Adventures of One of Our State Department Diplomats in Search of a Bug," *Daily Alta California*, April 30, 1890.

78. "Entomological: More Foes of Icerya," *Pacific Rural Press*, 1888.

79. A. Koebele, "Report of a Trip to Australia Made under Direction of the Entomologist to Investigate the Natural Enemies of the Fluted Scale," *Division of Entomology Bulletin* 21. (Washington, DC: USDA, 1890), 1–32.

80. J. C. Carr, "The Blessed Bugs," *Pacific Rural Press* 37, no. 20 (May 18, 1889): 481; and J. R. Dobbins, "Extracts from Correspondence: The Spread of the Australian Lady-Bird," *Insect Life* II (1889): 112.

81. L. E. Caltagirone and R. L. Doutt, "The History of the Vedalia Beetle Importation to California and Its Impact on the Development of Biological Control," *Annual Review of Entomology* 34 (1989): 1–16; and R. C. Sawyer, *To Make a Spotless Orange: Biological Control in California*, Henry Wallace Series on Agriculture and Rural Life (Ames: Iowa State University Press, 1996).

82. B. M. Lelong, "Improved Fumigating Apparatus," in *Annual Report* (Sacramento: State Board of Horticulture of the State of California, 1890), 469–72; and C. W. Woodworth, "Agricultural Experiment Station Bulletin 122: Orchard Fumigation" (Berkeley: University of California, 1899).

83. "Horticultural Commission: What the Australian Bugs Are Doing for Southern California," *Los Angeles Times*, September 8, 1889.

84. J. E. Bennet, "Black Scale Pest: Lively Enemy of the California Horticulturist," *Los Angeles Times*, March 1, 1896; "Hunting for Enemies of the Red Scale: Mischievous Foe of Oranges Is Hard to Combat," *Los Angeles Times*, November 23, 1902; "Purple Scale Disappearing: Speaker at Farmers' Institute Meeting Gives Encouraging Address on Tree Fumigation," *Los Angeles Times*, September 20, 1906; "After the Scale Pest: Black and Purple Varieties Especially

Guarded against by County Horticulturist," *Los Angeles Times*, July 26, 1912; C. C. Chapman, "The Purple Scale in Fullerton," *Claremont Pomological Club Proceedings* (March 22, 1909): 4–5; J. R. Horton, *Control of the Argentine Ant in Orange Groves*, Farmer's Bulletin, vol. 928 (Washington, DC: US Department of Agriculture, 1918); A. M. Boyce, "Studies on the Resistance of Certain Insects to Hydrocyanic Acid," *Journal of Economic Entomology* 21, no. 5 (1928): 715–20; G. P. Gray and A. Kirkpatrick, "The Resistance of Black Scale (Saissetia Oleae Bern.) to Hydrocyanic Acid Fumigation," *Journal of Economic Entomology* 22, no. 6 (1929): 893–97; R. S. Woglum, "The History of Hydrocyanic and Gas Fumigation as an Index to Progress in Economic Entomology," *Journal of Economic Entomology* 16, no. 6 (1923): 518–21; R. S. Woglum, "Observations on Insects Developing Immunity to Insecticides," *Journal of Economic Entomology* 18, no. 4 (1925): 593–97; and Essig, *History of Entomology*, 1933.

85. "The Night Process: The Gas Treatment in the Courts," *Los Angeles Times*, October 20, 1893.

86. "The Patent of the Gas Treatment Declared Void," *Pacific Rural Press* 47, no. 17 (April 28, 1894): 326.

87. Quoted in "The Night Process," *Los Angeles Times*, 1893.

88. D. W. Coquilett, "The Patent on Hydrocyanic Acid Gas Process Declared Invalid," *Insect Life* 7, no. 3 (1894): 257–58.

89. Coquilett, "The Patent on Hydrocyanic Acid Gas Process."

90. "A County Fumigation Outfit," *Pacific Rural Press* 56, no. 12 (September 17, 1898): 188; and "Will Study Fumigation: Berkeley Man Will Spend a Month Experimenting in the South," *San Francisco Chronicle*, August 18, 1902.

91. "Covina," *Los Angeles Times*, August 9, 1896.

92. C. W. Woodworth, "The Insecticide Industries in California," *Journal of Economic Entomology* 5, no. 4 (1912): 358–64; G. P. Gray, "The Workings of the California Insecticide Law," *Journal of Industrial and Engineering Chemistry* 6, no. 7 (1914): 590–94; and G. P. Gray, "The Consumption and Cost of Economic Poisons in California in 1916," *Industrial & Engineering Chemistry* 10, no. 4 (1918): 301–2.

93. E. Cooper, "Insects and Insecticides" (Sacramento: California State Commission of Horticulture, 1905), 1–23.

94. "The Land: Orchard, Farm, Garden, Rancho, and Stockyard," *Los Angeles Times*, October 5, 1900.

95. J. W. Jeffreys, "The Land: Orchard, Farm, Garden, Rancho and Stockyard," *Los Angeles Times*, August 17, 1900.

96. Sackman, *Orange Empire*, 2005.

97. G. H. Powell, "Causes of Fruit Decay," *Riverside Daily Press*, April 7, 1905; and G. H. Powell, "The Decay of Oranges While in Transit from California," in *Bulletin* (Washington, DC: USDA Bureau of Plant Industry, 1908), 1–79.

98. Coit, *Citrus Fruits*, 1915.

99. Jeffreys, "Land, Orchard, Farm," 1900; Webber and Batchelor, *Citrus Industry*, 1943; and W. Reuther, E .C. Calavan, and G. E. Carman, eds., *The Citrus Industry*, vol. V (Oakland: University of California, Agriculture and Natural Resources, 1989).

100. C. H. Shinn, "The Fruit Industry of California," *Popular Science Monthly* 44, no. December (1893): 200–217.

101. P. K. Wilson, "Headquarters for Defense," *Los Angeles Times*, March 13, 1932; A. Shoenfield, "Insect War Ceaseless: Man's Dominion Challenged," *Los Angeles Times*, October 6, 1929; E. O. Essig, "Insects and Agriculture," *Journal of Economic Entomology* 26, no. 4 (1933): 869–72; D. Aikman, "War to the Hilt on Insects!," *New York Times*, August 1, 1937; R. P. Brundage, "Orange Pests Develop Resistance to Poisons, Cost Growers Millions," *Wall Street Journal*, August 3, 1946; and J. E. McWilliams, *American Pests: Losing the War on Insects from Colonial Times to DDT* (New York: Columbia University Press, 2008).

102. Woodworth, "Agricultural Experiment Station Bulletin 122: Orchard Fumigation," 1899. By this time cyanide fumigation had also become a common industry practice of West Coast nurseries and quarantine operations. In 1894, L. O. Howard, recently appointed chief of the USDA Bureau of Entomology, introduced cyanide fumigation to East Coast nurserymen in a USDA circular, and by 1896 it was in limited but general use in the nursery trade across the United States. By 1900, there was a network of specialized buildings across the United States constructed for the sole purpose of fumigating nursery stock, creating a nodal geography of agroindustrial gas chambers. Cyanide fumigation was also introduced to other commercial orange-growing regions in the 1890s. For example, C. V. Riley, former chief of the Bureau of Entomology, introduced it to Montserrat, British West Indies, in 1894, and word of its success reached Cape Town, South Africa, about the same time. Although the UC Agriculture Extension and the USDA would eventually help the practice spread to citrus-growing regions around the world, early extension of the practice into other citrus-growing regions met with commercial failure, likely due in part to the lack of intensive and cooperative organizational structure of Southern California's industry and the lack of government subsidy (public research and county equipment) that first brought cyanide fumigation within reach of the average grower. R. S. Woglum of the USDA introduced Florida citrus to California's fumigation techniques in 1905. L. O. Howard, "An Important Enemy to Fruit Trees. The San Jose Scale (*Aspidiotus pernidosus*): Its Appearance in the Eastern United States; Measures to Be Taken to Prevent Its Spread and Destroy It," *Circular 3*, Second Series (Washington, DC: USDA Division of Entomology, 1894); L. O. Howard and C. L. Marlatt, "The San José Scale: Its Occurrence in the United States with a Full Account of Its Life History and the Remedies to Be Used against It," *Bulletin 3, New Series* (Washington, DC: USDA Division of Entomology, 1896); L. O. Howard, "Progress in Economic Entomology in the United States," in *Yearbook of Department of Agriculture for 1899* (Washington, DC: USDA, 1899); C. Pugsley, "Gas Treatment for Scale Insects: Treating of the Operations of the Horticultural's Board Fumigating Outfit, the Applicability of the Fumigation Process in Cape Colony, and Embodying a Full Description of the Equipment Necessary for Fumigation with Hydrocyanic Acid Gas," Horticultural Board of the Cape Colony (Cape Town, South Africa: Taylor Townshend, & Snashall, 1897); H. J. Quayle, "Correspondence between H. J. Quayle and the University of California Agricultural

Departments as Well as Horticultural and Entomological Agencies throughout the World, 1908–1914," 1910, Henry J. Quayle Papers, UC Riverside Special Collections, Riverside, CA; and Essig, *History of Entomology*, 1931.

103. Shinn, "Fruit Industry," 1893; and "Will Study Fumigation," *San Francisco Chronicle*, 1902.

104. "The Land: Orchard, Farm, Garden," *Los Angeles Times*, 1900.

105. "Hague Convention of 1899."

106. L. Raemaekers, "The Gas Fiend," in *Raemaekers' Cartoons with Accompanying Notes by Well-Known English Writers*, ed. F. Stopford (London: Doubleday, Page, 1916); and M. G. Dorsey, "More Than Just Taboo: The Legacy of the Chemical Warfare Prohibitions of the 1899 and 1907 Hague Conferences," in *War, Peace and International Order? The Legacies of the Hague Conference of 1899 and 1907*, ed. M. Abbenhuis, C. Barber, and A. Higgins (New York: Routledge, 2017), 86–102.

107. L. May, *War Crimes and Just War* (Cambridge: Cambridge University Press, 2007).

108. M. Walzer, *Just and Unjust Wars: A Moral Argument with Historical Illustrations* (New York: Basic Books, 1977); J. T. Johnson, *Just War Tradition and the Restraint of War: A Moral and Historical Inquiry* (Princeton, NJ: Princeton University Press, 1981); and R. Regan, *Just War: Principles and Cases*, 2nd ed. (Washington, DC: Catholic University of America Press, 2013).

109. J. Kosek, "Ecologies of Empire: On the New Uses of the Honeybee," *Cultural Anthropology* 25, no. 4 (2010): 650–78, 669.

110. R. Carson, "Women's National Press Club Speech," in *Lost Woods: The Discovered Writing of Rachel Carson*, ed. L. Lear (1962; rcpr., Boston: Beacon Press, 2002), 201–10.

111. R. H. Lutts, "Chemical Fallout: Rachel Carson's Silent Spring, Radioactive Fallout, and the Environmental Movement," *Environmental Review* 9, no. 3 (1985): 210–25; C. Glotfelty, "Cold War, Silent Spring: The Trope of War in Modern Environmentalism," in *And No Birds Sing: Rhetorical Analyses of Rachel Carson's Silent Spring*, ed. C. Waddell (Carbondale: Southern Illinois University Press, 2000), 157–73; and P. Cafaro, "Rachel Carson's Environmental Ethics," in *Linking Ecology and Ethics in a Changing World: Values, Philosophy, and Action*, ed. R. Rozzi, S. Pickett, C. Palmer, J. Armesto, and J. Callicott (New York: Springer, 2013), 163–72.

112. Carson, "Women's National Press Club Speech," 2002, 210.

113. Carson, *Silent Spring*, 2002.

114. D. Vail, *Chemical Lands: Pesticides, Aerial Spraying, and Health in North America's Grasslands since 1945* (Tuscaloosa: University of Alabama Press, 2018).

115. F. Davis, *Banned: A History of Pesticides and the Science of Toxicology* (New Haven, CT: Yale University Press, 2014), xi.

116. D. Zwerdling, "The Farm Labor Climax: Pesticides, Another Hazard for Farm Laborers," *Los Angeles Times*, September 9, 1973; J. B. Gordon, "Perilous DDT Ban," *New York Times*, September 16, 1972; and J. B. Flippen, "Pest, Pollution, and Politics: The Nixon Administration's Pesticide Policy," *Agricultural History* 71, no. 4 (1997): 442–56.

117. B. Williams, "'That We May Live': Pesticides, Plantations, and Environmental Racism in the United States South," *Environment and Planning E: Nature and Space* 1–2 (2018): 243–67.

118. Brundage, "Orange Pests Develop Resistance to Poisons," 1946.

CHAPTER 3. MANUFACTURING PETROTOXICITY

Paracelsus, *Dritte Defensio*, 1538.

1. Anonymous, Notecard, William H. Volck File, Pajaro Valley Historical Association, Watsonville, CA.

2. H. V. Moses, "Machines in the Garden: A Citrus Monopoly in Riverside, 1900–1936," *California History* 61, no. 1 (1982): 26–35; R. Tobey and C. Wetherell, "The Citrus Industry and the Revolution of Corporate Capitalism in Southern California, 1887–1944," *California History* 74, no. 1 (1995): 6–21; H. V. Moses, "'The Orange-Grower Is Not a Farmer': G. Harold Powell, Riverside Orchardists, and the Coming of Industrial Agriculture, 1893–1930," *California History* 74, no. 1 (1995): 22–37; and D. C. Sackman, *Orange Empire: California and the Fruits of Eden* (Berkeley: University of California Press, 2005).

3. B. Holden, *Charles W. Woodworth: The Remarkable Life of U.C. First Entomologist* (n.p.: Brian Holden Publishing, 2015).

4. "Establish Their Own Laboratory," *Berkeley Daily Gazette*, January 26, 1904, 8.

5. "What Two Young Men Did," *Pacific Rural Press* 98, no. 24 (December 13, 1919): 810.

6. "Fight Fruit Pests," *Berkeley Daily Gazette*, May 31, 1904, 1.

7. H. F. Williamson, R. L. Andreano, A. R. Daum, and G. C. Klose, *The American Petroleum Industry: The Age of Energy, 1899–1959* (Evanston, IL: Northwestern University Press, 1963).

8. P. Sabin, *Crude Politics: The California Oil Market, 1900–1940* (Berkeley: University of California Press, 2005).

9. Sabin, *Crude Politics*, 2005.

10. "Oceans of Oil," *Los Angeles Times*, September 24, 1907.

11. "Refining Business Makes Rapid Strides," *Los Angeles Times*, July 20, 1913.

12. "Scientists Will Tell How to Kill Scale Curse," *Oakland Tribune*, July 18, 1903, 14.

13. W. H. Volck, "Bulletin No. 153: Spraying with Distillates" (Sacramento: College of Agriculture, Agricultural Experiment Station, University of California, 1903).

14. L. A. Riehl, "The Use of Petroleum Oil Fractions as Insecticides on Citrus in California," in *The Third World Petroleum Congress Proceedings: Section V*, ed. E. J. Brill (The Hague: World Petroleum Congress, 1951), 204.

15. "Advises Caution in the Use of Oils: Too Much Will Ruin Trees, So Says Entomologist Volck," *San Francisco Call*, August 15, 1903.

16. C. Ellis, *The Chemistry of Petroleum Derivatives*, vol. 1 (New York: Chemical Catalog, 1934); and P. K. Frolich, "Chemical Trends in the Petroleum Industry," *Industrial & Engineering Chemistry* 30, no. 8 (1938): 916–22.

17. R. K. Vickery, "Petroleum Insecticides," *Journal of Economic Entomology* 13, no. 6 (1920): 444–47; E. R. De Ong, "Technical Aspects of Petroleum Oils and Oil Sprays," *Journal of Economic Entomology* 5, no. 1 (1926): 733–45; and N. Turner, "Standardized Oil Sprays," *Journal of Economic Entomology* 24, no. 4 (1931): 901–4.

18. For example, S. Frickel, *Chemical Consequences: Environmental Mutagens, Scientist Activism, and the Rise of Genetic Toxicology* (New Brunswick, NJ: Rutgers University Press, 2004); M. Murphy, *Sick Building Syndrome and the Problem of Uncertainty: Environmental Politics, Technoscience, and Women Workers* (Durham, NC: Duke University Press, 2006); L. Nash, *Inescapable Ecologies: A History of Environment, Disease, and Knowledge* (Berkeley: University of California Press, 2006); D. Rosner and G. Markowitz, "The Politics of Lead Toxicology and the Devastating Consequences for Children," *American Journal of Industrial Medicine* 50, no. 10 (2007): 740–56; K. Fortun and M. Fortun, "Scientific Imaginaries and Ethical Plateaus in Contemporary U.S. Toxicology," *American Anthropologist* 107, no. 1 (2008): 43–54; B. Walker, *Toxic Archipelago: A History of Industrial Disease in Japan* (Seattle: University of Washington Press, 2010); D. Arnold, "Pollution, Toxicity, and Public Health in Metropolitan India, 1850–1939," *Journal of Historical Geography* 42 (2013): 124–33; F. R. Davis, *Banned: A History of Pesticides and the Science of Toxicology* (New Haven, CT: Yale University Press, 2014); and E. Hepler-Smith, "Molecular Bureaucracy: Toxicological Information and Environmental Protection," *Environmental History* 24, no. 3 (2019): 534–60.

19. M. A. Gallo, "History and Scope of Toxicology," in *Casarett & Doull's Essential of Toxicology*, ed. C. D. Klaassen and J. B. Watkins III (New York: McGraw-Hill, 2015), 3–11.

20. G. P. Gray, "Economic Toxicology," *Science* 48, no. 12 (1918): 329–32.

21. C. W. Woodworth, "Fumigation Dosage," in *Bulletin 152*, ed. Experiment Station, College of Agriculture (Berkeley: University of California Publications, 1903); R. S. Woglum, "Bulletin No. 79—Fumigation Investigations in California" (Washington, DC: Bureau of Entomology, USDA, 1909); C. W. Woodworth, "Leakage of Fumigation Tents," *Journal of Economic Entomology* 4, no. 4 (1911): 376–80; C. W. Woodworth, "New Dosage Tables: Fumigation Studies No. 7" (Berkeley: College of Agriculture, Agricultural Experiment Station, University of California Publications, 1915), 1–20; C. W. Woodworth, "Theory of Toxicity," *Journal of Economic Entomology* 8, no. 6 (1915): 509–12; C. W. Woodworth, "The Toxicity of Insecticides," *Science* 41, no. 1053 (1915): 367–69; and R. S. Woglum, "Bulletin No. 907—Fumigation of Citrus Plants with Hydrocyanic Acid: Conditions Influencing Injury" (Washington, DC: USDA, 1920).

22. H. J. Quayle, "Are Scales Becoming Resistant to Fumigation?," *University of California Journal of Agriculture* 3, no. 8 (1916): 333–34, 358; and H. J. Quayle, "The Development of Resistance to Hydrocyanic Acid in Certain Scale Insects," *Hilgardia* 11, no. 5 (1938): 183–210.

23. "Sprays Damage Suit Opens: Horticultural Experts Gathered at Santa Ana in $40,000 Action Brought by Rancher," *Los Angeles Times*, February 16, 1926; H. Knight, J. C. Chamberlin, and C. D. Samuels, "On Some Limiting

Factors in the Use of Saturated Petroleum Oils as Insecticides," *Plant Physiology* 4, no. 3 (1929): 299–321; P. A. Young and H. E. Morris, "Injury to Apple by Petroleum-Oil Sprays," *Journal of Agricultural Research* 47, no. 7 (1933): 505–22; R. P. Tucker, "Oil Sprays: Chemical Properties of Petroleum Oil Unsaturates Causing Injury to Foliage," *Industrial & Engineering Chemistry* 28, no. 4 (1936): 458–61; and R. P. Brundage, "Orange Pests Develop Resistance to Poisons, Cost Growers Millions," *Wall Street Journal*, August 3, 1946.

24. J. G. Speight, *The Chemistry and Technology of Petroleum*, 5th ed. (Boca Raton, FL: Taylor & Francis, 2014).

25. G. T. Walker, *Petroleum: Its History, Occurrence, Production, Uses and Tests* (Minneapolis, MN: Imperial Printing, 1915); "Behind the Scenes in the Oil Industry," *Standard Oil Bulletin* 15, no. 8 (1927): 1; H. F. Williamson, A. R. Daum, and G. C. Klose, *The American Petroleum Industry: The Age of Illumination, 1859–1899* (Evanston, IL: Northwestern University Press, 1963); and S. Manager, *Living Oil: Petroleum Culture in the American Century* (Oxford: Oxford University Press, 2014).

26. G. Bridge and P. Le Billon, *Oil* (Cambridge, MA: Polity Press, 2013), I.

27. Ellis, *Petroleum Derivatives*, 1934.

28. C. Ellis, *The Chemistry of Petroleum Derivatives*, vol. 2 (New York: Reinhold, 1937).

29. W. Boyd, W. S. Prudham, and R. A. Schurman, "Industrial Dynamics and the Problem of Nature," *Society & Natural Resources* 7, no. 7 (2001): 555–70.

30. W. Isard and E. W. Schooler, "Location Factors in the Petrochemical Industry with Special Reference to the Future Expansion in the Arkansas-White-Red River Basins," US Department of Commerce (Washington, DC: Office of Technical Services, 1955); and G. Henderson, *California and the Fictions of Capital* (Oxford, UK: Oxford University Press, 1999).

31. "California Leads in Oil," *Los Angeles Herald*, December 22, 1907; "Oceans of Oil," *Los Angeles Times*, 1907; and Sabin, *Crude Politics*, 2005.

32. J. D. Gladding, "El Segundo to Be Big Oil Center," *Los Angeles Herald*, October 31, 1914.

33. "Oiling the Levees," *San Francisco Call*, October 22, 1903; "Oil's By-Products: Hundreds of Thousands of Dollars They Amount to Every Year in Los Angeles," *Los Angeles Times*, June 11, 1905; "Standard Oil to Double Capacity of Its Refinery," *San Francisco Call*, September 2, 1911; "Refining Business," *Los Angeles Times*, 1913; G. T. White, *Formative Years in the Far West: A History of Standard Oil Company and Predecessors through 1919* (New York: Appleton-Century-Crofts, 1962); Williamson, Daum, and Klose, *American Petroleum Industry*, 1963; and Sabin, *Crude Politics*, 2005.

34. C. V. Riley, "The Kerosene Emulsion: Its Origin, Nature, and Increasing Usefulness," *Proceedings of the Twelfth and Thirteenth Annual Meeting of the Society for the Promotion of Agricultural Science* (1892): 83–98; and E. G. Lodeman, *The Spraying of Plants: A Succinct Account of the History, Principles and Practice of the Application of Liquids and Powders to Plants for the Purpose of Destroying Insects and Fungi* (London: Macmillan, 1909).

35. "Crude Oil of Distillate Spray," *Pacific Rural Press* 61, no. 4 (January 26, 1901): 51; and P. R. Jones, "Oil Sprays—Five Years' Successful Use," *Better Fruit, Better Vegetables* 8, no. 7 (1914): 33–38.

36. "Crude Oil Emulsion Spraying," *Pacific Rural Press* 92, no. 24 (1916): 637.

37. "Oil Emulsion Too Strong," *Pacific Rural Press* 88, no. 20 (November 14, 1914).

38. A. L. Melander, "Can Insects Become Resistant to Sprays?," *Journal of Economic Entomology* 7, no. 2 (1914): 167–73.

39. Quayle, "Are Scales Becoming Resistant to Fumigation?," 1916; and Quayle, "Development of Resistance to Hydrocyanic Acid," 1938.

40. R. S. Woglum, "Observations on Insects Developing Immunity to Insecticides," *Journal of Economic Entomology* 18, no. 4 (1925): 593–97.

41. "After the Red Spider: Something More Terrible Than Horticulturalists Fighting Him," *Los Angeles Herald*, June 8, 1902; and H. J. Quayle, "Bulletin 234—Red Spiders and Mites of Citrus Trees" (Sacramento: College of Agriculture, Agricultural Experiment Station, University of California Publications, 1912).

42. "Working to Find Oil Insecticide," *La Habra Star*, December 18, 1925.

43. J. S. Ceccatti, "Natural Selection in the Field: Insecticide Resistance, Economic Entomology, and the Evolutionary Synthesis, 1914–1951," *Transactions of the American Philosophical Society* 99, no. 1 (2009): 199–217.

44. "Petroleum Orchard Sprays," *Standard Oil Bulletin* 11, no. 12 (1924): 2–3; M. B. Rounds, "Tests Show Value of Spraying for Control of Black Scale," *Los Angeles Times*, June 29, 1924; M. B. Rounds, "Get the Scale, Regardless of Methods," *Los Angeles Times*, October 18, 1925; R. S. Woglum, "The Use of Oil Sprays on Citrus Trees," *Journal of Economic Entomology* 19, no. 5 (1926): 733–45; de Ong, "Technical Aspects of Petroleum Oils," 1926; R. S. Woglum, "The Use of Oil Sprays on Citrus during 1926," *Journal of Economic Entomology* 21, no. 4 (1928): 530–31; and W. B. Herms, "An Analysis of Some of California's Major Entomological Problems," *Journal of Economic Entomology* 19, no. 2 (1926): 262–70.

45. Anonymous, "A Brief Chronological History of Ortho Division, Chevron Chemical Company," 1964, California Spray Chemical Company, Chevron Corporation Archive, Concord, CA; and L. R. Gardner, *The First Thirty Years: The Early History of the Company Now Known as Ortho Division, Chevron Chemical Company* (San Francisco, CA: Chevron Chemical Company, 1978).

46. For example, R. K. Vickery and A. C. Browne, *Handbook of Pest Control* (Watsonville: California Spray-Chemical Company, 1929); C. J. West, "Industrial Research Laboratories of the United States Including Consulting Research Laboratories," *Bulletin of the National Research Council* 81 (1931): 1–267; and W. H. Volck and R. W. Hunt, *Citrus Pests and Their Control: A Description of Various Citrus Pests of Economic Importance in California, with General Control Recommendations* (Berkeley: California Spray-Chemical Company, 1931).

47. C. W. Woodworth, "Petroleum Insecticides," *Journal of Economic Entomology* 23, no. 5 (1931): 848–51.

48. White, *Formative Years in the Far West*, 1962.

49. A. R. Hinton, "Development of California Petroleum Products," *Los Angeles Times*, January 1, 1916.

50. "The Romance of Gasoline: What Petroleum Gives Us Besides Gasoline," *Los Angeles Times*, July 26, 1925.

51. For example, "Advertisement for Oronite Cleaning Fluid: The Spotter," *Standard Oil Bulletin* 16, no. 3 (1928): 17.

52. "Understanding Oil Sprays," *Pacific Rural Press* 89, no. 11 (March 20, 1915): 360.

53. Vickery, "Petroleum Insecticides," 1920, 444.

54. E. R. de Ong (in cooperation with Shell Chemical Company), "Specifications for Petroleum Oils to Be Used on Plants," *Journal of Economic Entomology* 21, no. 5 (1928): 697–702.

55. Vickery, "Petroleum Insecticides," 1920, 444.

56. E. R. De Ong, *Chemistry and Uses of Insecticides* (New York: Reinhold Publishing Corporation, 1948).

57. G. P. Gray and E. R. de Ong, "California Petroleum Insecticides: Laboratory and Field Tests," *Industrial & Engineering Chemistry* 18, no. 2 (1926): 175–80; and Riehl, "Use of Petroleum Oil Fractions," 1951.

58. W. H. Volck, "Insecticide and Process of Making and Using the Same to Protect Plants," Patent #1,707,465, US Patent Office, 1929; W. H. Volck, "Fungicide," Patent #1,707,467, US Patent Office, 1929; and W. H. Volck, "Parasiticidal Oil," Patent #1,707,468, US Patent Office, 1929.

59. F. B. Herbert, "Spray Stimulation," *Journal of Economic Entomology* 17, no. 5 (1924): 567–72.

60. N. Rasmussen, "The Forgotten Promise of Thiamin: Merck, Caltech Biologists, and Plant Hormones in a 1930s Biotechnology Project," *Journal of the History of Biology* 32, no. 2 (1999): 245–61;and N. Rasmussen, "Plant Hormones in War and Peace: Science, Industry, and Government in the Development of Herbicides in 1940s America," *Isis* 92, no. 2 (2001): 291–316.

61. W. H. Volck, "Stimulation by Spraying," *Pacific Rural Press*, December 13, 1913.

62. W. S. Ballard and W. H. Volck, "Apple Powdery Mildew and Its Control in the Pajaro Valley (California)," in *United States Department of Agriculture Bulletin* 120 (Washington, DC: USDA, 1914).

63. W. H. Volck, "Process of Stimulating or Rejuvenating Plants and Composition for Use Therein," Patent #1,914,903, US Patent Office, 1933.

64. Herbert, "Spray Stimulation," 1924.

65. Jones, "Oil Sprays," 1914; W. C. Dutton, "The Effect of Some Spraying Materials upon the Rest Period of Fruit Trees," *Proceedings of the American Society of Horticultural Science* 21 (1925): 176–78; de Ong, "Technical Aspects of Petroleum Oils," 1926; E. R. de Ong, "Petroleum Oil as a Carrier for Insecticides and as a Plant Stimulant," *Industrial and Engineering Chemistry* 20, no. 8 (1928): 826–27; and M. W. Black, "Some Physiological Effects of Oil Sprays upon Deciduous Fruit Trees," *Journal of Pomology and Horticultural Science* 14, no. 2 (1937): 175–202.

66. M. Rothstein, "A British Firm on the American West Coast, 1869–1914," *Business History Review* 37, no. 4 (1963): 392–415; and M. Rothstein,

"West Coast Farmers and the Tyranny of Distance: Agriculture on the Fringes of the World Market," *Agricultural History* 49, no. 1 (1975): 272–80.

67. Herbert, "Spray Stimulation," 1924.

68. Williamson, Daum, and Klose, *American Petroleum Industry*, 1963, 188.

69. W. H. Volck, "Insecticide and Method of Making the Same," Patent #1,707,466, US Patent Office, 1929.

70. "Spraying Makes Bigger Fruit Crops—Do It Early," *Pacific Rural Press* 94, no. 3 (November 3, 1917): 437; and Woglum, "Use of Oil Sprays on Citrus Trees," 1926.

71. E. R. de Ong and H. Knight, "Emulsifying Agents as an Inhibiting Factor in Oil Sprays," *Journal of Economic Entomology* 18, no. 2 (1925): 424–26; and E. R. de Ong, H. Knight, and J. C. Chamberlin, "A Preliminary Study of Petroleum Oil as an Insecticide for Citrus Trees," *Hilgardia* 2, no. 9 (1927): 351–86.

72. S. Stoll, "Insects and Institutions: University Science and the Fruit Business in California," *Agricultural History* 69, no. 2 (1995): 216–39, 237n61.

73. International Apple Shippers Association, "Report of Officers and Executive Committee," 1926, Western Cooperative Spray Project Records, 1921–1952, Washington State University Manuscripts, Archives, & Special Collections, Pullman; A. L. Quaintance, P. B. Dunbar, and L. S. Tenny, "Confidential Minutes of Conference between Representatives of the US Department of Agriculture, the Insecticide and Fruit Industries and Others Relative to Arsenical Spray Residues of Fruits," 1926, Western Cooperative Spray Project Records, 1921–1952, Washington State University Manuscripts, Archives, & Special Collections, Pullman; and R. G. Phillips, Letter to Yakima Fruit Growers Association, 1926, Western Cooperative Spray Project Records, 1921–1952, Washington State University Manuscripts, Archives, & Special Collections, Pullman.

74. R. L. Webster, Letter to Professor G. W. Herrick, Cornell University, 1926, Western Cooperative Spray Project Records, 1921–1952, Washington State University Manuscripts, Archives, & Special Collections, Pullman; and G. W. Herrick, Letter to Professor R. L. Webster, Washington State University, 1926, Western Cooperative Spray Project Records, 1921–1952, Washington State University Manuscripts, Archives, & Special Collections, Pullman.

75. Webster, Letter to Herrick, 1926.

76. Tolerance in this case means simply the maximum amount a food may have of a particular ingredient, for example lead or arsenic, not how much the human body can tolerate. Anonymous, "Statement of Facts and Observations Pertaining to Spray Residue Matters Presented on the Part of the Fruit Growing Industry of the State of Washington at the Spokane Conference," 1933, Western Cooperative Spray Project Records, 1921–1952, Washington State University Manuscripts, Archives, & Special Collections, Pullman.

77. Webster, Letter to Herrick, 1926.; and R. L. Webster, "Outline of U.S. Spray Residue History," 1933, Western Cooperative Spray Project Records, 1921–1952, Washington State University Manuscripts, Archives, & Special Collections, Pullman.

78. W. B. White, "Poisonous Spray Residues on Vegetables," *Industrial & Engineering Chemistry* 25, no. 6 (1933): 621–23; and H. A. Wallace, Letter

to Growers and Shipper of Apples and Pears, 1937, Western Cooperative Spray Project Records, 1921–1952, Washington State University Manuscripts, Archives, & Special Collections, Pullman.

79. R. L. Webster, Letter to Professor G. W. Herrick, Cornell University, 1934, Western Cooperative Spray Project Records, 1921–1952, Washington State University Manuscripts, Archives, & Special Collections, Pullman.

80. There was no understanding of what compounds in the oil were toxic, and even if there were, there were no analytical tools for measuring them.

81. *Grower Pamphlet: Scientific Control of Orchard Pests* (Watsonville: California Spray-Chemical Company, 1926).

82. D. F. Fisher, E. L. Green, and E. J. Newcomer, "The Western Cooperative Spray Oil Project," 1928, Western Cooperative Spray Project Records, 1921–1952, Washington State University Manuscripts, Archives, & Special Collections, Pullman.

83. D. F. Fisher, "Suggested Outline for Typical Oil Spray Project," 1927, Western Cooperative Spray Project Records, 1921–1952, Washington State University Manuscripts, Archives, & Special Collections, Pullman; and D. F. Fisher, "Physiological Investigations—Cooperative Oil Spray Project," 1927, Western Cooperative Spray Project Records, 1921–1952, Washington State University Manuscripts, Archives, & Special Collections, Pullman.

84. They continue to do so every few years until the cooperative project's dissolution in the early 1950s. Minutes of the 10th Annual Meeting of the Northwest Oil Spray Project, 1937, Western Cooperative Spray Project Records, 1921–1952, Washington State University Manuscripts, Archives, & Special Collections, Pullman; and Minutes of the Sixteenth Annual Meeting of the Western Cooperative Spray Conference, 1942, Western Cooperative Spray Project Records, 1921–1952, Washington State University Manuscripts, Archives, & Special Collections, Pullman.

85. "Oil Insecticide," *La Habra Star*, 1925; and E. R. de Ong, Letter to E. J. Newcomer, November 8, 1927, Western Cooperative Spray Project Records, 1921–1952, Washington State University Manuscripts, Archives, & Special Collections, Pullman.

86. J. B. Terry, Letter from the Chief Chemist, Standard Oil of California, to Northwestern Entomologists, 1930, Western Cooperative Spray Project Records, 1921–1952, Washington State University Manuscripts, Archives, & Special Collections, Pullman.

87. Fisher, Green, and Newcomer, "The Western Cooperative Spray Oil Project," 1928.

88. Anonymous, "History of Ortho Division," 1964; and Gardner, *First Thirty Years*, 1978.

89. E. R. De Ong, "Present Trend of Oil Sprays," *Journal of Economic Entomology* 24, no. 5 (1931): 978–85.

90. K. Crist, "A Battle That Never Ends," *Los Angeles Times*, July 22, 1934.

91. "Arming for War on Pests," *Standard Oil Bulletin* 19, no. 8 (1931): 3–11.

92. K. W. Smith, "Standard in New Venture: California Company Again Expands Activities by Entering Spray-Chemical Field," *Los Angeles Times*,

August 16, 1931; and "Standard Oil of California: Chemical Spray Company Using Mineral Oils Organized as New Subsidiary," *Wall Street Journal*, August 24, 1931.

93. Gardner, *First Thirty Years*, 1978.

94. "Annual Statement to Stockholder 1931," *Standard Oil Bulletin* 19, no. 12 (1932): 1–9.

95. "Arming for War on Pests," *Standard Oil Bulletin* 19, no. 8 (1931): 3–11, 16.

96. Anonymous, "History of Ortho Division," 1964. Standard Oil of California provided feedstocks for its largest plant at Richmond, California, and Standard Oil Company (New Jersey) provided feedstocks for its Bayway, New Jersey, and East St. Louis, Missouri (via contracts with Standard Oil of Indiana) plants.

97. Gardner, *First Thirty Years*, 1978, 43; L. R. Gardner, "Petroleum-Derived Products in Agriculture Pest Control," in *Agricultural Applications of Petroleum Products*, ed. Industrial and Engineering Chemistry (Washington, DC: American Chemical Society, 1952), 100–104; and L. R. Gardner, "Entomology in the Pacific Branch—Plus and Minus Fifty Years: Industrial Contributions," *Bulletin of the Entomological Society of America* 13, no. 1 (1967): 24–26.

98. R. C. Roark, "Insecticides and Fungicides," *Industrial & Engineering Chemistry* 27, no. 5 (1935): 530–32.

99. A. S. Crafts and H. G. Reiber, "Herbicidal Properties of Oils," *Hilgardia* 18, no. 2 (1948): 77–156.

100. A. S. Crafts and H. G. Reiber, "Herbicidal Uses of Oils," in *Agricultural Applications of Petroleum Products*, ed. Industrial and Engineering Chemistry (Washington, DC: American Chemical Society, 1952), 70–75.

101. Crafts and Reiber, "Herbicidal Properties," 1948; and A. S. Crafts, "Oil Sprays for Weeding Carrots and Related Crops," Circular 136, California Agricultural Extension Service (Berkeley: College of Agriculture, University of California, 1947).

102. J. Van Overbeek and R. Blondeau, "Mode of Action of Phytonomic Oils," *Weeds* 3, no. 1 (1954): 55–65.

103. "Weeding Onions," *Western Grower and Shipper: The Business Magazine of the Western Row Crop Industries* 15, no. 9 (1944): 10–11, 26–27; and Van Overbeek and Blondeau. "Mode of Action of Phytonomic Oils," 1954.

104. Anonymous, "History of Ortho Division," 1964; and Gardner, *First Thirty Years*, 1978.

105. Staff of Industrial and Engineering Chemistry, ed., *Agricultural Applications of Petroleum Products* (Washington, DC: American Chemical Society, 1952).

106. Brundage, "Orange Pests Develop Resistance to Poisons," 1946.

107. M. Buteler and T. Stadler, "A Review of the Mode of Action and Current Use of Petroleum Distilled Sprays Oils," in *Pesticides in the Modern World: Trends in Pesticide Analysis*, ed. M. Stoytcheva (Rijeka, Croatia: InTech, 2011), 119–36; A. J. Najar-Rodríguez et al., "The Toxicological Effects of Petroleum Spray Oils on Insects—Evidence for an Alternative Mode of Action and Possible

New Control Options," *Food and Chemical Toxicology* 46, no. 9 (2008): 3003–14; P. Taverner, "Drowning or Just Waving? A Perspective on the Ways Petroleum-Derived Oils Kill Anthropod Pests of Plants," in *Spray Oils Beyond 2000: Sustainable Pest and Disease Management*, ed. G. A Beattie, D. M. Watson, M. L Stevens, D. J. Rae, and R. N. Sponner-Hart (Penrith, Australia: University of Western Sydney, 2002), 78–87; and G. P. Ebbon, "Environmental and Health Aspects of Agricultural Spray Oils," in *Spray Oils Beyond 2000: Sustainable Pest and Disease Management*, ed. G. A. Beattie, D. M. Watson, M. L Stevens, D. J. Rae, and R. N. Sponner-Hart (Penrith, Australia: University of Western Sydney, 2002), 232–46.

108. A. Cózar et al., "Plastic Debris in the Open Ocean," *Proceedings of the National Academy of Sciences* 111, no. 28 (2014): 10239–44; and E. S. Bernhardt, E. J. Rosi, and M. O. Gessner, "Synthetic Chemicals as Agents of Global Change," *Frontiers in Ecology and the Environment* 15, no. 2 (2017): 84–90.

109. P. H. Spitz, *Petrochemicals: The Rise of an Industry* (New York: John Wiley & Sons, 1988).

110. G. P. Gray, "The Workings of the California Insecticide Law," *Journal of Industrial and Engineering Chemistry* 6, no. 7 (1914): 590–94; W. P. Tufts, "The Rich Pattern of California Crops," in *California Agriculture by Members of the Faculty of the College of Agriculture University of California*, ed. C. B. Hutchinson (Berkeley: University of California Press, 1946), 113–238; R. E. Smith et al., "Protecting Plants from Their Enemies," in *California Agriculture by Members of the Faculty of the College of Agriculture University of California*, ed. C. B. Hutchinson (Berkeley: University of California Press, 1946), 239–317.

111. Gray, "Workings of the California Insecticide Law," 1914.

CHAPTER 4. PUBLIC-PRIVATE PARTNERSHIPS

Cushman quoted in National Research Council, Minutes of the Conference of Plant Pathologists, Entomologists, and Manufacturers of Insecticides and Fungicides at The Hotel Seneca, Rochester, NY, June 30, 1920, National Research Council, Institutions: Associations, Individuals, Archive of the National Academy of Sciences, Washington, DC.

1. "America Manufactures Dyes on Big Scale," *Wall Street Journal*, October 7, 1918; "Review of the Year: Chemistry," *Scientific American* 120, no. 1 (1918): 9; B. M. Baruch, *American Industry in the War: A Report of the War Industries Board* (New York: Prentice-Hall, 1921); V. S. Clark, *History of the Manufactures in the United States: 1893–1928*, vol. III (New York: McGraw-Hill, 1929); W. Haynes, *American Chemical Industry: The World War I Period, 1912–1922*, vol. III (New York: D. Van Nostrand, 1945); L. F. Haber, *The Chemical Industry, 1900–1930: International Growth and Technological Change* (Oxford: Oxford University Press, 1971); and K. Steen, *The American Synthetic Organic Chemicals Industry: War and Politics, 1910–1930* (Chapel Hill: University of North Carolina Press, 2014).

2. Haber, *Chemical Industry, 1900–1930*, 1971, 184.

3. Haynes, *American Chemical Industry: World War I Period*, 1945; "Coal Tar Products Fill Daily Needs: Almost Every Luxury and Necessity Has

Something Derived from the Substance That Gives Heat," *New York Times*, June 15, 1914; and J. L. Howe, "War of Chemicals Reaches a Climax," *New York Times*, June 16, 1918.

4. Haynes, *American Chemical Industry: World War I Period*, 1945, 36.

5. "Coal Tar Basis of Defense: Its Products Needed for High Explosives," *Los Angeles Times*, February 13, 1916; "Chemical Preparedness," *New York Times*, February 25, 1917; "Chemists Gain Advantage: Americans Have Outdone Germany in Chemical Products," *New York Times*, February 17, 1918; B. Crowell, *America's Munitions 1917–1918: Report of Benedict Crowell, the Assistant Secretary of War, Director of Munitions* (Washington, DC: Government Printing Office, 1919); Haynes, *American Chemical Industry: World War I Period*, 1945; and Haber, *Chemical Industry, 1900–1930*, 1971.

6. Haynes, *American Chemical Industry: World War I Period*, 1945.

7. The NRC was composed of military representatives and scientific and business representatives from civilian departments, universities, research foundations, and industrial firms. G. E. Hale, "War Services of the National Research Council," in *The New World of Science: Its Development during the War*, ed. R. M. Yerkes (1920; repr., Freeport, NY: Books for Libraries Press, 1969), 13–30; J. R. Angell, "The National Research Council," in *The New World of Science: Its Development during the War*, ed. R. M. Yerkes (1920; repr., Freeport, NY: Books for Libraries Press, 1969), 417–38; and R. C. Cochrane, *The National Academy of Sciences, the First Hundred Years 1863-1963* (Washington, DC: National Academy of Sciences, 1978).

8. "A Council of National Defense is established, for the coordination of industries and resources for the national security and welfare, to consist of the Secretary of the Army, the Secretary of the Navy, the Secretary of the Interior, the Secretary of Agriculture, the Secretary of Commerce, and the Secretary of Labor" (50 U.S.C. § 1: Creation, purpose, and composition of council).

9. "Wizardries of Modern Chemistry Shown: Remarkable Work of the National Research Council Is Presented in Nontechnical Manner," *Washington Post*, March 20, 1921; and Cochrane, *National Academy of Sciences*, 1978. The NRC's 1916 and 1917 operations were funded by private organizations such as the Rockefeller Foundation, the Carnegie Corporation, the Mellon Foundation, and the Engineering Foundation, which gives some insight into the industrially cooperative nature that framed the creation of the NRC.

10. V. Kellogg, "The National Research Council," *International Conciliation* 7 (1920): 423–30; V. Kellogg, "The National Research Council," *North American Review* 212, no. 78 (1920): 754–56; and V. Kellogg, "The United States National Research Council," *Nature* 105, no. 2637 (1920): 332–33.

11. G. E. Hale, "War Services," 1920.

12. Y. M. Rabkin and J. J. Lafitte-Houssat, "Cooperative Research in Petroleum Chemistry," *Scientometrics* 1, no. 4 (1979): 327–38; and Y. M. Rabkin, "Chemicalization of Petroleum Refining in the United States: The Role of Cooperative Research, 1920–1950," *Sociology of Science* 19, no. 4-5 (1980): 833–50.

13. Kellogg, "National Research Council," *Nature*, 1920, 333.

14. V. Kellogg, "Isolation or Cooperation in Research," *Reprint and Circular Series of National Research Council* 67 (1925): 1–7.

15. For example, L. A. Jones and D. Durand, *Mortgage Lending Experience in Agriculture*, National Bureau of Economic Research Financial Research Program (Princeton, NJ: Princeton University Press, 1954); and W. W. Cochrane, *The Development of American Agriculture: A Historical Analysis* (Minneapolis: University of Minnesota Press, 1993).

16. M. S. Wildman, *Prices of Food*, History of Prices during the War (Washington, DC: Government Printing Office, 1919).

17. V. L. Perkins, *Crisis in Agriculture: The Agricultural Adjustment Administration and the New Deal, 1933*, vol. 81 (Berkeley: University of California Press, 1969).

18. L. J. Alston, "Farm Foreclosures in the United States During the Interwar Period," *Journal of Economic History* 43, no. 4 (1983): 885–903.

19. L. O. Howard, *The Insect Menace* (New York: D. Appleton-Century Company, 1933); J. E. McWilliams, *American Pests: Losing the War on Insects from Colonial Times to DDT* (New York: Columbia University Press, 2008).

20. L. O. Howard, "War Against Insects," *Nature* 109, no. 2725 (1922): 79–80; L. O. Howard, "Two Billion Crop Loss Spur Fight on Insects: Entomologists Waging War on a Hundred Agricultural Pests, Half of Foreign Origin—Changes in Methods of Growing and Harvesting Urged," *New York Times*, February 24, 1924; "Fighting Insects," *Popular Mechanics* 44, no. 4 (1925): 567–71; J. C. Whorton, *Before Silent Spring: Pesticides and Public Health in Pre-DDT America* (Princeton, NJ: Princeton University Press, 1974); and E. O. Russell, "'Speaking of Annihilation': Mobilizing for War against Human and Insect Enemies," *Journal of American History* 82, no. 4 (1996): 1505–29.

21. NRC, Minutes of the Conference, 1920.

22. W. B. Herms, "An Analysis of Some of California's Major Entomological Problems," *Journal of Economic Entomology* 19, no. 2 (1926): 262–70; E. O. Essig, *A History of Entomology* (New York: Hafner Publishing, 1931); and S. Stoll, *The Fruits of Natural Advantage: Making the Industrial Countryside in California* (Berkeley: University of California Press, 1998).

23. For example, H. H. Dow, Letter from Herbert Dow to Luther Burbank on Sodium Benzoate, 1906, and H. H. Dow, Letter from Herbert Dow to Fred Snyder on Sodium Benzoate, 1906, Herbert H. Dow Papers, Science History Institute, Philadelphia, PA.

24. G. P. Gray, "The Workings of the California Insecticide Law," *Journal of Industrial and Engineering Chemistry* 6, no. 7 (1914): 590–94.

25. Like many biologists at the time, Vernon Kellogg was a eugenicist. In particular, he was concerned with how wars affected "race-deterioration" because war killed off the fittest men and was thus a form of unnatural selection. V. Kellogg, "Eugenics and Militarism," *Atlantic* 112 (July 1913): 99–108. He began the war as a pacifist and humanitarian, but by 1917 his experiences interacting with the German Army during relief work led him to fully support the war. V. Kellogg, *Headquarters Nights: A Record of Conversations and Experiences at the Headquarters of the German Army in France and Belgium* (Boston: Atlantic Monthly Press. 1917); V. Kellogg, A. E. Taylor, and H. Hoover, *The Food Problem* (Bedford, MA: Applewood Books, 1917); Kellogg, "National Research Council," *Nature*, 1920; and V. Kellogg, "The Food Problem," in *A New World*

of Science: Its Development during the War, ed. R. M. Yerkes (1920; repr., Freeport, NY: Books for Libraries Press, 1969).

26. Dr. H. P. Armsby (1920), quoted in Kellogg, " Food Problem," 1969.

27. W. C. O'Kane, *The Crop Protection Institute: A Get-Together Movement on the Part of Three Great Groups, the Intelligent Grower, the Scientist, and the Businessman* (Durham, NH: Crop Protection Institute, 1920); and Crop Protection Institute, "The Establishment of the Crop Protection Institute: A Get Together Movement on the Part of Three Great Groups, the Intelligent Grower, the Scientist, and the Businessman," Pamphlet Sent to Members of the American Association of Economic Entomology (Durham, NC: Crop Protection Institute, 1920).

28. Angell, "National Research Council," 1969; and Cochrane, *National Academy of Sciences*, 1978.

29. NRC, "Minutes of the Conference," 1920.

30. "War on Insects," *New York Times*, February 13, 1921.

31. NRC, Minutes of the Conference," 1920.

32. Founders of the CPI saw potential for chemicals in all arenas, including food processing, storage, and transportation.

33. Crop Protection Institute, "Constitution and By-Laws of the Crop Protection Institute," 1920, National Research Council, Institutions: Associations, Individuals, Archive of the National Academy of Sciences, Washington, DC.

34. O'Kane, "*Crop Protection Institute*; Crop Protection Institute, "Investigations of Industrial Organizations" (Washington, DC: Crop Protection Institute, 1921); and "The Crop Protection Institute," *Crop Protection Digest* 1, no. 1 (1921).

35. V. Kellogg, Letter from V. Kellogg, Permanent Secretary of NRC, to P. J. O'Gara, American Smelting and Refining Company, 1921, National Research Council, Institutions: Associations, Individuals, Archive of the National Academy of Sciences, Washington, DC.

36. C. E. McClung, Letter from to C. E. McClung, Chairman Division of Biology and Agriculture, NRC, to H. E. Howe, Chairman Division of Research Extension, NRC, January 29, 1921, National Research Council, Institutions: Associations, Individuals, Archive of the National Academy of Sciences, Washington, DC.

37. G. R. Lyman, Letter from to G. R. Lyman to H. E. Howe, January 29, 1921, National Research Council, Institutions: Associations, Individuals, Archive of the National Academy of Science, Washington, DC.

38. W. C. O'Kane, "The Crop Protection Institute: Its Organization, Plan and Procedure, and Work Accomplished," *Journal of Economic Entomology* 29, no. 1 (1936): 6–20.

39. The project record was compiled from the archives of the NRC at the National Academy of Sciences, from the published bulletins and internal circulars of the CPI, from the minutes and reports of the annual meetings of the American Association of Economic Entomology and the Association of Official Agricultural Chemists, and from various other publications and patents and LGU archives. The records of the CPI become very limited after 1942.

40. For example, C. W. Woodworth, "The Toxicity of Insecticides," *Science* 41, no. 1053 (1915): 367–69. See also chapter 3.

41. Crop Protection Institute, "Pamphlet—Industrial Organizations," 1921; National Research Council, "Sixth Annual Report of the National Research Council" (Washington, DC: National Research Council, 1922); "The Crop Protection Institute," *Science* 55, no. 1410 (1922): 14–15; W. C. O'Kane, "One Year of the Crop Protection Institute," *Journal of Economic Entomology* 15, no. 3 (1922): 209–13; Crop Protection Institute, "Cooperative Dusting and Spraying Experiment of 1921," *Crop Protection Institute Digest* 2 (1922): 1–30; National Research Council, "NRC Report of the Crop Protection Institute for 1922," 1923, National Research Council, Institutions: Associations, Individuals, Archive of the National Academy of Sciences, Washington, DC; F. D. Frome and F. J. Schneiderhan, "Cooperative Dust Spraying Experiment of 1922," *Crop Protection Institute Digest* 4 (1924): 1–36.

42. M. P. Zappe and E. M. Stoddard, "Results of Dusting Versus Spraying in Connecticut Apple and Peach Orchards in 1922," *Connecticut Experiment Station Bulletin* 245 (1923): 229–44.

43. NRC, "NRC Report of the Crop Protection Institute for 1922," 1923.

44. L. Haseman, "Testing Commercial Insecticides," *Journal of Economic Entomology* 21, no. 1 (1928): 115–17.

45. National Research Council, Minutes of the Crop Protection Institute Annual Meeting, 1923, National Research Council, Institutions: Associations, Individuals, Archive of the National Academy of Sciences, Washington, DC; and E. B. Lambert, H. A. Rodenhiser, and H. H. Flor, "The Effectiveness of Various Fungicides in Controlling the Covered Smuts of Small Grains," *Phytopathology* 26, no. 6 (1926): 393–411.

46. M. F. Guyer, "Research Fellowships Administered through the Division of Biology and Agriculture of the National Research Council," *Science* 55, no. 1433 (1922): 636; National Research Council, "Sulfur Fellows of the Crop Protection Institute, October 22," 1922, National Research Council, Institutions: Associations, Individuals, Archive of the National Academy of Sciences, Washington, DC; H. C. Young, "The Toxic Property of Sulphur," *Annals of Missouri Botanical Garden* 9 (1922): 403–5; H. C. Young, "Colloidal Sulfur as a Spray Material," *Annals of Missouri Botanical Garden* 12 (1925): 133–43; H C. Young, "Colloidal Sulfur: Preparation and Toxicity," *Annals of Applied Biology* 12 (1925): 381–418; H. C. Young and R. C. Walton, "Spray Injury to Apple," *Phytopathology* 15, no. 7 (1925): 404–15; and H. C. Young and R. Williams, "Pentathionic Acid, the Fungicidal Factory of Sulfur," *Science* 62, no. 1723 (1928): 19–20.

47. E. S. Salmon, "Discussion on 'the Fungicidal Action of Sulphur,'" *Annals of Applied Biology* 13 (1926): 308–18.

48. W. C. O'Kane, "Chemistry in the Control of Plant Enemies: New Achievement and Future Possibilities," *Industrial & Engineering Chemistry* 15, no. 9 (1923): 911–13.

49. W. C. O'Kane and P. Moore, "Fungicide and Insecticide," Patent #1,515,803, US Patent Office, CPI, 1924; F. Wilcoxin, "Fungicide," Patent #1,849,778, US Patent Office, CPI, 1932; and A. Hartzell and F. Lathrop, "Process and Apparatus for Making Colloidal Substances," Patent #1,870,727, US Patent Office, CPI, 1932. Several other companies would run with this

information. In California, which had a much more sophisticated network of private-public research by this time, the Pacific Gas and Electric Company (PG&E) funded the research of the UC Berkeley agricultural chemist E. R. de Ong into the use of sulfur as a pesticide. The Western Sulphur Company funded the research of J. D. Hayes at the Oregon State Agricultural College. On the East Coast, which lacked established private-public networks, the CPI continued to administer further investigation of sulfur across a great number of states with funds from the Koppers Company of Pittsburgh, which was very impressed by the ability of the CPI to coordinate the project across a wide geographic and great number of local environmental conditions. V. Sauchelli, "Flotation Sulfur in Agriculture," *Industrial & Engineering Chemistry* 25, no. 4 (1933): 363–68.

50. P. Moore, Letter to Dr. Kellogg, Permanent Secretary of NRC, from P. Moore, Secretary of NRC, February 5, 1925; V. Kellogg, Letter from V. Kellogg, Permanent Secretary of the NRC, to Gano Dunn, Chairman of NRC, March 6, 1925; V. Kellogg, Letter from V. Kellogg, Permanent Secretary of the NRC, to Gano Dunn, Chairman of NRC, March 6, 1925; P. Moore, Letter from P. Moore, Secretary of CPI, to V. Kellogg, Permanent Secretary of NRC, June 16, 1925; V. Kellogg, Letter from V. Kellogg, Permanent Secretary of NRC, to G. Dunn, Chairman of NRC, June 17, 1925; G. Dunn, Letter from G. Dunn, Chairman of NRC, to Vernon Kellogg, June 18, 1925, National Research Council, Institutions: Associations, Individuals, Archive of the National Academy of Sciences, Washington, DC.

51. G. Dunn, Letter from G. Dunn, Chairman of NRC, to Albert L. Barrows, Esq., August 7, 1925, National Research Council, Institutions: Associations, Individuals, Archive of the National Academy of Sciences, Washington, DC.

52. W. C. O'Kane quoted in National Research Council, Annual Meeting of the Crop Protection Institute for 1925, Franklin Square Hotel, December 31, 1925, National Research Council, Institutions: Associations, Individuals, Archive of the National Academy of Sciences, Washington, DC.

53. Haynes, *American Chemical Industry: World War I Period*, 1945; and Haber, *Chemical Industry, 1900–1930*, 1971.

54. Dow Chemical Company, *Dow in the West* (Walnut Creek, CA: Dow Chemical Company, 1977).

55. C. K. Good and N. Pensky, "Halowax Acne ('Cable Rash'): A Cutaneous Eruption in Marine Electricians Due to Certain Chlorinated Napthalenes and Diphenyls," *Archives of Dermatology and Syphilology* 48, no. 3 (1943): 251–57.

56. "The use of chlorinated naphthalenes and compounds of allied pharmacological possibilities is extremely wide, and [with] the steady growth of the use of electricity is certainly to expand much farther." C. Drinker, M. F. Warren, and G. Bennett, "The Problem of Possible Systemic Effects Form Certain Chlorinated Hydrocarbons," *Journal of Industrial Hygiene* 19, no. 7 (1937): 283–99.

57. S. Brown, "Chlorination Apparatus," Patent #1,566,044, US Patent Office, Halowax Corporation, 1925; S. Brown, "Process of Chlorination," Patent #1,672.878, US Patent Office, Halowax Corporation, 1928; S. Brown and E. R. Hanson, "Purification of Chlornapthalenes," Patent #1,953,070, US Patent Office, Halowax Corporation, 1934; and E. R. Hanson and S. Brown,

"Light Colored Liquid Chlorinated Napthalene and Production Thereof," Patent #2,025,742, US Patent Office, Halowax Corporation, 1935.

58. They were also sold under the trade names Nibren waxes, Seekay waxes, Clonacire waxes, N-Oil, N-Wax, and Cerifal materials.

59. G. L. Hockenyos, "Monochloronapthalenes as an Insecticide," *Crop Protection Digest* 31 (1931): 1–38. MCN may still be used as a synergistic additive to chloronicotyl, a neonicotinoid. Bayer AgroSciences has multiple patents on doing this, but since active ingredients are the only ones that have to be reported, it is hard to tell how extensively it is used.

60. E. P. Breakey, "Halowax as Contact Insecticide," *Journal of Economic Entomology* 27, no. 2 (1934): 393–98.

61. Two years later, A. M. Boyce of the UC Citrus Experiment Station would use this recommended emulsion in experiments in the control of the citrus red spider mite. He obtained very promising results for control, but the Halowax mixtures caused too much foliage injury to be considered promising for use in commercial control of the red spider mite on citrus. A. M. Boyce, "The Citrus Red Mite Paratetranychus Citri Mcg. in California, and Its Control," *Journal of Economic Entomology* 29, no. 1 (1936): 125–30.

62. E. P. Breakey and A. C. Miller, "Halowax as an Ovicide," *Journal of Economic Entomology* 28, no. 2 (1935): 358–65.

63. E. P., Breakey and A. C. Miller, "Halowax (Chlorinated Napthalene) as an Ovicide for Codling Moth and Oriental Fruit Moth," *Journal of Economic Entomology* 29, no. 5 (1936): 820–26.

64. Good and Pensky, "Halowax Acne," 1943.

65. Drinker, Warren, and Bennett, "Problem of Possible Systemic Effects," 1937.

66. "These experiments leave no doubt as to the possibility of systemic effects of chlorinated naphthalenes and chlorinated diphenyls." Drinker, Warren, and Bennett, "Problem of Possible Systemic Effects," 1937, 298; and J. Falandysz, "Polychlorinated Napthalenes: An Environmental Update," *Environmental Pollution* 101, no. 1 (1998): 77–90.

67. Haynes, *American Chemical Industry: World War I Period*, 1945.

68. A. Hamilton, "Dinitrophenol Poisoning in Munition Works in France," *Monthly Labor Review* 7, no. 3 (1918): 718–26; R. G. Perkins, "A Study of the Munitions Intoxications in France," *Public Health Review* 24, no. 43 (1919): 2335–2430; and F. Olsen and J. C. Goldstein, "The Preparation of Picric Acid from Phenol," *Industrial & Engineering Chemistry* 16, no. 1 (1924): 66–71. DNP was sparingly consumed in the synthesis of sulfur black and blue dyes. L. E. Vlies, "Colouring Matters and Their Apbplication," *Journal of the Society of Dyers and Colourists* 29, no. 11 (1913): 316–21.

69. In 1933 multiple health companies introduced DNP as a diet pill. M. L. Tainter, W. C. Cutting, and A. B. Stockton, "Use of Dinitrophenol in Nutritional Disorders: A Critical Survey of Clinical Results," *American Journal of Public Health* 24, no. 10 (1934): 1045–53.

70. E. C. Britton and L. E. Mills, "Dinitro-Ortho-Cyclohexylphenol," Patent #1,880,404, US Patent Office, Dow Chemical Company, 1932; E. C. Britton and L. E. Mills, "Manufacture of Cyclohexlphenols," Patent #1,862,075, US

Patent Office, Dow Chemical Company, 1932; E. C. Britton and R. P. Perkins, "Method for Manufacture of Cyclohexlphenols," Patent #1,917,823, US Patent Office, Dow Chemical Company, 1933; L. E. Mills, "Nicotine Salts of 2,4-Dinitrophenol and Substituted Derivatives Thereof," Patent #1,963,471, US Patent Office, Dow Chemical Company, 1934; F. B. Smith and W. W. Sunderland, "Esters of 2,4-Dintro-6-Cyclohexyl-Phenol," Patent #2,097,136, US Patent Office, Dow Chemical Company, 1937; L. E. Mills, "Insecticidal Compositions Comprising Dinitro-Cresols," Patent #2,121,039, US Patent Office, Dow Chemical Company, 1938; E. C. Britton and C. L. Moyle, "N-Substituted-2-Amino Nitro-Phenols," Patent #2,155,356, US Patent Office, Dow Chemical Company, 1939; E. C. Britton et al., "Arylamino-Derivatives of 2,4-Dintro-Phenol," Patent #2,158.956, US Patent Office, Dow Chemical Company, 1939; E. C. Britton and F. B. Smith, "Amine Salts of Nitro-Phenols," Patent #2,225,618, US Patent Office, Dow Chemical Company, 1940; and J. W. Britton and F. B. Smith, "Insecticidal Composition," Patent #2,225,619, US Patent Office, Dow Chemical Company, 1940.

71. Anonymous, "Kagy, John F.," undated, Dow Chemical Historical Collection, 1897–2006, Personnel Files, Science History Institute, Philadelphia, PA; and K. Barrons, "The Ag Labs," undated, in Dow Chemical Historical Collection, 1897–2006, Personnel Files, Science History Institute, Philadelphia, PA.

72. J .F. Kagy, "Toxicity of Some Nitro-Phenols as Stomach Poisons for Several Species of Insects," *Journal of Economic Entomology* 29, no. 2 (1936): 397–405; J. F. Kagy, "Laboratory Method of Comparing the Toxicity of Substances to San Jose Scale," *Journal of Economic Entomology* 29, no. 2 (1936): 393–97; and J. F. Kagy, "Ovicidal and Scalicidal Properties of Solutions of Dinitro-O-Cyclohexylphenol in Petroleum Oil," *Journal of Economic Entomology* 29, no. 1 (1936): 52–61.

73. W. C. Dutton, "Orchard Trials of Dinitro-O-Cylohexylphenol in Petroleum Oil for Control of Rosy Apple Aphis and San Jose Scale," *Journal of Economic Entomology* 29, no. 1 (1936): 62–65. Dutton left Michigan State to work for Dow following the publication. F. Z. Hartzell and J. B. Moore, "Control of Oyster-Shell Scale on Apple by Means of Tar Oils, Tar-Lubricating Oils, and Lubricating Oils Containing Dinitro-O-Cyclohexylphenol," *Journal of Economic Entomology* 30, no. 4 (1937): 651–55; F. Z. Hartzell, J. B. Moore, and D. E. Greenwood, "Control of Eye-Spotted Budmoth on Apple by Lubricating Oil Containing Dintro-O-Cyclohexylphenol," *Journal of Economic Entomology* 31, no. 2 (1938): 249–53; and R. L. Wain, "Toxic Polynitro Derivatives in Pest Control," *Annals of Applied Biology* 29, no. 3 (1942): 301–8.

74. The CPI also arranged for Dow to send it to Dr. H. Huckett at Cornell.

75. Boyce, "Citrus Red Mite," 1936.

76. A. M. Boyce, J. F. Kagy, and J. W. Hansen, "Studies with Dinitro-O-Cyclohexylphenol," *Journal of Economic Entomology* 32, no. 3 (1939): 432–49; A. M. Boyce et al., "Dinitro-O-Cyclohexylphenol in the Control of Mites on Citrus and Persian Walnuts," *Journal of Economic Entomology* 32, no. 3 (1939): 450–66; and J. F. Kagy, "The Relative Toxicity of Some 2,4-Dinitro-6-R-Phenols," *Journal of Economic Entomology* 34, no. 4 (1941): 660–68.

77. L. E. Mills, "Insecticidal Compositions," 1938; Britton and Smith, "Insecticidal Composition," 1940; A. M. Boyce, "Dusting Composition," Patent #2,166,121, US Patent Office, 1939; A. M. Boyce, "Dusting Composition," Patent #2,191,421, US Patent Office, 1940; and J. W. Britton and R. C. Dosser, "Manufacture of 2,4-Dintro-6-Cyclohexl-Phenol," Patent #2,384,365, US Patent Office, Dow Chemical Company, 1945.

78. H. P. Barss, "NRC Report of the Crop Protection Institute for 1939," 1940, National Research Council, Institutions: Associations, Individuals. Archive of the National Academy of Sciences, Washington, DC; M. F. Ohman, "Great Western Division, General Student and Sales Trainee Program," 1950, Dow Chemical Historical Collection, 1897–2006, Educational Department Dow Chemical Company, Science History Institute, Philadelphia, PA; and Dow Chemical Company, *Dow in the West*, 1977.

79. Ohman, "Great Western Division," 1950.

80. H. E. Morrison and J. D. Vertrees, "Hop Pests and Their Control: A Report of the Control of the Hop Red Spider and Other Closely Related Problems during the Season of 1940" (Corvallis: Oregon Agricultural Experiment Station, 1940).

81. In 1936, Dow took its first major step toward the development of an agrochemical R&D division and established a small experimental farm in New Haven, Michigan.

82. A. C. Simpson, "Control of the Red Spider Mite," *Nature* 155, no. 3930 (1945): 241; Dow Chemical Company, "Red Mite Research and the Dinitros," *Down to Earth: A Review of Agricultural Chemical Progress* 1, no. 1 (1945): 6–9; Dow Chemical Company, "DN-111 Used with DDT Controls Red Mite," *Down to Earth: A Review of Agricultural Chemical Progress* 2, no. 1 (1946): 5–6; and Dow Chemical Company, "Chemical News for Western Agriculture," Papers of Alden S. Crafts, UC Davis Special Collections, Davis, CA.

83. Dow Chemical Company, *Dow in the West*, 1977. At Dow he joined his former colleagues D. Pendergast, S. Braucher, and B. Underhill, all of whom had worked under him and Boyce at the UC Citrus Experiment Station.

84. L. J. Meuli, "Herbicides," Patent #2,392,859A, US Patent Office, Dow Chemical Company, 1946.

85. Dow Chemical Company, Great Western Division, "Dow Contact Herbicide Pamphlet," 1944, Papers of Alden S. Crafts, UC Davis Special Collections, Davis, CA; and E. M. Hildebrand, "War on Weeds," *Science* 103, no. 2677 (1946): 465–68, 492.

86. Dow Chemical Company, "Dow Manual on Spraying and Dusting,' 1945, Dow Chemical Historical Collection, 1897–2006, Science History Institute, Midland, MI; A. S. Crafts, "A New Herbicide, 2,4, Dinitro 6 Secondary Butyl Phenol," *Science* 101, no. 2625 (1945): 417–18; A. S. Crafts, "Toxicity of Ammonium Dintro-O-Sec-Butyl," *Hilgardia* 19, no. 5 (1949): 159–69; and A. S. Crafts, "Weed Control Research: Past, Present, and Future," *Weeds* 8, no. 4 (1960): 535–40.

87. W. A. Westgate and R. N. Raynor, "Bulletin 634—A New Selective Spray for the Control of Certain Weeds" (Berkeley: UC Agricultural Experiment Station, 1940). The Caterpillar Company and the Campbell-Budlong Company

furnished the tractors and hand sprayers, and the Hawke Dusting Corporation and the Independent Dusting Corporation provided the airplanes.

88. The Standard Chemical Company did commercialize Sinox in the mid-1940s and opened an office in Sacramento, but DOW dominated the market. Standard Agricultural Chemicals Inc., "For Selective Weed Control—Sinox," Papers of Alden S. Crafts, UC Davis Special Collections, Davis, CA.

89. E. C. Britton, "Insecticide," Patent #1,907,493, US Patent Office, Dow Chemical Company, 1933.

90. Dow learned a lesson from the commercialization of DN-111 that different salts of their target compounds had differing commercial toxicological potential and had A. S. Crafts selectively look at the herbicidal potential of various salts of DNOC that they synthesized at their facility in Midland, MI.

91. Dow Chemical Company, Great Western Division, "Dow Selective Herbicide Pamphlet," 1944, Papers of Alden S. Crafts, UC Davis Special Collections, Davis, CA.

92. Dow Chemical Company, *Dow in the West*, 1977.

93. Barss, "NRC Report of the Crop Protection Institute," 1940; and H. P. Barss, "NRC Report of the Crop Protection Institute for 1941," 1942, National Research Council, Institutions: Associations, Individuals, Archive of the National Academy of Sciences, Washington, DC.

94. Barss, "NRC Report of the Crop Protection Institute," 1940.

95. W. H. MacIntire, "Report of the Representative on Board of Governors, Crop Protection Institute," *Journal of the Association of Official Agricultural Chemists* 35, no. 1 (1952): 107.

96. R. J. Norton, "Obituary: Walter Collins O'Kane 1877–1973," *Journal of Economic Entomology* 67, no. 1 (1974): 144–45.

97. Farrar quoted in H. J. Patterson, "Report of the Representatives on the Board of Governors of the Crop Protection Institute of the National Research Council," *Journal of the Association of Agricultural Chemists* 30, no. 1 (1947): 109.

98. M. D. Farrar, "Relation of Chemical Research Laboratories to Development of New Insecticides and Fungicides," *Industrial & Engineering Chemistry* 40, no. 4 (1948): 680–81.

99. K. Barrons, "The Function of Agricultural Chemical Development," 2000, Dow Chemical Historical Collection, 1897–2006, Dow Chemical Company, Science History Institute, Philadelphia, PA.

100. R. Carson, *Silent Spring* (1962; repr., New York: Mariner Books, 2002); A. M. Chiapella et al., "Toxic Chemical Governance Failure in the United States: Key Lessons and Paths Forward," *BioScience* 69, no. 8 (2019): 615–30; and J. L. Harrison, "Pesticide Purveyors and Corporate Power," in *Bite Back: People Taking on Corporate Food and Winning*, ed. K. DeMaster and S. Jayaraman (Oakland: University of California Press, 2020), 51–63.

101. J. Hightower, *Hard Times, Hard Tomatoes: A Report of the Agribusiness Accountability Project on the Failure of America's Land Grant College Complex* (Cambridge, MA: Schenkman Publishing Company, 1973); W. Robbins, "Study Finds Agricultural Fails to Aid Consumers or Rural Towns," *New York Times*, June 1, 1972, 39; R. Van Den Bosch, *The Pesticide Conspiracy*

(Berkeley: University of California Press, 1978); and C. Gorney, "University Is Sued over Development of Sophisticated Harvesting Machines," *Washington Post*, January 18, 1979, A11.

102. B. H. Jennings, "The Killing Fields: Science and Politics at Berkeley, California, USA," *Agriculture and Human Values* 14, no. 3 (1997): 259–71.

103. M. Weber, "The American Way of Farming: Pioneer Hi-Bred and Power in Postwar America," *Agricultural History* 92, no. 3 (2018): 394.

104. Barss, "NRC Report of the Crop Protection Institute," 1940; and Barss, "NRC Report of the Crop Protection Institute," 1942.

CHAPTER 5. FROM OIL WELL TO FARM

Shell Union Oil Corporation, *Shell . . . Soldier and Civilian* (San Francisco, CA: Shell Union Oil Corporation and Associate Companies, 1945); and "Shell Oil Testing Soil Fumigants: New Chemical Shows Success in Treating Peach Tree 'Replant Disease,'" *New York Times*, September 15, 1950.

1. J. Guthman, *Wilted: Pathogens, Chemicals, and the Fragile Future of the Strawberry Industry* (Berkeley: University of California Press, 2019).

2. G. Thorne, *Principles of Nematology* (Ithaca, NY: Cornell University Press, 1961).

3. J. Liebig, *Familiar Letters on Chemistry, and Its Relation to Commerce, Physiology, and Agriculture* (Walton & Maberly, 1859); Thorne, *Principles of Nematology*, 1961; J. B. Foster, "Marx's Theory of Metabolic Rift: Classical Foundations for Environmental Sociology 1," *American Journal of Sociology* 105, no. 2 (1999): 366–405; and R. Naylor, "Losing the Links between Livestock and Land," *Science* 310, no. 5754 (2005): 1621–22.

4. Quoted in "Treatment of the Soil," *New York Times*, January 26, 1947.

5. W. Isard and E. W. Schooler, "Location Factors in the Petrochemical Industry with Special Reference to the Future Expansion in the Arkansas-White-Red River Basins," US Department of Commerce (Washington, DC: Office of Technical Services, 1955); K. Chapman, *The International Petrochemical Industry: Evolution and Location* (Oxford: Blackwell Publishing, 1991); and P. H. Spitz, *Petrochemicals: The Rise of an Industry* (New York: John Wiley & Sons, 1988).

6. In petroleum refining, cracking is the process by which the complex organic molecules of crude oil are broken down into simpler, smaller, and lighter hydrocarbons, such as gasoline, naptha, diesel, and jet fuel. H. F. Williamson et al., *The American Petroleum Industry: The Age of Energy, 1899–1959* (Evanston, IL: Northwestern University Press, 1963). Royal Dutch/Shell's expansion into California is considered "formidable" by economic historians and was financed through profit reinvestment and by floating Royal Dutch/Shell shares in the United States. M. Wilkins, *The History of Foreign Investment in the United States, 1914–1945* (Cambridge, MA: Harvard University Press, 2004). For thresholds and value, see B T. Brooks, "Petroleum as a Chemical Raw Material," *Industrial & Engineering Chemistry* 16, no. 2 (1924): 185–89; B. T. Brooks, "Synthetic Organic Chemicals from Petroleum: An American Development," *Industrial & Engineering Chemistry* 31, no. 5 (1939): 514–19;

and R. E. Wilson, "Refinery Gas: A Raw Material of Growing Importance," *Journal of the Society of Chemical Industry* 58, no. 51 (1939): 1095–101.

7. Quoted in R. J. Forbes and D. R. O'Beirne, *The Technical Development of Royal Dutch Shell: 1890–1940* (The Hague: Royal Dutch Petroleum Company, 1957), 456.

8. V. Smil, *Enriching the Earth: Fritz Haber, Carl Bosch, and the Transformation of World Food Production* (Cambridge, MA: MIT Press, 2004).

9. Smil, *Enriching the Earth*, 2004.

10. P. Sabin, *Crude Politics: The California Oil Market, 1900–1940* (Berkeley: University of California Press, 2005).

11. T. Priest, *The Offshore Imperative: Shell Oil's Search for Petroleum in Postwar America* (College Station: Texas A&M University Press, 2007).

12. "Natural Gas: The Future Fuel of Southern California," *Los Angeles Times*, January 1, 1888, 17; "Wealth of Natural Gas Resources in State: Oil Fields Can Yield Sufficient to Supply the Needs of Every City and Town in Southern California," *Los Angeles Times*, June 29, 1913; H. C. Kegley, "By-Products from Oil Well Vapors of Great Value: Wet Gas Conversion Gains," *Los Angeles Times*, December 15, 1924; "Wet Gas Assets of California: Survey Shows Progress in Gasoline Recovery," *Los Angeles Times*, November 19, 1928, 17; and "Natural 'Gas' in California: Survey Shows Progress Made in Recovery Methods over the Past Few Years," *Wall Street Journal*, November 23, 1928. Dry gas refers to methane, or natural gas, while wet gas refers to the collection of saturated and unsaturated hydrocarbons containing ~2–5 carbon atoms, such as ethane, propene, and butane.

13. J. Teeple, "Raw Materials–Waste and by-Products," *Industrial & Engineering Chemistry* 8, no. 11 (1926): 1187–90.

14. Sabin, *Crude Politics*, 2005, 123.

15. "Shell Union Offers $50,000,000 Bonds," *New York Times*, September 13, 1929; and Priest, *Offshore Imperative*, 2007.

16. When Shell Oil and Union Oil merged in 1922, the Simplex Refining Company, with its associated patents, owned by Union Oil, was excluded from the merger. Asiatic of New York rechartered the Oakland, California–based Simplex Refining Company in 1926 as a Delaware corporation. In 1927, the Shell Union Oil Company of California acquired the research laboratories, patents, and personnel of the Simplex Refining Company, which was reformed as the Shell Development Company in 1928 with an enlarged research and capital base. K. Beaton, *Enterprise in Oil: A History of Shell in the United States* (New York: Appleton-Century-Crofts, 1957), 517.

17. Shell had also considered Long Beach as a California location. R. Williams, "Proposed Royal Dutch Shell Synthetic Ammonia Plant," 1929, Records of E. I. du Pont de Nemours & Co., series II, part 2, Du Pont Ammonia Corporation, Hagley Museum and Library, Wilmington, DE; "Nitrogen Plant Site Purchased," *Los Angeles Times*, November 20, 1929; Beaton, *Enterprise in Oil*, 1957, 521–23; and Forbes and O'Beirne, *Technical Development*, 1957, 464–69.

18. "Shell Chemical Company," *Wall Street Journal*, March 22, 1929.

19. Beaton, *Enterprise in Oil*, 1957, 519–20; Forbes and O'Beirne, *Technical Development*, 1957, 503–5; Chapman, *International Petrochemical Industry*,

1991, 56; and A. S. Travis, "High Pressure Industrial Chemistry: The First Steps, 1909–1913," in *Determinants in the Evolution of the European Chemical Industry*, ed. A. S. Travis, H. G. Schröter, E. Homburg, and J. T. Morris (Boston: Kluwer Academic Publishers, 1998), 3–21.

20. The overall chemistry is the same. The engineering and management of the ammonia plant was different, as well as the pressure of the reaction. Beaton, *Enterprise in Oil*, 1957; L. F. Haber, *The Chemical Industry, 1900–1930: International Growth and Change* (Oxford: Clarendon Press, 1971); and Smil, *Enriching the Earth*, 2004.

21. Smil, *Enriching the Earth*, 2004.

22. Travis, "High Pressure," 1998, 15; Beaton, *Enterprise in Oil*, 1957, 520; Forbes and O'Beirne, *Technical Development*, 1957, 503–4.

23. Travis, "High Pressure," 1998, 15

24. H. M. Smith, "Possible Utilization of Natural Gas for the Production of Chemical Products" (Washington, DC: US Department of Commerce, Bureau of Mines, 1930); and H. C. Miller, "Function of Natural Gas in the Production of Oil: A Report of the Bureau of Mines in Cooperation with the American Petroleum Institute" (Washington, DC: US Department of Commerce, Bureau of Mines, 1929).

25. Smil, *Enriching the Earth*, 2004.

26. Forbes and O'Beirne, *Technical Development*, 1957, 515–16; and Beaton, *Enterprise in Oil*, 1957, 522.

27. D. Pyzel, "Producing Ammonia," Patent #1,849,357, US Patent Office, Shell Development Company, 1928; D. Pyzel, "Process and Apparatus for the Production of Ammonia," Patent #1,957,849, US Patent Office, Shell Development Company, 1932; D. Pyzel, "Process for the Absorption and Distillation of Ammonia," Patent #1,999,546, US Patent Office, Shell Development Company, 1932; F. M. Pyzel, "Process for the Manufacture of Ammonium Sulphate," Patent #2,035,920, US Patent Office, Shell Development Company, 1933; and F. M. Pyzel and J. D. Ruys, "Manufacture of Ammonium Sulfate," Patent #2,026,250, US Patent Office, Shell Development Company, 1934.

28. Carbon black is a semicrystalline form of carbon that results from the incomplete combustion of hydrocarbons. Different hydrocarbons result in different forms of carbon black.

29. F. M. Pyzel, "Process for the Thermal Decomposition of Hydrocarbons," Patent #1,983,992, US Patent Office, Shell Development Company, 1931; F. M. Pyzel, "Process of Producing Hydrogen," Patent #1,896,420, US Patent Office, Shell Development Company, 1933; D. Pyzel, "Process for the Removal of Acetylene," Patent #1,985,548, US Patent Office, Shell Development Company, 1934; W. Haynes, *The American Chemical Industry: The Chemical Companies*, vol. 6 (New York: D. Van Nostrand, 1949); Forbes and O'Beirne, *Technical Development*, 1957; and Beaton, *Enterprise in Oil*, 1957.

30. Forbes and O'Beirne, *Technical Development*, 516. The principal byproduct of the ammonia sulfate plant was carbon black. Carbon black was an important feedstock for steel and rubber manufacture. Shell Chemical Company, *Shell Carbon: Its Properties and Uses in the Rubber Industry* (San Francisco: Shell Chemical Company, 1939); and Beaton, *Enterprise in Oil*, 1957, 528.

31. W. Haynes, *The American Chemical Industry: Decade of New Products, 1930–1939*, vol. 5 (New York: D. Van Nostrand, 1945); Forbes and O'Beirne, *Technical Development*, 1957; and Beaton, *Enterprise in Oil*, 1957.

32. F. H. Leavitt, "Agricultural Ammonia Equipment Development and History," in *Agricultural Anhydrous Ammonia: Technology and Use*, ed. M. H. McVickar, W. P. Martin, I. E. Miles, and H. H. Tucker, 125–68 (Memphis, TN: Agricultural Ammonia Institute, 1966).

33. Pyzel and Ruys, "Manufacture of Ammonium Sulfate," 1934; J. van der Valk, "Acid Recovery Process," Patent #2,441,521, US Patent Office, Shell Development Company, 1944; and Forbes and O'Beirne, *Technical Development*, 1957.

34. By 1929, there were 4.7 million acres of irrigated land in the top ten agricultural counties in California. G. Henderson, *California and the Fictions of Capital* (Oxford: Oxford University Press, 1999). Anhydrous ammonia is a pure ammonia with no water. It is a gas at standard temperature and pressure. Aqua ammonia is a highly concentrated solution of ammonia in water.

35. D. D. Waynick, "Anhydrous Ammonia as a Fertilizer," *California Citrograph* 19, no. 11 (1934): 295, 310–11; Leavitt, "Agricultural Ammonia," 1966, 125–33; and R. E. Warnock, "Ammonia Application in Irrigation Water," in *Agricultural Anhydrous Ammonia: Technology and Use*, ed. M. H. McVickar, W. P. Martin, I. E. Miles, and H. H. Tucker, 115–24 (Memphis, TN: Agricultural Ammonia Institute, 1966).

36. E. L. Prizer and J. A. Prizer, "Method of Supplying Soluble Fertilizing Agents to Soil," Patent #1,868,913, US Patent Office, 1932; and Leavitt, "Agricultural Ammonia," 125–26. Shell was also able to break from the patent by introducing ammonia into irrigation water at a substantially higher concentration and faster rate than specified in the patent.

37. Waynick, "Anhydrous Ammonia," 1934, 295; F. Kortland, "Flow Meter," Patent #2,038,511, US Patent Office, Shell Development Company, 1936; A. B. Beaumont and G. J. Larsinos, "Aqua Ammonia as a Nitrogen Fertilizer," *American Fertilizer* 76 (1932): 9–10; and Leavitt, "Agricultural Ammonia," 1966.

38. C. B. deBuyn, "Process of Fertilizing Soil," Patent #2,020,824, US Patent Office, Shell Development Company, 1935; Beaton, *Enterprise in Oil*, 1957; Forbes and O'Beirne, *Technological Development*, 1957; Warnock, "Ammonia Application," 1966; and Leavitt, "Agricultural Ammonia," 1966.

39. F. H. Leavitt, "Nitrogation, Nitrojection, and Soil Fumigation: Their Application and Their Results," *American Fertilizer* 110, no. 2 (1949): 3; and Leavitt, "Agricultural Ammonia," 1966.

40. Leavitt, "Agricultural Ammonia," 1966.

41. Leavitt, "Nitrogation, Nitrojection," 1949, 7–8; and Leavitt, "Agricultural Ammonia," 1966.

42. C. J. Brand, "Recovery in the Fertilizer Industry," *Industrial & Engineering Chemistry* 27, no. 4 (1935): 372–78; Beaton, *Enterprise in Oil*, 1957; and Leavitt, "Agricultural Ammonia," 1966.

43. Shell tended to commercialize chemical products before they had a solid understanding of their efficacy. See *Buckley v. Shell Chemical Company*, 32

Cal.App.2d 209 (1939), for a picture into some of the issues that followed from this practice.

44. L. Rosenstein, "Increased Yields Obtained from Shell Agricultural Ammonia (NH₃) in Irrigated Agriculture," *Shell Chemical Bulletin* 1 (1936): 1–23.

45. J. R. Adams and M. S. Anderson, "Liquid Nitrogen Fertilizers for Direct Applications" (Washington, DC: USDA, Agricultural Research Service, 1961), 1–44.

46. Leavitt, "Nitrogation, Nitrojection," 1949; Leavitt, "Agricultural Ammonia," 1966; and Forbes and O'Beirne, *Technical Development*, 1957.

47. Leavitt, "Nitrogation, Nitrojection," 1949; and Leavitt, "Agricultural Ammonia," 1966.

48. Shell Chemical Division, Agricultural Products Departments, Shell Union Oil Corporation. "Nitrojection: A New Method of Soil Fertilization" (San Francisco: National Agricultural Library, 1945).

49. Leavitt, "Agricultural Ammonia," 1966.

50. Shell had also been gifting UC Berkeley small amounts ($500–$1,000) to undertake studies to determine the nitrogen requirements of various crops, particularly food trees. "U.C. Receives $10,000,000 Gift," *Los Angeles Times*, October 11, 1941; and "University Berth Filled," *Los Angeles Times*, December 14, 1940.

51. "Improved Fertilizer That Mixes with Irrigating Water Helps Farmers Boost Their War Output," *Wall Street Journal*, September 7, 1943; L. S. Hannibal, "Soil Injector," Patent #2,598,121, US Patent Office, Shell Development Company, 1952; and J. R. Turner, "Device for Distributing Mixtures of Vapors and Liquid," Patent #2,650,556, US Patent Office, Shell Development Company, 1953.

52. H. I. Forde and E. L. Proebsting, "Utilization of Ammonia Supplied to Peaches and Prunes at Different Seasons," *Hilgardia* 16 (1945): 411–25; Leavitt, "Nitrogation, Nitrojection," 1949; and Leavitt, "Agricultural Ammonia," 1966.

53. W. B. Andrews, F. E. Edwards, and J. G. Hammons, "Bulletin 451— Ammonia as a Source of Nitrogen" (Oxford: Mississippi Agricultural Experiment Station, 1947); W. B. Andrews, J. A. Neely, and F. E. Edwards, "Bulletin 482— Anhydrous Ammonia as Source of Nitrogen," 39 (Oxford: Mississippi Agricultural Experiment Station, 1951); R. L. Beacher, "Arkansas Rice Tests Prove Ammonia Successful in Mississippi River Delta," *Agricultural Ammonia News* 5, no. 2 (1955): 9–11; and W. B. Andrews, "Anhydrous Ammonia as a Fertilizer," in *Advances in Agronomy*, ed. A. G. Norman (New York: Academic Press, 1956), 62–125.

54. W. Carter, "Fumigation of Soil in Hawaii," in *Yearbook of Agriculture*, 126–29 (Washington, DC: USDA, 1953); and D. P. Bartholomew, R. A. Hawkins, and J. A. Lopez, "Hawaii Pineapple: The Rise and Fall of an Industry," *HortScience* 47, no. 10 (2012): 1390–98.

55. Carter quoted in B. Clark, "D-D Saves Crops from Foes," *Science News Letter* (October 1946): 234–35.

56. Carter quoted in Clark, "D-D Saves"; W. Carter, "A Promising New Soil Amendment and Disinfectant," *Science* 97, no. 2051 (1943): 383–84; W. Carter,

"Soil Treatments with Special Reference to Fumigation with DD Mixture," *Journal of Economic Entomology* 38, no. 1 (1945): 35–44; and W. Carter, "Soil Fumigant Comprising 1,3-Dichloropropene and 1,2-Dichloropropane," Patent #2,502,244, US Patent Office, 3, 1950.

57. M. O. Johnson and G. H. Godfrey. "Chloropicrin for Nematode Control," *Industrial & Engineering Chemistry* 24, no. 3 (1932): 311–13; Carter, "Promising New Soil Amendment," 1943; Carter, "Soil Treatments," 1945; and Carter, "Soil Fumigant," 1950.

58. Clark, "D-D Saves," 1946; Carter, "Soil Treatments," 1945; and Carter, "Fumigation of Soil," 1953.

59. W. L. Laurence, "Say Drugs Checks Tubercle Bacilli: Chemists Also Hear Synthetic Glycerine Can Now Be Made from Petroleum Gases," *New York Times*, April 6, 1939. While DD was the first chemical from this by-product series to enter agricultural production, many others eventually did as well. Allyl alcohol became a weed seed killer, and methallyl chloride became a commodity and warehouse fumigant. Shell Chemical Corporation, "Specimen Labels," Agricultural Chemicals Division, Shell Chemical Company, AA-1 (New York: Shell Chemical Company, Agricultural Chemicals Division, 1964). DD was originally composed of ~30–33% low boiling point 1,3-dichloroproene; ~30–33% high boiling point 1,3-dichloropropene; ~30–35% 1,2-dichlorpropane; and ~5% heavy trichlorides of propane. Shell Chemical Company, "Shell D-D," *Bulletin* 3 (1944), unpaginated.

60. They are also present in the wet gas fraction of oil well gases.

61. R. M. Deansley, "Process for the Inhibition of Halogen Substitution Reactions," Patent #1,952,122, US Patent Office, Shell Development Company, 1934; R. M. Deansley, "Halogenation Process," Patent #1,991,600, US Patent Office, Shell Development Company, 1935; R. M. Deansley and W. Engs, "Process for the Preparation of Substantially Pure Tertiary Olefins," Patent #2,012,785, US Patent Office, Shell Development Company, 1935; H. Groll and G. Hearne, "Halo-Substitution of Unsaturated Organic Compounds," Patent #2,130,084, US Patent Office, Shell Development Company, 1938; H. Groll and G. Hearne, "Halogenation of Hydrocarbons: Substitution of Chlorine and Bromine into Straight Chain Olefins," *Industrial & Engineering Chemistry* (December 1939): 1531–39; H. Groll et al., "Halogenation of Hydrocarbons: Chlorination of Olefins and Olefin-Paraffin Mixtures at Moderate Temperatures; Induced Substitution," *Industrial & Engineering Chemistry* 31, no. 10 (1939): 1238–44; F. Rust and W. Vaughn, "The High-Temperature Chlorination of Olefin Hydrocarbons," *Journal of Organic Chemistry* 5, no. 5 (1940): 472–503; W. Vaughn and F. Rust, "The High-Temperature Chlorination of Parrafin Hydrocarbons," *Journal of Organic Chemistry* 5, no. 5 (1940): 449–71; E. C. Williams, "Creating Industries, 1919–1939, Petroleum," *Chemical Industries* 44 (1939): 495–501; E. C. Williams, "Synthetic Glycerol from Petroleum: A Contribution from the Research Laboratories of Shell Development Company," *Transactions of the American Institute of Chemical Engineers* 37 (1942): 157–208; W. Engs and S. Wik, "Process for Producing and Recovering Halogenated Organic Compounds," Patent #2,321,472, US Patent Office, Shell Development Company, 1943; and K. D. Detling, "Production of Organic

Halogen Compound," Patent #2,501,597, US Patent Office, Shell Development Company, 1950.

62. Clark, "D-D Saves," 1946.

63. Clark, "D-D Saves," 1946.

64. Carter, "Soil Fumigant," 1950; and Thorne, *Principles of Nematology*, 1961.

65. Carter, "Promising New Soil Amendment," 1943, 384.

66. "DD Found Effective against Wireworms," *Science News Letter* 48, no. 19 (1945): 296; and "New Chemical Kills Nematodes, Soil Pests," *Science News Letter* 50, no. 23 (1946): 367.

67. J. A. Pinckard, "Soil Fumigant Effective against Root-Knot and Meadow Nematodes," *Seed World* 54, no. 10 (1943): 10, 12–13, 46; "Control of Nematodes," *California Cultivator* 91, no. 21 (1944): 520; "Controlling Beet Nematode," *California Cultivator* 92, no. 1 (1945): 8; USDA, Agricultural Research Administration, "Report of the Administrator of Agricultural Research," 6, 215 (Washington, DC: USDA, ARS, 1944); T. W. Evans, "Toxic Composition," Patent #2,411,566, US Patent Office, Shell Development Company, 1946; C. J. Tonkin, "Soil Improving Method," Patent #2,424,520, US Patent Office, Shell Development Company, 1947; W. H. Lange Jr., "Notes and Correspondence of W. H. Lange Jr.," William H. Lange Jr. Papers, UC Davis Shields Library, Department of Special Collections, Davis, CA, D-288, box 1, folders 1–10.

68. J. S. Houser, "Some Problems in Economic Entomology," *Journal of Economic Entomology* 25, no. 1 (1932): 28–39; Clark, "DD Saves," 1946; F. C. Bishopp, "The Insecticide Situation," *Journal of Economic Entomology* 39, no. 4 (1946): 444–59; J. A. Pinckard, "Soil Fumigant Effective against Nematodes," *Food Packer* 25, no. 1 (1944): 43–44; R. P. Brundage, "Citrus Troubles: West Coast Growers Worried about Market Sizes, Tree Diseases," *Wall Street Journal*, September 6, 1946.

69. J. A. Hyslop, "Soil Fumigation," *Journal of Economic Entomology* 7, no. 4 (1914): 305–12; W. B. Herms, "An Analysis of Some of California's Major Entomological Problems," *Journal of Economic Entomology* 19, no. 2 (1926): 262–70; "A Feast for Wire Worms–Sow Calcium Cyanide between Rows," *Los Angeles Times*, September 20, 1925; M. W. Stone and R. E. Campbell, "Chloropicrin as a Soil Insecticide for Wireworms," *Journal of Economic Entomology* 26, no. 1 (1933): 237–43; R. S. Lehman, "Laboratory Experiments with Various Fumigants against the Wireworm Limonius (Pheletes) Californicus Mann," *Journal of Economic Entomology* 26, no. 6 (1933): 1042–51; R. S. Lehman, "Laboratory Tests of Organic Fumigants for Wireworms," *Journal of Economic Entomology* 35 (1942): 659–61; C. G. Lincoln, H. H. Schwardt, and C. E. Palm, "Methyl Bromide-Dichloroethyl Ether Emulsion as a Soil Fumigant," *Journal of Economic Entomology* 35, no. 2 (1942): 238–39.

70. Leavitt, "Nitrogation, Nitrojection," 1949; and Leavitt, "Agricultural Ammonia," 1966. M. Stone of the USDA undertook the first experiments with DD outside of Hawaii in a Ventura lab a few months prior to the first field tests. M. W. Stone, "Dichloropropane-Dichloropropylene, a New Soil Fumigant for Wireworms," *Journal of Economic Entomology* 37, no. 2 (1944): 297–99.

71. W. H. Lange Jr., "Ethylene Dibromide and Dichloropropane-Dichloropropene Mixture for Wireworm Control," *Journal of Economic Entomology* 38, no. 6 (1945): 643–45. Henry Lange Jr. played a critical role in the commercialization of soil fumigants, especially DD, ethylene dibromide, and benzene hexachloride. Lange was thanked for his work by Shell donations to UC, which funded his travels and talks, which in turn helped convince more growers of the promise of soil fumigation, expanding the market for Shell.

72. Leavitt, "Nitrogation, Nitrojection," 1949; Leavitt, "Agricultural Ammonia," 1966; and F. H. Leavitt, "Method and Apparatus for Protecting Subsurface Ground Tools," Patent #2,306,339, US Patent Office, Shell Development Company, 1942.

73. They also trialed Dow Chemical's 1,2-dibromoethane (ethylene dibromide) at the same time, but it was not as effective against nematodes. EDB would also go on to be a critical soil and commodity fumigant around the world after World War II. EDB was not a novel chemical; it was one of the main components of ethyl fluid, the antiknock agent, which came into general use in the United States in the late 1920s. See D. Seyferth, "The Rise and Fall of Tetraethyllead," *Organometallics* 22 (2003): 5154–78.

74. See G. Thorne and V. Jensens, "A Preliminary Report on the Control of Sugar-Beet Nematode with Two Chemicals D-D and Dowfume W15," *Proceedings of the American Sugar Beet Technologists* 4 (1947): 322–29; H. L. Fletcher, "Sugar Beet Nematode (*Heterodera Schachtii*) Control Studies in Ontario" (paper presented at the American Society of Sugar Beet Technologists, 1947); Lange, "Notes and Correspondence of W. H. Lange Jr.," 1943–1951, William H. Lange Jr. Papers, UC Davis Shields Library, Department of Special Collections, D-288, box 1, folders 1–10.

75. Thorne, "Preliminary Report," 1947; and Leavitt, "Nitrogation, Nitrojection," 1949.

76. Clark, "D-D Saves," 1946.

77. Haynes, *American Chemical Industry*, vol. 6, 1949.

78. G. C. Martin, "'DD' as a Means of Controlling Heterodera Rostochiensis (Woll.)," *Nature* 160, no. 720 (1947): 160; M. W. Allen and D. J. Raski, "Chemical Control of Nematodes," *California Agriculture* 4, no. 10 (1950): 5, 15; and A. L. Taylor, "Nematocides and Nematicides—a History," *Nematropica* 33, no. 2 (2003): 225–32.

79. "Supreme Commander for the Allied Powers, Scientific and Economic Section, Foreign Trade and Commerce Division, Chemical and Drug File, 1946–1950," 1947, box no. 651, file D. D. J1-51,407, National Archives, Washington, DC, RG 331.

80. Clark, "DD- Saves," 1946; F. B. Gilbreth, "New Soil Fumigant Hailed as Farm Boon; Sponsors Say to Revolutionize Rotation," *News and Courier*, July 21, 1948; and "Shell Oil Testing Soil Fumigants," *New York Times*, 1950.

81. Quote from M. Pollan, *The Botany of Desire: A Plant's Eye View of the World* (New York: Random House, 2001), 217. The active ingredient 1,3-dichloropropene remains one of the most used fumigants in the United States. D. Atwood and C. Paisley Jones, "Pesticide Industry Sales and Usage 2008–2012 Market Estimates" (Washington, DC: Environmental Protection Agency, 2017).

82. "Shell Will Establish Agricultural Laboratory on the Pacific Coast," *Wall Street Journal*, June 22, 1944; and Shell Oil Company, Agricultural Laboratory, *Better Farming through Research* (San Francisco, CA: Shell Union Oil and Associate Companies, 1946).

83. "Headlines of the Month," *Industrial & Engineering Chemistry* 42, no. 11 (1946): 2385–86; and "New Laboratory Opened by Shell: California Institutions Is Called One of the World's Largest Oil Research Facilities," *New York Times*, November 23, 1950.

84. Shell Oil Company, *Better Farming*, 1946; and "Shell Oil Testing Soil Fumigants," *New York Times*, 1950.

85. Shell Oil Company, *Better Farming*, 1946.

86. Thorne, *Principles of Nematology*, 1961.

87. Guthman, *Wilted*, 2019.

88. Thorne, *Principles of Nematology*, 1961.

CONCLUSION

J. B. Smith, "Cultivation and Susceptibility to Insect Attack," *Journal of Economic Entomology* 1, no. 1 (1908): 15–17.

1. E. D. Mellilo, *Strangers on Familiar Soil: Rediscovering the Chile-California Connection* (New Haven, CT: Yale University Press, 2015), 109.

2. R. Altman, "On What We Bury," *Interdisciplinary Studies on Literature and Environment* 21, no. 1 (2014): 88.

3. M. Nestle, *Food Politics: How the Food Industry Influences Nutrition and Health* (Berkeley: University of California Press, 2002); W. W. Cochrane, *The Curse of American Agricultural Abundance: A Sustainable Solution* (Lincoln: University of Nebraska Press, 2003); and J. Guthman, *Weighing In: Obesity, Food Justice, and the Limits of Capitalism* (Berkeley: University of California Press, 2011).

4. S. Giedion, *Mechanization Takes Command: A Contribution to Anonymous History* (New York: Oxford University Press, 1948), 256.

5. R. Carson, *Silent Spring* (1962; repr., New York: Mariner Books, 2002), 9.

6. R. A. Mullen, "Why Poison Bugs, Foes or Surpluses?," *Washington Post*, June 25, 1933.

7. C. Hiç et al., "Food Surplus and Its Climate Burdens," *Environmental Science and Technology* 50, no. 8 (2016): 4269–77.

8. D. Fitzgerald, *Every Farm a Factory: The Industrial Ideal in American Agriculture* (New Haven, CT: Yale University Press, 2005), 190.

9. Carson, *Silent Spring*, 2002.

10. Guthman, *Weighing In*, 2011.

Bibliography

Abernathy, J. R. "Role of Arsenical Chemicals in Agriculture." In *Arsenic: Industrial, Biomedical, Environmental Perspectives*, edited by W. H. Lederer and R. J. Fensterheim, 57–62. New York: Van Nostrand Reinhold, 1983.

Adams, J. R., and M. S. Anderson. "Liquid Nitrogen Fertilizers for Direct Applications." Washington, DC: US Department of Agriculture, Agricultural Research Service, 1961.

Agamben, G. *Homo Sacer: Sovereign Power and Bare Life*. Translated by D. Heller-Roazen. Palo Alto, CA: Stanford University Press, 1998.

Aikman, D. "War to the Hilt on Insects!" *New York Times*, August 1, 1937.

Alden, J. C. "The Continuing Need for Inorganic Arsenical Pesticides." In *Arsenic: Industrial, Biomedical, Environmental Perspectives*, edited by W. H. Lederer and R. J. Fensterheim, 63–70. New York: Van Nostrand Reinhold, 1983.

Allen, M. W., and D. J. Raski. "Chemical Control of Nematodes." *California Agriculture* 4, no. 10 (1950): 5, 15.

Alston, L. J. "Farm Foreclosures in the United States During the Interwar Period." *Journal of Economic History* 43, no. 4 (1983): 885–903.

Altman, R. "On What We Bury." *Interdisciplinary Studies on Literature and Environment* 21, no. 1 (2014): 85-95.

———. "How the Benzene Tree Polluted the World." *Atlantic*, October 4, 2017. www.theatlantic.com/science/archive/2017/10/benzene-tree-organic-compounds/530655/.

Ambruster, H. W. "Arsenic." In *The Mineral Industry: Its Statistics, Technology and Trade during 1926*, edited by A. B. Butts and G. A. Roush, 54–65. New York: McGraw-Hill, 1927.

———. "Arsenic." In *The Mineral Industry: Its Statistics, Technology and Trade during 1937*, edited by G. A. Roush, 54–65. New York: McGraw-Hill, 1938.

Anaconda Mining Company. "Arsenic Daily Report, Year-to-Date." 1920. Anaconda Copper Mining Company Records, Collection no. 169, box 265-2, Montana Historical Society Research Center, Helena.

Andrews, W. B. "Anhydrous Ammonia as a Fertilizer." In *Advances in Agronomy*, edited by A. G. Norman, 62–125. New York: Academic Press, 1956.

Andrews, W. B., F. E. Edwards, and J. G. Hammons. "Bulletin 451—Ammonia as a Source of Nitrogen." Oxford: Mississippi Agricultural Experiment Station, 1947.

Andrews, W. B., J. A. Neely, and F. E. Edwards. "Bulletin 482—Anhydrous Ammonia as Source of Nitrogen." Oxford: Mississippi Agricultural Experiment Station, 1951.

Angell, J. R. "The National Research Council." In *The New World of Science: Its Development During the War*, edited by R. M. Yerkes, 417–38. Freeport, NY: Books for Libraries Press, 1969. First published 1920.

Anonymous. "Fumigating Equipment, Workers and Children in a Citrus Orchard, Ca. 1892-1910." 1895. California Historical Society Collection, 1860–1960, CHS-1376, USC Digital Archive, Los Angeles.

———. "Everett Smelter." State of Washington Department of Ecology, 1905. https://ecology.wa.gov/Spills-Cleanup/Contamination-cleanup/Cleanup -sites/Toxic-cleanup-sites/Everett-Smelter/Site-history.

———. "Mr. Volck and Mr. Luther Experimenting on the Charles Rodgers Ranch, Watsonville, CA." 1910. William Volck File, Pajaro Valley Historical Association, Synder Archive Photograph Collection, Watsonville, CA.

———. "Anaconda Mining Company Parade Wagon Advertising 99.90% White Arsenic for Sale." 1915. Anaconda Mining Company, Montana Historical Society Research Center Digital Archives, Helena.

———. "California Spray Chemical Company Manufacturing Plant." 1915. William Volck File, Pajaro Valley Historical Association, Synder Archive Photograph Collection, Watsonville, CA.

———. "Stacks and Treater, Collecting Electrodes." 1919. Anaconda Mining Company, Montana Historical Society Research Center Digital Archives, Helena.

———. "Arsenic Plant, Barrell Filling Devices." 1923. Anaconda Mining Company, Montana Historical Society Research Center Digital Archives, Helena.

———. "Dust Settling over Cotton Plants in the Wake of the Airplane." 1925. Crop and Soil Science—Pest Control, Special Collections Research Center at NCSU Libraries, Raleigh, NC.

———. "Statement of Facts and Observations Pertaining to Spray Residue Matters Presented on the Part of the Fruit Growing Industry of the State of Washington at the Spokane Conference." 1933. Western Cooperative Spray Project Records, 1921–1952, Washington State University Manuscripts, Archives, & Special Collections, Pullman, WA.

———. "Fighting Our Insect Enemies: Achievement of Professional Entomology." In *Agriculture Information Bulletin* no. 121. Washington, DC: US Department of Agriculture, Agricultural Research Service, 1954.

———. "A Brief Chronological History of Ortho Division, Chevron Chemical Company." 1964. California Spray Chemical Company, Chevron Corporation Archive, Concord, CA.

———. Notecard. Undated. William H. Volck File, Pajaro Valley Historical Association, Watsonville, CA.

———. "Kagy, John F." Undated. Dow Chemical Historical Collection, 1897–2006, Personnel Files, Science History Institute, Philadelphia, PA.

Arnold, D. "Pollution, Toxicity, and Public Health in Metropolitan India, 1850–1939." *Journal of Historical Geography* 42 (2013): 124–33.

Atlanta Constitution. "Arsenic Factories: Habits Acquired by People Who Work in Them." January 24, 1902.

———. "Farms and Farmers: Don't Believe in Scientific Farming." April 14, 1913.

Atwood, D., and C. Paisley Jones. "Pesticide Industry Sales and Usage 2008–2012 Market Estimates." Washington, DC: Environmental Protection Agency, 2017.

Ayres, R. U. "Industrial Metabolism." In *Technology and Environment*, edited by J. H. Ausubel and H. E. Sladovich, 23–49. Washington, DC: National Academy Press, 1989.

Ball, P. *Bright Earth: Art and the Invention of Color.* Chicago: University of Chicago Press, 2003.

Ballard, W. S., and W. H. Volck. "Apple Powdery Mildew and Its Control in the Pajaro Valley (California)." In *United States Department of Agriculture Bulletin* 120. Washington, DC: US Department of Agriculture, 1914.

Bannister, R. *Social Darwinism: Science and Myth in Anglo-American Social Thought.* Atlanta, GA: Temple University Press, 2010.

Barles, S. "History of Waste Management and the Social and Cultural Representations of Waste." In *The Basic Environmental History*, edited by M. Agnoletti and S. Serneri, 199–226. New York: Springer, 2014.

Barrons, K. "The Function of Agricultural Chemical Development." 2000. Dow Chemical Historical Collection, 1897–2006, Post Street Archives, Dow Chemical Company, Science History Institute, Philadelphia, PA.

———. "The Ag Labs." Undated. Dow Chemical Historical Collection, 1897–2006, Personnel Files, Dow Chemical Company, Science History Institute, Philadelphia, PA.

Barrows, H. D. "William Wolfskill, the Pioneer." *Annual Publication of the Historical Society of Southern California and of the Pioneers of Los Angeles County* (1902): 287–94.

Barss, H. P. "NRC Report of the Crop Protection Institute for 1939." 1940. National Research Council, Institutions: Associations, Individuals, Archive of the National Academy of Sciences, Washington, DC.

———. "NRC Report of the Crop Protection Institute for 1941." 1942. National Research Council, Institutions: Associations, Individuals, Archive of the National Academy of Sciences, Washington, DC.

Barta, T. "Discourses of Genocide in Germany and Australia: A Linked History." *Aboriginal History* 25, no. 1 (2001): 37–57.

Bartholomew, D. P., R. A. Hawkins, and J. A. Lopez. "Hawaii Pineapple: The Rise and Fall of an Industry." *HortScience* 47, no. 10 (2012): 1390–98.

Barton, D. B. *A History of Tin Mining in Devon and Cornwall*. Cornwall, UK: Truro Bookshop, 1967.

———. *A History of Copper Mining in Cornwall and Devon*. Cornwall, UK: Truro Bookshop, 1968.

Bartrip, P. W. "How Green Was My Valence? Environmental Arsenic Poisoning and the Victorian Domestic Ideal." *English History Review* 109, no. 433 (1994): 891–913.

Baruch, B. M. *American Industry in the War: A Report of the War Industries Board*. New York: Prentice-Hall, 1921.

Bass, L. W. "Chemical Economics." In *Annual Survey of American Chemistry*, edited by C. J. West, 582–600. New York: National Research Council, Chemical Catalog Company, 1931.

Beacher, R. L. "Arkansas Rice Tests Prove Ammonia Successful in Mississippi River Delta." *Agricultural Ammonia News* 5, no. 2 (1955): 9–11.

Beard, J. "DDT and Human Health." *Science of the Total Environment* 355 (2006): 78–89.

Beaton, K. *Enterprise in Oil: A History of Shell in the United States*. New York: Appleton-Century-Crofts, 1957.

Beaumont, A. B., and G. J. Larsinos. "Aqua Ammonia as a Nitrogen Fertilizer." *American Fertilizer* 76 (1932): 9–10.

Beeman, R. "'Chemivisions': The Forgotten Promises of the Chemurgy Movement." *Agricultural History* 68, no. 4 (1994): 23–45.

Bennet, J. E. "Black Scale Pest: Lively Enemy of the California Horticulturist." *Los Angeles Times*, March 1, 1896.

Berkeley Daily Gazette. "Establish Their Own Laboratory." January 26, 1904, 8.

———. "Fight Fruit Pests." May 31, 1904, 1.

Bernhardt, E. S., E. J. Rosi, and M. O. Gessner. "Synthetic Chemicals as Agents of Global Change." *Frontiers in Ecology and the Environment* 15, no. 2 (2017): 84–90.

Biringuccio, V. *The Pirotechnia*. Translated by C. Smith and M. Gnudi. New York: American Institute of Mining and Metallurgical Engineers, 1942. First published 1540.

Bishopp, F. C. "The Insecticide Situation." *Journal of Economic Entomology* 39, no. 4 (1946): 449.

Black, M. W. "Some Physiological Effects of Oil Sprays upon Deciduous Fruit Trees." *Journal of Pomology and Horticultural Science* 14, no. 2 (1937): 175–202.

Blanchette, A. *Porkopolis: American Animality, Standardized Life, and the Factory Farm*. Durham, NC: Duke University Press, 2020.

Bohme, S. R. *Toxic Injustice: A Transnational History of Exposure and Struggle*. Berkeley: University of California Press, 2015.

Bowles, O. "Arsenic." In *The Mineral Industry: Its Statistics, Technology and Trade during 1929*, edited by A. B. Butts and G. A. Roush, 36–42. New York: McGraw-Hill, 1930.

Boyce, A. M. "Studies on the Resistance of Certain Insects to Hydrocyanic Acid." *Journal of Economic Entomology* 21, no. 5 (1928): 715–20.

———. "The Citrus Red Mite Paratetranychus Citri Mcg. in California, and Its Control." *Journal of Economic Entomology* 29, no. 1 (1936): 125–30.

———. "Dusting Composition." Patent #2,166,121, US Patent Office, 1939.

———. "Dusting Composition." Patent #2,191,421, US Patent Office, 1940.

Boyce, A. M., J. F. Kagy, and J. W. Hansen. "Studies with Dinitro-O-Cyclohexylphenol." *Journal of Economic Entomology* 32, no. 3 (1939): 432–49.

Boyce, A. M., D. T. Prendergast, J. F. Kagy, and J. W. Hansen. "Dinitro-O-Cyclohexylphenol in the Control of Mites on Citrus and Persian Walnuts." *Journal of Economic Entomology* 32, no. 3 (1939): 450–66.

Boyd, W., W. S. Prudham, and R. A. Schurman. "Industrial Dynamics and the Problem of Nature." *Society & Natural Resources* 7, no. 7 (2001): 555–70.

Brand, C. J. "Recovery in the Fertilizer Industry." *Industrial & Engineering Chemistry* 27, no. 4 (1935): 372–78.

Braun, F. W. "The Manufacture of Sodium Cyanide." Paper presented at the School of Fumigation, Conducted by C. W. Woodworth, University of California, Pomona, 1915.

Breakey, E. P. "Halowax as Contact Insecticide." *Journal of Economic Entomology* 27, no. 2 (1934): 393–98.

Breakey, E. P., and A. C. Miller. "Halowax as an Ovicide." *Journal of Economic Entomology* 28, no. 2 (1935): 358–65.

———. "Halowax (Chlorinated Napthalene) as an Ovicide for Codling Moth and Oriental Fruit Moth." *Journal of Economic Entomology* 29, no. 5 (1936): 820–26.

Bridge, G., and P. Le Billon. *Oil.* Cambridge, MA: Polity Press, 2013.

Bristol, S. "The Oleander and Orange Scale-Bug." *Southern California Horticulturist* 1, no. 12 (1878): 374–75.

Britton, E. C. "Insecticide." Patent #1,907,493, US Patent Office, Dow Chemical Company, 1933.

Britton, E. C., and L. E. Mills. "Dinitro-Ortho-Cyclohexylphenol." Patent #1,880,404, US Patent Office, Dow Chemical Company, 1932.

———. "Manufacture of Cyclohexlphenols." Patent #1,862,075, US Patent Office, Dow Chemical Company, 1932.

Britton, E. C., and C. L. Moyle. "N-Substituted-2-Amino Nitro-Phenols." Patent #2,155,356, US Patent Office, Dow Chemical Company, 1939.

Britton, E. C., and R. P. Perkins. "Method for Manufacture of Cyclohexlphenols." Patent #1,917,823, US Patent Office, Dow Chemical Company, 1933.

Britton, E. C., and F. B. Smith. "Amine Salts of Nitro-Phenols." Patent #2,225,618, US Patent Office, Dow Chemical Company, 1940.

Britton, E. C., F. B. Smith, J. E. Livak, and W. W. Sunderland. "Arylamino-Derivatives of 2,4-Dintro-Phenol." Patent # 2,158.956, US Patent Office, Dow Chemical Company, 1939.

Britton, J. W., and R. C. Dosser. "Manufacture of 2,4-Dintro-6-Cyclohexl-Phenol." Patent #2,384,365, US Patent Office, Dow Chemical Company, 1945.

Britton, J. W., and F. B. Smith. "Insecticidal Composition." Patent # 2,225,619, US Patent Office, Dow Chemical Company, 1940.

Brooks, B. T. "Petroleum as a Chemical Raw Material." *Industrial & Engineering Chemistry* 16, no. 2 (1924): 185–89.

———. "Synthetic Organic Chemicals from Petroleum: An American Development." *Industrial & Engineering Chemistry* 31, no. 5 (1939): 514–19.

Brown, J. J., R. C. Berckmans, and T. G Hudson. "Georgia Refuses to Buy Arsenate at Present Price: Situation Declared by Entomology Board to Be the Result of Manipulation of the Market." *Atlanta Constitution*, December 14, 1922.

Brown, S. "Chlorination Apparatus." Patent #1,566,044, US Patent Office, Halowax Corporation, 1925.

———. "Process of Chlorination." Patent #1,672.878, US Patent Office, Halowax Corporation, 1928.

Brown, S., and E. R. Hanson. "Purification of Chloronapthalenes." Patent #1,953,070, US Patent Office, Halowax Corporation, 1934.

Browne, C. A. "Chronological Table of Some Leading Events in the History of Industrial Chemistry in America from the Earliest Colonial Settlements Until the Outbreak of the World War." *Industrial & Engineering Chemistry* 18, no. 9 (1926): 884–93.

Browne, J. R., and J. W. Taylor. *Reports upon the Mineral Resources of the United States*. Washington, DC: US Government Printing Office, 1867.

Brundage, R. P. "Orange Pests Develop Resistance to Poisons, Cost Growers Millions." *Wall Street Journal*, August 3, 1946.

———. "Citrus Troubles: West Coast Growers Worried About Market Sizes, Tree Diseases." *Wall Street Journal*, September 6, 1946.

Buckley v. Shell Chemical Company, 32 Cal.App.2d 209 (1939).

Bureau of the Census. *Historical Statistics of the United States 1789–1945, a Supplement to the Statistical Abstract of the United States*. Washington, DC: US Department of Commerce, 1949.

Burrow, J. "'Photo: The Centre of the Cornish Mining District.'" In *Pictorial England and Wales with upwards of Three Hundred and Twenty Copyright Illustrations*, 320. London: Cassel, 1897.

Buteler, M., and T. Stadler. "A Review of the Mode of Action and Current Use of Petroleum Distilled Sprays Oils." In *Pesticides in the Modern World: Trends in Pesticide Analysis*, edited by M. Stoytcheva, 119–36. Rijeka, Croatia: InTech, 2011.

Cafaro, P. "Rachel Carson's Environmental Ethics." In *Linking Ecology and Ethics in a Changing World: Values, Philosophy, and Action*, edited by R. Rozzi, S. Pickett, C. Palmer, J. Armesto, and J. Callicott, 163–72. New York: Springer, 2013.

California Cultivator. "Control of Nematodes." 91, no. 21 (1944): 520.

———. "Controlling Beet Nematode." 92, no. 1 (1945): 8.

California Farmer and Journal of Useful Sciences. "Orange Culture." 49, no. 4 (September 5, 1878).

California State Agricultural Society. *Table of Statistics: Transactions of the California State Agricultural Society*. Sacramento: California State Agricultural Society, 1872.

Caltagirone, L. E., and R. L. Doutt. "The History of the Vedalia Beetle Importation to California and Its Impact on the Development of Biological Control." *Annual Review of Entomology* 34 (1989): 1–16.

Calvert, C. C. "Arsenicals in Animal Feeds and Wastes." In *Arsenical Pesticides*, edited by E. A. Woolson, 70–80. Washington, DC: American Chemical Society, 1975.

Carr, J. C. "The Blessed Bugs." *Pacific Rural Press* 37, no. 20 (May 18, 1889): 481.

Carson, R. *Silent Spring.* New York: Mariner Books, 2002. First published 1962.

———. "Women's National Press Club Speech." In *Lost Woods: The Discovered Writing of Rachel Carson,* edited by L. Lear, 201–10. Boston: Beacon Press, 2002. First published 1962.

Carter, J. E., and G. E. Scattergood. "Agreement of Sale to the Henry Bower Chemical Manufacturing Company." 1911. Carter and Scattergood Business Records, Hagley Library and Archive, Wilmington, DE.

———. "Transfer Leger Binder." 1913. Carter and Scattergood Business Records, Hagley Library and Archive, Wilmington, DE.

Carter, R. H., and R. C. Roark. "Composition of Fluorides and Fluorosilicates Sold as Insecticides." *Journal of Economic Entomology* 21, no. 5 (1928): 762–73.

Carter, W. "A Promising New Soil Amendment and Disinfectant." *Science* 97, no. 2051 (1943): 383–84.

———. "Soil Treatments with Special Reference to Fumigation with DD Mixture." *Journal of Economic Entomology* 38, no. 1 (1945): 35–44.

———. "Soil Fumigant Comprising 1,3-Dichloropropene and 1,2-Dichloropropane." Patent #2,502,244, US Patent Office, 1950.

———. "Fumigation of Soil in Hawaii." In *Yearbook of Agriculture,* 126–29. Washington, DC: US Department of Agriculture, 1953.

Casagrande, R. A. "The Colorado Potato Beetle: 125 Years of Mismanagement." *American Entomologist* 33, no. 3 (1987): 142–50.

CC Pierce & Co. "Drawing Depicting William Wolfskill's Pasadena Orange and Lemon Grove and Residence, between Alameda and San Pedro Streets, Los Angeles, CA 1882." 1882. California Historical Society Collection, CHS-7310, USC Digital Archive, Los Angeles.

Cecil, P. F. *Herbicidal Warfare: The Ranch Hand Project in Vietnam.* New York: Praeger, 1986.

Chapman, A. C. "Letter to the Editor." *Pacific Rural Press* 33, no. 25 (June 18, 1887): 539.

Chapman, C. C. "The Purple Scale in Fullerton." *Claremont Pomological Club Proceedings* (March 22, 1909): 4–5.

Chapman, K. *The International Petrochemical Industry: Evolution and Location.* Oxford: Blackwell Publishing, 1991.

Checkland, S. G. *The Mines of Tharsis: Roman, French and British Enterprise in Spain.* London: George Allen & Unwin, 1967.

Chemical Markets. "Just So Long as the Weather Holds the Boll Weevil in Check, the Calcium Arsenate Is a Drug on the Market, but the Potential Demand Is 100,000,000 Lbs." 19, no. 13 (1926): 517–18, 564.

———. "Where Arsenic Is Produced." 19, no. 33 (1926): 1364.

———. "Chemical Costs." 19, no. 23 (1926): 933.

———. "Weevil Causing Some Concern in Texas." 21, no. 2 (1927): 58.

Chevron Chemical Company. "A Brief Chronological History of the Ortho Division, Chevron Chemical Company." 1964. California Spray Chemical Company, Chevron Chemical Company, Chevron Corporation Archive, Concord, CA.

Chiapella, A. M., Z. J. Grabowski, M. A. Rozance, A. D. Denton, M. A. Alattar, and E. F. Granek. "Toxic Chemical Governance Failure in the United States: Key Lessons and Paths Forward." *BioScience* 69, no. 8 (2019): 615–30.

Clark, B. "D-D Saves Crops from Foes." *Science News Letter*, October 1946, 234–35.

Clark, V. S. *History of the Manufactures in the United States: 1893–1928.* Vol. 3. New York: McGraw-Hill, 1929.

Coad, B. R. "Killing Boll Weevils with Poison Dust." In *Yearbook for 1920*, 241–52. Washington, DC: US Department of Agriculture, 1921.

Coates, P. *American Perceptions of Immigrant and Invasive Species: Strangers on the Land.* Berkeley: University of California Press, 2006.

Cochrane, R. C. *The National Academy of Sciences, the First Hundred Years, 1863–1963.* Washington, DC: National Academy of Sciences, 1978.

Cochrane, W. W. "Farm Technology, Foreign Surplus Disposal and Domestic Supply Control." *Journal of Farm Economics* 41, no. 5 (1959): 885–89.

———. *The Development of American Agriculture: A Historical Analysis.* Minneapolis: University of Minnesota Press, 1993.

———. *The Curse of Agricultural Abundance: A Sustainable Solution.* Lincoln: University of Nebraska Press, 2003.

Coit, J. E. *Citrus Fruits: An Account of the Citrus Industry with Special Reference to California Requirement and Practices and Similar Conditions.* New York: Macmillan, 1915.

Constitution. "Slandered Insects." August 1, 1876.

Cook, A. J. "Bulletin No. 58—Insecticides." Ann Arbor: University of Michigan Agricultural Experiment Station, 1890.

Cooper, E. "Insects and Insecticides." Pamphlet. Sacramento: California State Commission of Horticulture, 1905.

Cooper, T. "Recycling Modernity: Waste and Environmental History." *History Compass* 8, no. 9 (2010): 1114–25.

Coquilett, D. W. "The Patent on Hydrocyanic Acid Gas Process Declared Invalid." *Insect Life* 7, no. 3 (1894): 257–58.

———. "Farm and Range: Cotton Cushiony Scale, Experiments with Remedies for Their Destruction." *Los Angeles Times*, July 18, 1886.

———. "US Department of Agriculture Report for 1886." Washington, DC: US Department of Agriculture, 1887.

———. "Talks with Citizens." *Los Angeles Times*, May 27, 1888.

———. "Insect Killing by Fumigation: An Essay Read at the Santa Barbara Convention of Fruit Growers." *Pacific Rural Press* 35, no. 18 (May 5, 1888): 404.

———. "Report on the Gas Treatment for Scale Insects." In *Agriculture Yearbook for 1887*, 123–42. Washington, DC: US Department of Agriculture, 1888.

———. "Another Foe for Icerya." *Pacific Rural Press* 40, no. 26 (December 27, 1890): 551.

———. "Entomological: Origin of the Gas Treatment for Scale Insect." *Pacific Rural Press* 35, no. 18 (September 5, 1891): 193.

Cottrell, F. C. "Progress Report to Anaconda Smelter Commission." 1913. Anaconda Copper Mining Company Records, Collection no. 169, box 261-2, 1-7, Montana Historical Society Research Center, Helena.

Cózar, A., F. Echevarría, J. I. González-Gordillo, X. Irigoien, B. Úbeda, S. Hernández-León, Á. T. Palma, et al. "Plastic Debris in the Open Ocean." *Proceedings of the National Academy of Sciences* 111, no. 28 (2014): 10239–44.

Crafts, A. S. "A New Herbicide, 2,4, Dinitro 6 Secondary Butyl Phenol." *Science* 101, no. 2625 (1945): 417–18.

———. "Oil Sprays for Weeding Carrots and Related Crops." Circular 136, California Agricultural Extension Service. Berkeley: College of Agriculture, University of California, 1947.

———. "Toxicity of Ammonium Dintro-O-Sec-Butyl." *Hilgardia* 19, no. 5 (1949): 159–69.

———. "Weed Control Research: Past, Present, and Future." *Weeds* 8, no. 4 (1960): 535–40.

Crafts, A. S., and H. G. Reiber. "Herbicidal Properties of Oils." *Hilgardia* 18, no. 2 (1948): 77–156.

———. "Herbicidal Uses of Oils." In *Agricultural Applications of Petroleum Products*, edited by Industrial and Engineering Chemistry, 70–75. Washington, DC: American Chemical Society, 1952.

Crist, K. "A Battle That Never Ends." *Los Angeles Times*, July 22, 1934.

Cronon, W. *Nature's Metropolis: Chicago and the Great West*. New York: W. W. Norton, 1991.

Crop Protection Digest. "The Crop Protection Institute," 1, no. 1 (1921).

Crop Protection Institute. "Constitution and By-Laws of the Crop Protection Institute." 1920. National Research Council, Institutions: Associations, Individuals, Archive of the National Academy of Sciences, Washington, DC.

———. "The Establishment of the Crop Protection Institute: A Get Together Movement on the Part of Three Great Groups, the Intelligent Grower, the Scientist, and the Businessman." Pamphlet Sent to Members of the American Association of Economic Entomology. Durham, NC: Crop Protection Institute, 1920.

———. "The Crop Protection Institute." *Crop Protection Digest* 1, no. 1 (1921).

———. "Investigations of Industrial Organizations." Washington, DC: Crop Protection Institute, 1921.

———. "Cooperative Dusting and Spraying Experiment of 1921." *Crop Protection Institute Digest* 2 (1922): 1–30.

Crowell, B. *America's Munitions 1917–1918: Report of Benedict Crowell, the Assistant Secretary of War, Director of Munitions*. Washington, DC: Government Printing Office, 1919.

Culver, J. P. "Tree Cover and Fumigator." Patent #367,134, US Patent Office, 1887.

Daily, G. C., ed. *Nature's Services: Societal Dependence on Natural Ecosystems*. Washington, DC: Island Press, 1997.

Daily, G. C., and K. Ellison. *The New Economy of Nature*. New York: Island Press, 2002.

Daily Alta California (DAC). "Later from the South: Arrival of the Southerner." September 5, 1854.

———. "Wolfskill of Los Angeles and His Vineyard." December 20, 1858.

———. "California Wine-Growers Association: Secretary's Report." June 25, 1863.

———. "Death of William Wolfskill." October 5, 1866.

———. "Agricultural Notes." February 28, 1885.

———. "State Notes." June 30, 1886.

———. "Horticulture: The Fumigation of Trees without the Use of Carbonate of Soda." December 9, 1887.

———. "Chasing a Beetle: Our Foreign Relations with the Icerya Purchase, an Enthusiastic Entomologist, Surprising Adventures of One of Our State Department Diplomats in Search of a Bug." April 30, 1890.

Daily Constitution. "Arsenic: Devon, England." February 2, 1875.

Danbom, D. *The Resisted Revolution: Urban American and the Industrialization of Agriculture, 1900–1930.* Ames: Iowa State University Press, 1979.

Davis, F. R.. *Banned: A History of Pesticides and the Science of Toxicology.* New Haven, CT: Yale University Press, 2014.

Davis, J. J. "The Value of Crude Arsenious Oxide in Poison Bait for Cutworms and Grasshoppers." *Journal of Economic Entomology* 12, no. 2 (1919): 200–203.

Day, J. "Copper, Zinc, and Brass Production." In *The Industrial Revolution in Metals*, edited by J. Day and R. F. Tylecote, 131–99. London: Institute of Metals, 1991.

De Ong, E. R. "Technical Aspects of Petroleum Oils and Oil Sprays." *Journal of Economic Entomology* 5, no. 1 (1926): 733–45.

———. "Petroleum Oil as a Carrier for Insecticides and as a Plant Stimulant." *Industrial and Engineering Chemistry* 20, no. 8 (1928): 826–27.

———. "Present Trend of Oil Sprays." *Journal of Economic Entomology* 24, no. 5 (1931): 978–85.

———. *Chemistry and Uses of Insecticides.* New York: Reinhold, 1948.

———. Letter to E. J. Newcomer. November 8, 1927. Western Cooperative Spray Project Records, 1921–1952, Washington State University Manuscripts, Archives, & Special Collections, Pullman, WA.

De Ong, E. R., and H. Knight. "Emulsifying Agents as an Inhibiting Factor in Oil Sprays." *Journal of Economic Entomology* 18, no. 2 (1925): 424–26.

De Ong, E. R., H. Knight, and J. C. Chamberlin. "A Preliminary Study of Petroleum Oil as an Insecticide for Citrus Trees." *Hilgardia* 2, no. 9 (1927): 351–86.

Deansley, R. M. "Process for the Inhibition of Halogen Substitution Reactions." Patent #1,952,122, US Patent Office, Shell Development Company, 1934.

———. "Halogenation Process." Patent #1,991,600, US Patent Office, Shell Development Corporation, 1935.

Deansley, R. M., and W. Engs. "Process for the Preparation of Substantially Pure Tertiary Olefins." Patent #2,012,785, US Patent Office, Shell Development Company, 1935.

deBuyn, C. B. "Process of Fertilizing Soil." Patent #2,202,824, US Patent Office, Shell Development Company, 1934.

Dennis, W. H. *A Hundred Years of Metallurgy.* Chicago: Aldine, 1964.

Detling, K. D. "Production of Organic Halogen Compound." Patent #2,501,597, US Patent Office, Shell Development Corporation, 1950.

Dickens, C. *Our Mutual Friend: Book the First*. New York: Charles Scribner's Sons, 1901. First published 1864.

Dimmock, G. "The Effect of a Few Common Gases on Arthropods." *Psyche: A Journal of Entomology* 2, nos. 35–36 (1877): 19–22.

Dines, H. G. *The Metalliferous Mining Region of South-West England*. Memoirs of Geological Survey of Great Britain, vol. 1. London: Her Majesty's Stationary Office, 1956.

Dingle, A. E. "'The Monster Nuisance of All': Landowners, Alkali Manufacturers, and Air Pollution, 1828–1864." *Economic History Review* 35, no. 4 (1982): 529–48.

Dinzelbacher, D. "Animal Trials: A Multidisciplinary Approach." *Journal of Interdisciplinary History* 32, no. 3 (2002): 405–21.

Dobbins, J. R. "Extracts from Correspondence: The Spread of the Australian Lady-Bird." *Insect Life* 2 (1889): 112.

Dorsey, M. G. "More Than Just Taboo: The Legacy of the Chemical Warfare Prohibitions of the 1899 and 1907 Hague Conferences." In *War, Peace and International Order? The Legacies of the Hague Conference of 1899 and 1907*, edited by M. Abbenhuis, C. Barber and A. Higgins, 86–102. New York: Routledge, 2017.

Douglas, E. "Millions Are Slain. Farmers Turn on Grasshopper Horde." *Los Angeles Times*, July 2, 1933.

Douglas, M. *Purity and Danger: An Analysis of the Concepts of Pollution and Taboo*. New York: Ark Paperbacks, 1988. First published 1966.

Doutt, R. L. "Vice, Virtue, and Vedalia." *Bulletin of the Entomological Society of America* 4, no. 4 (1958): 119–23.

Dow, H. H. Letter from Herbert Dow to Luther Burbank on Sodium Benzoate. 1906. Herbert H. Dow Papers, Post Street Archives, Science History Institute, Philadelphia, PA.

———. Letter from Herbert Dow to Fred Snyder on Sodium Benzoate. 1906. Herbert H. Dow Papers, Post Street Archives, Science History Institute, Philadelphia, PA.

Dow Chemical Company. "Red Mite Research and the Dinitros." *Down to Earth: A Review of Agricultural Chemical Progress* 1, no. 1 (1945): 6–9.

———. "Dow Manual on Spraying and Dusting." 1945. Dow Chemical Historical Collection, 1897–2006, Dow Chemical Company, Science History Institute, Midland, MI.

———. "DN-111 Used with DDT Controls Red Mite." *Down to Earth: A Review of Agricultural Chemical Progress* 2, no. 1 (1946): 5–6.

———. "Chemical News for Western Agriculture." 1949. Papers of Alden S. Crafts, Dow Chemical Company, Great Western Division, UC Davis Special Collections, Davis, CA.

———. *Dow in the West*. Walnut Creek, CA: Dow Chemical Company, 1977.

———. "Personnel—Kagy, John F." Undated. In Dow Chemical Historical Collection, 1897–2006, Dow Chemical Company, Science History Institute, Midland, MI.

Dow Chemical Company, Great Western Division. "Dow Contact Herbicide Pamphlet." 1944. In Papers of Alden S. Crafts, UC Davis Special Collections, Davis, CA.

———. "Dow Selective Herbicide Pamphlet." 1944. Papers of Alden S. Crafts, UC Davis Special Collections, Davis, CA.

Drinker, C., M. F. Warren, and G. Bennett. "The Problem of Possible Systemic Effects Form Certain Chlorinated Hydrocarbons." Journal of Industrial Hygiene 19, no. 7 (1937): 283–99.

Drug & Chemical Markets. "May Be Shortage in Arsenate." 14, no. 3 (1924): 167.

———. "Is Arsenic Down to Stay? Demoralization of Present Market Had Driven Prices to Lowest Level of the Last Ten Years." 27, no. 2 (1925): 77–78.

Dunn, G. Letter from G. Dunn, Chairman of NRC, to Albert L. Barrows, Esq. August 7, 1925. National Research Council, Institutions: Associations, Individuals, Archive of the National Academy of Sciences, Washington, DC.

———. Letter from G. Dunn, Chaiman of NRC, to Vernon Kellogg. June 18, 1925. National Research Council, Institutions: Associations, Individuals, Archive of the National Academy of Sciences, Washington, DC.

DuPont. "Digest, R&H Chemical Company, Subsidiaries and Affiliates." 1930. Absorbed Companies, Records of E. I. du Pont de Nemours, Hagley Museum, Wilmington, DE.

Dutton, W. C. "The Effect of Some Spraying Materials upon the Rest Period of Fruit Trees." Proceedings of the American Society of Horticultural Science 21 (1925): 176–78.

———. "Orchard Trials of Dinitro-O-Cylohexylphenol in Petroleum Oil for Control of Rosy Apple Aphis and San Jose Scale." Journal of Economic Entomology 29, no. 1 (1936): 62–65.

Earl, B. Cornish Mining: The Techniques of Metal Mining in the West of England, Past and Present. Cornwall, UK: D. Bradford Barton, 1968.

———. "Arsenic Winning and Refining Methods in the West of England." Journal of the Trevithick Society 10 (1983): 9–29.

———. The Cornish Arsenic Industry. Cornwall, UK: Penhellick Publications, 1996.

Ebbon, G. P. "Environmental and Health Aspects of Agricultural Spray Oils." In Spray Oils Beyond 2000: Sustainable Pest and Disease Management, edited by G. A. Beattie, D. M. Watson, M. L Stevens, D. J. Rae, and R. N. Sponner-Hart, 232–46. Penrith, Australia: University of Western Sydney, 2002.

Effland, A. B. "'New Riches from the Soil': The Chemurgic Ideas of Wheeler McMillen." Agricultural History 69, no. 2 (1995): 288–97.

Eichers, T. D., R. Jenkins, and A. Fox. "DDT Used in Farm Production." Agricultural Economics Report no. 158. Washington, DC: US Department of Agriculture Economic Research Service, 1971.

Ellis, C. The Chemistry of Petroleum Derivatives. Vol. 1. New York: Chemical Catalog, 1934.

———. The Chemistry of Petroleum Derivatives. Vol. 2. New York: Reinhold, 1937.

Elton, J., W. Welch, and E. Dunn. "Blueprints of Proposed New Arsenic Plant Design, Recommendations for Improved Arsenic Plant Operation at the Washoe Reduction Works of the Anaconda Copper Mining Company."

1913. In Anaconda Copper Mining Company Records, Collection no. 169, box 261-6, Montana Historical Society Research Center, Helena.

Engs, W., and S. N. Wik. "Process for Producing and Recovering Halogenated Organic Compounds." Patent #2,321,472, US Patent Office, Shell Development Company, 1943.

Essig, E. O. *A History of Entomology*. New York: Hafner Publishing, 1931.

———. "Farm Machinery in Relation to Insect Pest Control." *Journal of Economic Entomology* 26, no. 4 (1933): 864–68.

———. "Insects and Agriculture." *Journal of Economic Entomology* 26, no. 4 (1933): 869–72.

Evans, E. P. *The Criminal Prosecution and Punishment of Animals: The Lost History of Europe's Animals Trials*. London: Faber and Faber, 1987. First published 1906.

Evans, T. W. "Toxic Composition." Patent #2,411,566, US Patent Office, Shell Development Company, 1946.

Everitt, E. P. "Orange Grove, Showing Southern Pacific Passenger Train Moving in the Background, Ca.1880." 1880. California Historical Society Collection, 1860–1960, CHS-43696, USC Digital Archive, Los Angeles, CA.

Falandysz, J. "Polychlorinated Napthalenes: An Environmental Update." *Environmental Pollution* 101, no. 1 (1998): 77–90.

Farrar, M. D. "Relation of Chemical Research Laboratories to Development of New Insecticides and Fungicides." *Industrial & Engineering Chemistry* 40, no. 4 (1948): 680–81.

Fay, A. H., ed. *The Mineral Industry, Its Technology and Trade during 1910*. Vol. 19. New York: McGraw-Hill, 1911.

"Financial Records 2297–2299." 1900. Yellow Aster Mining and Milling Company Records, 1898–1918, California State Library, Sacramento.

Fine, G. A., and L. Christoforides. "Dirty Birds, Filthy Immigrants, and the English Sparrow War: Metaphorical Linkage in Constructing Social Problems." *Symbolic Interaction* 14, no. 4 (1991): 375–93.

Finlay, M. "The Failure of Chemurgy in Depression-Era South: The Case of Jesse F. Jackson and the Central of Georgia Railroad." *Georgia Historical Quarterly* 81, no. 1 (1997): 78–102.

———. "Old Efforts at New Uses: A Brief History of Chemurgy and the American Search for Biobased Materials." *Journal of Industrial Ecology* 7, nos. 3–4 (2008): 33–46.

Finlay, Mark R. "The Industrial Utilization of Farm Products and By-Products: The USDA Regional Research Laboratories." *Agricultural History* 64, no. 2 (1990): 41–52.

Fisher, D. F. "Suggested Outline for Typical Oil Spray Project." 1927. Western Cooperative Spray Project Records, 1921–1952, Washington State University Manuscripts, Archives, & Special Collections, Pullman.

———. "Physiological Investigations—Cooperative Oil Spray Project." 1927. Western Cooperative Spray Project Records, 1921–1952, Washington State University Manuscripts, Archives, & Special Collections, Pullman.

———. "Arsenical and Other Fruit Injuries of Apples Resulting from Washing." Technical Bulletin 245. Washington, DC: US Department of Agriculture, 1931.

Fisher, D. F., E. L. Green, and E. J. Newcomer. "The Western Cooperative Spray Oil Project." 1928. Western Cooperative Spray Project Records, 1921–1952, Washington State University Manuscripts, Archives, & Special Collections, Pullman.

Fitzgerald, D. *Every Farm a Factory: The Industrial Ideal in American Agriculture.* New Haven, CT: Yale University Press, 2005.

Fleming, W. E. "Fluorosilicates as Insecticides for the Japanese Beetle." *Journal of Economic Entomology* 20, no. 5 (1927): 685–91.

Fletcher, H. L. "Sugar Beet Nematode (Heterodera Schachtii) Control Studies in Ontario." Paper presented at the American Society of Sugar Beet Technologists, 1947.

Flippen, J. B. "Pest, Pollution, and Politics: The Nixon Administration's Pesticide Policy." *Agricultural History* 71, no. 4 (1997): 442–56.

Forbes, R. J., and D. R. O'Beirne. *The Technical Development of Royal Dutch Shell: 1890–1940.* The Hague: Royal Dutch Petroleum Company, 1957.

Forde, H. I., and E. L. Proebsting. "Utilization of Ammonia Supplied to Peaches and Prunes at Different Seasons." *Hilgardia* 16, no. 9 (1945): 411–25.

Fordyce, J., I. Rosen, and C. Myers. "Quantitative Studies in Syphilis from a Clinical and Biologic Point of View II: Normal Arsenic." *Archives of Internal Medicine* 31, no. 5 (1923): 739–57.

Fortun, K., and M. Fortun. "Scientific Imaginaries and Ethical Plateaus in Contemporary U.S. Toxicology." *American Anthropologist* 107, no. 1 (2008): 43–54.

Foster, J. B. "Marx's Theory of Metabolic Rift: Classical Foundations for Environmental Sociology 1." *American Journal of Sociology* 105, no. 2 (1999): 366–405.

Francis, G. G. *The Smelting in the Copper in the Swansea District of South Wales, from the Time of Elizabeth to the Present Day.* 2nd ed. London: Henry Southern, 1881.

Frankenberger, W. T., ed. *The Environmental Chemistry of Arsenic.* New York: Marcel Decker, 2002.

Frickel, S. *Chemical Consequences: Environmental Mutagens, Scientist Activism, and the Rise of Genetic Toxicology.* New Brunswick, NJ: Rutgers University Press, 2004.

Friedlander, H. *The Origins of Nazi Genocide: From Euthanasia to the Final Solution.* Chapel Hill: University of North Carolina Press, 1995.

Frolich, P. K. "Chemical Trends in the Petroleum Industry." *Industrial & Engineering Chemistry* 30, no. 8 (1938): 916–22.

Frome, F. D., and F. J. Schneiderhan. "Cooperative Dust Spraying Experiment of 1922." *Crop Protection Institute Digest* 4 (1924): 1–36.

Gabrys, J. "Sink: The Dirt of Systems." *Environment and Planning D: Society and Space* 27, no. 4 (2009): 666–81.

Gallo, M. A. "History and Scope of Toxicology." In *Casarett & Doull's Essential of Toxicology,* edited by C. D. Klaassen and J. B. Watkins III, 3–11. New York: McGraw-Hill, 2015.

Gardner, L. R. "Petroleum-Derived Products in Agriculture Pest Control." In *Agricultural Applications of Petroleum Products,* edited by Industrial and

Engineering Chemistry, 100–104. Washington, DC: American Chemical Society, 1952.

———. "Entomology in the Pacific Branch—Plus and Minus Fifty Years: Industrial Contributions." *Bulletin of the Entomological Society of America* 13, no. 1 (1967): 24–26.

———. *The First Thirty Years: The Early History of the Company Now Known as Ortho Division, Chevron Chemical Company.* San Francisco: Chevron Chemical Company, 1978.

Garelick, H., H. Jones, A. Dybowska, and E. Valsami-Jones. "Arsenic Pollution Sources." In *Reviews of Environmental Contamination and Toxicology: Arsenic, Pollution and Remediation, an International Perspective,* edited by D. M. Whitacre, 17–60. New York: Springer, 2008.

Gee, K. "America's Dairy Farmers Dump 43 Million Gallons of Excess Milk." *Wall Street Journal,* October 13, 2016.

Gibby, D., W. Scheer, S. Collmen, and G. Pinyuh. "The Master Gardener Program: A WSU Extension Success Story, Early History from 1973." Pullman: Washington State University Extension, 2008.

Giedion, S. *Mechanization Takes Command: A Contribution to Anonymous History.* New York: Oxford University Press, 1948.

Gilbreth, F. B. "New Soil Fumigant Hailed as Farm Boon; Sponsors Say to Revolutionize Rotation." *News and Courier,* July 21, 1948.

Gille, Z. *From the Cult of Waste to the Trash Heap of History: The Politics of Waste in Socialist and Postsocialist Hungary.* Bloomington: Indiana University Press, 2007.

———. "Actor Networks, Modes of Production, and Waste Regimes: Reassembling the Macro-Social." *Environment and Planning A: Economy and Space* 42, no. 5 (2010): 1049–64.

Glacken, G. J. "Reflections on the Man-Nature Theme as a Subject for Study." In *Future Environments of North America,* edited by F. F. Darling and J. P. Milton, 355–71. Garden City, NY: Natural History Press, 1966.

Gladding, J. D. "El Segundo to Be Big Oil Center." *Los Angeles Herald,* October 31, 1914.

Glotfelty, C. "Cold War, Silent Spring: The Trope of War in Modern Environmentalism." In *And No Birds Sing: Rhetorical Analyses of Rachel Carson's Silent Spring,* edited by C. Waddell, 157–73. Carbondale: Southern Illinois University Press, 2000.

Good, C. K., and N. Pensky. "Halowax Acne ("Cable Rash"): A Cutaneous Eruption in Marine Electricians Due to Certain Chlorinated Napthalenes and Diphenyls." *Archives of Dermatology and Syphilology* 48, no. 3 (1943): 251–57.

Goodman, D., B. Sorj, and J. Wilkinson. *From Farming to Biotechnology: A Theory of Agro-industrial Development.* Oxford: Basil Blackwell, 1987.

Gordon, J. B. "Perilous DDT Ban." *New York Times,* September 16, 1972.

Gorney, C. "University Is Sued over Development of Sophisticated Harvesting Machines." *Washington Post,* January 18, 1979, A11.

Gray, G. P. "The Workings of the California Insecticide Law." *Journal of Industrial and Engineering Chemistry* 6, no. 7 (1914): 590–94.

———. "Economic Toxicology." *Science* 48, no. 12 (1918): 329–32.
———. "The Consumption and Cost of Economic Poisons in California in 1916." *Industrial & Engineering Chemistry* 10, no. 4 (1918): 301–2.
Gray, G. P., and E. R. de Ong. "California Petroleum Insecticides: Laboratory and Field Tests." *Industrial & Engineering Chemistry* 18, no. 2 (1926): 175–80.
Gray, G. P., and A. Kirkpatrick. "The Resistance of Black Scale (Saissetia Oleae Bern.) to Hydrocyanic Acid Fumigation." *Journal of Economic Entomology* 22, no. 6 (1929): 893–97.
Gregson, N., and M. Crang. "Materiality and Waste: Inorganic Vitality in a Networked World." *Environment and Planning A* 42, no. 5 (2010): 1026–32.
Griswold, E. "How 'Silent Spring' Ignited the Environmental Movement." *New York Times*, September 21, 2012.
Groll, H., G. Hearne, F. F. Rust, and W. E. Vaughn. "Halogenation of Hydrocarbons: Chlorination of Olefins and Olefin-Paraffin Mixtures at Moderate Temperatures; Induced Substitution." *Industrial & Engineering Chemistry* 31, no. 10 (1939): 1238–44.
Groll, H. P. A., and G. Hearne. "Halo-Substitution of Unsaturated Organic Compounds." Patent #2,130,084, US Patent Office, Shell Development Company, 1938.
———. "Halogenation of Hydrocarbons: Substitution of Chlorine and Bromine into Straight Chain Olefins." *Industrial & Engineering Chemistry* 31, no. 12 (1939): 1531–39.
Grower Pamphlet: Scientific Control of Orchard Pests. Watsonville: California Spray-Chemical Company, 1926.
Guinn, J. M. "From Cattle Ranch to Orange Grove." *Annual Publication of the Historical Society of Southern California* 8, no. 3 (1912): 145–57.
Gundersen, C., B. Kreider, and J. Pepper. "The Economics of Food Insecurity in the United States." *Applied Economic Perspectives and Policy* 33, no. 3 (2011): 281–303.
Guthman, J. *Agrarian Dreams: The Paradox of Organic Farming in California.* Berkeley: University of California Press, 2004.
———. *Weighing In: Obesity, Food Justice, and the Limits of Capitalism.* Berkeley: University of California Press, 2011.
———. *Wilted: Pathogens, Chemicals, and the Fragile Future of the Strawberry Industry.* Berkeley: University of California Press, 2019.
Guyer, M. F. "Research Fellowships Administered through the Division of Biology and Agriculture of the National Research Council." *Science* 55, no. 1433 (1922): 636.
Haber, L. F. *The Chemical Industry during the Nineteenth Century: A Study of the Economic Aspect of Applied Chemistry in Europe and North America.* Oxford: Oxford University Press, 1958.
———. *The Chemical Industry, 1900–1930: International Growth and Technological Change.* Oxford: Oxford University Press, 1971.
"Hague Convention of 1899." Adopted at Hague Peace Conference, Netherlands.
Hale, G. E. "War Services of the National Research Council." In *The New World of Science: Its Development During the War*, edited by R. M. Yerkes, 13–30. Freeport, NY: Books for Libraries Press, 1969. First published 1920.

Hale, W. J. "When Agriculture Enters the Chemical Industry." *Industrial & Engineering Chemistry* 22, no. 12 (1930): 1311–15.

Hamilton, A. "Dinitrophenol Poisoning in Munition Works in France." *Monthly Labor Review* 7, no. 3 (1918): 718–26.

Hannibal, L. S. "Soil Injector." Patent #2,598,121, US Patent Office, Shell Development Company, 1948.

Hansen and Solano Co. "Moulton Crystal Springs Property of J. W. Wolfskill on the East Side of the Los Angeles River." 1888. Maps, Huntington Digital Library, San Marino, CA.

Hanson, E. R., and S. Brown. "Light Colored Liquid Chlorinated Napthalene and Production Thereof." Patent #2,025,742, US Patent Office, Halowax Corporation, 1935.

Harris, J. R. "Copper and Shipping in the Eighteenth Century." *Economic History Review* 19, no. 3 (1966): 550–68.

Harrison, J. L. "Pesticide Purveyors and Corporate Power." In *Bite Back: People Taking on Corporate Food and Winning*, edited by K. DeMaster and S. Jayaraman, 51–63. Berkeley: University of California Press, 2020.

Hartzell, A., and F. Lathrop. "Process and Apparatus for Making Colloidal Substances." Patent #1,870,727, US Patent Office, Crop Protection Institute, 1932.

Hartzell, F. Z., and J. B. Moore. "Control of Oyster-Shell Scale on Apple by Means of Tar Oils, Tar-Lubricating Oils, and Lubricating Oils Containing Dinitro-O-Cyclohexylphenol." *Journal of Economic Entomology* 30, no. 4 (1937): 651–55.

Hartzell, F. Z., J. B. Moore, and D. E. Greenwood. "Control of Eye-Spotted Budmoth on Apple by Lubricating Oil Containing Dintro-O-Cyclohexylphenol." *Journal of Economic Entomology* 31, no. 2 (1938): 249–53.

Haseman, L. "Testing Commercial Insecticides." *Journal of Economic Entomology* 21, no. 1 (1928): 115–17.

Haynes, W. "The Chemical Era of Modern Industry." *Chemical Markets* 21, no. 2 (1927): 43–44.

———. *Chemical Economics*. New York: D. Van Nostrand, 1933.

———. *American Chemical Industry: The World War I Period, 1912–1922*. Vol. 3. New York: D. Van Nostrand, 1945.

———. *The American Chemical Industry: Decade of New Products, 1930–1939*. Vol. 5. New York: D. Van Nostrand, 1945.

———. *The American Chemical Industry: The Chemical Companies*. Vol. 6. New York: D. Van Nostrand, 1949.

Haywood, J. K. "The Composition and Analysis of London Purple." *Journal of the American Chemical Society* 22, no. 12 (1900): 800–809.

———. "Injury to Vegetation and Animal Life by Smelter Fumes." *Journal of the American Chemical Society* 29, no. 7 (1907): 998–1009.

Heikes, V. C. "Arsenic." In *The Mineral Industry: Its Statistics, Technology and Trade during 1924*, edited by A. B. Butts and G. A. Roush, 63–70. New York: McGraw-Hill, 1925.

Helms, D. "Technological Methods for Boll Weevil Control." *Agricultural History* 53, no. 1 (1979): 286–99.

Hempel, S. *The Inheritor's Powder: A Tale of Arsenic, Murder, and the New Forensic Science*. New York: W. W. Norton, 2013.

Henderson, G. *California and the Fictions of Capital.* Oxford: Oxford University Press, 1999.

Henderson, R. R. "Agricultural Insecticides: Raw Materials and Methods of Manufacture." *Chemical Age* 29, nos. 257–60 (1921): 167–69.

———. "Arsenic, Calcium Arsenate, and the Boll-Weevil." *Chemical Age* 31, no. 12 (1923): 547–48.

Henke, C. R. *Cultivating Science, Harvesting Power: Science and Industrial Agriculture in California.* Cambridge, MA: MIT Press, 2008.

Henry, W. A. "Pacific Coast Work of the Division of Entomology." *Insect Life* 2, no. 5 (1889): 141–44.

Hepler-Smith, E. "Molecular Bureaucracy: Toxicological Information and Environmental Protection." *Environmental History* 24, no. 3 (2019): 534–60.

Hepp, N. M., W. R. Mindak, J. G. Gasper, C. B. Thompson, and J. N. Barrows. "Survey of Cosmetics for Arsenic, Cadmium, Chromium, Cobalt, Lead, Mercury, and Nickel Content." *Journal of Cosmetic Science* 65 (May/June 2014): 125–45.

Herbert, F. B. "Spray Stimulation." *Journal of Economic Entomology* 17, no. 5 (1924): 567–72.

Herms, W. B. "An Analysis of Some of California's Major Entomological Problems." *Journal of Economic Entomology* 19, no. 2 (1926): 262–70.

Herrick, G. W. Letter to Professor R. L. Webster, Washington State University. 1926. Western Cooperative Spray Project Records, 1921–1952, Washington State University Manuscripts, Archives, & Special Collections, Pullman.

Hiç, C, P. Pradhan, D. Rybski, and J. P. Kropp. "Food Surplus and Its Climate Burdens." *Environmental Science and Technology* 50, no. 8 (2016): 4269–77.

Hightower, J. *Hard Times, Hard Tomatoes: A Report of the Agribusiness Accountability Project on the Failure of America's Land Grant College Complex.* Cambridge, MA: Schenkman Publishing, 1973.

Hildebrand, E. M. "War on Weeds." *Science* 103, no. 2677 (1946): 465–68, 492.

Hilgard, E. "Science in the Orchard." *Riverside Daily Press,* April 16, 1895.

Hills, P. *Venetian Colour: Marble Mosaic, Painting and Glass, 1250–1550.* New Haven, CT: Yale University Press, 1999.

Hinds, W. E. "Presidential Address: Some Achievements in Economic Entomology." *Journal of Economic Entomology* 27, no. 1 (1934): 37–52.

Hinton, A. R. "Development of California Petroleum Products." *Los Angeles Times,* January 1, 1916.

Hockenyos, G. L. "Monochloronapthalenes as an Insecticide." *Crop Protection Digest* 31 (1931): 1–38.

Hofman, H. O. *Metallurgy of Copper.* New York: McGraw-Hill, 1914.

Holden, B. *Charles W. Woodworth: The Remarkable Life of U.C. First Entomologist.* n.p.: Brian Holden Publishing, 2015.

Holt, L. M. "Orange Tree Diseases." *Southern California Horticulturist* 1, no. 2 (1877): 61–62.

———. "The Red Scale on Citrus Trees." *Pacific Rural Press* 19, no. 5 (1880): 67.

Horton, J .R. *Control of the Argentine Ant in Orange Groves.* Farmer's Bulletin, vol. 928. Washington, DC: US Department of Agriculture, 1918.

Houser, J. S. "Some Problems in Economic Entomology." *Journal of Economic Entomology* 25, no. 1 (1932): 28–39.

Howard, L. O. "An Important Enemy to Fruit Trees, San Jose Scale (Asidioutus Pernidosus): Its Appearance in the Eastern United States; Measure to Be Taken to Prevent Its Spread and Destroy It." Circular 3, Second Series. Washington, DC: US Department of Agriculture, Division of Entomology, 1894.

———. "Progress in Economic Entomology in the United States." In *Yearbook of the United States Department of Agriculture for 1899*, 135–56. Washington, DC: US Government Printing Office, 1900.

———. "War against Insects." *Nature* 109, no. 2725 (1922): 79–80.

———. "Two Billion Crop Loss Spur Fight on Insects: Entomologists Waging War on a Hundred Agricultural Pests, Half of Foreign Origin—Changes in Methods of Growing and Harvesting Urged." *New York Times*, February 24, 1924.

———. *A History of Applied Entomology (Somewhat Anecdotal)*. Washington, DC: Smithsonian Institution, 1930.

———. *The Insect Menace*. New York: D. Appleton-Century, 1933.

Howard, L. O., and C. L. Marlatt. "The San José Scale: Its Occurrence in the United States with a Full Account of Its Life History and the Remedies to Be Used against It." Bulletin 3, New Series. Washington, DC: US Department of Agriculture, Division of Entomology, 1896.

Howe, H. E., and J. V. Antwerpen. "Utilization of Industrial Wastes." *Industrial & Engineering Chemistry* 31, no. 11 (1939): 1323–30.

Howe, J. L. "War of Chemicals Reaches a Climax." *New York Times*, June 16, 1918.

Howell, P. "Animals, Agency, and History." In *The Routledge Companion to Animal-Human History*, edited by H. Kean and O. Howell, 197–221. New York: Taylor & Francis, 2018.

Hyde, C. K. *Copper for America: The United States Copper Industry from Colonial Times to the 1990s*. Tucson: University of Arizona Press, 1998.

Hyslop, J. A. "Soil Fumigation." *Journal of Economic Entomology* 7, no. 4 (1914): 305–12.

Imperial Mineral Resources Bureau. *The Mineral Industry of the British Empire and Foreign Countries: War Period; Arsenic (1913–1919)*. London: His Majesty's Stationery Office, 1920.

Industrial & Engineering Chemistry. "History of American Chemical Industries: Roessler and Hasslacher–Partners." 21, no. 10 (1929): 989–91.

———. "Headlines of the Month." 42, no. 11 (1946): 2385–86.

Ingallis, W. R., ed. *The Mineral Industry: Its Statistics, Technology, and Trade during 1905*. Vol. 14. New York: Engineering and Mining Journal, 1906.

———. *The Mineral Industry: Its Statistics, Technology, and Trade during 1909*. Vol. 18. New York: Engineering and Mining Journal, 1910.

International Apple Shippers Association. "Report of Officers and Executive Committee." 1926. Western Cooperative Spray Project Records, 1921–1952, Washington State University Manuscripts, Archives, & Special Collections, Pullman, WA.

Isard, W., and E. W. Schooler. "Location Factors in the Petrochemical Industry with Special Reference to the Future Expansion in the Arkansas-White-Red River Basins." US Department of Commerce. Washington, DC: Office of Technical Services, 1955.

Jeffreys, J. W. "The Land: Orchard, Farm, Garden, Rancho and Stockyard." *Los Angeles Times*, August 17, 1900.

Jennings, B. H. "The Killing Fields: Science and Politics at Berkeley, California, USA." *Agriculture and Human Values* 14, no. 3 (1997): 259–71.

Johnson, J. T. *Just War Tradition and the Restraint of War: A Moral and Historical Inquiry*. Princeton, NJ: Princeton University Press, 1981.

Johnson, M. O., and G. H. Godfrey. "Chloropicrin for Nematode Control." *Industrial & Engineering Chemistry* 24, no. 3 (1932): 311–13.

Jones, H. *Steam Engines: An International History*. London: Ernest Benn Limited, 1973.

Jones, L. A., and D. Durand. *Mortgage Lending Experience in Agriculture*. National Bureau of Economic Research Financial Research Program. Princeton, NJ: Princeton University Press, 1954.

Jones, P. R. "Oil Sprays—Five Years' Successful Use." *Better Fruit, Better Vegetables* 8, no. 7 (1914): 33–38.

Journal of Industrial and Engineering Chemistry. "The Wide Use of Arsenic." 4, no. 9 (1912): 696–97.

Kagy, J. F. Undated. Dow Chemical Historical Collection. 1897–2006. Personnel Files, Science History Institute, Philadelphia, PA.

Kagy, J. F. "Toxicity of Some Nitro-Phenols as Stomach Poisons for Several Species of Insects." *Journal of Economic Entomology* 29, no. 2 (1936): 397–405.

———. "Laboratory Method of Comparing the Toxicity of Substances to San Jose Scale." *Journal of Economic Entomology* 29, no. 2 (1936): 393–97.

———. "Ovicidal and Scalicidal Properties of Solutions of Dinitro-O-Cyclohexylphenol in Petroleum Oil." *Journal of Economic Entomology* 29, no. 1 (1936): 52–61.

———. "The Relative Toxicity of Some 2,4-Dinitro-6-R-Phenols." *Journal of Economic Entomology* 34, no. 4 (1941): 660–68.

———. "Method for Maturing Cotton." Patent #2,416,259, US Patent Office, Dow Chemical Company, 1947.

Kallet, A., and F. J. Schlink. *100,000,000 Guinea Pigs: Dangers in Everyday Foods, Drugs, and Cosmetics*. New York: Vanguard Press, 1933.

Keeling, A. "Urban Wastes Sinks as a Natural Resource: The Case of the Fraser River." *Urban History Review* 34, no. 1 (2005): 57–70.

Kegley, H. C. "By-Products from Oil Well Vapors of Great Value: Wet Gas Conversion Gains." *Los Angeles Times*, December 15, 1924.

Kellogg, V. "Eugenics and Militarism." *Atlantic* 112, no. July (1913): 99–108.

———. *Headquarters Nights: A Record of Conversations and Experiences at the Headquarters of the German Army in France and Belgium*. Boston: Atlantic Monthly Press, 1917.

———. "The National Research Council." *North American Review* 212, no. 78 (1920): 754–56.

———. "The National Research Council." *International Conciliation* 7 (1920): 423–30.

———. "The United States National Research Council." *Nature* 105, no. 2637 (1920): 332–33.

———. Letter from V. Kellogg, Permanent Secretary of NRC to P. J. O'Gara, American Smelting and Refining Company. 1921. National Research Council, Institutions: Associations, Individuals, Archive of the National Academy of Sciences, Washington, DC.

———. Letter from V. Kellogg, Permanent Secretary of the NRC, to Gano Dunn, Chairman of NRC, March 6. 1925. National Research Council, Institutions: Associations, Individuals, Archive of the National Academy of Science, Washington, DC.

———. Letter from V. Kellogg, Permanent Secretary of NRC, to G. Dunn, Chairman of NRC. June 17, 1925. National Research Council, Institutions: Associations, Individuals, Archive of the National Academy of Sciences, Washington, DC.

———. Memo from V. Kellogg, Permanent Secretary of the NRC, to V. Kellogg. June 17, 1925. National Research Council, Institutions: Associations, Individuals, Archive of the National Academy of Sciences, Washington, DC.

———. "Isolation or Cooperation in Research." *Reprint and Circular Series of National Research Council* 67 (1925): 1–7.

———. "The Food Problem." In *A New World of Science: Its Development during the War*, edited by R. M. Yerkes, 265–71. Freeport, NY: Books for Libraries Press, 1969. First published 1920.

Kellogg, V., A. E. Taylor, and H. Hoover. *The Food Problem*. Bedford, MA: Applewood Books, 1917.

Kercheval, A. F. "What Shall We Do about the Scale?" *Los Angeles Times*, March 22, 1885.

———. "Shall the White Scale Go, or Shall We?" *Los Angeles Times*, July 11, 1886.

———. "Letters to the Times: Are the Bugs Sick?" *Los Angeles Times*, October 4, 1888.

Kloppenburg, J. R. *First the Seed: The Political Economy of Plant Biotechnology*. Madison: University of Wisconsin Press, 2004.

Knight, H., J. C. Chamberlin, and C. D. Samuels. "On Some Limiting Factors in the Use of Saturated Petroleum Oils as Insecticides." *Plant Physiology* 4, no. 3 (1929): 299–321.

Knox, G. C. "Map of the Wolfskill Orchard." 1886. Maps, Huntington Digital Library, San Marino, CA.

Koebele, A. "US Department of Agriculture Report for 1886." Washington, DC: US Department of Agriculture, 1887.

———. "Report of a Trip to Australia Made under Direction of the Entomologist to Investigate the Natural Enemies of the Fluted Scale." In *Division of Entomology Bulletin* 21, 1–32. Washington, DC: US Department of Agriculture, 1890.

Kortland, F. "Flow Meter." Patent #2,038,511, US Patent Office, Shell Development Company, 1934.

Kosek, J. "Ecologies of Empire: On the New Uses of the Honeybee." *Cultural Anthropology* 25, no. 4 (2010): 650–78.

Kreps, T. J. "Joint Costs in the Chemical Industry." *Quarterly Journal of Economics* 44, no. 3 (1930): 416–61.

Kurz, H. "Classical and Early Neoclassical Economists on Joint Production." *Metroeconomica* 38, no. 1 (1986): 1–37.

Lamb, R. *The American Chamber of Horrors: The Truth about Food and Drugs.* New York: Farrar & Rinehart, 1936.

Lambert, E. B., H. A. Rodenhiser, and H. H. Flor. "The Effectiveness of Various Fungicides in Controlling the Covered Smuts of Small Grains." *Phytopathology* 26, no. 6 (1926): 393–411.

Landes, D. *The Unbound Prometheus: Technological Change and Industrial Development in Western Europe from 1750 to the Present.* New York: Cambridge University Press, 1969.

Lange, W. H., Jr. "Notes and Correspondence of W. H. Lange, Jr." 1943–1945. William H. Lange Jr. Papers, UC Davis Shields Library, Department of Special Collections, Davis, CA.

———. "Ethylene Dibromide and Dichloropropane-Dichloropropene Mixture for Wireworm Control." *Journal of Economic Entomology* 38, no. 6 (1945): 643–45.

———. "The Use of Two New Soil Fumigants D-D and EDB for Wireworm Control." Berkeley: University of California, College of Agriculture, Agricultural Experiment Station, 1946.

Lanman, S. W. "Colour in the Garden: 'Malignant Magenta.'" *Garden History* 28, no. 2 (2000): 209–21.

Larkin, B. "The Politics and Poetics of Infrastructure." *Annual Review of Anthropology* 42 (2013): 327–43.

Laurence, W. L. "Say Drugs Checks Tubercle Bacilli: Chemists Also Hear Synthetic Glycerine Can Now Be Made from Petroleum Gases." *New York Times*, April 6, 1939.

Lawson, H. G. "Death in the Fields: Phosphate Pesticides Suspected in Poisoning of Some Farmhands." *Wall Street Journal*, July 16, 1971.

Le, X. C. "Arsenic Speciation in the Environment and Humans." In *The Environmental Chemistry of Arsenic*, edited by W. T. Frankenberger, 95–116. New York: Marcel Dekker, 2002.

Lear, L. "Rachel Carson's Silent Spring." *Environmental History Review* 17, no. 2 (1993): 23–48.

Leavitt, F. H. "Method and Apparatus for Protecting Subsurface Ground Tools." Patent #2,306,339, US Patent Office, Shell Development Company, 1942.

———. "Nitrogation, Nitrojection, and Soil Fumigation: Their Application and Their Results." *American Fertilizer* 110, no. 2 (1949): 3.

———. "Agricultural Ammonia Equipment Development and History." In *Agricultural Anhydrous Ammonia: Technology and Use*, edited by M. H. McVickar, W. P. Martin, I. E. Miles, and H. H. Tucker, 125–68. Memphis, TN: Agricultural Ammonia Institute, 1966.

LeCain, T. "The Limits of 'Eco-Efficiency': Arsenic Pollution and the Cottrell Electrical Precipitator in the U.S. Copper Smelting Industry." *Environmental History* 5, no. 3 (2000): 336–51.

Leech, J. "Fatal Facility." *Punch, or the London Charivari* 17 (July–September 1849).

Legge, R. T. "Occupational Hazards in the Agricultural Industries." *American Journal of Public Health* 25, no. 4 (1935): 457–62.

Lehman, R. S. "Laboratory Experiments with Various Fumigants against the Wireworm Limonius (Pheletes) Californicus Mann." *Journal of Economic Entomology* 26, no. 6 (1933): 1042–51.

———. "Laboratory Tests of Organic Fumigants for Wireworms." *Journal of Economic Entomology* 35, no. 5 (1942): 659–61.

Lelong, B. M. "Improved Fumigating Apparatus." In *Annual Report*, 469–72. Sacramento: State Board of Horticulture of the State of California, 1890.

Leopold, A. "What Is a Weed?" In *The River of the Mother of God and Other Essays*, edited by B. Callicott and S. Flader, 306–9. Madison: University of Wisconsin Press, 1992. First published 1943.

Leslie, E. *Synthetic Worlds: Nature, Art, and the Chemical Industry*. London: Reaktion Books, 2005.

Liboiron, M. *Pollution Is Colonialism*. Durham, NC: Duke University Press, 2021.

Liebig, J. *Familiar Letters on Chemistry, and Its Relation to Commerce, Physiology, and Agriculture*. London: Walton & Maberly, 1859.

Lincoln, C. G., H. H. Schwardt, and C. E. Palm. "Methyl Bromide-Dichloroethyl Ether Emulsion as a Soil Fumigant." *Journal of Economic Entomology* 35, no. 2 (1942): 238–39.

Lodeman, E. G. *The Spraying of Plants: A Succinct Account of the History, Principles and Practice of the Application of Liquids and Powders to Plants for the Purpose of Destroying Insects and Fungi*. London: Macmillan, 1909.

Los Angeles Herald. "Growing Interest—the Money in Raising Oranges." August 25, 1878.

———. "History of the Orange in Los Angeles." April 5, 1882.

———. "The White Scale: Some Terribly Infested Orange Groves; Where Are the Inspectors?" June 12, 1886.

———. "Patent Twilight: The Orange Tree Fumigator Patent to Be Bought." May 30, 1891.

———. "After the Red Spider: Something More Terrible Than Horticulturalists Fighting Him." June 8, 1902.

———. "Codling Moth Crusade." December 23, 1903.

———. "California Leads in Oil." December 22, 1907.

———. "Domestic Arsenic." December 15, 1907.

Los Angeles Times. "Natural Gas: The Future Fuel of Southern California." January 1, 1888.

———. "Horticultural Commission: What the Australian Bugs [Are] Doing for Southern California." September 8, 1889.

———. "Poison by the Ton." December 24, 1893.

———. "The Night Process: The Gas Treatment in the Courts." October 20, 1893.

———. "In an Arsenic Mine." July 4, 1894.

———. "Paris Green." November 2, 1895.

———. "Covina." August 9, 1896.

———. "Gleaners of Poison: Arsenic Picked up by the Roadside and Made by the Ton in Cornwall." September 5, 1897.

———. "The Land: Orchard, Farm, Garden, Rancho, and Stockyard." October 5, 1900.

———. "Hunting for Enemies of the Red Scale: Mischievous Foe of Oranges Is Hard to Combat." November 23, 1902.

———. "Oil's By-Products: Hundreds of Thousands of Dollars They Amount to Every Year in Los Angeles." June 11, 1905.

———. "Purple Scale Disappearing: Speaker at Farmers' Institute Meeting Gives Encouraging Address on Tree Fumigation." September 20, 1906.

———. "Oceans of Oil." September 24, 1907.

———. "After the Scale Pest: Black and Purple Varieties Especially Guarded against by County Horticulturist." July 26, 1912.

———. "Refining Business Makes Rapid Strides." July 20, 1913.

———. "Wealth of Natural Gas Resources in State: Oil Fields Can Yield Sufficient to Supply the Needs of Every City and Town in Southern California." June 29, 1913.

———. "Wide Use of Arsenic: Is Principally Employed in Glass Making and in Insecticides, as Well as Paints and Medicines." May 10, 1914.

———. "Coal Tar Basis of Defense: Its Products Needed for High Explosives." February 13, 1916.

———. "Arsenic in 1924." June 5, 1925.

———. "The Romance of Gasoline: What Petroleum Gives Us Besides Gasoline." July 26, 1925.

———. "Mass Attack of Worms Stopped at Trenches." August 16, 1925.

———. "A Feast for Wire Worms—Sow Calcium Cyanide between Rows." September 20, 1925.

———. "Sprays Damage Suit Opens: Horticultural Experts Gathered at Santa Ana in $40,000 Action Brought by Rancher." February 16, 1926.

———. "Wet Gas Assets of California: Survey Shows Progress in Gasoline Recovery." November 19, 1928.

———. "Nitrogen Plant Site Purchased." November 20, 1929.

———. "The Endless Battle." August 2, 1931.

———. "University Berth Filled." December 14, 1940.

———. "U.C. Receives $10,000,000 Gift." October 11, 1941.

Loughheed, A. L. "The Anatomy of an International Cyanide Cartel: Cyanide, 1897–1927." *Prometheus* 19, no. 1 (2001): 1–10.

Luther, E. E., and W. H. Volck. "Process of Making Lead Arsenate." Patent #892,603, US Patent Office, 1908.

———. "Process of Making Arsenate of Lead." Patent #903,389, US Patent Office, 1908.

———. "Manufacture of Lead Arsenate." Patent #929,962, US Patent Office, 1909.

Lutts, R. H. "Chemical Fallout: Rachel Carson's Silent Spring, Radioactive Fallout, and the Environmental Movement." *Environmental Review* 9, no. 3 (1985): 210–25.

Luyssaert, S., E. D. Schulze, A. Börner, A. Knohl, D. Hessenmöller, B. E. Law, P. Ciais, and Grace. J. "Old-Growth Forests as Global Carbon Sinks." *Nature* 455, no. 7210 (2008): 213–15.

Lyman, G. R. Letter from to G. R. Lyman to H. E. Howe. January 29, 1921. National Research Council, Institutions: Associations, Individuals, Archive of the National Academy of Science, Washington, DC.

Lynch, M. *Mining in World History*. London: Reaktion Books, 2002.

Lynch, W. D., C. C. McDonnell, J. K. Haywood, and M. B. Waite. "Bulletin 127—Poisonous Metals on Sprayed Fruits and Vegetables." US Department of Agriculture. Washington, DC: US Government Printing Office, 1922.

MacArthur, J. S. "Gold Extraction by Cyanide: A Retrospective." *Journal of the Society of Chemical Industry* 24, no. 7 (1905): 311–15.

MacIntire, W. H. "Report of the Representative on Board of Governors, Crop Protection Institute." *Journal of the Association of Official Agricultural Chemists* 35, no. 1 (1952): 107.

Mackintosh, S. A., N. G. Dodder, N. J. Shaul, L. I. Aluwihare, K. A. Maruya, S. J. Chivers, K. Danil, D. W. Weller, and E. Hoh. "Newly Identified DDT-Related Compounds Accumulating in Southern California Bottlenose Dolphins." *Environmental Science and Technology* 50, no. 22 (2016): 12129–37.

MacMillan, D. *Smoke Wars: Anaconda Copper, Montana Air Pollution, and the Courts, 1890–1924*. Helena: Montana Historical Society Press, 2000.

Manager, S. *Living Oil: Petroleum Culture in the American Century*. Oxford: Oxford University Press, 2014.

Manchester Guardian. "The Cotton Worm in the South." August 9, 1880.

Mandal, B. K., and K. T. Suzuki. "Arsenic Round the World: A Review." *Talanta* 58, no. 1 (2002): 201–35.

Mann, S. A. *Agrarian Capitalism in Theory and Practice*. Chapel Hill: University of North Carolina Press, 1990.

Marcosson, I. F. *Metal Magic: The Story of the American Smelting an Refining Company*. New York: Farrar, Straus, 1949.

Marsh, G. P. *Man and Nature, or, Physical Geography Modified by Human Action*. Seattle: University of Washington Press, 2003.

Martin, G. C. "DD as a Means of Controlling Heterodera Rostochiensis (Woll.)." *Nature* 160, no. 720 (1947): 702.

Marx, K. *Capital: A Critique of Political Economy*. Vol. 1. New York: Penguin Books, 1976.

———. *Capital: A Critique of Political Economy*. Vol 3. New York: Penguin Books, 1981.

Mattingley, C. *Survival in Our Own Land: "Aboriginal" Experiences in "South Australia" since 1836*. Adelaide, Australia: Wakefield Press, 1988.

May, L. *War Crimes and Just War*. Cambridge: Cambridge University Press, 2007.

McClung, C. E. Letter from to C. E. Mcclung, Chairman Division of Biology and Agriculture, NRC to H. E. Howe, Chairman Division of Research Extension, NRC. January 29, 1921. National Research Council, Institutions: Associations, Individuals, Archive of the National Academy of Sciences, Washington, DC.

McDonnell, C. C. "Recent Progress in Insecticides and Fungicides." *Industrial & Engineering Chemistry* 16, no. 10 (1924): 1007–12.

McLean, H. C., A. L. Weber, and J. S. Joffe. "Arsenic Content of Vegetables Grown in Soils Treated with Lead Arsenate." *Journal of Economic Entomology* 37, no. 2 (1944): 315–16.

McMillen, W. "Chemurgy: Utilization of Farm Products in the American Way." *Industrial & Engineering Chemistry* 31, no. 5 (1939): 1–9.

McWilliams, C. *Factories in the Field*. Vol. 342. Berkeley: University of California Press, 1935.

———. *Southern California: An Island on the Land*. Salt Lake City, UT: Gibbs Smith, 1946.

McWilliams, J. E. *American Pests: Losing the War on Insects from Colonial Times to DDT*. New York: Columbia University Press, 2008.

Meharg, A. A. *Venomous Earth: How Arsenic Caused the World's Worst Mass Poisoning*. New York: Macmillan, 2005.

Melander, A. L. "Can Insects Become Resistant to Sprays?" *Journal of Economic Entomology* 7, no. 2 (1914): 167–73.

Melillo, E. D. "The First Green Revolution: Debt Peonage and the Making of the Fertilizer Trade, 1840–1930." *American Historical Review* 117, no. 4 (2012): 1028–60.

Mellilo, E. D. *Strangers on Familiar Soil: Rediscovering the Chile-California Connection*. New Haven, CT: Yale University Press, 2015.

Merchant, C. *The Death of Nature: Women, Ecology, and the Scientific Revolution*. New York: HarperCollins, 1990.

Meuli, L. J. "Herbicides." Patent #2,392,859A, US Patent Office, Dow Chemical Company, 1946.

Millennium Ecosystem Assessment, *Ecosystems and Human Well-Being*. Washington, DC: Island Press, 2005.

Miller, H. C. "Function of Natural Gas in the Production of Oil: A Report of the Bureau of Mines in Cooperation with the American Petroleum Institute." Washington, DC: US Department of Commerce, Bureau of Mines, 1929.

Mills, L. E. "Nicotine Salts of 2,4-Dinitrophenol and Substituted Derivatives Thereof." Patent #1,963,471, US Patent Office, Dow Chemical Company, 1934.

———. "Insecticidal Compositions Comprising Dinitro-Cresols." Patent #2,121,039, US Patent Office, Dow Chemical Company, 1938.

Minkoff-Zern, L. A. "Hunger amidst Plenty: Farmworker Food Insecurity and Coping Strategies in California." *Local Environments* 19, no. 2 (2014): 204–19.

Mintz, S. W. *Sweetness and Power: The Place of Sugar in Modern History*. New York: Penguin Books, 1986.

Minutes of the 10th Annual Meeting of the Northwest Oil Spray Project. 1937. Western Cooperative Spray Project Records, 1921–1952, Washington State University Manuscripts, Archives, & Special Collections, Pullman.

Minutes of the Sixteenth Annual Meeting of the Western Cooperative Spray Conference. 1942. Western Cooperative Spray Project Records, 1921–1952, Washington State University Manuscripts, Archives, & Special Collections, Pullman.

Mitchell, T. *Rule of Experts: Egypt, Techno-Politics, Modernity*. Berkeley: University of California Press, 2002.

Moore, J. W. *Capitalism in the Web of Life: Ecology and the Accumulation of Capital*. New York: Verso, 2015.

Moore, P. Letter from P. Moore, Secretary of CPI, to V. Kellogg, Permanent Secretary of NRC. February 5, 1925. National Research Council, Institutions: Associations, Individuals, Archive of the National Academy of Sciences, Washington, DC.

———. Letter from P. Moore, Secretary of CPI, to V. Kellogg, Permanent Secretary of NRC. June 16, 1925. National Research Council, Institutions: Associations, Individuals, Archive of the National Academy of Sciences, Washington, DC.

Moore, P. B. "Copper Arsenides at Mohawk, Michigan." *Rocks & Minerals* 27, nos. 1/2 (1962): 24–26.

Moore, S. A. "Garbage Matters: Concepts in New Geographies of Waste." *Progress in Human Geography* 36, no. 6 (2012): 780–99.

Morin, B. M. *The Legacy of American Copper Smelting: Industrial Heritage versus Environmental Policy*. Knoxville: University of Tennessee Press, 2013.

Morrison, H. E., and J. D. Vertrees. "Hop Pests and Their Control: A Report of the Control of the Hop Red Spider and Other Closely Related Problems during the Season of 1940." Corvallis: Oregon Agricultural Experiment Station 1940.

Morse, F. W. "The Uses of Gases against Scale Insects." *California Agricultural Experiment Station Bulletin* 71 (1887): 1–3.

———. "Use of Hydrocyanic Acid against Scale Insects." *California Agricultural Experiment Station Bulletin* 73 (1887): 1–3.

———. "Doses of Acids of Different Strengths." *Pacific Rural Press* 34, no. 10 (September 3, 1887): 182.

———. "Scale Insects: The Use of Hydrocyanic Acid to Exterminate Them." *Sacramento Daily Union*, September 3, 1887.

———. "Entomological: Comments by Mr. Morse." *Pacific Rural Press* 42, no. 10 (September 5, 1891): 193.

Moses, H. V. "'The Orange-Grower Is Not a Farmer': G. Harold Powell, Riverside Orchardists, and the Coming of Industrial Agriculture 1893–1930." *California History* 74, no. 1 (1995): 22–37.

Moses, H. V. "Machines in the Garden: A Citrus Monopoly in Riverside, 1900–1936." *California History* 61, no. 1 (1982): 26–35.

Mullen, R. A. "Why Poison Bugs, Foes or Surpluses?" *Washington Post*, June 25, 1933.

Multhauf, R. P. "Industrial Chemistry in the Nineteenth Century." In *Technology in Western Civilization: The Emergence of Modern Industrial Society Earliest Times to 1900*, edited by M. Kranzberg and C. W. Pursell, 468–88. New York: Oxford University Press, 1967.

Murphy, M. *Sick Building Syndrome and the Problem of Uncertainty: Environmental Politics, Technoscience, and Women Workers*. Durham, NC: Duke University Press, 2006.

Murray, J. "The Once Despised Cottonseed Now Gives Cottonseed Oil to Make Soap and Many Other Products." *Chemical Markets* 19, no. 33 (1926): 1361–62.

Myers, C. N., B. Throne, F. Gustafson, and J. Kingsbury. "Significance and Danger of Spray Residue." *Industrial & Engineering Chemistry* 25, no. 6 (1933): 624–29.

Najar-Rodríguez, A. J., N. A. Lavidis, R. K. Mensah, P. T. Choy, and G. H. Walter. "The Toxicological Effects of Petroleum Spray Oils on Insects—Evidence for an Alternative Mode of Action and Possible New Control Options." *Food and Chemical Toxicology* 46, no. 9 (2008): 3003–14.

Nash, L. *Inescapable Ecologies: A History of Environment, Disease, and Knowledge.* Berkeley: University of California Press, 2006.

National Research Council. Minutes of the Conference of Plant Pathologists, Entomologists, and Manufacturers of Insecticides and Fungicides at The Hotel Seneca, Rochester, NY. June 30, 1920. National Research Council, Institutions: Associations, Individuals, Archive of the National Academy of Sciences, Washington, DC.

———. Minutes of the Conference of Plant Pathologists, Entomologists, and Manufacturers of Insecticides and Fungicides at the National Academy of Sciences, Washington, DC. September 28, 1920. National Research Council, Institutions: Associations, Individuals, Archive of the National Academy of Sciences, Washington, DC.

———. Minutes of the Crop Protection Institute Annual Meeting. December 6, 1920. National Research Council, Institutions: Associations, Individuals, Archive of the National Academy of Sciences, Washington, DC.

———. "Sixth Annual Report of the National Research Council." 1922. National Research Council, Institutions: Associations, Individuals, Archive of the National Academy of Sciences, Washington, DC.

———. "Sulfur Fellows of the Crop Protection Institute, October 22." 1922. National Research Council, Institutions: Associations, Individuals, Archive of the National Academy of Sciences, Washington, DC.

———. "NRC Report of the Crop Protection Institute for 1922." 1923. National Research Council, Institutions: Associations, Individuals, Archive of the National Academy of Sciences, Washington, DC.

———. Minutes of the Crop Protection Institute Annual Meeting. 1923. National Research Council, Institutions: Associations, Individuals, Archive of the National Academy of Sciences, Washington, DC.

———. Annual Meeting of the Crop Protection Institute for 1925, Franklin Square Hotel, December 31, 1925. National Research Council, Institutions: Associations, Individuals, Archive of the National Academy of Sciences, Washington, DC.

———. "Report of the Committee on Persistent Pesticides, Division of Biology and Agriculture, National Research Council to U.S. Department of Agriculture." Washington, DC: National Academy of Sciences, 1969.

Naylor, R. "Losing the Links between Livestock and Land." *Science* 310, no. 5754 (2005): 1621–22.

Nelson, K. "Industrial Contributions of Arsenic to the Environment." *Environmental Health Perspectives* 19 (1977): 31–34.

Nestle, M. *Food Politics: How the Food Industry Influences Nutrition and Health.* Berkeley: University of California Press, 2002.

New York Times. "Millions of Fish and Fowl Dying, Results of the Use of Paris Green." August 9, 1878.

———. "May Sue Copper Company: President Will Learn If Poisonous Fumes Can Be Prevented." December 6, 1908.

———. "Montana Smelters Sued: Government Action against Anaconda Company to Protect Forests." March 17, 1910.

———. "Coal Tar Products Fill Daily Needs: Almost Every Luxury and Necessity Has Something Derived from the Substance That Gives Heat." June 15, 1914.

———. "Chemical Preparedness." February 25, 1917.

———. "Chemists Gain Advantage: Americans Have Outdone Germany in Chemical Products." February 17, 1918.

———. "Our Super-Poison Gas: First Story of Compound 72 Times Deadlier Than 'Mustard,' Manufactured Secretly by the Thousands of Tons." April 20, 1919.

———. "War on Insects." February 13, 1921.

———. "Holds Chemistry Is Farmers' Hope." August 12, 1926.

———. "Humans Face Insect War." June 20, 1926.

———. "Shell Union Offers $50,000,000 Bonds." September 13, 1929.

———. "Calls Man to War on Insect Pests: Entomologist Pictures Bugs as Driving Humanity Off the Planet Unless Halted." September 10, 1931.

———. "Treatment of the Soil." January 26, 1947.

———. "Shell Oil Testing Soil Fumigants: New Chemical Shows Success in Treating Peach Tree 'Replant Disease.'" September 15, 1950.

———. "New Laboratory Opened by Shell: California Institutions Is Called One of the World's Largest Oil Research Facilities." November 23, 1950.

Nighman, C. E. "Arsenic." In *Minerals Resources of the United States,* 743–51. Washington, DC: US Bureau of Mines, Geological Survey, 1944.

Norman, S. "Problem Solved: Smelting Process Kills All Fumes." *New York Times,* February 16, 1908, II13.

Norton, R. J. "Obituary: Walter Collins O'Kane 1877–1973." *Journal of Economic Entomology* 67, no. 1 (1974): 144–45.

Nriagu, J. O. "Arsenic Poisoning through the Ages." In *Environmental Chemistry of Arsenic,* edited by W. T. Frankenberger, 2. New York: Marcel Dekker, 2002.

Nriagu, J. O., and J. M. Azcue. "Food Contamination with Arsenic in the Environment." In *Food Contamination from Environmental Sources,* edited by J. O. Nriagu and M. S. Simmons. Advances in Environmental Science and Technology. New York: John Wiley and Sons, 1990.

Oakland Tribune. "Scientists Will Tell How to Kill Scale Curse." July 18, 1903.

Observer. "War on Insect Pests. Poison, Petrol, and 'Planes.'" September 22, 1935.

Ohman, M. F. "Great Western Division, General Student and Sales Trainee Program." 1950. Dow Chemical Historical Collection, 1897–2006, Educational Department, Dow Chemical Company, Science History Institute, Philadelphia, PA.

O'Kane, W. C. *The Crop Protection Institute: A Get-Together Movement on the Part of Three Great Groups, the Intelligent Grower, the Scientist, and the Businessman*. Durham, NH: Crop Protection Institute, 1920.

———. "The Common Ground of Science and Industry: The Fundamental Basis for the Organization of the Crop Protection Institute." *Crop Protection Digest* 1 (April 1921): 1–16.

———. "One Year of the Crop Protection Institute." *Journal of Economic Entomology* 15, no. 3 (1922): 209–13.

———. "Chemistry in the Control of Plant Enemies: New Achievement and Future Possibilities." *Industrial & Engineering Chemistry* 15, no. 9 (1923): 911–13.

———. "The Crop Protection Institute: Its Organization, Plan and Procedure, and Work Accomplished." *Journal of Economic Entomology* 29, no. 1 (1936): 6–20.

O'Kane, W. C., and P. Moore. "Fungicide and Insecticide." Patent #1,515,803, US Patent Office, Crop Protection Institute, 1924.

Oxford English Dictionary. "By-Product." Oxford: Oxford University Press, 2018.

———. "Pest." Oxford: Oxford University Press, 2018.

———. "Sink." Oxford: Oxford University Press, 2018.

Olsen, F., and J. C. Goldstein. "The Preparation of Picric Acid from Phenol." *Industrial & Engineering Chemistry* 16, no. 1 (1924): 66–71.

Pacific R&H Chemical Corporation. "Useful Information on Fumigation of Citrus Trees for Growers and Fumigators." Los Angeles, 1923.

Pacific Rural Press. "Agricultural Notes: California—Los Angeles." 3, no. 14 (April 6, 1872): 213.

———. "Horticulture: Los Angeles Fruit Growers Association." 13, no. 20 (May 19, 1877): 307.

———. "Agricultural Notes: California—Los Angeles." 13, no. 9 (March 3, 1877): 133.

———. "Entomological: Citrus Scale and Their Foes." 25, no. 10 (March 10, 1883): 205.

———. "The Gas Treatment for Scales." 33, no. 21 (July 30, 1887): 85.

———. "Entomological: More Foes of Icerya." 36, no. 26 (December 29, 1888): 556.

———. "The Patent of the Gas Treatment Declared Void." 47, no. 17 (April 28, 1894): 326.

———. "A County Fumigation Outfit." 56, no. 12 (September 17, 1898): 188.

———. "Crude Oil of Distillate Spray." 61, no. 4 (January 26, 1901): 51.

———. "The Codling Moth Work at Watsonville." August 6, 1904.

———. "Oil Emulsion Too Strong." 88, no. 20 (November 14, 1914).

———. "Understanding Oil Sprays." 89, no. 11 (March 20, 1915): 360.

———. "Crude Oil Emulsion Spraying." 92, no. 24 (1916): 637.

———. "Spraying Makes Bigger Fruit Crops—Do It Early." 94, no. 3 (November 3, 1917): 437.

———. "What Two Young Men Did." 98, no. 24 (December 13, 1919): 810.

Paine, F. W. "Copper." In *Political and Commercial Geology and the World's Mineral Resources*, edited by J. E. Spurr, 223–60. New York: McGraw-Hill, 1920.

Paracelsus. *Dritte Defensio (Third Defense)*, 1538. In *Four Treatises of Theophrastus Von Hohenheim Called Paracelsus*, edited by H. Siegersit, L. Temkion, G. Rosen, and G. Zilboorg. Baltimore, MD: Johns Hopkins University Press, 1941.

Parsons, C. L. "Miscellaneous Mineral Wastes." *Industrial & Engineering Chemistry* 4, no. 3 (1912): 185–88.

Patterson, H. J. "Report of the Representatives on the Board of Governors of the Crop Protection Institute of the National Research Council." *Journal of the Association of Agricultural Chemists* 30, no. 1 (1947): 109.

Pementel, D., C. Kirby, and A. Shroff. "The Relationship between 'Cosmetic Standards' for Foods and Pesticide Use." In *The Pesticide Question: Environment, Economics, and Ethics*, edited by D. Pimentel and H. Lehman, 85–105. New York: Chapman and Hall, 1993.

Perkins, J. H. "Insects, Food, and Hunger: The Paradox of Plenty for Us Entomology, 1920–1970." *Environmental History Review* 7, no. 1 (1983): 71–96.

Perkins, R. G. "A Study of the Munitions Intoxications in France." *Public Health Review* 24, no. 43 (1919): 2335–430.

Perkins, V. L. *Crisis in Agriculture: The Agricultural Adjustment Administration and the New Deal, 1933*. Vol. 81 Berkeley: University of California Press, 1969.

Petroleum Times. "Notes of a Speech of J B August Kessler to the Institution of Petroleum Technologists." 28, no. October 15 (1932): 371–77.

Pettengill, R. B. "The United States Copper Industry and the Tariff." *Quarterly Journal of Economics* 46, no. 1 (1931): 141–57.

Phillips, R. G. Letter to Yakima Fruit Growers Association. 1926. Western Cooperative Spray Project Records, 1921–1952, Washington State University Manuscripts, Archives, & Special Collections, Pullman, WA.

Pictorial England and Wales with upwards of Three Hundred and Twenty Copyright Illustrations. London: Cassel, 1897.

Pinckard, J. A. "Soil Fumigant Effective against Root-Knot and Meadow Nematodes." *Seed World* 54, no. 10 (1943): 10, 12–13, 46.

———. "Soil Fumigant Effective against Nematodes." *Food Packer* 25, no. 1 (1944): 43–44.

Pollan, M. *The Botany of Desire: A Plant's Eye View of the World*. New York: Random House, 2001.

Poppendick, J. *Breadlines Knee-Deep in Wheat: Food Assistance in the Great Depression*. Berkeley: University of California Press, 2014.

Popular Mechanics. "Fighting Insects." 44, no. 4 (1925): 567–71.

Powell, G. H. "Causes of Fruit Decay." *Riverside Daily Press*, April 7, 1905.

———. "The Decay of Oranges While in Transit from California." Bulletin 123. Washington, DC: US Department of Agriculture, Bureau of Plant Industry, 1908.

Priest, T. *The Offshore Imperative: Shell Oil's Search for Petroleum in Postwar America*. College Station: Texas A&M University Press, 2007.

Prizer, E. L., and J. A. Prizer. "Method of Supplying Soluble Fertilizing Agents to Soil." Patent #1,868,913, US Patent Office, 1932.

Pugsley, C. "Gas Treatment for Scale Insects: Treating of the Operations of the Horticultural Board's Fumigating Outfit, the Applicability of the Fumigation Process in Cape Colony, and Embodying a Full Description of the Equipment Necessary for Fumigation with Hydrocyanic Acid Gas." Cape Town, South Africa: Horticultural Board of the Cape Colony, 1897.

Pyzel, D. "Producing Ammonia." Patent #1,849,357, US Patent Office, Shell Development Company, 1928.

———. "Process and Apparatus for the Production of Ammonia." Patent #1,957,849, US Patent Office, Shell Development Company, 1932.

———. "Process for the Absorption and Distillation of Ammonia." Patent #1,999,546, US Patent Office, Shell Development Company, 1932.

———. "Process for the Removal of Acetylene." Patent #1,985,548, US Patent Office, Shell Development Company, 1934.

Pyzel, F. M. "Process for the Thermal Decomposition of Hydrocarbons." Patent #1,983,992, US Patent Office, Shell Development Company, 1931.

———. "Process for the Manufacture of Ammonium Sulphate." Patent #2,035,920, US Patent Office, Shell Development Company, 1933.

———. "Process of Producing Hydrogen." Patent #1,896,420, US Patent Office, Shell Development Company, 1933.

Pyzel, F. M., and J. D. Ruys. "Manufacture of Ammonium Sulfate." Patent #2,026,250, US Patent Office, Shell Development Company, 1934.

Quaintance, A. L., P. B. Dunbar, and L. S. Tenny. "Confidential Minutes of Conference between Representatives of the US Department of Agriculture, the Insecticide and Fruit Industries and Others Relative to Arsenical Spray Residues of Fruits." 1926. Western Cooperative Spray Project Records, 1921–1952, US Department of Agriculture, Washington State University Manuscripts, Archives, & Special Collections, Pullman.

Quayle, H. J. "Correspondence between H. J. Quayle and the University of California Agricultural Departments as Well as Horticultural and Entomological Agencies throughout the World, 1908–1914." 1910. Henry J. Quayle Papers, UC Riverside Special Collections.

———. "Bulletin 234—Red Spiders and Mites of Citrus Trees." Sacramento: College of Agriculture, Agricultural Experiment Station, University of California Publications, 1912.

———. "Are Scales Becoming Resistant to Fumigation?" *University of California Journal of Agriculture* 3, no. 8 (1916): 333–34.

———. "The Development of Resistance to Hydrocyanic Acid in Certain Scale Insects." *Hilgardia* 11, no. 5 (1938): 183–210.

Rabkin, Y. M. "Chemicalization of Petroleum Refining in the United States: The Role of Cooperative Research 1920–1950." *Sociology of Science* 19, nos. 4–5 (1980): 833–50.

Rabkin, Y. M., and J. J. Lafitte-Houssat. "Cooperative Research in Petroleum Chemistry." *Scientometrics* 1, no. 4 (1979): 327–38.

Raemaekers, L. "The Gas Fiend." In *Raemaekers' Cartoons with Accompanying Notes by Well-Known English Writers*, edited by F. Stopford. London: Doubleday, Page, 1916.

Raffles, H. "Jews, Lice, and History." *Public Culture* 19, no. 3 (2007): 521–66.

Rasmussen, N. "The Forgotten Promise of Thiamin: Merck, Caltech Biologists, and Plant Hormones in a 1930s Biotechnology Project." *Journal of the History of Biology* 32, no. 2 (1999): 245–61.

——— "Plant Hormones in War and Peace: Science, Industry, and Government in the Development of Herbicides in 1940s America." *Isis* 92, no. 2 (2001): 291–316.

Raymer, R. G. "Early Copper Mining in Arizona." *Pacific Historical Review* 4, no. 2 (1935): 123–30.

Reed, P. *Acid Rain and the Rise of the Environmental Chemist in Nineteenth-Century Britain: The Life and Work of Robert Angus Smith*. New York: Routledge, 2014.

Regan, R. *Just War: Principles and Cases*. 2nd ed. Washington, DC: Catholic University of America Press, 2013.

Renick, A. "Arsenic." In *Minerals Resources of the United States*, 162–66. Washington, DC: US Bureau of Mines, Geological Survey, 1931.

Reno, J. "Waste and Waste Management." *Annual Review of Anthropology* 44 (2015): 557–72.

Reuter, M. J. "The Arsenic Problem: Report of a Case of Arsenic Dermatitis from Wearing Apparel." *Archives of Dermatology and Syphilology* 31, no. 6 (1935): 811–18.

Reuther, W., E. C. Calavan, and G. E. Carman, eds. *The Citrus Industry*. Vol. V. Oakland, CA: University of California, Agriculture and Natural Resources, 1989.

Richter, F. E. "The Copper-Mining Industry in the United States, 1845–1925." *Quarterly Journal of Economics* 41, no. 2 (1927): 236–91.

Rickard, T. A. *A History of American Mining*. New York: McGraw-Hill, 1932.

Riehl, L. A. "The Use of Petroleum Oil Fractions as Insecticides on Citrus in California." In *The Third World Petroleum Congress Proceedings: Section V*, edited by E. J. Brill, 204–17. The Hague: World Petroleum Congress, 1951.

Riley, C. V. *The Colorado Potato Beetle: With Suggestions for Its Repression and Methods of Destruction*. London: George Routledge and Sons, 1877.

———. "Insecticides: Summer and Spring Washes and Remedies against Pests." *Los Angeles Times*, May 3, 1887.

———. "Bulletin No. 10—Our Shade Trees and Their Insect Defoliators." Division of Entomology, US Department of Agriculture. Washington, DC: US Government Printing Office, 1887.

———. "Importation of Icerya Enemies from Australia." *Pacific Rural Press* 38, no. 25 (December 21, 1889): 570.

———. "The Kerosene Emulsion: Its Origin, Nature, and Increasing Usefulness." *Proceedings of the Twelfth and Thirteenth Annual Meeting of the Society for the Promotion of Agricultural Science* (1892): 83–98.

Roark, R. C. "United States Insecticide Statistics for 1928." *Journal of Economic Entomology* 22, no. 4 (1929): 699–701.

———. "Insecticides and Fungicides." *Industrial & Engineering Chemistry* 27, no. 5 (1935): 530–32.

230 | Bibliography

Robbins, W. "Study Finds Agricultural Fails to Aid Consumers or Rural Towns." *New York Times,* June 1, 1972, 39.

Robert, R. O. "The Development and Decline of the Non-ferrous Metal Smelting Industries in South Wales." In *Industrial South Wales, 1750–1914,* 264. London: Frank Cass, 1969.

Robinson, R. H. "New Solvents for the Removal of Arsenical Spray Residue." *Industrial & Engineering Chemistry* 21, no. 11 (1929): 1132–36.

Romero, A. "Beyond the Mother Lode: Synthetic Cyanide and the Chemicalization of California Gold Mining (1885–1905)." *California History* 95, no. 1 (2018): 2–24.

Rosen, C. M. "'Knowing' Industrial Pollution: Nuisance Law and the Power of Tradition in a Time of Rapid Economic Change." *Environmental History* 8, no. 4 (2003): 565–97.

———. "The Role of Pollution Regulation and Litigation in the Development of the U.S. Meatpacking Industry, 1865–1880." *Enterprise & Society* 8, no. 2 (2007): 297–347.

———. "Fact Versus Conjecture in the History of Industrial Waste Utilization." *Econ Journal Watch* 9, no. 2 (2012): 112–21.

Rosenstein, L. "Increased Yields Obtained from Shell Agricultural Ammonia (Nh3) in Irrigated Agriculture." *Shell Chemical Bulletin* 1 (1936): 1–23.

Rosner, D., and G. Markowitz. "The Politics of Lead Toxicology and the Devastating Consequences for Children." *American Journal of Industrial Medicine* 50, no. 10 (2007): 740–56.

Rothstein, M. "A British Firm on the American West Coast, 1869–1914." *Business History Review* 37, no. 4 (1963): 392–415.

———. "West Coast Farmers and the Tyranny of Distance: Agriculture on the Fringes of the World Market." *Agricultural History* 49, no. 1 (1975): 272–80.

Rothwell, R. P., ed. *The Mineral Industry: Its Statistics, Technology, and Trade in the United States and Other Countries to the End of 1897.* Vol. 6. New York: Scientific Press, 1898.

Rothwell, R. P., and J. Struthers, eds. *The Mineral Industry: Its Statistics, Technology, and Trade in the United States and Other Countries to the End of 1901.* Vol. 10. New York: Engineering and Mining Journal, 1902.

Rounds, M. B. "Tests Show Value of Spraying for Control of Black Scale." *Los Angeles Times,* June 29, 1924.

———. "Get the Scale, Regardless of Methods." *Los Angeles Times,* October 18, 1925.

Roush, G. A., ed. *The Mineral Industry: Its Statistics, Technology, and Trade during 1915.* Vol. 24. New York: McGraw-Hill, 1916.

Roush, G. A., and A. B. Butts, eds. *The Mineral Industry: Its Statistics, Technology, and Trade during 1918.* Vol. 27. New York: McGraw-Hill, 1919.

———, eds. *The Mineral Industry: Its Statistics, Technology, and Trade during 1920.* Vol. 29. New York: McGraw-Hill, 1921.

———, eds., *The Mineral Industry: Its Statistics, Technology, and Trade during 1921.* Vol. 30. New York: McGraw-Hill, 1922.

Russell, E. "War on Insects: Warfare, Insecticides, and Environmental Change in the United States, 1870–1945." PhD diss., University of Michigan, 1993.

———. *War and Nature: Fighting Humans and Insects with Chemicals from World War I to Silent Spring.* Cambridge: Cambridge University Press, 2001.

Russell, E. O. "'Speaking of Annihilation': Mobilizing for War against Human and Insect Enemies." *Journal of American History* 82, no. 4 (1996): 1505–29.

Rust, F. F., and W. E. Vaughn. "The High-Temperature Chlorination of Olefin Hydrocarbons." *Journal of Organic Chemistry* 5, no. 5 (1940): 472–503.

Sabin, P. *Crude Politics: The California Oil Market, 1900–1940.* Berkeley: University of California Press, 2005.

Sackman, D. C. *Orange Empire: California and the Fruits of Eden.* Berkeley: University of California Press, 2005.

Sacramento Daily Union. "Advertisement: Grape Cuttings: Grape Cuttings." April 9, 1851.

———. "Pacific Coast Items." March 18, 1874.

———. "Practical Agriculture: Orange Culture in California." January 3, 1880.

Sadtler, S. P. "Early Chemical Manufacture in Philadelphia." *Journal of Industrial and Engineering Chemistry* 8, no. 12 (1916): 1153–57.

Salmon, E. S. "Discussion on 'the Fungicidal Action of Sulphur.'" *Annals of Applied Biology* 13 (1926): 308–18.

San Francisco Call. "Advises Caution in the Use of Oils: Too Much Will Ruin Trees, So Says Entomologist Volck." August 15, 1903.

———. "Oiling the Levees." October 22, 1903.

———. "Standard Oil to Double Capacity of Its Refinery." September 2, 1911.

San Francisco Chronicle. "Will Study Fumigation: Berkeley Man Will Spend a Month Experimenting in the South." August 18, 1902.

———. "Arsenic Poison Spray Used to Destroy Weeds." November 15, 1915.

Sauchelli, V. "Flotation Sulfur in Agriculture." *Industrial & Engineering Chemistry* 25, no. 4 (1933): 363–68.

Sawyer, R. C. *To Make a Spotless Orange: Biological Control in California.* Henry Wallace Series on Agriculture and Rural Life. Ames: Iowa State University Press, 1996.

Scheidel, E. M. "The Cyanide Process: Its Practical Application and Economical Results." In *California State Mining Bureau Bulletin,* Sacramento, CA: J. J. Crawford, 1894.

Schmitz, C. "The Rise of Big Business in the World Copper Industry, 1870–19301." *Economic History Review* 39, no. 3 (1986): 392–410.

Science. "The Crop Protection Institute." 55, no. 1410 (1922): 14–15.

Science News Letter. "DD Found Effective against Wireworms." 48, no. 19 (1945): 296.

———. "New Chemical Kills Nematodes, Soil Pests." 50, no. 23 (1946): 367.

Scientific American. "Review of the Year: Chemistry." 120, no. 1 (1918): 9.

Seyferth, D. "The Rise and Fall of Tetraethllead." *Organometallics* 22 (2003): 5154–78.

Shell Chemical Company. *Shell Carbon: Its Properties and Uses in the Rubber Industry.* San Francisco: Shell Chemical Company, 1939.

———. "Shell D-D." *Bulletin* 3 (1944): unpaginated.

Shell Chemical Corporation. "Specimen Labels." Agricultural Chemicals Division, Shell Chemical Company, AA-1. New York: Shell Chemical Company, Agricultural Chemicals Division, 1964.

Shell Chemical Division, Agriculture Products Departments, Shell Union Oil Corporation. "Nitrojection: A New Method of Soil Fertilization." San Francisco: National Agricultural Library, 1945.

Shell Oil Company, Agricultural Laboratory. *Better Farming through Research*. San Francisco, CA: Shell Union Oil Corporation and Associate Companies, 1946.

Shell Union Oil Corporation. *Shell . . . Soldier and Civilian*. San Francisco, CA: Shell Union Oil Corporation and Associate Companies, 1945.

Shinn, C. H. "The Fruit Industry of California." *Popular Science Monthly* 44, no. December (1893): 200–217.

Shinozuka, J. N. "Deadly Perils: Japanese Beetles and the Pestilent Immigrant, 1920s–1930s." *American Quarterly* 65, no. 4 (2013): 831–52.

Shoenfield, A. "Insect War Ceaseless: Man's Dominion Challenged." *Los Angeles Times*, October 6, 1929.

Simpson, A. C. "Control of the Red Spider Mite." *Nature* 155, no. 3930 (1945): 241.

Siverson, H. S. "Arsenic Breakfasts Ready for 'Hoppers': Middle West Preparing for Grasshopper Swarms Predicted by Experts to Be Greatest in Many Years of Farm History." *Washington Post*, May 16, 1937.

Smil, V. *Enriching the Earth: Fritz Haber, Carl Bosch, and the Transformation of World Food Production*. Cambridge, MA: MIT Press, 2004.

Smith, F. B., and W. W. Sunderland. "Esters of 2,4-Dintro-6-Cyclohexyl-Phenol." Patent #2,097,136, US Patent Office, Dow Chemical Company, 1937.

Smith, H. M. "Possible Utilization of Natural Gas for the Production of Chemical Products." Washington, DC: US Department of Commerce, Bureau of Mines, 1930.

Smith, J. B. "Cultivation and Susceptibility to Insect Attack." *Journal of Economic Entomology* 1, no. 1 (1908): 15–17.

Smith, K. W. "Standard in New Venture: California Company Again Expands Activities by Entering Spray-Chemical Field." *Los Angeles Times*, August 16, 1931.

Smith, R. E., H. S. Smith, H. J. Quayle, and E. O. Essig. "Protecting Plants from Their Enemies." In *California Agriculture by Members of the Faculty of the College of Agriculture University of California*, edited by C. B. Hutchinson, 239–317. Berkeley: University of California Press, 1946.

Solano, A. "Land of L. Wolfskill in the Rancho Santa Anita." 1871. Maps, Huntington Digital Library, San Marino, CA.

Southern California Horticulturist. "The Red Scale." 2, no. 9 (1879): 280.

Spalding, W. *The Orange: Its Culture in California, with a Brief Discussion of the Lemon*. Riverside, CA: Press and Horticulturist Steam Press, 1885.

———. "Early Chapters in the History of California Citrus Culture." *California Citrograph* 7, no. 4 (1922): 94–95.

Spear, R. *The Great Gypsy Moth War: A History of the First Campaign in Massachusetts to Eradicate the Gypsy Moth, 1890–1901*. Boston: University of Massachusetts Press, 2005.

Speight, J. G. *The Chemistry and Technology of Petroleum*, 5th ed. Boca Raton, FL: Taylor & Francis, 2014.

Spitz, P. H. *Petrochemicals: Rise of an Industry.* New York: John Wiley & Sons, 1988.

Standard Agricultural Chemicals, Inc. "For Selective Weed Control—Sinox." 1944. Papers of Alden S. Crafts, UC Davis Special Collections, Davis, CA.

Standard Oil Bulletin. "Petroleum Orchard Sprays." 11, no. 12 (1924): 2–3.

———. "Behind the Scenes in the Oil Industry." 15, no. 8 (1927): 1.

———. "Advertisement for Oronite Cleaning Fluid: The Spotter." 16, no. 3 (1928): 17.

———. "Arming for War on Pests." 19, no. 8 (1931): 3–11.

———. "Annual Statement to Stockholder 1931." 19, no. 12 (1932): 1–9

Steen, K. *The American Synthetic Organic Chemicals Industry: War and Politics, 1910–1930.* Chapel Hill: University of North Carolina Press, 2014.

Steinbeck, J. *The Chrysanthemums and Other Stories.* New York: Penguin Books, 1996.

Stellman, J. M., S. D. Stellman, R. Christian, T. Weber, and C. Tomasallo. "The Extent and Patterns of Usage of Agent Orange and Other Herbicides in Vietnam." *Nature* 422, no. 6933 (2003): 681–87.

Stoll, S. *The Fruits of Natural Advantage: Making the Industrial Countryside in California.* Berkeley: University of California Press, 1998.

Stone, M. W. "Dichloropropane-Dichloropropylene, a New Soil Fumigant for Wireworms." *Journal of Economic Entomology* 37, no. 2 (1944): 297–99.

Stone, M. W., and R. E. Campbell. "Chloropicrin as a Oil Insecticide for Wireworms." *Journal of Economic Entomology* 26, no. 1 (1933): 237–43.

Street, R. S. *Beasts of the Field: A Narrative History of California Farmworkers, 1769–1913.* Stanford, CA: Stanford University Press, 2004.

Sunday Times. "Melancholy Effects of Poison." March 30, 1823.

———. "Profligate Seduction and Suicide." December 26, 1824, 4.

———. "Sheep Dipping, and Sheep Killing, with Corrosive Sublimate of Arsenic." September 12, 1858.

"Supreme Commander for the Allied Powers, Scientific and Economic Section, Foreign Trade and Commerce Division, Chemical and Drug File, 1946–1950." 1947. box no. 651, file D. D. J1-51,407, National Archives, Washington, DC. RG 331.

Swain, R. E. "Atmospheric Pollution by Industrial Wastes." *Industrial & Engineering Chemistry* 15, no. 3 (1923): 296–301.

Symons, T. B. "Should State Departments Conduct Public Sprayers." *Journal of Economic Entomology* 1, no. 2 (1908): 106–10.

Sze, J. *Noxious New York: The Racial Politics of Urban Health and Environmental Justice.* Cambridge, MA: MIT Press, 2006.

Taber, I. W. "Wolfskill Orange Grove." 1885. Riverside and Los Angeles Area Views, circa 1880–1889, BANC PIC 1905.06211:18, Bancroft Library, Berkeley, CA.

Tacoma News Tribune. "Tacoma's Poison Factory Is Interesting Industry." April 6, 1927.

Tainter, M. L., W. C. Cutting, and Stockton A. B. "Use of Dinitrophenol in Nutritional Disorders: A Critical Survey of Clinical Results." *American Journal of Public Health* 24, no. 10 (1934): 1045–53.

Tarr, J. "From City to Farm: Urban Wastes and the American Farmer." *Agricultural History* 49, no. 4 (1975): 598–612.

———. "The Search for the Ultimate Sink: Urban Air, Land, and Water Pollution in Historical Perspective." *Records of the Columbia Historical Society* 51 (1984): 1–29.

Tarr, J. A. "Searching for a 'Sink' for an Industrial Waste: Iron Making Fuels and the Environment." *Environmental History Review* 18, no. 1 (1994): 9–34.

Taverner, P. "Drowning or Just Waving? A Perspective on the Ways Petroleum-Derived Oils Kill Anthropod Pests of Plants." In *Spray Oils Beyond 2000: Sustainable Pest and Disease Management,* edited by G. A Beattie, D. M. Watson, M. L Stevens, D. J. Rae, and R. N. Sponner-Hart, 78–87. Penrith, Australia: University of Western Sydney, 2002.

Taylor, A. L. "Nematocides and Nematicides–a History." *Nematropica* 33, no. 2 (2003): 225–32.

Taylor, D. *Toxic Communities: Environmental Racism, Industrial Pollution, and Residential Mobility.* New York: New York University Press, 2014.

Teeple, J. "Waste Pine Wood Utilization." *Journal of Industrial and Engineering Chemistry* 7, no. 11 (1913): 929–30.

———. "Raw Materials—Waste and By-Products." *Industrial & Engineering Chemistry* 8, no. 11 (1926): 1187–90.

———. "Economic Factors in the Chemical Industry." *Industrial & Chemical Engineering* 19, no. 10 (1927): 1085–87.

Tepper, L., and J. H. Tepper. "The Rise and Fall of the Tacoma Arsenic Industry." *Journal of the Society of Industrial Archeology* 39, nos. 1/2 (2013): 65–78.

Terry, J. B. Letter from the Chief Chemist, Standard Oil of California, to Northwestern Entomologists. 1930. Western Cooperative Spray Project Records, 1921–1952, Washington State University Manuscripts, Archives, & Special Collections, Pullman.

Thomas, D., S. Fowler, and V. Johnson. *The Silence of the Archive.* London: Facet Publishing, 2017.

Thorne, G. *Principles of Nematology.* Ithaca, NY: Cornell University Press, 1961.

Thorne, G., and V. Jensens. "A Preliminary Report on the Control of Sugar-Beet Nematode with Two Chemicals D-D and Dowfume W15." *Proceedings of the American Sugar Beet Technologists* 4 (1947): 322–29.

Thorsheim, P. *Inventing Pollution: Coal, Smoke and Culture in Britain since 1800.* Athens: Ohio University Press, 2006.

Thucydides. *History of the Peloponnesian War.* Translated by R Crawley. New York: E. P. Dutton, 1910.

Tobey, R. and C. Wetherell. "The Citrus Industry and the Revolution of Corporate Capitalism in Southern California, 1887–1944." *California History* 74, no. 1 (1995): 6–21.

Tonkin, C. J. "Soil Improving Method." Patent #2,424,520, US Patent Office, Shell Development Company, 1947.

Travis, A. S. "High Pressure Industrial Chemistry: The First Steps, 1909–1913." In *Determinants in the Evolution of the European Chemical Industry,* edited by A. S. Travis, H. G. Schröter, E. Homburg, and J. T. Morris, 392. Boston: Kluwer Academic Publishers, 1998.

Tredinnick, R. *A Review of Cornish Copper Mining Enterprise, with a Description of the Most Important Dividend and Progressive Copper and Tin Mines of Cornwall and Devon, and Detailed Account of the Buller and Bassest District.* 2nd ed. London: Thompson and Vincent, 1858.

Tucker, J. B. *War of Nerves: Chemical Warfare from World War I to Al-Qaeda.* New York: Pantheon Books, 2006.

Tucker, R. P. "Oil Sprays: Chemical Properties of Petroleum Oil Unsaturates Causing Injury to Foliage." *Industrial & Engineering Chemistry* 28, no. 4 (1936): 458–61.

Tufts, W. P. "The Rich Pattern of California Crops." In *California Agriculture by Members of the Faculty of the College of Agriculture University of California*, edited by C. B. Hutchinson, 113–238. Berkeley: University of California Press, 1946.

Turner, J. R. "Device for Distributing Mixtures of Vapors and Liquid." Patent #2,650,566, US Patent Office, Shell Development Company, 1953.

Turner, N. "Standardized Oil Sprays." *Journal of Economic Entomology* 24, no. 4 (1931): 901–4.

Tyler, P. M., and C. N. Gerry. "Arsenic." In *Minerals Resources of the United States*, 319–27. Washington, DC: US Bureau of Mines, Geological Survey, 1931–1932.

Tyrrell, I. R. *True Gardens of the Gods: Californian-Australian Environmental Reform, 1860–1930.* Berkeley: University of California Press, 1999.

Underwood, K. D. "Mining Wars: Corporate Expansion and Labor Violence in the Western Desert 1876–1920." PhD diss., University of Nevada, Las Vegas, 2009.

United States Department of Agriculture, Agricultural Research Administration. "Report of the Administrator of Agricultural Research." Washington, DC: US Department of Agriculture, Agricultural Research Administration, 1944.

United States Geological Survey. "Historical Statistics for Mineral and Material Commodities in the United States." Department of the Interior, 2019. http://minerals.usgs.gov/minerals/pubs/historical-statistics.

Vail, D. *Chemical Lands: Pesticides, Aerial Spraying, and Health in North America's Grasslands since 1945.* Tuscaloosa: University of Alabama Press, 2018.

Van Den Bosch, R. *The Pesticide Conspiracy.* Berkeley: University of California Press, 1978.

van der Valk, J. "Acid Recovery Process." Patent #2,441,521, US Patent Office, Shell Development Company, 1944.

Van Overbeek, J., and R. Blondeau. "Mode of Action of Phytonomic Oils." *Weeds* 3, no. 1 (1954): 55–65.

van Siclen, A. P., and C. N. Gerry. "Arsenic." In *Minerals Resources of the United States*, 496–501. Washington, DC: US Bureau of Mines, Geological Survey, 1935.

Vaughn, W. E., and F. F. Rust. "The High-Temperature Chlorination of Parrafin Hydrocarbons." *Journal of Organic Chemistry* 5, no. 5 (1940): 449–71.

Vickery, R. K. "Petroleum Insecticides." *Journal of Economic Entomology* 13, no. 6 (1920): 444–47.

Vickery, R. K., and A. C. Browne. *Handbook of Pest Control.* Watsonville: California Spray-Chemical Company, 1929.

Vilensky, J. A. *Dew of Death: The Story of Lewisite, America's World War I Weapon of Mass Destruction.* Bloomington: Indiana University Press, 2005.

Vlies, L. E. "Colouring Matters and Their Application." *Journal of the Society of Dyers and Colourists* 29, no. 11 (1913): 316–21.

Vogel, K. "The Significance of Arsenic in the Excretions." *American Journal of the Medical Sciences* 176, no. 2 (1928): 215–24.

Volck, W. H. "Bulletin No. 153: Spraying with Distillates." Sacramento: College of Agriculture, Agricultural Experiment Station, University of California, 1903.

———. "The Significance of Lead Arsenate Composition." *Science* 33, no. 857 (1911): 866–70.

———. "Stimulation by Spraying." *Pacific Rural Press*, December 13, 1913.

———. "Insecticide and Process of Making and Using the Same to Protect Plants." Patent #1,707,465, US Patent Office, 1929.

———. "Fungicide." Patent #1,707,467, US Patent Office, 1929.

———. "Insecticide and Method of Making the Same." Patent #1,707,466, US Patent Office, 1929.

———. "Parasiticidal Oil." Patent #1,707,468, US Patent Office, 1929.

———. "Process of Stimulating or Rejuvenating Plants and Composition for Use Therein." Patent #1,914,903, US Patent Office, 1933.

Volck, W. H., and R. W. Hunt. *Citrus Pests and Their Control: A Description of Various Citrus Pests of Economic Importance in California, with General Control Recommendations.* Berkeley: California Spray-Chemical Company, 1931.

von Driel, J. "Ashes to Ashes: The Stewardship of Waste and Oeconomic Cycles of Agricultural and Industrial Improvement, 1750–1800." *History and Technology* 30, no. 3 (2014): 177–206.

Wain, R. L. "Toxic Polynitro Derivatives in Pest Control." *Annals of Applied Biology* 29, no. 3 (1942): 301–8.

Walker, B. *Toxic Archipelago: A History of Industrial Disease in Japan.* Seattle: University of Washington Press, 2010.

Walker, G. T. *Petroleum: Its History, Occurrence, Production, Uses and Tests.* Minneapolis, MN: Imperial Printing, 1915.

Walker, R. *The Conquest of Bread: 150 Years of Agribusiness in California.* New York: New Press, 2004.

Wall, W. B., M. S. Jones, and A. D. Bishop. "Process of Fumigating Trees and Other Plants." Patent #445,342, US Patent Office, 1891.

Wall Street Journal. "The Washoe Smelter: Believed That There Is Not Danger of the Plant Being Closed." December 21, 1908.

———. "America Manufactures Dyes on Big Scale." October 7, 1918.

———. "Increasing Use Calcium Arsenate." January 28, 1924.

———. "Natural 'Gas' in California: Survey Shows Progress Made in Recovery Methods over the Past Few Years." November 23, 1928.

———. "Shell Chemical Company." March 22, 1929.

———. "Shell Chemical Plant: Nitrogen Works Site Served by Three Railroads." June 30, 1930.

———. "Standard Oil of California: Chemical Spray Company Using Mineral Oils Organized as New Subsidiary." August 24, 1931.

———. "Improved Fertilizer That Mixes with Irrigating Water Helps Farmers Boost Their Water Output." September 7, 1943.

———. "Shell Will Establish Agricultural Laboratory on the Pacific Coast." June 22, 1944.

Wallace, H. A. "Extension Service Review—May." Washington, DC: US Department of Agriculture, 1933.

———. "Notice to Producers and Consumer of Apples and Pears." 1935. Western Cooperative Spray Project Records, 1921–1952, US Department of Agriculture, Washington State University Manuscripts, Archives, & Special Collections, Pullman, WA.

———. Letter to Growers and Shipper of Apples and Pears. 1937. Western Cooperative Spray Project Records, 1921–1952, Washington State University Manuscripts, Archives, & Special Collections, Pullman.

Wallace, R. Farming Industries of the Cape Colony. Johannesburg, South Africa: J. C. Juta and Co., 1896.

Walzer, M. Just and Unjust Wars: A Moral Argument with Historical Illustrations. New York: Basic Books, 1977.

Warnock, R. E. "Ammonia Application in Irrigation Water." In Agricultural Anhydrous Ammonia: Technology and Use, edited by M. H. McVickar, W. P. Martin, I. E. Miles, and H. H. Tucker, 115–24. Memphis, TN: Agricultural Ammonia Institute, 1966.

Warren, K. Chemical Foundations: The Alkali Industry in Britain to 1926. Oxford: Clarendon Press, 1980.

Washington, S. H. Packing Them In: An Archeology of Environmental Racism in Chicago, 1865–1954. Lanham, MD: Lexington Books, 2004.

Washington Post. "Crazed by the Use of Arsenic." July 11, 1878.

———. "Pheasants Die by Poison: Wheat Soaked in Arsenic Kills Nearly Fifteen Hundred Birds." August 26, 1897.

———. "Dust Is Worth Millions: Fortunes Now Obtained from What Formerly Waste Matter." August 17, 1913.

———. "Wizardries of Modern Chemistry Shown: Remarkable Work of the National Research Council Is Presented in Nontechnical Manner." March 20, 1921.

———. "40 Ships Carrying Australian Apples to British Market: Dominion Taking Advantage of Disfavor American Fruit Has Met." May 2, 1926.

Waynick, D. D. "Anhydrous Ammonia as a Fertilizer." California Citrograph 19, no. 11 (1934): 295, 310–11.

Webber, H. J., and L. D. Batchelor. The Citrus Industry. Vol. I, History, Botany and Breeding. Berkeley: University of California Press, 1943.

Weber, M. "The American Way of Farming: Pioneer Hi-Bred and Power in Postwar America." Agricultural History 92, no. 3 (2018): 380–403.

Webster, R. L. Letter to Professor G. W. Herrick, Cornell University. 1926. Western Cooperative Spray Project Records, 1921–1952, Washington State University Manuscripts, Archives, & Special Collections, Pullman, WA.

———. "Outline of U.S. Spray Residue History." 1933. Western Cooperative Spray Project Records, 1921–1952, Washington State University Manuscripts, Archives, & Special Collections, Pullman, WA.

———. Letter to Professor G. W. Herrick, Cornell University. 1934. Western Cooperative Spray Project Records, 1921–1952, Washington State University Manuscripts, Archives, & Special Collections, Pullman, WA.

———. "Insecticide Situation in the Pacific Northwest." *Journal of Economic Entomology* 37, no. 6 (1944): 818–21.

Weed, W. H. *The Copper Mines of the World.* New York: Hill Publishing, 1907.

———. "Copper Deposits of the United States." In *The Copper Mines of World*, 253–367. New York: Hill Publishing, 1908.

West, C. J. "Industrial Research Laboratories of the United States Including Consulting Research Laboratories." *Bulletin of the National Research Council* 81 (1931): 1–267.

Western Grower and Shipper: The Business Magazine of the Western Row Crop Industries. "Weeding Onions." 15, no. 9 (1944): 10–11, 26–27.

Westgate, W. A., and R. N. Raynor. "Bulletin 634—A New Selective Spray for the Control of Certain Weeds." Berkeley: UC Agricultural Experiment Station, 1940.

Westing, A. H. "Agent Blue in Vietnam." *New York Times*, July 12, 1971.

White, G. T. *Formative Years in the Far West: A History of Standard Oil Company and Predecessors through 1919.* New York: Appleton-Century-Crofts, 1962.

White, W. B. "Poisonous Spray Residues on Vegetables." *Industrial & Engineering Chemistry* 25, no. 6 (1933): 621–23.

Whorton, J. "Insecticide Residue of Foods as a Public Health Problem: 1865–1938." PhD diss., University of Wisconsin, 1969.

———. *Before Silent Spring: Pesticides and Public Health in Pre-DDT America.* Princeton, NJ: Princeton University Press, 1974.

———. *The Arsenic Century: How Victorian Britain Was Poisoned at Home, Work, and Play.* Oxford: Oxford University Press, 2010.

Wilcoxin, F. "Fungicide." Patent #1,849,778, US Patent Office, Crop Protection Institute, 1932.

Wildman, M. S. *Prices of Food.* History of Prices during the War, edited by W. C. Mitchell. Washington, DC: US Government Printing Office, 1919.

Wiley, H. W. *The History of a Crime against the Food Law: The Amazing Story of the National Food and Drugs Law Intended to Protect the Health of the People, Perverted to Protect the Adulteration of Foods and Drugs.* Washington, DC: Self-published, 1929.

Wilkins, M. *The History of Foreign Investment in the United States, 1914–1945.* Cambridge, MA: Harvard University Press, 2004.

Williams, B. "'That We May Live': Pesticides, Plantations, and Environmental Racism in the United States South." *Environment and Planning E: Nature and Space* 1–2 (2018): 243–67.

Williams, E. C. "Creating Industries, 1919–1939, Petroleum." *Chemical Industries* 44 (1939): 495–501.

———. "Synthetic Glycerol from Petroleum: A Contribution from the Research Laboratories of Shell Development Company." *Transactions of the American Institute of Chemical Engineers* 37 (1942): 157–208.

Williams, R. "Proposed Royal Dutch Shell Synthetic Ammonia Plant." 1929. Records of E. I. du Pont de Nemours & Co., series II, part 2, Du Pont Ammonia Corporation, Hagley Museum and Library, Wilmington, DE.

———. *Key Words: A Vocabulary of Culture and Society.* 2nd ed. Oxford: Oxford University Press, 1983.

Williamson, H. F., R. L. Andreano, A. R. Daum, and G. C. Klose. *The American Petroleum Industry: The Age of Energy 1899–1959.* Evanston, IL: Northwestern University Press, 1963.

Wilson, H. F., and C. E. Holmes. "Little Danger in Eating Arsenic-Fed Chickens." *Journal of Economic Entomology* 29, no. 5 (1936): 1008–14.

Wilson, I. A. "Early Southern California Viniculture 1830–1865." *Historical Society of Southern California Quarterly* 39, no. 3 (1957): 242–50.

Wilson, I. H. *William Wolfskill, 1798–1866: Frontier Trapper to California Ranchero.* Glendale, CA: Arthur H. Clark, 1965.

Wilson, P. K. "Headquarters for Defense." *Los Angeles Times,* March 13, 1932.

Wilson, R. E. "Refinery Gas: A Raw Material of Growing Importance." *Journal of the Society of Chemical Industry* 58, no. 51 (1939): 1095–1101.

Wines, R. *Fertilizer in America: From Waste Recycling to Resource Exploitation.* Philadelphia: Temple University Press, 1985.

Woglum, R. S. "Bulletin No. 79—Fumigation Investigations in California." Washington, DC: Bureau of Entomology, US Department of Agriculture, 1909.

———. "Bulletin No. 907—Fumigation of Citrus Plants with Hydrocyanic Acid: Conditions Influencing Injury." Washington, DC: US Department of Agriculture, 1920.

———. "The History of Hydrocyanic and Gas Fumigation as an Index to Progress in Economic Entomology." *Journal of Economic Entomology* 16, no. 6 (1923): 518–21.

———. "Observations on Insects Developing Immunity to Insecticides." *Journal of Economic Entomology* 18, no. 4 (1925): 593–97.

———. "The Use of Oil Sprays on Citrus Trees." *Journal of Economic Entomology* 19, no. 5 (1926): 733–45.

———. "The Use of Oil Sprays on Citrus during 1926." *Journal of Economic Entomology* 21, no. 4 (1928): 530–31.

Wolcott, G. N. "The Status of Economic Entomology in Peru." *Bulletin of Entomological Research* 20, no. 2 (1929): 225–31.

Wolf, M. *It All Began in Frankfurt: Landmarks in the History of Degussa Ag.* Frankfurt am Main, West Germany: Degussa AG, 1985.

Wolfskill, J. J. "William Wolfskill, the Pioneer." *Daily Alta California,* October 12, 1866.

Wolfskill, W. "Petition for Guillermo Wolfskill for Grant of Agricultural Parcel." 1836. Los Angeles City Archives, 1836–1872, USC Digital Archive.

Woodworth, C. W. "Agricultural Experiment Station Bulletin 122: Orchard Fumigation." Berkeley: University of California, 1899.

———. "Fumigation Dosage." In *Bulletin 152*, edited by Experiment Station, College of Agriculture. Berkeley: University of California Publications, 1903.

———. "Codling Moth Control in California." *Journal of Economic Entomology* 3, no. 6 (1910): 470–73.

———. "The Battle of the Arsenicals." *Pacific Rural Press*, November 26, 1910.

———. "Leakage of Fumigation Tents." *Journal of Economic Entomology* 4, no. 4 (1911): 376–80.

———. "The Insecticide Industries in California." *Journal of Economic Entomology* 5, no. 4 (1912): 358–64.

———. "New Dosage Tables: Fumigation Studies No. 7." Berkeley: College of Agriculture, Agricultural Experiment Station, University of California Publications, 1915.

———. "Theory of Toxicity." *Journal of Economic Entomology* 8, no. 6 (1915).

———. "The Toxicity of Insecticides." *Science* 41, no. 1053 (1915): 367–69.

———. "Petroleum Insecticides." *Journal of Economic Entomology* 23, no. 5 (1931): 848–51.

Woodworth, C. W., and M. B. Messenger. "Introductory Lecture: School of Fumigation." Paper presented at the School of Fumigation, conducted by C. W. Woodworth, University of California, Pomona, 1915.

Yagi, K., J. Williams, N. Wang, and R. Cicerone. "Atmospheric Methyl Bromide (Ch3br) from Agricultural Soil Fumigations." *Science* 267, no. 5206 (1995): 1979–81.

Young, H. C. "The Toxic Property of Sulphur." *Annals of Missouri Botanical Garden* 9 (1922): 403–5.

———. "Colloidal Sulfur: Preparation and Toxicity." *Annals of Applied Biology* 12 (1925): 381–418.

———. "Colloidal Sulfur as a Spray Material." *Annals of Missouri Botanical Garden* 12 (1925): 133–43.

Young, H. C., and R. C. Walton. "Spray Injury to Apple." *Phytopathology* 15, no. 7 (1925): 404–15.

Young, H. C., and R. Williams. "Pentathionic Acid, the Fungicidal Factory of Sulfur." *Science* 62, no. 1723 (1928): 19–20.

Young, P. A., and H. E. Morris. "Injury to Apple by Petroleum-Oil Sprays." *Journal of Agricultural Research* 47, no. 7 (1933): 505–22.

Zappe, M. P., and E. M. Stoddard. "Results of Dusting Versus Spraying in Connecticut Apple and Peach Orchards in 1922." *Connecticut Experiment Station Bulletin* 245 (1923): 229–44.

Zimring, C. A. *Clean and White: A History of Environmental Racism in the United States.* New York: New York University Press, 2017.

Zwerdling, D. "The Farm Labor Climax: Pesticides, Another Hazard for Farm Laborers." *Los Angeles Times*, September 9, 1973.

Index

Founded in 1893,
UNIVERSITY OF CALIFORNIA PRESS
publishes bold, progressive books and journals
on topics in the arts, humanities, social sciences,
and natural sciences—with a focus on social
justice issues—that inspire thought and action
among readers worldwide.

The UC PRESS FOUNDATION
raises funds to uphold the press's vital role
as an independent, nonprofit publisher, and
receives philanthropic support from a wide
range of individuals and institutions—and from
committed readers like you. To learn more, visit
ucpress.edu/supportus.